The Democrats

The Democrats

A Critical History
Updated Edition

Lance Selfa

Haymarket Books
Chicago, Illinois

First published in 2008 by Haymarket Books.
This edition published in 2012 by
Haymarket Books
P.O. Box 180165, Chicago, IL 60618
773-583-7884
info@haymarketbooks.org
www.haymarketbooks.org

Cover design by Josh On

Trade distribution:
In the U.S. through Consortium Book Sales, www.cbsd.com
In the UK, Turnaround Publisher Services, www.turnaround-psl.com
In Australia, Palgrave MacMillan, www.palgravemacmillan.com.au
All other countries, Publishers Group Worldwide, www.pgw.com/home/worldwide.aspx

Special discounts are available for bulk purchases by organizations and institutions. Please
contact Haymarket Books for more information at 773-583-7884 or
info@haymarketbooks.org.

Printed in the United States by union labor on FSC certified stock

LIBRARY OF CONGRESS CATALOGING-IN-PUBLICATION DATA
Selfa, Lance.
The Democrats : a critical history / Lance Selfa.
p. cm.
Includes bibliographical references and index.
ISBN 978-1-931859-55-4 (pbk.)
1. Democratic Party (U.S.)--History. I. Title.
JK2316.S45 2008
324.2736--dc22
                              2008036839

10 9 8 7 6 5 4 3 2 1

SUSTAINABLE FORESTRY INITIATIVE

Certified Sourcing
www.sfiprogram.org
SFI-01234

Contents

Introduction

What Happened to the New Era?

When Haymarket Books published the first edition of *The Democrats: A Critical History* in the fall of 2008, political pundits and analysts expected the Democrats to post a huge win that November. The outgoing Bush administration had discredited itself in numerous ways, from its incompetent handling of 2005's Hurricane Katrina to its championing of the widely unpopular, and falsely justified, war in Iraq. In September 2008, the collapse of major financial institutions (Lehman Brothers, Washington Mutual, and American Insurance Group, among others) added another disaster to the Bush administration's resumé: ushering in what came to be called the Great Recession. By Election Day 2008, the question for analysts wasn't whether the Democrats would win. The question was: by how much?

In any event, the Democrats—with Barack Obama leading the way to become the nation's first African-American president—scored a massive victory. The Obama-Biden ticket defeated the Republican McCain-Palin ticket by more than 7 percentage points (52.9 percent to 45.6 percent) and by nearly ten million votes (69.5 million for Obama, 59.9 million for McCain). Obama became the first Democrat since Jimmy Carter, and only the second since Franklin Roosevelt, to win an outright majority (i.e., more than 50 percent of the electorate). The Democrats won states like Indiana, North Carolina, and Virginia that

1

had been solidly GOP states for most of the last generation. At the same time, Obama brought with him the largest Democratic majority in the House of Representatives since 1992 and the largest Democratic majority in the Senate since 1977. By the standards of recent American politics, where it was common to describe the country as polarized nearly fifty-fifty between "red" and "blue," the 2008 election counted as a landslide. Obama's election set off jubilant multiracial celebrations in cities across the country.

Liberals looked forward to a new era of activist government along the lines that President Franklin Delano Roosevelt traced when he assumed power during the Great Depression. In his book *Obama's Challenge*, which also appeared in the fall of 2008, Robert Kuttner boldly stated:

> Barack Obama could be the first chief executive since Lyndon Johnson with the potential to be a transformative progressive president. By that I mean a president who profoundly alters American politics and the role of government in American life—one who uses his office to appeal to our best selves to change our economy, society and democracy for the better. That achievement requires a rendezvous of a critical national moment with rare skills of leadership. There have been been perhaps three such presidents since Lincoln.[1]

For conservatives, the prospect of a new New Deal presented something of a nightmare scenario. In a *Financial Times* op-ed entitled "Beware the Coming Democratic Sea-Change," conservative former Bush speechwriter David Frum warned:

> The stage has been set for the boldest and most dramatic redirection of US politics since Reagan's first year in office. Of course, there are no guarantees in politics. An inept president could bungle his or her chances. Unexpected events could intrude: a nuclear test in Iran, a major terrorist attack on US soil or some attention-grabbing political scandal. But given moderate luck and skill, the next president could join Reagan, Lyndon Johnson and Franklin Roosevelt as one of the grand reshapers of politics and government.[2]

As I write this, in the fall of 2011, the great liberal expectations and conservative trepidation of fall 2008 seem as if they took place decades ago. Seven out of ten Americans believe the country is moving in the wrong direction, and only about four in ten Americans approve of the job Obama is doing.[3] There is a very real chance that the "Obama era" will end in 2012, as Obama joins Jimmy Carter, George H. W. Bush, and Herbert Hoover on the list of one-term failed presidents.

In the midterm election of 2010, Republican revanchists—stoked with the energy of their "base" in the guise of the Tea Party—staged their comeback. In the biggest congressional midterm landslide since 1938, the Republicans captured sixty-three seats, ending the four-year Democratic majority in the House of Representatives. The GOP failed to gain the Senate. But that was the only consolation for the Democrats. The Republican sweep was so broad that the GOP emerged holding nineteen state legislatures outright, twenty-nine governorships, and the largest percentage of state legislative seats since 1928.[4] As a result of the worst recession since the Great Depression, the Republicans now hold more power at the state level than they have at any time since before the Black Friday crash of 1929! Working people soon discovered what those state-level gains meant, as Republican governors and legislatures move to outlaw decades-old collective bargaining gains for public sector workers. At the federal level, austerity and deficit-cutting dominated the national debate.

Although the GOP touted its gains as proof that Americans rejected President Obama's "socialist" agenda, rejection of the Democrats had a less ideological explanation. It started with the economy's terrible state. The recession, which officially lasted from December 2007 to June 2009, left wreckage that will take years to clean up. Sixteen to 17 percent of the US workforce remained unemployed or underemployed, with record numbers remaining unemployed for periods of six months or longer. Median family income declined 7 percent to $49,445 between 2000 and 2009, with income levels returning to 1996 levels. At the same time, the nation posted the highest number of Americans living in poverty in fifty years.[5] By mid-2011, lenders owned almost a million homes lost to foreclosure, with another million homes undergoing foreclosure.[6] Only two years after the economic crisis punctured all the neoliberal and conservative myths about the free market and gave a Democratic administration the opportunity to change course, it seemed that not much had changed.

This produced what pollsters and pundits referred to as "the enthusiasm gap" between conservative voters who couldn't wait to throw out the Democratic bums in 2010 and the traditional Democratic "base" groups (such as youth, African Americans and trade unionists), who showed much less interest in the election then they did in 2008. Patricia Elizondo, president of a Milwaukee International Association of Machinists United Lodge 66, told the *New York Times* that the union had trouble motivating its members to get out the vote for the Democrats. "People have been unemployed for two years, and they're unhappy that the health care bill was not as good as they expected," she said. "Two years ago, I had many members going door-to-door to campaign. Now they're saying, 'Why should I? We supported that candidate, but he didn't follow through.'"[7]

ABC's polling expert Gary Langer calculated that twenty-nine million Obama voters in 2008 stayed home during the midterms, compared to 19.5 million McCain voters in 2008.[8] As a result, the electorate that turned up for the November 2010 midterms was much whiter, wealthier, older, and more conservative than either the 2008 electorate or the U.S. population as a whole. The result was predictable: a conservative landslide.

As Democrats gear up for Obama's 2012 reelection campaign, they will have to contend with the skepticism and demoralization that has set in among their constituencies. For most of the period of unified Democratic control of Washington (2009–2010), Obama and the Democrats assumed the role as saviors of a corporate system teetering on the edge of abyss. Even though the Obama administration was not the originator of the massive bailouts of the Wall Street banks and the likes of insurance giant AIG, it became the chief defender of those programs.

It's very likely that the massive government backing of the financial system saved it from meltdown, but that was cold comfort for millions of Americans who suffered from high unemployment, loss of retirement wealth, and a massive foreclosure crisis. Obama and the Democrats legitimized massive government spending without changing any of their neoliberal assumptions. Instead, the administration pursued a kind of "neoliberal Keynesianism"—putting trillions of taxpayer dollars at the disposal of private business and trying to "incentivize" business to carry out social policy. It didn't work. The banks and big corporations were happy to take the money, but they didn't commit to lending it, saving homes, or hiring workers.

The behavior of the Democrats in power illustrated one side of the party's Janus-faced[9] role in the American political system—as the hopes and aspirations of 2008 illustrated the other side. The Democratic Party's mythological role as the "party of the people," positioned against the "party of the rich," the Republicans, clashed against the reality of the Democrats as one of the two big-business parties in the American system. Election atmospherics—and the very real hopes that millions placed in Obama—aside, support for Obama within many business sectors represented their calculation about how the president could help them to preserve the status quo.

About this Book

An understanding of the two sides of the Democratic Party illustrated here—the harbinger of hope for millions fed up with war and economic distress and the selfsame betrayer of those hopes—is central to the main themes of this book. I hope to show that the Democratic Party of today is the latest incarnation of an institution that appeals to "the people" while looking out for the interests of corporations. In the two-party system of American government, the Democrats have historically played the role of the party that appeals to immigrants, the oppressed, and working-class Americans with the promise of policies that increase economic and social opportunity. Jerome Armstrong and Markos Moulitsas Zúniga, two influential Democratic "netroots" bloggers, have described this positioning in somewhat idealized tones: "The [Democratic] New Deal . . . brought the nation out of the Great Depression by reforming the U.S. economy, strengthening labor unions, employing millions of unemployed Americans in public works projects, creating Social Security, and generally proving that government can be a force for good."[10]

Yet after the heyday of Democratic dominance from the 1930s to the 1960s, millions of working-class Americans—particularly African Americans—felt left out of the "great society" that Democratic administrations promised. Organized labor had provided much of the human force that transformed the Democrats into a viable political institution reaching from the White House to Main Street. But it felt alienated enough by the Democrats' pro-business policies to consider itself locked into what Mike Davis described as a "barren marriage" with the Democrats.[11]

The contention of this book is that these Democratic "betrayals" are not primarily the result of unscrupulous politicians or office holders who "sell out"—although there are plenty of each of those in the Democratic Party. Rather, they are the inevitable outcome of a political institution that socialists have long described as a capitalist party that only pretends to be a friend of working people. To develop this argument, I rely on much historical and analytical data. Nevertheless, this book does not purport to be a definitive or exhaustive history of the Democrats. It does not try to profile leading personalities or relate "insider" stories about Democratic administrations. Nor is it an attempt at muckraking, exposing Democratic corruption and double-dealing. Many books have done this far more effectively than I can here. And anyone interested in reading about John F. Kennedy's peccadilloes or Bill Clinton's affair with Monica Lewinsky will find dozens of other books to choose from.

This book presents an analysis, informed by Marxism, of one of the leading political institutions in the United States. Chapter 1 outlines the socialist case for why the main liberal reform party in the United States should be understood as a capitalist institution. Chapter 2 traces the Democratic Party's two-hundred-plus-year past, as it evolved from the party of slavery in the nineteenth century to the party of Social Security and Medicare in the twentieth. Chapter 3 focuses on the Democratic Party of the last generation, during the conservative ascendancy that found its echo in a "right turn" in the Democratic Party. Chapter 4, newly added for this edition, situates the Obama presidency in the overall analysis.

Chapters 5 and 6 take up more topical concerns about the Democratic Party's roles both in and out of office. Chapter 5 addresses the Democrats' record as the party to which most progressive social movements of the last century have looked for support. Chapter 6 looks at Democratic administrations' record in their conduct of the foreign policy of the United States as it rose to superpower status. Chapter 6 emphasizes Nobel Peace Prize winner Obama's role in continuing and institutionalizing—rather than burying—the foreign policy of his predecessor, President George W. Bush.

Chapters 7 and 8 take on the vexing question of the relationship between the Democratic Party, which in common parlance represents the "left" of the political mainstream, and those activists committed to a genuine left or transformational project. Chapter 7 discusses the strategies and histories of those on the left who have unsuccessfully sought to use the Democratic Party as a vehicle for social change. Chapter 8 provides a brief post-1960s history to explain why no alternative to the Democrats resulted from that era's radicalization. The book concludes with a brief sketch of how we can expect real social change to be accomplished, regardless of which party is occupying the White House.

Socialists understand that the Democratic Party is the default option for millions of Americans who want positive social change. Indeed, the two-party setup of mainstream American politics practically forces this choice, as it blocks the emergence of independent parties committed to popular and pro-working class policies. But as the history recounted here shows, millions who have started down the path of participation in Democratic politics—from antiwar activists in the First World War to labor activists in the 1930s and civil rights activists in the 1960s—have drawn the conclusion that the Democratic Party is not an effective vehicle for genuine social change.

My aim with this book is to provide a new generation who want to fight for a better world the political and historical tools they will need to understand the Democratic Party today. Whatever happens in 2012, the attraction of the Democratic Party will remain one of the chief political challenges to anyone attempting to build an alternative on the left in the United States. I hope this book helps in some small way to meet those challenges.

Acknowledgments

All books are a collective effort of many people's time, energy, and ideas. This one is no different.

My editor Sharon Smith helped to streamline my arguments and to make them accessible to a wider readership. Chapter 1 benefited from astute comments from Sam Farber. Sherry Wolf provided me with material on the LGBT movement and the Democrats. At various points, Joe Allen, Joel Geier, Phil Gasper, Shaun Harkin, Eric Ruder, Todd Chretien, Paul Street, Keeanga-Yamahtta Taylor, Jessie Kindig, and Ashley Smith came up with factoids, ideas, or sources that helped me to make or to tie down an argument.

The folks at Haymarket Books deserve special recognition. Thanks to Anthony Arnove and Julie Fain, who encouraged me to bring this all together into a book. And thanks to Rachel Cohen, Sarah Grey, and Dao X. Tran for their careful proofreading and production work.

This book is also a product of more than two decades of collaboration with a group of talented activists and writers for *Socialist Worker* newspaper and the *International Socialist Review*. So special thanks are due to Alan Maass, Ahmed Shawki, Paul D'Amato, Lee Sustar, Elizabeth Schulte, Nicole Colson, David Whitehouse, Bill Roberts, Eric Ruder, Adam Turl, Joel Geier, and Sherry Wolf. Their insights, advice, and critiques have shaped my understanding of U.S. politics. My work is better as a result.

Last, but certainly not least, I'd like to thank Carole Ramsden, without whose love and support this book wouldn't have become a reality.

Chapter One

"History's Second-Most Enthusiastic Capitalist Party"

As he geared up for his 2012 reelection campaign, President Barack Obama roasted the Republicans who opposed the administration's plans to spend billions to hire workers to repair the nation's crumbling infrastructure. Appearing at the foot of the Brent Street Bridge in Cincinnati, Obama decried a tax system tilted toward the rich.

"In the United States of America, a construction worker making fifty thousand dollars shouldn't pay higher taxes than somebody pulling in fifty million dollars," he told a raucous crowd filled with union members. "That's not fair. It's not right. And it has to change."

"The Republicans in Congress call this class warfare," Obama continued. "Well, you know what? If asking a billionaire to pay the same tax rate as a plumber or a teacher makes me a warrior for the middle class, I'll wear that charge as a badge of honor.

"I'm a warrior for the middle class; I'm happy to fight for working people," Obama shouted to the cheers of the crowd. "Because the only class warfare I've seen is the battle that's been waged against the middle class in this country for a decade."[1]

Obama's speech tapped the wellspring of Democratic Party support—the notion that the Democrats represent "the people," while the Republican Party represents big business and the rich. At the beginning of what looked to be difficult reelection effort, it was easy to forget that

Obama—not his 2008 Republican opponent, Arizona Senator John McCain—raked in the lion's share of corporate, business, and wealthy individuals' contributions in 2008. Officially, Obama raised more than three quarters of a billion dollars—doubling McCain's haul. Obama bested McCain by factors of two, three, and four to one from industries as diverse as lawyers and lobbyists; communications/electronics, finance, insurance and real estate (a.k.a. Wall Street), and defense. And while he received overwhelming support from labor organizations, Obama's total from the labor sector amounted to $585,000, compared to forty-two million dollars from Wall Street.[2]

As this chapter and the next two will show, the contradiction between Obama's "class warrior" rhetoric and his corporate backing is no accident. The Democratic Party is one of the two major political parties that have shared in governing the United States at all levels of government since the Civil War. The Democrats' reputation as the "party of the people" follows largely from the party's "Golden Age," the New Deal period (1933–1945), in which Democratic president Franklin Delano Roosevelt enacted a number of important social reforms. The 1960s "Great Society," under which Democratic administrations inaugurated Medicare and the "War on Poverty," solidified the identification of the Democratic Party with the downtrodden.

Yet, viewed with a wider lens, this history of Democratic reform on behalf of "the people" spans only about forty of the 150 years since the Civil War era. Even in the last generation, when working-class living standards have been cut, unions have been destroyed, and the majority of American workers have lost their belief that their children will have a better life then they did, the Democrats have done little to stem that tide. Since 1973, when the median wage in real terms peaked, the Democrats have held the White House for half as long as the Republicans have, but they have held the majority in Congress and the state legislatures for most of that time. Yet they did little to reverse the conservative-inspired offensive against working people's living standards. Kevin Phillips, a former Republican operative who turned against the dominant conservatism of the Reagan era, explained the persistence of the assault on working people in 1990:

> Much of the new emphasis in the 1980s on tax reduction and the aggressive accumulation of wealth reflected the Republican Party's long record of support for unabashed capitalism. It was no fluke that three important Republican

supremacies coincided with and helped generate the Gilded Age, the Roaring Twenties and the Reagan-Bush years.

Part of the reason survival-of-the-fittest periods are so relentless, however, rests on the performance of the Democrats as history's second-most enthusiastic capitalist party. They do not interfere with capitalist momentum, but wait for excesses and the inevitable popular reaction.

In the United States, elections arguably play a more important cultural and economic role than in other lands. Because we lack a hereditary aristocracy or Establishment, our leadership elites and the alignment of wealth are more the product of political cycles than they are elsewhere. Capitalism is maneuvered more easily in the United States, pushed in new regional and sectoral directions. As a result, the genius of American politics—failing only in the Civil War—has been to manage through ballot boxes the problems that less fluid societies resolve with barricades and with party structures geared to class warfare.[3]

So despite their (at times) populist rhetoric and support for social reform legislation, the Democrats are at their core an elite party concerned with sharing the responsibility of ruling the United States with the GOP. The differences that separate the Democrats and Republicans are minor in comparison to the fundamental commitments that unite them. To be sure, if there weren't differences between the two parties, there would be no justification for a two-party system. But for corporate America, which generally supports the Republicans more fervently than the Democrats, the two-party system plays an essential role. If one party falls out of favor with the voters, there's always the other one—with predictable policies—waiting in the wings. Even as the New Deal rearranged mainstream American politics, a well-known radical social commentator, Ferdinand Lundberg, stressed that the underlying nature of U.S. politics hadn't changed: "The United States can be looked upon as having, in effect, a single party: the Property Party. This party can be looked upon as having two subdivisions: The Republican Party, hostile to accommodating adjustments (hence dubbed 'Conservative') and the Democratic Party, of recent decades favoring such adjustments (hence dubbed 'Liberal')."[4]

A Bosses' Party: What Does This Mean?

Although the Democratic Party is one of the longest-existing mainstream parties in the world, it doesn't really compare to many of the world's political parties on the most basic levels. It has no fixed membership or membership requirements. Voters are Democrats if they vote for Democrats in elections. The party has no stated set of principles or programs. The closest approximation to a "program" is the party platform approved at the party convention every four years. As party conventions have developed into little more than trade shows rolling out that year's model (the presidential candidate), the party platform is usually synonymous with the candidate's talking points. In any event, Democratic Party candidates—from the presidency to the city council—are free to follow or to ignore the party platform in their election drives. It has no official political leadership outside of its candidate for president and important Democratic congressional officials. The Democratic National Committee, composed of hundreds of elected politicians, union leaders, lobbyists, and campaign donors, exists mainly to raise money for Democratic candidates. Its role in policy making or determining the direction of the party is fairly minimal. In essence, the Democratic Party is a loose federation of candidate-based local and state electoral machines.[5]

The Democratic Party isn't a membership organization or a mass party of the type developed by reform socialists in the late 1800s in Europe, in which party members joined a myriad of organizations, from singing clubs to trade unions, and subscribed to a party press that analyzed events from the party's ideological point of view.[6] It is more accurate to describe the Democratic Party as something closer to what mainstream political scientist Maurice Duverger described as a "caucus-cadre" party of "notables." In this type of party, a vestige of pre-twentieth-century forms, small groups of prominent people (politicians and business leaders) hire themselves activists (i.e., a cadre) to maintain the mechanisms of a party (getting out the vote, distributing patronage). These prominent people (the notables) aren't interested in involving more people or expanding democratic participation—in fact, they view voters and constituents as passive objects of the party's operation. The cadre is motivated to work for the party less because of a commitment to shared values or ideology than for career advancement—the possibility that they could climb the ranks of the party to become part of the circle of notables.[7]

While this description may seem theoretical, it becomes clearer when illustrated by its most visible example: a Democratic Party–run urban political machine. In the classic case of the machine of Richard J.

Daley that dominated Chicago from the 1950s to the 1970s, Democratic Party "members" started out as "doorbell ringers, working in the jobs their sponsors got for them, pushing the ward book [of tickets to party fundraisers], buying the tickets, doing the favors, holding the coats, opening the doors, putting in the fix, and inching their way up the organizational ladder, waiting for somebody to die and the chance to go on to the legislature, into the City Council, and maybe someday something even bigger."[8] A modernized version of this system, where city contracts played the role that patronage armies once did, operated in Chicago under the heir to the family dynasty, Richard M. Daley.[9] As we will discuss later (in chapter 7), generations of reformers who have thought that they could change the Democratic Party from within find out that this operation is highly effective at defusing their demands for increased democracy or for social change.

The party platform, an amalgam of general rhetoric, attacks on the Republicans, and a laundry list of specific policy recommendations, changes with every convention—and with the political winds. The 1972 Democratic platform, written when the 1960s' movements exerted influence on public opinion, would seem radical when compared with today's Democratic policy statements. For the 1988 election, pitting the technocratic liberal Massachusetts governor Michael Dukakis against George H. W. Bush, the Democrats produced a platform that included such right-wing staples as a call for a drug "czar," a call for a strengthened federal role in local law enforcement in order to secure "the safety of our neighborhoods and homes," endorsements of "fiscal responsibility," and warnings against the "Soviet threat" (when, ironically, the Soviet Union stood on the verge of collapse).[10] The current statement of the "Democratic vision" reads: "The Democratic Party is committed to keeping our nation safe and expanding opportunity for every American. That commitment is reflected in an agenda that emphasizes the security of our nation, strong economic growth, affordable health care for all Americans, retirement security, honest government, and civil rights."[11]

How can this seemingly ramshackle and decentralized operation act as one of the two parties by which the U.S. capitalist class exercises its rule? Describing the Democratic Party as a "bosses'" or "capitalist" party doesn't mean that it is a cog in a conspiracy in which a Wall Street cabal or top industrialists give orders for the party to follow. The relationship between capitalists and the Democratic Party is very open and often a source of tension with other major party donors and interest groups, such as organized labor. To answer the question about how the Democratic Party can be described as a capitalist party, we must step back and consider what, in theory, a bourgeois political party is.

The standard picture of a political party handed down to us from civics and political science classes is one of a collective body of people organizing to get from government what they can't get as individuals. The political party in a democracy represents the citizens, who indicate their preferences about what they want from government when they vote to put the party's candidates in office. And yet it's clear that this oversimplified model does not reflect reality.

A recent case in point would be the experience and aftermath of the 2006 congressional midterm elections that handed the Congress back to the Democrats after twelve years of Republican rule. Even the most mainstream analysts ascribed the Democratic victory to a public desire to end the war in Iraq. In polls taken immediately after the election, the public's desire to see the end of the Iraq War increased. Almost six in ten Americans supported a "timetable for withdrawal" from Iraq, and 73 percent of Americans said the United States should withdraw from Iraq within a year if the Iraqis wanted it, according to an early December 2006 poll conducted for the University of Maryland's Program on International Policy Attitudes. In fact, a September 2006 poll of Iraqis, conducted by the same polling outlet, found that 71 percent of Iraqis wanted the United States out within a year. So the majority of Iraqis and Americans agreed: the United States must leave Iraq—the sooner the better.[12] Yet less than a year after that historic election, the Democratic leadership in Congress had already folded on setting a timetable and, to the outrage of its most consistent supporters, had approved more than $120 million in continued war spending—providing even more money than President Bush initially requested. At the same time, the leading Democratic contenders for the presidential nomination were engaged in a process of redefining "withdrawal" from Iraq to render the term meaningless, in an effort to shift public opinion to approving a continued long-term occupation of the country.[13] Clearly, this isn't the way political science textbooks describe the operation of a democracy or a "responsible" political party.[14]

Meanwhile, the party that claims to be a "party of the people" has acted against the people time and again. Bill Clinton came to Washington promising to reverse twelve years of Reagan-Bush "trickle-down economics" and to "put people first." Expectations were so high that the Rainbow Coalition's Reverend Jesse Jackson, the standard-bearer for Democratic liberals at the time, told *Jet* magazine that "Bill Clinton and a Congress controlled by the Democrats have the opportunity to put America back to work and rebuild America with jobs, education, housing, health care and cleaning up the environment."[15] But Clinton insiders knew all along what the administration had in store. Only days after Clinton's 1992 election, an unnamed Clinton spokesperson told the *New York Times*: "Labor, minorities, environmentalists, Blacks, Hispanics, women, retired people, you name it, all see the pot of gold at the end of the rainbow. And somebody is going to be very disappointed."[16]

Indeed, one year into the administration, Treasury Secretary Lloyd Bentsen summarized its achievements: "When was the last time that you saw a Democrat who could stake his political career over a free trade agreement as this president over NAFTA? Who would have predicted a year ago that this administration would tackle one of business's number one concerns, that of deficit reduction? . . . Who would have expected a Democratic administration to propose cutting 252,000 jobs over the next five years, and bringing that one about?"[17]

Who would have thought? Certainly not the millions of people who voted in 1992 for Clinton's message of "change." These Democratic Party actions are perfectly understandable, however, if one evaluates them from a different conception of mainstream political parties. This conception sees the Democrats not as a representative of "voters" or "the people," but as one of the leading institutions that sustain the U.S. political system on behalf of the ruling capitalist class. To understand what this means, it is useful to understand the relationship among the state, social classes, and government that James Petras and Morris Morley used to analyze the 1980s' transition from dictatorship to electoral democracy in Latin America:

> The state refers to the permanent institutions of government and the concomitant ensemble of class relations which have been embedded in these same institutions. The permanent institutions include those which exercise a monopoly over the means of coercion (army, police, judiciary), as well as those that control the economic levers of the accumulation process. The "government" refers

to those political officials that occupy the executive and legislative positions and are subject to renewal or replacement.[18]

Petras and Morley go on to contrast the continuity of the state while highlighting "changes at the level of the regime." In other words, governments can change, while the state, the crucial determinant of the "long-term large-scale policies of a political system," remains intact.[19] Despite much antigovernment rhetoric that emanates from business sectors, the ruling class needs a capitalist state to guarantee its property and its influence against rival capitalist classes. As long as the regime's political parties remain committed to maintaining that state, big business can abide by changes in government. But just to assure that governments do not enact policies that work too much to the detriment of business, the capitalists attempt to shape and control the political parties that regularly compete to run the government. James O'Connor describes this as one way by which the capitalist class mediates conflicting goals and agendas:

> Because conflicts within the corporate ruling class must be reconciled and compromised and because of the complex and wide-ranging nature of the interests of this class, policy is dictated not by a single directorate but by a multitude of private, quasipublic, and public agencies. Policy is formulated within the highly influential Business Council, in key universities and policy-planning agencies such as the Foreign Policy Association and the Committee for Economic Development, and by the corporate-dominated political parties. This policy is a key input into the formulation of legislation initiated by the executive branch.[20]

The government—and in particular, the executive branch, acting as what Karl Marx called "a committee for managing the common affairs of the whole bourgeoisie"—pursues policies that balance short-term economic and political needs, and even sections of capital. "In this important sense, the capitalist state is not an 'instrument' but a 'structure.'"[21]

Applying these concepts to U.S. political parties, it is easy to see that the Democrats are concerned with the staffing of the government but not with altering the state. The Democratic Party, like the Republican Party, plays the role of helping big business to articulate its priorities through government while maintaining the power and stability of the political status quo. In many ways, these relationships between ruling party and ruling class are not ideological. They could easily describe the Republican Party as well as the Democratic Party. But they help to explain why so often the "party of the people" carries out the wishes of big business or the military-industrial complex instead.

Big Business and the Democrats: A Sound Investment?

Most great American fortunes were made by capitalists who used the power of government to gain advantages over competitors or to profit from public resources. Most of the Gilded Age plutocrats—the Vanderbilts, the Astors, the Stewarts, the Goulds—built their railroad-based fortunes on the foundation of a hundred million dollars in federal and state grants and two hundred million acres of federal land grants. The DuPont chemical empire owed much to the United States' seizure of German chemical patents and government assistance in building its plants during the First World War.[22] The modern nuclear power industry and the Internet are both products of the privatization of technologies developed in government laboratories. Many similar stories could be recounted, but the point is clear. Despite the free-market rhetoric that pits "Big Government" and "Big Business" against each other, big business has always found it useful to invest in politicians and their political parties to win government policies that improve their bottom lines. No wonder Marx's collaborator Frederick Engels described American political parties in 1891 as "two great gangs of political speculators, who alternately take possession of the state power and exploit it by the most corrupt means and for the most corrupt ends—and the nation is powerless against these two great cartels of politicians, who are ostensibly its servants, but in reality exploit and plunder it."[23]

In the political system of 1896—the system that organized American politics until the New Deal—it was generally the case that industrial firms that benefited from protectionism supported Republicans: "At the center of the Republican Party under the System of '96 was a massive block of major industries, including steel, textiles, coal, and, less monolithically, shoes, whose labor-intensive production processes automatically made them deadly enemies of labor and paladins of laissez-faire social policy."[24] Meanwhile the Democrats tended to organize a section of New York finance, Southern agriculture, and Western oil. As a result of the First World War's transformations of the U.S. economy, two different sets of business interests arose: one, capital-intensive industries, such as auto and electronics, that looked for opportunities to export their products to a world market; and two, internationally oriented banks taking advantage of the transition of the United States from a debtor to a creditor nation. These changes created what political scientist Thomas Ferguson called a "multinational bloc" that broke up the old party system and underpinned the new party system issuing from the New Deal. To Ferguson, the development of capital-intensive industries whose profits depended less on the cost of labor than on overall production conditions gave impetus to schemes for labor-management cooperation and "industrial democracy." This multinational bloc of businesses became the core capitalist supporters of the Democratic Party, whose New Deal program incorporated ameliorations for labor alongside an encouragement of free trade. After the Democrats lost the 1928 presidential election, two leading capitalists, John J. Raskob of General Motors and Pierre du Pont of DuPont Chemical Corporation, moved to professionalize the Democratic National Committee. With thousands of corporate dollars, Raskob and Du Pont gave the DNC its first permanent staff in preparation for the 1932 election.[25] At the same time, leading banks, such as National City (now Citibank) and Lehman Brothers, moved into the Democratic camp.

The onset of the Great Depression in 1929 created a demand in corporate America for action to reflate the economy. While incumbent President Herbert Hoover took some steps to meet business's demands, he followed the lead of the J. P. Morgan banking empire and refused a full program of reflation. In this context, "virtually all of the non-Morgan investment banks in America lined up behind Roosevelt" and a "powerful group of industrialists, large farm organizations, and retailers organized" to campaign for a program of government action to help the economy. In addition to Du Pont and Raskob, other leading "New Deal capitalists" included Gerard D. Swope of General Electric; Thomas Watson of IBM; Julius Rosenwald of Sears, Roebuck; Edward Filene of Filene's department stores; and Walter Teagle of Standard Oil Company of New Jersey (the future Exxon). In the First New Deal (1933–1934), the Democrats' programs of agricultural adjustment, separating investment and commercial banking (i.e., the Glass-Steagall Act), the "oil depletion allowance" (i.e., price controls on oil), and the cartelization of major industry (i.e., the National Recovery Administration) reflected the active support and policy advice of the main industries involved: the non-Morgan banking houses, East Texas oil, and desperate industrial firms looking for government protection. Representatives of these major corporate interests made their influence felt in campaign contributions to FDR, in their support of liberal foundations, and in helping to devise the legislation that FDR and Congress would enact in the first one hundred days of his administration. However, this coalition of business interests proved unstable and fell apart rapidly in the political battle over the NRA—and in the face of an emerging workers' struggle in the early 1930s.[26]

At this point, Ferguson argues, a "capital-intensive-led" coalition of businesses came together to prop up the Second New Deal, which produced the Social Security Act and the Wagner National Labor Relations Act. Teagle and Swope, who had pioneered various schemes of "welfare capitalism" in their companies in the 1920s, were appointed to the Commerce Department's Business Advisory Council, which held the responsibility to draft the Social Security Act. Meanwhile, Teagle, Swope, Filene, George Mead of Mead Paper, and representatives of Northeastern shoe and textile firms worked behind the scenes—or through liberal foundations—in support of the Wagner Act. Why did these "welfare capitalists" help to erect the New Deal while many of the rest in their class were coalescing to tear it down? Edward Berkowitz and Kim McQuaid explain:

> Welfare capitalists now lived with the knowledge that their company programs required a substantial federal underpinning to be effective. The NRA experiment had revealed the limits of voluntary business organization to solve the nation's problems. Businessmen lacked the unity necessary to defend themselves successfully against challenges to their authority, particularly challenges from organized labor. In addition, this business disunity was an implicit invitation for the federal government to solve the nation's welfare problems on its own, without the benefit of business advice. Still, by 1935 government had not accepted the invitation, and continued business control of America's social welfare system was as likely a possibility as any.[27]

While these "welfare capitalists" were certainly a minority of their class, they proved far-sighted enough to endorse the incorporation of labor into the political system at a time when class struggle was on the rise and the capitalist system was at risk of rebellion from below. The majority of the capitalist class reacted with fury to the New Deal and the rising labor movement. In 1935 the Du Ponts defected from the Democrats and joined with the House of Morgan and labor-intensive manufacturing firms to form the Liberty League, a right-wing lobby dedicated to sinking the New Deal. The Liberty League hoped to win the 1936 Republican candidate to its anti–New Deal, protectionist program.

This corporate counterattack might have worked but for the fact that Roosevelt cannily moved in two directions at once. On one hand, he reached out for support offered from the new labor movement through its newly formed Labor's Non-Partisan League. As Sharon Smith writes about the first prong of this strategy, "Roosevelt needed the working-class vote in order to win reelection in 1936, and he shrewdly tailored his campaign to win the hearts and minds of workers."[28] On the other hand, he adopted an aggressive promotion of "free trade" by which secretary of state Cordell Hull would be given the authority to lower U.S. tariffs in exchange for lowered tariffs abroad—forcing open markets to U.S. goods around the world. The second prong of the strategy was nearly as important as the first, and it produced similar results:

> [On October 29, 1936] at a mass meeting in the heart of the Wall Street District, about 200 business leaders, most of whom described themselves as Republicans, enthusiastically endorsed . . . the foreign trade policy of the Roosevelt Administration and pledged themselves to work for the President's reelection.
> They contended that if Landon [the 1936 Republican candidate] were elected and Secretary Hull's treaties were revoked, there would be a revolution among conservative businessmen.[29]

FDR won the 1936 election in a landslide, illustrating how the modern Democratic Party had perfected its appeal to working-class voters while loyally pursuing the interests of capital. While Roosevelt attacked the "economic royalists" of the Liberty League, he simultaneously benefited from the support of capitalists who themselves benefited from export markets and from Keynesian policies of demand stimulation in the United States.

The New Deal order organized American politics for the next two generations, including the agendas of both major parties. In 1967 the socialist Hal Draper explained this process well, and it is worth quoting him at length:

> A profound change has taken place in this country since the days of the New Deal—has taken place in the nature of capitalist politics, and therefore in the two historic wings of capitalist politics, liberalism and conservatism. In the 1930s there was a genuine difference in the programs put before capitalism by its liberal and conservative wings. The New Deal liberals proposed to save capitalism, at a time of deepgoing crisis and despair, by statification—that is, by

increasing state intervention into the control of the economy from above. It is notorious that some of the most powerful sectors of the very class that was being saved hated Roosevelt like poison. (This added to the illusions of the "Roosevelt revolution" at the time, of course.) Roosevelt himself always insisted that a turn toward state-capitalist intervention was necessary to save capitalism itself; and he was right. In fact, the New Deal conquered not only the Democratic but the Republican Party. When Roosevelt's New Deal and Truman's Fair Deal were succeeded by Eisenhower's regime, the free-enterprise-spouting Republican continued and even intensified exactly the same social course that Roosevelt had begun. (This is the reality behind the Birchite charge that Eisenhower is a "card-carrying Communist"!)

In the three and a half decades since 1932, and before, during and after a second world war which intensified the process, the capitalist system itself has been going through a deepgoing process of bureaucratic statification. The underlying drives are beyond the scope of this article; the fact itself is plain to see. The liberals who sparked this transformation were often imbued with the illusion that they were undermining the going system; any child can now see that they knew not what they did. The conservatives who denounced all the steps in this transformation, and who had to be dragged kicking and screaming into the new stage, were also imbued with the very same illusion. But even Eisenhower—who has never been accused of being an egghead, and who, before he was nominated for the presidency, made exactly the same sort of free-enterprise-hurrah speeches as [then-California governor Ronald] Reagan was paid to make for General Electric—even he was forced to act, in the highest office, no differently from a New Deal Democrat. Because that is the only way the system can now operate.[30]

Draper was a little shortsighted. Only a few years after he wrote these words, the system did indeed find a different way to operate. The New Deal order gave way to the conservative-dominated order that laid the groundwork for Ronald Reagan's election in 1980. This turnover wasn't the product of a change in popular attitudes. Instead, it marked a shift inside big business, under pressure from the worst recession in the postwar era (1973–75), away from accepting the regulated capitalism of the New Deal to promoting a more cutthroat neoliberalism. Chapter 3 discusses this shift in greater detail.

Political scientists Thomas Ferguson and Joel Rogers argue that since "tensions within the Democrats' ranks made them a less efficient vehicle for business aspirations than the Republicans," the GOP was the main beneficiary of the right turn in U.S. politics beginning in the mid-1970s.[31] But the Democrats were not content to let this situation stand. As the pillars of the New Deal coalition dissolved, the Democrats remade their party. Particularly in the 1990s, Democratic Party leaders under Bill Clinton reoriented the institution to the emerging sectors of the "New Economy" so that "the onetime party of Jefferson and Jackson emerged as the clear choice of many of the new Internet and telecommunications rich headed to the top of the *Forbes* 400."[32] After reviewing campaign finance data from the 2000 presidential election, Mike Davis drew a balance sheet of what "materially grounds partisan difference in the early twenty-first century":

> The Republicans . . . remain solidly grounded in the Old Economy sectors: indeed, the [George W.] Bush administration is virtually an executive committee of the energy, construction, and defense industries. On the other hand, the Democrats, primarily in the Clinton/Rubin years, have made spectacular gains in the New Economy. Meanwhile, Wall Street old money veers Republican while the new money is marginally Democratic. The health care sector, which favored Clinton in 1992, remains a competitive terrain for Democratic fund-raisers.[33]

Federal Election Commission data offer some insight into the political contributions to the two parties' national committees and congressional campaign committees during the 2010 election cycle. The Democrats showed strength in the "new economy" sectors, such as the communications and electronics sectors, which gave $21.2 million to Democrats and only $7.3 million to Republicans, in addition to traditional Democratic funders like organized labor and trial lawyers. The GOP remained anchored in such "old economy" sectors as agribusiness (with $7.6 million to the Democrats' $2.9) and energy (with $10.8 million to the Democrats' $4.5). Despite the contentious Washington debates over health care reform and financial services reform—or perhaps because of them—those industries tended to split their contributions between the two parties.[34]

Nevertheless, it would be misleading to conclude from these data that the Democrats simply represent one section or coalition of business while Republicans represent another. The operation of the two-party system assures that these divisions within American business are ad hoc and do not congeal into permanent ideological camps. Business must learn to operate within the federal system, which means that industries that may be big Republican donors at the presidential level may also support local Democratic political machines. Secondly, corporations like to increase their bargaining power. They want to get as much as they can from their political involvement and it helps them to be able to play one party off the other. Finally, corporations seeking government favors subscribe to "lesser evilism" as much as voters do. The congressional majority party, which for decades was the Democratic Party, usually is assured the majority of campaign finance contributions as well. Since its politicians will be in positions of authority in Congress with the power to advance legislation, business will contribute to the majority in order to maintain "access" to its congressional leaders.

What does corporate America expect for its investment? In total, the 2004 presidential election cost somewhere approaching four billion dollars. While this seems like a staggering sum, and, indeed, represents a twenty-fold increase in the cost of the presidential election in just eight years, it is equivalent to the size of an average "mid-cap" company. When Microsoft tycoon Bill Gates is worth more than fifty billion dollars and a company like Google is valued (in early 2008) at nearly two hundred billion dollars, the cost of buying the Oval Office appears to be a bargain. What is most notable is how much a relatively small investment in politicians will bring in returns for their "investors."

In fact, a 2007 study analyzing corporate donations and company stock performance between 1979 and 2004 found that corporations that contributed the most to political candidates had stock prices that beat the overall stock market by an average of 2.5 percentage points annually. And while corporations generally gave more to Republicans than to Democrats in this period, the study's authors found that contributions to Democrats actually had a bigger payoff for corporations. Prudential Equity Group analyst Charles Gabriel, commenting on the study's findings, explained: "If you are trying to assemble a critical mass of votes, that marginal Democratic vote is worth a lot. Democrats are the ones that get you over the hump."[35]

Consider the Telecommunications Act of 1996, one of the main legislative achievements that President Bill Clinton claimed in that election year. The bill, passed overwhelmingly with little public debate and quickly signed by Clinton, took down barriers of ownership and transmission rights of content among major media, radio, phone, and Internet companies. Although the industry promised a new era of competition that would lead to lower prices and greater choice for consumers, the exact opposite developed. The Telecommunications Act unleashed a bacchanal of media mergers and industry consolidation. In the decade following the act's passage, cable TV rates jumped by almost 50 percent and local phone charges increased by 20 percent. Under the

Telecommunications Act, the government gave to broadcasters *for free* digital TV licenses that were at the time valued at seventy billion dollars. One can only guess what they are worth today. All this for a total industry investment in the Democratic Party of about $309 million. At the head of the gravy train was Clinton, who bounced back from the 1994 loss of Congress to the GOP to win easy reelection in 1996. Ferguson observed:

> In the end, however, the best-kept secret of the 1996 election is that, more than any other single bloc, it was the telecommunications sector that rescued Bill Clinton. In my sample of large firms, this staggeringly profitable sector (which I treat as distinct from both the computer and software industries) stands out in its support for Clinton: Forty-six percent of the firms in my sample contributed to the president's re-election campaign through either individual contributions from top executives or soft money to the Democratic Party.[36]

Given the affinity between the telecommunications industry and the Democrats, it was no surprise that Roy Neel, a top aide to Vice President Al Gore and President Clinton, moved from the White House to the presidency of the United States Telecom Association, one of the main industry lobbying groups. While tending to the industry's needs, Neel took time out to briefly run "insurgent" Howard Dean's presidential campaign in 2004. Later that year, Neel directed the Democratic Party's legal and financial campaign to keep left-wing independent presidential candidate Ralph Nader off as many state ballots as it could.[37]

Pulling the Levers of Power

The notion that Democrats and Republicans are committed to capitalism and to advancing U.S. interests overseas is hardly news. But the capitalist class takes nothing for granted. It exerts constant pressure on the political parties to ensure that its interests are carried out. While there are numerous tentacles that tie the Democrats to big business, we briefly consider two major areas of corporate influence here: candidate selection and corporate lobbying and policy advice.

Candidate Selection

Elections are an expensive business. Anyone hoping to mount a successful campaign needs millions of dollars. In the 2006 congressional election, when the Democrats overturned a twelve-year-old Republican majority, the average House winner spent almost $1.3 million for his/her seat. The average Senate winner spent $8.8 million. Only twenty years before, in 1986, a House seat could be bought for $193,000 and a Senate seat cost $1.39 million.[38] The expense of electioneering means that both major parties look to wealthy individuals and to corporations for their funding. In fact, the major parties often decide to back particular candidates based on their ability to raise money.

For most of the period of GOP ascendancy (especially in the 1980s and 1990s), the Democrats lagged behind the Republicans in winning contributions from "small" donors—people who gave contributions of fifty or a hundred dollars. By the end of the Clinton administration, the Democrats leaned more heavily on "soft" money, a small number of huge contributions given by rich individuals for "party building" activity. Perhaps nothing better exemplified the spirit of the Clinton-Gore years than the May 24, 2000, Democratic fundraiser held in Washington, D.C.'s MCI Center. Pulling in a record $26.5 million in one evening, the Democrats paid tribute to their fundraiser-in-chief, outgoing President Bill Clinton. But unlike the blue-blooded Republicans, who dined extravagantly at their 2000 fundraiser, the Democrats ate barbecue served on paper plates. In keeping with this fake populism, organizers encouraged all who attended to wear blue jeans.[39]

The MCI Center spectacle typified the administration it honored. Like the Clinton-Gore administration, the Democratic Party itself hid its pro-corporate agenda behind a fog of populist rhetoric. Like the administration, it beat the Republicans at their own game. Campaign finance reform legislation passed in 2002 outlawed soft money contributions. The day after the law passed—but before it went into effect—media mogul Haim Saban, a children's entertainment billionaire, handed a check for seven million dollars to Terry McAuliffe, then DNC chairman. It is still considered the largest single campaign contribution ever given to a political party in U.S. history.[40] As the Democrats adjusted to the post–soft money era, they benefited from largesse from the likes of liberal hedge-fund billionaire George Soros, who spent an estimated $26 million to underwrite get-out-the-vote efforts in the 2004 election.[41]

Why would prominent capitalists and wealthy individuals give money to a party that is traditionally thought of as the "party of the people?" Certainly there are rich, liberal individuals who, for reasons of personal conviction or background, support Democrats over Republicans. Soros, for example, backed Kerry because, he said, "President Bush is endangering our safety, hurting our vital interests and undermining American values."[42] Billionaire investor Warren Buffett tends to support Democrats, and he campaigns against Republican-inspired plans to abolish the estate tax. Yet there are limits to what the likes of Soros and Buffett will support. As sociologist G. William Domhoff, writing about the "limousine liberals" of the early 1970s, put it, they "want a little touching up of the socioeconomic system around the ragged edges, but they don't want anybody tampering with sacred corporate institutions."[43]

While actions like Saban's check writing or Soros's spending in 2004 grab headlines, they are not the crucial measuring stick for corporate control of the Democratic Party. Perhaps it's obvious that donations from Democratic fat cats like Oracle's Larry Ellison, DreamWorks' David Geffen, or supermarket mogul Ron Burkle are proof that corporate America has nothing to fear from the Democratic Party. But the more central evidence of the Democrats' fealty to corporate America can be seen in the day-to-day accounting of the party's financial lifeblood. Although labor unions send about 90 percent of their political contributions to Democratic candidates, labor union money is not decisive in Democratic fundraising. In fact, of the $283.4 million in 2010 election contributions to the Democrats that could be associated with an industry or sector, only about one-quarter of them ($71.6 million) came from labor and liberal groups. The rest came from business sectors. During the 2008 Democratic sweep, the $83.7 million in contributions to Democrats from a single business sector (finance/insurance/real estate) dwarfed the contributions from labor and liberal interest groups ($74.6 million) *combined*.[44] Former Senator Russell Long (D-LA), the longtime chairman of the Senate Finance Committee, was not far from the mark when he said: "It would be my guess that about 95 percent of campaign funds at the congressional level are derived from businessmen."[45]

In parties like the British Labour Party, rules once specified that trade unions could cast blocs of votes for particular party candidates or for particular platform positions. Until Tony Blair's "New Labour" transformed the institution so that it would function more like the U.S. Democratic Party, almost no business money flowed into the

Labour Party's coffers. Accordingly, the trade unions influenced almost all of what happened in the pre-Blair British Labour Party. The Democratic Party has no such provisions. It is not the political expression of the trade unions—and the trade union leadership—like the Labour Party in its pre-Blair days. Even if the AFL-CIO supports whomever it considers to be the "pro-labor" candidate in Democratic primaries, it will generally back whichever Democratic candidate is chosen—even the most pro-business one. Thus, any money or campaigning support the AFL-CIO or other unions deliver to the Democrats is offered among all the other sources of money and support, predominantly corporate, that the party's candidates receive. It is little wonder that Democratic officials have time and again ignored union demands.

Business funding for the Democratic Party assures that it, like the Republican Party, will remain a loyal corporate representative in government. A chief Democratic financier, Richard A. Kline, executive director of the Council of Active Independent Oil & Gas Producers, explained why he helped to rally business contributions to the Democratic Congressional Campaign Committee for the 1986 elections: "A great danger in America is if we go the way of the British, with a labor party and a business party. And that's what's going to happen if the Democrats get no business money."[46] Kline needn't have worried, because the system of organized bribery that finances American political parties ensures that no one who might challenge this status quo becomes a serious contender. "Any candidate that expects to show up on the PAC lists is well aware of the need to tailor, if not eliminate, any populist leanings," a Democratic congressional aide told investigative journalists Alexander Cockburn and Ken Silverstein. "It's not a formula that opens the door to any but establishment candidates."[47]

The dwindling crop of sincere liberals among elected Democrats—people like representatives Barbara Lee of California and Raul Grijalva of Arizona—are exceptions that prove the rule. Federal Election Commission data shows that these two representatives receive most of their funds from labor unions and from committed individuals. Although they have long tenures in Congress and hail from "safe" seats, they would not even be in the running for leadership roles in Congress. But their value to the Democratic Party lies elsewhere. This point will be taken up later when we consider what makes the Democrats different from the Republicans.

Corporate Lobbying and Policy Advice

Once in office, Democratic (and Republican) administrations are subject to constant pressure from big business to adopt pro-corporate policies. Since the 1930s, the Business Council, an advisory organization composed of chief executive officers of major U.S. corporations, has acted as a sounding board and proponent for pro-business policies within every presidential administration. All U.S. presidents have regularly consulted the Council, and other organizations like the Committee for Economic Development (CED). Democratic and Republican administrations have appointed council and CED members to government advisory panels and to government administrative positions.

The business interests represented by such organizations as the council, the CED, and the Trilateral Commission have generally supported a limited government role in the economy and an interventionist foreign policy. For these reasons they coexisted quite well with Democratic administrations. Business Council influence was crucial in winning administration endorsement for a number of "Democratic" policies since the 1930s: Social Security, the Marshall Plan aid to post–Second World War European governments, and the 1964–65 Kennedy-Johnson tax cut plan.[48] In 1981 the Democrats inaugurated the Democratic Business Council (DBC), a constituency group inside the party, with a few dozen Democratic-leaning businesspeople. Today, the Democratic National Committee maintains a Small Business Owners Council and, at the state level, Democratic Business Councils organize thousands of businesspeople to contribute money and other resources to the party.

Business sustains these kinds of organizations, along with others like the Conference Board, the Chamber of Commerce, and the National Association of Manufacturers, to be able to develop class-wide positions on a range of issues. These can then be presented to the government through elected politicians and through executive branch agencies. Business isn't always successful in getting everything it wants, but it always gets what it can. Socialist Harry Braverman, writing in 1952 at the height of the Cold War with the USSR, explained this process well:

> The fact that the capitalist class or individual capitalists cannot get everything

they want from the capitalist state does not at all impress Marxists. They can't because circumstances make it impossible, not because the state power is against them. This is particularly true in the present period, when corporations must surrender a large portion of their profit to the war machine in order to safeguard the rest of it. Some thoughtless and irresponsible (from their own viewpoint) capitalists try to make an anti-regime platform of this, but they have been rejected by the overwhelming majority of the capitalist class in both the Republican and Democratic parties. For the rest, the capitalist class as a whole keeps up a running fire against high taxes, not because it could or would alter the tax structure fundamentally, but in order to keep its share as low as possible within the limits dictated by present circumstances.[49]

By many indicators, business devotes more money and time to lobbying and advocacy than it does to electioneering. This is because the real bonanza to companies is reaped from actions that take place behind closed doors, often in the arcane minutia of legislation and regulations. Companies seek favors for themselves, or, equally as important, win rewrites of regulations that allow them to profit. Here, a single line in legislation or a regulation can undo or render meaningless a politician's campaign promise. It's also the place where working people and the non-rich are completely overmatched. During the 2001 "debate" on the Bush tax cuts, Capitol Hill was crawling with lobbyists from every conceivable industry seeking favorable tax treatment. At the same time, the AFL-CIO had one lobbyist working quarter-time against tax cuts for the rich.[50]

When politicians seek to develop policies on any particular topic, they find business think tanks ready to offer up advice. One particularly crude example was that of former Democratic senator Bill Bradley, who represented New Jersey when it played host to ten of the eighteen largest pharmaceutical companies. Bradley's speeches "parrot[ed], sometimes virtually verbatim, background material produced by the Pharmaceutical Research and Manufacturers of America, the industry's chief lobbying group."[51] For years, hawkish senator Henry Jackson of Washington was known as the "senator from Boeing" for looking out for the largest military contractor in his state. Old bull Representative John Dingell (D-MI) had by 2006 served a half-century in Congress as a loyal servant of Detroit's auto industry. For decades Dingell almost single-handedly blocked regulations to increase auto fuel-efficiency standards.

Whatever their regional or local commitments, the two parties define the parameters of mainstream political debate and the horizons of policy alternatives that are put before the government. A good example of this was the failed 1994 health care reform effort led by Hillary Clinton. For months Clinton led a secret task force of five hundred experts, with insurance industry representatives placed strategically throughout. Although a few health care activists and advocates of a government-run single-payer system were included in the task force, the guiding principles of its recommendations came from big insurance companies' plans for "managed competition" between private health insurance plans.[52]

As a sop to progressive opinion, Vicente Navarro, an expert and advocate for a single-payer system, gained appointment to the task force. In an insightful account of his experience, Navarro described an encounter with Hillary Clinton:

> I told Mrs. Clinton that the only way of winning, and of neutralizing the enormous power of the insurance industry and large employers, was for the President and the Democratic Party leadership to make the issue one of the people against the establishment. It was a class war strategy that the Republicans most feared. My good friend David Himmelstein, a founder of Physicians for a National Health Program, told Mrs. Clinton the same thing. And as I judged by her response, she seemed to think we did not understand how politics works in the U.S. The problem is, we understood only too well how power operates.

Navarro approached Alain Enthoven, known as "the father of managed competition," to ask why, with the single-payer system proven to be more efficient and equitable, the United States didn't consider it. Enthoven replied, "The U.S. Political System is incapable of forcing changes in such powerful constituencies as the insurance industry." Navarro remarked, "Such candid admission of the profoundly undemocratic nature of the U.S. political system was refreshing."[53]

All things considered, big business prefers Republicans, whose generally open pro-business stances are not usually balanced against appeals to labor or the poor. But business is decidedly nonpartisan when it comes to protecting its interests, and Democratic politicians are also skilled at asking big business to open its wallet. When he headed the Democratic Congressional Campaign Committee, former California representative Tony Coelho mastered this pitch. Coehlo described his modus operandi to the *Atlantic*'s Gregg Easterbrook in 1986:

The thing to do with business men and women is to appeal to their business sense . . . You can't sell them H. R. 1236. You can't sell them a legislative program. People aren't interested in that. Business men and women want to be associated with success. If they see you are going to be successful, they latch on to you. I basically went out and said, 'I'm an entrepreneur in politics. I'm going to get the Democratic Party into direct mail, media centers, computers.' . . . I went to Texas and California. Where are the entrepreneurs in this country? The big numbers are in those states. I went to New York and later Florida, as well, but Texas and California the most. Some people will say that was where to find oil and gas money or conservative money. But I was going after a mentality. It's just like anybody else who starts a new business. Where do they find people who will invest in them? Among the entrepreneurs.

What I wanted was to make the DCCC like a business. What I have now is a business that is successful. My business had no assets, and today has five million dollars in assets. My business had no income, and today we open up our doors every month and get three hundred thousand dollars in direct mail. The business of politics is what I'm all about.[54]

When the GOP ran Congress from 1995 to 2007, it pioneered the "K Street Project,"[55] then–House majority leader Tom DeLay's plan to enforce Republican hegemony on the lobbying industry, which had practiced a "bipartisan" approach to Congress and the executive branch before the GOP took over Congress in 1995. As a cost of doing business with the new GOP majority, the GOP leadership demanded that corporations and lobbying firms hire Republican loyalists and contribute to campaign funds controlled by the congressional leadership. In this way the GOP leadership built a patronage machine that assured they always had the votes needed to pass through the GOP-corporate agenda.[56] But as soon as it became clear that the GOP would lose control of Congress in 2006, business returned to its "bipartisan" ways. In June 2006, five months before the election, the *Wall Street Journal* reported, "Some big companies are boosting their share of campaign contributions to Democrats this year, a sign that executives may be starting to hedge their political bets after a decade of supporting congressional Republicans."[57] Not to look a gift horse in the mouth, Representative Steny Hoyer, who took DeLay's position as majority leader when the Democrats won Congress, announced that he would start a fundraising operation that the *Hill* magazine dubbed "Hoyer's K Street Project." Hoyer appointed his top legislative adviser, who doubled as his liaison to corporations and lobbyists, to run the operation. And, the *Hill* noted, Hoyer "has sought to make himself the first contact for K Street."[58]

On K Street itself, the end of the Republican era meant new job opportunities for Democrats. With business anticipating that the 2008 presidential election would produce a Democratic Congress and White House, its lobbies were on the hunt for Democratic talent: "It's a bull market for Democrats, especially those who have worked for the Congressional leadership," a lobbyist told the *New York Times*. Even the Pharmaceutical Research and Manufacturers of America, whose executive director is former Republican congressman Billy Tauzin, hired several Democratic lobbyists so that its roster was balanced between the parties. All this activity ensures that no matter which party is officially in power, big business's interests will be attended to. A conservative military analyst, giving his assessment of the 2008 presidential election, bluntly admitted this: "Defense contractors have not only begun to prepare for the next administration. They have begun to shape it. They've met with Hillary Clinton and other candidates."[59]

What Makes the Democrats Different from Other Parties?

Up to this point, this chapter has illustrated how similar the Democrats and Republicans are. But the two-party system would not work the way it is supposed to if the two parties were identical. There must be at least some differences between the parties to give voters a stake in choosing which of the two will be in power after each election. So in early twenty-first-century America, the Democrats are the "pro-choice" party and the GOP mostly opposes reproductive rights. The Democrats tend to be friendlier to organized labor than the Republicans. Democrats tend to support provisions for immigrants to win a "path to citizenship," while the GOP harbors many more open nativists in its midst. Aside from providing these kinds of issue contrasts, a crucial role of the political parties is "binding citizens to the established political system. In a lesser fashion, they have sought to adjust conflicts among the dominant groups and accommodate pressures from the disadvantaged."[60]

Here is where the Democratic Party asserts its difference from the Republicans—and its usefulness to the "Property Party" that controls it. As chapter 5 will show in greater detail, modern-day Democrats have provided the bulk of political space where certain "out" groups in society—such as Blacks or labor unions—have been accepted into the political mainstream. Although labor organizations in the Democratic Party don't carry the weight that corporations do, the fact that organized labor has virtually no presence in the GOP creates institutional loyalty of organized labor and its members to the Democrats. This loyalty has only grown stronger as labor increasingly represents the public sector, whose support is more likely found among Democrats than Republicans. Likewise, African Americans vote overwhelmingly for Democrats—a legacy of the New Deal and Democratic support in the North for 1960s civil rights legislation.

But more important to the Democratic Party as an institution is the fact that organizations with grassroots followings, like the AFL-CIO, the National Organization for Women, the National Association for the Advancement of Colored People (NAACP), and the Sierra Club, provide the more "liberal" party with a social base. These groups don't have anywhere near the clout in the party that big business does, but they are important to giving the Democratic Party its appeal. The people who head these organizations have a stake in the Democratic Party's electoral success and, as a result, have an incentive to make sure that their followers continue to vote for Democrats. In fact, it is often in the realm of Democratic politics that these organizations of "the people" fall under corporate influence.

Writing in the early 1970s, Domhoff observed, "The benevolent rich among the power elite have several political fronts, most of which serve as support agencies for liberal Democrats even though they remain formally separate from the party and claim to be on the lookout for deserving liberal Republicans. These organizations also are a major avenue by means of which the high-toned liberals relate to their labor-union and middle-class allies."[61] At the time Domhoff was referring to organizations like the Field Foundation (of the Marshall Field department store fortune), Americans for Democratic Action (an anticommunist, liberal membership organization formed in 1947 to draw the Cold War line among liberals), and the Taconic Foundation (which funded some civil rights activism in the 1960s). Today these organizations are not the players they were, and liberal philanthropy is an industry that goes far beyond the vanities of individual rich people. But the same basic processes that Domhoff described are at work. The fate of the environmental movement provides a modern example. In the 1980s, when corporate foundations were extending their donations to environmental causes, one-time grassroots environmental groups like Friends of the Earth and the Wilderness Society responded by reinventing themselves as Washington-based policy shops. By the mid-1990s, according to muckrakers Alexander Cockburn and Ken Silverstein, environmental organizations were receiving about forty million dollars annually from oil company funded–foundations, and the Pew Charitable Trusts earmarked twenty million dollars a year to environmental organizations. All this created what Cockburn and Silverstein called a "Green establishment" that mimicked the "iron triangle" of special-interest politics during Bill Clinton's administration:

> In the Clinton era, the contours of environmental politics in Washington Babylon has settled into a triangulated landscape, bounded by the Executive Office Building and its agency outlets (where administrative fiats are handed down with devastating finality); the committee rooms of the Congress ... the grey mansions of the special interest lobbies, both environmental and industrial. ... Daily, the inhabitants of these centers of power determine the levels of lead in the blood of children in south-central L.A. ...
> At the top of the Executive pyramid now squats Bill Clinton.[62]

Cockburn and Silverstein go on to describe how the Clinton administration used its influence with leading environmental lobbyists—most of them Democrats—to persuade them to support the North American Free Trade Agreement and a Clinton-sponsored "compromise" that opened Northwestern old-growth forests to logging.[63]

Green Party activist Howie Hawkins, who ran against Hillary Rodham Clinton in the 2006 New York Senate race, aptly characterizes the people who head up these satellites of the Democratic Party as "professional liberals." Commenting on the stampede of all the leading liberal organizations into John Kerry's presidential campaign in 2004, Hawkins wrote:

> [Professional liberals include] ... the paid staff and leaders of the unions and the big environmental, peace, civil rights, women's, gay, and community organizing groups. Selling out to the Democratic Party pays off for the professional liberals in the form of career opportunities and funding. These material benefits flow through social and organizational networks that connect the professional liberals in nongovernmental organizations (NGOs) to their peers in Democratic administrations and the corresponding party organizations that are built from the top down by Democratic patronage and preferment. Corporate funding—grants for the NGOs, universities, and progressive media, and campaign cash for the Democrats—cements it all together, co-opting institutionalized progressivism into the service of the corporate-dominated Democratic coalition.[64]

Hawkins's crucial point must be considered when evaluating the actual, existing Democratic Party. As argued earlier, the Democratic Party is an institution of capitalist rule, but capitalists don't mobilize voters as effectively as the local trade union official or church leader does. Those activists are very important to the entire operation of liberalism in American politics. This is not just because they're the people who get out the vote on Election Day (using funds provided from party coffers stuffed with corporate money), but also because they're the ones who give liberalism any sort of appeal for a social base. That's why liberals and Democrats sustain people like the Reverends Jesse Jackson or Al Sharpton. A Jackson or a Sharpton may at times lead an oppositional movement or may dissent from the mainstream Democrats. Likewise, people like Barbara Lee and Dennis Kucinich may propose programs and use rhetoric that push the left-most boundaries of "acceptable" opinion. But every time a figure like a Jackson or a Lee uses his or her credibility as an advocate for liberal causes to promote a mainstream Democratic candidate, it helps to convey to their bases that there are important differences between the two parties—or at least differences enough to allow the Democrats to present themselves as a lesser evil to the Republicans.

Many sincere activists work in liberal organizations and unions and on behalf of their members. But in the liberal universe, these organizations are part of an apparatus of control that ensures that the political demands they raise are never too far from what Democratic politicians consider "acceptable." More often than not, these organizations become transmission belts for Democratic Party talking points rather than acting as champions of their constituencies. Perhaps the most extreme example of this occurred during the disputed 2000 Florida presidential recount struggle, when Reverend Jesse Jackson and the AFL-CIO mobilized to defend the votes of thousands of African-American and working-class Floridians disenfranchised by pro-Bush Florida officials. Thomas Harrison recounted the sorry aftermath:

> Apparently, Jackson threatened at one point to lead demonstrations in Florida, and he was told by the Democratic National Committee to back off—meanwhile leaving the field clear for mobs of Republican congressional staffers who were flown down to intimidate vote counters.
>
> The Democrats' fear of disruptive protest was consistent with the overall conservatism and defeatism that the leadership displayed in this election and, particularly since the Reagan era, has become the party's distinguishing

feature. . . . The party's leaders do not want street demonstrations, nor do they want to give the world the impression that American "democracy" runs with anything less than clockwork precision. Therefore, the rabble are not to get involved. Everything must be done though the proper channels. In a "mature democracy" such as ours, the proper function of ordinary citizens is to vote and go home and leave the really important business of the nation—keeping down the standard of living (a.k.a. "preventing the economy from overheating"), policing the world and creating optimal conditions for capital accumulation—to their betters. It is crucial that this business be carried on with as little fuss as possible.

Although the Democratic Party might have benefited from a fight for democracy in Florida, the party bosses pulled back. And liberal leaders grudgingly went along with them. As the late New York senator and Democratic Party "wise man" Daniel Patrick Moynihan said, perhaps admitting more than he intended: "It doesn't so much matter who wins. The important thing is the legitimacy of the system."[65]

The Politics of Lesser Evilism

Minimal political differences between the two main parties and the fact that leading liberal organizations are tied to the Democratic Party form the basis of the politics of "lesser evilism"—of voting for the lesser of two evils. In a country where working people have not developed a party of their own, most voters are left to decide their vote on Election Day according to which choice they dislike least—or to stay home, abstaining from political action. Political scientist Walter Dean Burnham has for decades argued that the huge "party of nonvoters"— which dwarfs the vote for either main party and which is overwhelmingly working-class and poor—represents millions who would vote if the U.S. system offered them a choice of a workers' or labor party.[66]

Leading liberals operate in this environment and have come to accept its limitations. "We support what's possible," they'll say, "not what's desirable." After Bill Clinton endorsed the 1996 bill repealing Aid to Families with Dependent Children, a program that grew out of FDR's Social Security Act, *Nation* columnist Katha Pollitt denounced her fellow liberals for holding their fire against Clinton because they feared what the Republicans would do:

> These liberal groups are caught up in mainstream electoral politics, which in practice means clinging to Clinton and the Democratic Party. . . . Meanwhile, they preach the gospel of the lesser of two evils, that ever-downward spiral that

has brought us to this pass and that will doubtless end with liberals in hell organizing votes for Satan because Beelzebub would be even worse.[67]

Democrats know that, no matter how much liberals complain, they will accept the Democrats as the lesser evil on each Election Day. Indeed, the stability of the corporate-dominated two-party system rests on this, as political scientist Sheldon S. Wolin, noted:

> The timidity of a Democratic Party mesmerized by centrist precepts points to the crucial fact that, for the poor, minorities, the working class, anticorporatists, pro-environmentalists, and anti-imperialists, there is no opposition party working actively on their behalf. And this despite the fact that these elements are recognized as the loyal base of the party. By ignoring dissent and by assuming that the dissenters have no alternative, the party serves an important, if ironical, stabilizing function and in effect marginalizes any possible threat to the corporate allies of the Republicans.[68]

The Democrats agree with the Republicans on all fundamental issues, even if they disagree on specific policies. If Democrats argue that social programs should not be cut as deeply as the Republicans desire, they agree that such programs must be cut to demonstrate "fiscal responsibility." If Democrats campaign for slightly less regressive tax programs, they and the Republicans agree that tax breaks for the rich will stimulate investment. Both want to preserve a "good business climate." In times of economic expansion, this means confining social welfare expenditures and programs within business-defined limits. In times of economic contraction, this means cutting back on social spending and attacking working-class living standards. If they disagree on a particular use of military power, they are no less committed than the Republicans to extending U.S. influence around the world. In the meantime, the severe crises facing millions of Americans, including lack of affordable health care and declining living standards, remain unaddressed. For the bosses the arrangement is ideal: two capitalist parties help to uphold their rule, with one masquerading as the friend of labor and the poor. But for workers, every election presents a choice between two options, neither of them desirable.

Chapter Two

The Party of Slavery Becomes the "Party of the People"

The Democrats' reputation as "the party of the people" flows largely from the party's "Golden Age"—the New Deal period (1933–1945) when Democrats passed a series of unprecedented pro-working-class reforms. The mythic status of President Franklin Roosevelt's Depression-era platform, remembered for its public works, employment, and Social Security programs, perpetuates this view. The "Great Society" of the 1960s reinforced the identification of the Democratic Party with reform, as Democratic presidents passed voting rights legislation while also inaugurating Medicare and the "War on Poverty."

But the real history of the Democratic Party—in particular, its close identification with both plantation slavery and racial segregation—belies this progressive reputation. Many of the party "traditions" that most Democratic candidates pledge to defend are not particularly admirable. Although it is true that some Democratic administrations have helped to create important social welfare programs, others have helped to dismantle them. Furthermore, some Republican presidents have also spurred social reform. These reforms have not been unique to the United States, but have paralleled (or lagged behind) similar moves in all developed capitalist countries. In the period of economic boom following the Second World War, all capitalist countries, regardless of governmental party, increased spending for education and employment security—programs considered necessary to boost the productivity of labor. In addition, social reforms were passed in response to the demands of working-class struggle from below.

Indeed, the Democratic Party's effectiveness in containing progressive movements helps to explain its resilience over the past fifty years. If today's labor, women's rights, and civil rights activists look to the Democrats, it is because the Democrats have succeeded in co-opting much of the leadership of those particular struggles. To the extent that it has succeeded, the Democratic Party has been able to channel the radical energies of mass social movements into Democratic electoral campaigns.

The Origins of the Modern Democratic Party

Just about every year, and certainly during every election year, local Democratic Party organizations around the country hold "Jefferson-Jackson" dinners in honor of Thomas Jefferson and Andrew Jackson, presidents who are considered in many ways to be the founders of the Democratic Party. The organization that became the Democratic Party actually began life as the Democratic-Republican Party, founded in 1792, and also known as the Republican Party (yet another example of the interchangeability of the two main U.S. parties!). It emerged from the anti-Federalist wing of President George Washington's administration, the first government under the U.S. Constitution. The Democratic-Republicans, led by Jefferson, organized an opposition to a treaty with Great Britain negotiated by John Jay in 1794, and transformed the party from a loose grouping of politicians and interests into a more self-conscious political party. The details of the fight over Jay's treaty are less important than how it polarized the Washington administration and led to the formation, around Jefferson and James Madison, of the parliamentary and electoral predecessor of today's Democratic Party.[1] After 1824 the Democratic-Republican Party became known simply as the Democrats. It held under its banner a heterogenous coalition of forces, but its core was the Southern slaveholding aristocracy that Jefferson and Madison embodied. Harry Braverman's Marxist analysis of the American party system of the early nineteenth century, written in 1946, provides an excellent summary of the class alignments of the period:

We must recall that the policy of the Jeffersonian party had been to take the reins of the national government and draw into cooperation with the planters, sections of the Northern capitalist class. So successful had been this policy that the bourgeois Federalist Party was virtually dissolved in the Jeffersonian party during the administrations of Jefferson, Madison, Monroe and the second Adams. The Eastern planters grew accustomed in this so-called "era of good feeling" to secure their rule by means of this alliance at the cost of some concessions to the New England merchant capitalists. However, the fundamental antagonism between the two systems could not forever be repressed. In the North an aggressive manufacturing bourgeoisie was supplanting the merchant class. Paralleling this was the rise of an aggressive cotton slavocracy in the Southwest. Here were the chief contenders in the coming irrepressible conflict.[2]

In fact, as Braverman goes on to explain, Andrew Jackson, the champion of the "aggressive cotton slaveocracy in the Southwest," was in many ways the founder of the modern Democratic Party. "Jacksonian democracy" pioneered many of the trappings of modern bourgeois democratic politics: mass electioneering, the spoils system, urban patronage machines (especially New York's Tammany Hall), political conventions, and primary elections among them.

Jacksonian democracy took root in the first half of the nineteenth century, an era of enormous—and brutal—social change. This included the vast expansion of slave plantation agriculture ("King Cotton") toward the West, dispossession and genocide against Native Americans in the eastern and central parts of the country, and the seizure from Mexico of the territory that laid open a path to the Pacific. And as a result of industrialization, workers began forming organizations to defend their interests against their employers. Throughout this period of massive change, Jacksonian democracy maintained its reactionary, slavery-based core while gaining a mass following based on near-universal suffrage of white males:

The original home of this political art was in the Northern wing of the planters' Democratic Party—an auxiliary in enemy territory. It fought the bourgeoisie through sections of the urban petty-bourgeois and proletarian masses, who were mobilized by means of democratic and even anti-capitalist slogans. The planting class, resting on unorganized, unrepresented, almost unmentioned slave labor, could afford to countenance reforms which struck against the Northern bourgeoisie. The ten-hour day for workers, extension of the vote to the proletariat, attacks upon the factory system and other such agitations, typical of the Jackson period, represented no direct economic threat to the planters. During the Jackson period the planters put on their best democratic garb . . . in the North. But during that very same time, barbarous slave legislation multiplied on the statute books in the South. The concessions in the North were part of the slaveholder system of maintaining national power. John Randolph, the erratic phrasemaker of the planter bloc in Congress, gave clear expression to this strategy. "Northern gentlemen," he taunted, "think to govern us by our black slaves, but let me tell them, we intend to govern them by their white slaves!"[3]

The Democrats' populist rhetoric of "anti-monopolism" and "producerism" attracted the "producing classes" (yeoman farmers, workers, self-made men, and immigrants) opposed to "bloodsuckers" (bankers, lawyers, and speculators), while uniting this diverse Democratic base with the slavocracy. The slavocracy, in turn, had its own reasons to oppose industrial capital, represented in the antebellum era by the Whig Party.[4] Despite its populist ranting,

> The Democratic Party's professed egalitarianism was for whites only. Its commitment to slavery and racism was blatant in the North as well as the South. . . . At the other end of the social scale, Democratic leaders in New York included many bankers and merchants who had nothing in common with the Irish-American masses in the tenements except their allegiance to the same party.[5]

In the antebellum era, the slavocracy's quest for expansion to the West found its highest expression in the policies of "manifest destiny" proclaimed by Democratic president James K. Polk, who had commanded U.S. forces in their seizure of northern Mexico in 1847–48. Southern Democrats also controlled the Supreme Court, which issued its *Dred Scott* ruling in 1857—arguably the most appalling decision in the Court's entire history—revealing the Democratic Party's bottom-line fealty to the slavocracy in the antebellum era. The *Dred Scott* decision declared that "a black man has no rights that a white man is bound to respect," while upholding the federal Fugitive Slave Act, which gave slaveholders a right to reclaim their human property even in states that had outlawed slavery. This decision came at the end of a series of patched-together compromises (e.g., the Kansas-Nebraska Act of 1854) between the increasingly hostile slavocracy and the growing forces of industrial capital—which embraced the notion of "free soil" and "free labor." The "irrepressible conflict" wasn't simply based on sectional or regional disputes, but at root was a class conflict that helped to pull apart the Democratic coalition. As Peter Camejo wrote,

> [In the 1850s, the slavocracy's] political ally up to that time, the small farmer of the Midwest, was trying to acquire the same lands it wanted for the expansion of the Cotton Kingdom. This competition became so intense that for a time it

dominated national politics. In Kansas the struggle turned bloody ... with John Brown waging guerrilla warfare against the proslavery forces.[6]

In the 1850s the U.S. polity was clearly heading for an irreversible split over the issue of slavery. The Democratic Party divided its own forces between Northern Democrats such as Illinois senator Stephen Douglas, who proposed an arrangement preserving the old North-South/farmer-slaver alliance, and Southern fire-breathers, including Mississippi senator Jefferson Davis, who became the leaders of the Confederate States of America.

The Civil War of 1861–1865 forged modern American politics. While one section of the Democrats ruled the Confederacy, the Northern wing of the party formed the opposition to the Civil War effort led by Republican president Abraham Lincoln. "The Republican Party became the means for mobilizing war resources, raising taxes, creating a new financial system, initiating emancipation, and enacting conscription. Democrats opposed most of these measures," James McPherson wrote.[7] The leading Northern Democratic opponents of the war, nicknamed the Copperheads, engaged in activities that were openly treasonous. Copperhead activism and Democratic-led street-level organization lit the fuse of the racist New York City draft riots in 1863. During the riots, predominantly immigrant mobs not only destroyed symbols of federal authority, but also lynched ordinary Blacks.[8] Until the Los Angeles rebellion of 1992, following the Rodney King verdict, the draft riots were the largest urban insurrection in U.S. history. But it illustrated yet again the paradox of the Democratic Party: a political organization composed at its base of ordinary working-class people but serving the interests of a reactionary minority.

From Reconstruction to the New Deal

The Civil War's outcome established the dominance of industrial capital over the entire country by eliminating the major obstacle to its expansion, the Southern slaveholders, and opening the road to a modern capitalist economy. It also established the overwhelming predominance of the two major government parties, the Republicans and Democrats, while cementing the coalitions that backed them. The defeat of post–Civil War Reconstruction in the 1870s established the Democratic Party, now the party of the plantation owners, as the segregationist ruling class of the South. Though largely disenfranchised, Blacks who could vote supported the Republicans as the party of Lincoln, who "freed the slaves." From the 1880s through the early 1900s, the working class divided its loyalties between the Republicans and Democrats—although for the two decades after 1901, the Socialist Party of America drew significant support among workers and poor farmers. Native-born Protestant workers tended to support the Republicans, leaving immigrant workers, often Catholics from Ireland, Italy, or Poland, to the Democratic urban political machines that consolidated in Northern cities at the turn of the twentieth century. As Mike Davis explains:

> The ensuing split in the U.S. working class lasted until the eve of the New Deal, with consequences that were inimical to the development of class consciousness. Native Protestant workers rallied to the leadership of their Protestant bosses and exploiters while Catholic immigrants forged an unholy alliance with Southern reaction.[9]

Thus, both major parties allied specific segments of the capitalist class with sections of the working class. In these alliances the capitalist interests—which supplied money, candidates, and expertise to the parties—were in command, while the working class was expected to play a passive role as voters.

The major bloc that controlled the Democratic Party's policy decisions comprised the remnants of the Confederacy, Southern business interests. Until 1936 the party's "two-thirds" majority rule for voting guaranteed that these reactionary Jim Crow forces held virtual veto power over the party's presidential nominee. Meanwhile, the Democrats' monopoly of Southern state and congressional representation meant that Southern Democrats formed a persistent conservative bloc in Congress and in the Supreme Court.

The 1929 stock market crash and the onset of the Great Depression followed a decade-long employers' offensive against the labor movement that reduced trade union membership from 19.4 percent of the nonagricultural workforce in 1920 to 10.2 percent in 1930.[10] The labor movement seemed dead, with no new strategies and nowhere to turn for new members. Unemployment hit one-quarter of all workers in 1933.

The economic crisis was Roosevelt's cue to produce a program to save American capitalism. He enlisted the help of some of the country's leading businessmen, including General Electric's Gerard Swope and Walter Teagle of Standard Oil of New Jersey, who argued that crisis conditions required state intervention to control the excesses of private capitalism. The "New Deal capitalists" urged Roosevelt to adopt reforms modeled on private-sector benefit and insurance plans. The Social Security Act, passed in 1936, took as its inspiration a number of "welfare capitalism" programs that some of the country's leading corporations established in the 1920s.

Despite some capitalists' complaints that the New Deal represented a step toward "socialism," Roosevelt and the New Dealers had no such intention. In fact, Roosevelt argued to his business critics, "I am the best friend the profit system ever had." In campaign speeches in 1936 he proclaimed himself the "savior" of "the system of private profit and free enterprise."[11]

Roosevelt's "New Deal" coalition was launched in this context. While popularly perceived as an alliance of Blacks, labor, urban dwellers, and other "popular" constituencies, behind it all was a fundamental recasting of the alignment of business forces in American politics. The New Deal coalition involved not

> the millions of farmers, Blacks and poor that have preoccupied liberal commentators, nor even the masses of employed or striking workers who pressured the government from below . . . but something else—a new power bloc of capital-intensive industries, investment banks and internationally oriented commercial banks.[12]

Despite the fact that the New Deal represented, in essence, a political rearrangement of American capital, it succeeded only by striking a new arrangement with the system's traditional victims. Clause 7a of the New Deal's National Industrial Recovery Act, which granted the right of workers "to organize and bargain collectively," represented part of the arrangement. While the Roosevelt administration initially aimed to create company unions that would aid the hoped-for economic recovery, union organizers took advantage of Clause 7a to build genuine unions.

The 1933–34 industrial upturn brought workers back into the manufacturing plants where they could feel their collective strength, giving them greater confidence to fight back. By the end of the 1930s, a mass radicalization—exemplified by the 1934 general strikes in Minneapolis, San Francisco, and Toledo, followed by the 1936–37 wave of sit-down strikes and factory occupations—had rebuilt the labor movement. For the first time, under the banner of the Congress of Industrial Organizations (CIO), American workers created industrial unions across broad sections of industry. In 1940 unions represented just under 27 percent of all U.S. workers, and by 1945 union membership reached its high-water mark of almost 36 percent of non-agricultural workers.[13]

The New Deal: Myth and Reality

The New Deal and its reforms emerged as part of a program to save a capitalist system facing its greatest crisis ever during the Great Depression. Between 1929 and 1933, U.S. industrial production dropped by almost 50 percent. Unemployment expanded to nearly eighteen million workers by March 1933, when Roosevelt took office. The crisis forced the government to act, breaking from decades of "laissez-faire" capitalism and the unbridled rule of employers over their workers. Roosevelt's "New Deal was a recognition that capitalism in its monopoly stage could no longer solve its problems without systematic state intervention."[14] But even as Roosevelt and his "brain trust" were improvising the policies that became known as the New Deal, much of the Democratic Party itself had still not broken from its small-government, states'-rights past. During the 1932 campaign, Roosevelt's running mate, John Nance Garner, argued, "Had it not been for the steady encroachment of the federal government on the rights and duties for [sic] the states, we perhaps would not have the present spectacle of the people rushing to Washington to set right whatever goes wrong." And John W. Davis, the Democrats' unsuccessful presidential nominee in 1924, even denounced incumbent Republican President Herbert Hoover for "following the road to socialism."[15]

But the views of Garner and Davis were clearly out of step with what the crisis demanded. The half-century before the 1929 stock market crash represented the greatest concentration and centralization of capital in American history. On the eve of the crash, the two hundred largest corporations in the country accounted for one-half the corporate wealth and 20 percent of national wealth.[16] Yet at that time the U.S. government was composed of a patchwork of state and federal-level agencies, impeding a national response to the scale of crisis the Depression necessitated. The outgoing Republican Hoover administration took tentative steps in the direction of greater state intervention in the economy. It created the Reconstruction Finance Corporation to provide government loans to failing businesses. It promoted trade association industrial cartels. And it experimented with short-term public works projects. But the Hoover administration never broke from the view that the private market should lead economic recovery. In contrast, FDR was willing to consider greater government intervention into the private market in order to save capitalism.

The centerpiece of Roosevelt's first recovery program was the National Industrial Recovery Act (NIRA), which assumed that economic stabilization would flow from coordination between large-scale businesses. Rather than "bust trusts," the federal government would oversee the formation of industry-level codes to regulate wages, prices, and production. At least some of FDR's advisers saw a connection between industrial concentration and provision of a "social wage" to workers.

Adolph Berle and Louis Faulkner, two of FDR's economic advisers, argued in a 1932 memo to candidate Roosevelt that an economic recovery policy predicated on facilitating industry concentration and regulation should also include some social-welfare provisions: "Although apparently differentiated from problems of concentration, insurance against old age, unemployment and sickness really becomes necessary as a result of concentration. . . . In concentrated industry, the individual has no real liberty of action; he is at the mercy of a uniform system with which he cannot possibly cope."[17]

After Roosevelt's election in November 1932, Berle pressed FDR to act boldly because "we may have anything on our hands from a recovery to a revolution. The chance is about even either way. My impression is that the country wants and would gladly support a rather daring program."[18] Despite his patrician origins, Roosevelt shrewdly exploited popular discontent to win support for his program. In fact, the very name of this program, the New Deal, owed to Roosevelt's crafty co-optation of dissent, as brain truster Samuel I. Rosenman recounted.[19]

As Rosenman told the story, Roosevelt was awaiting the Democratic nomination in Chicago from the governor's mansion in Albany, New York. Meanwhile, hundreds of First World War veterans were marching on Washington to demand that Hoover advance the payment of their veteran bonus to help them cope with unemployment. Like Hoover, Roosevelt had opposed paying the bonus. In Albany, Roosevelt received a call from Louisiana's populist governor Huey "Kingfish" Long. Long told

Roosevelt that he would clinch the nomination if he embraced the bonus marchers. As Rosenman recounted the conversation:

> Long: "I think you should issue a statement immediately, saying that you are in favor of a soldiers' bonus to be paid as soon as you become President."
>
> Roosevelt: "I am afraid I cannot do that because I am not in favor of the bonus."
>
> Long: "Well, whether you believe in it or not, you'd better come out for it with a statement, otherwise you haven't got a chance for the nomination."

When Roosevelt still refused, Long hung up, telling FDR that he was "a gone goose." FDR's staff "began to think that the Kingfish might have been right." So they crafted a speech for Roosevelt that, while not openly endorsing the demands of the bonus marchers or of other ordinary people, pledged more vaguely—but no less powerfully—"to a new deal for the American people."[20]

Roosevelt's first one hundred days in office focused on aid to banks and other businesses. After Congress passed an act setting up the Federal Deposit Insurance Corporation, one congressman remarked that Roosevelt "drove the money changers out of the Capitol on the 4th [March 4, Inauguration Day]— and they were all back in on the 9th."[21]

The NIRA initially received the backing of both capital and labor. FDR garnered labor support with the NIRA's Clause 7a and its perceived collective bargaining rights for workers. Unionists read in Clause 7a support for genuine trade unions. The United Mine Workers of America recruited new members with leaflets announcing, "The president wants you to join a union."[22] Capitalists, meanwhile, read in Clause 7a government approval for their schemes to promote phony company unions.

For most of the first two years of Roosevelt's administration, the National Recovery Administration (NRA, the organization that implemented the NIRA) disappointed its working-class supporters. In particular, the emerging labor movement found that NRA administrators consistently sided with companies against unions. Unionists took to calling the NRA "the National Run-Around."[23] But the 1934 strike wave showed that workers were willing to fight for genuine trade unions, with or without government support. The three breakthrough strikes in Toledo, Minneapolis, and San Francisco showed common characteristics: mass picketing, self-defense against police and scabs, and radical leadership. All of them had quickly escaped control of the conservative American Federation of Labor union leaders. Indeed, the 1934 strike movement demonstrated the threat to the system that a mass working-class movement posed.[24]

The radical labor movement that exploded in 1934 pushed the Roosevelt administration and its friends in Congress to enact the "second New Deal" of labor and social reform in 1935 and 1936. Proponents of reforms like the National Labor Relations Act (NLRA) and the Social Security Act endorsed them as necessary to short-circuit radicalization. Representative Connery, speaking in 1934 *in support* of the NLRA, warned, "You have seen strikes in Toledo, you have seen Minneapolis, you have seen San Francisco, and you have seen some of the southern textile strikes . . . but you have not yet seen the gates of hell opened, and that is what is going to happen from now on" if the NLRA wasn't passed.[25] Meanwhile, labor leaders like the United Mine Workers' John L. Lewis and the Amalgamated Clothing Workers' Sidney Hillman sought to institutionalize a system of genuine collective bargaining.

To be sure, the NLRA, passed in 1935, represented a significant gain for the entire working class. It marked the first time the federal government guaranteed workers the right to organize. But these reforms also held political benefits for Roosevelt and the Democrats in addition to helping preserve social peace. At the start of the 1930s, the Democratic Party had been the minority party in the American political system since the decisive establishment of Republican dominance in 1896. The party represented little more than a collection of urban machines in the Northeast and the "solid South," whose Democratic majorities rested on the disenfranchisement of Blacks. But the 1930s created the conditions for a massive shift of party loyalties among farmers, Black voters, and urban, working-class ethnic voters into the Democratic camp. In three consecutive national elections between 1932 and 1936, the Democratic majority in Congress and in the electorate swelled. By the end of the 1930s, the Democratic Party had established itself as the majority capitalist party that would dominate the next two generations of American politics.

Most corporate leaders opposed the New Deal reforms—especially pro-labor legislation. They continued to contribute money and support to the Republican Party despite the fact that voters rejected the Republicans. But not all capitalists opposed the New Deal. In particular, prominent "welfare capitalists" like General Electric's Gerald Swope and Standard Oil's Walter Teagle took part in a presidential advisory panel that drafted the Social Security Act. Ferguson and Rogers argue that the New Deal won support from capital-intensive industrial corporations, internationally oriented commercial banks, and investment banks in particular.[26]

In 1935, secretary of state Cordell Hull pressed for and won from Congress the ability to negotiate bilateral "free-trade" treaties between the United States and other countries. This policy helped open wide the gap in the business class between "isolationists" who supported old Republican protectionist policies and those who began to see promotion of U.S. exports as a road to economic recovery. J. P. Morgan banking interests and isolationist firms such as DuPont Chemical bankrolled the Liberty League, an anti–New Deal organization with clear anticommunist—and pro-fascist—sympathies. The league supported FDR's 1936 Republican challenger Alf Landon. But Landon and the Republicans were fighting a rear-guard battle. Hull's free trade policy attracted to the Democrats businessmen who did not otherwise support the administration's social-reform policies. The most dramatic example of this is the one already mentioned: leading Wall Streeters, most of them Republicans, showed their support for Roosevelt's and Hull's "open door" foreign trade policies in a rally held in New York's financial district only a week before the 1936 election. This was a clear portent foretelling Landon's landslide loss.[27]

CIO leaders Lewis and Hillman meanwhile sought to use the government's labor-relations machinery to rein in radical activity in the labor movement. The new CIO created Labor's Non-Partisan League (LNPL) in the 1936 election, forging a crucial link between the labor movement and the Democratic Party. Hillman and Lewis consciously established LNPL to channel votes to Roosevelt's reelection—while forestalling the development of a third-party challenge to the Democrats. The scale of the 1934–37 class struggle, combined with rising radicalization among working-class militants, threatened the two-party status quo. Democratic officials noted that regular Democratic parties in New York and Michigan were suffering mass defections as newly politicized workers searched for an alternative political voice in mainstream politics. FDR adviser Berle worried that the Democratic Party would break into factions, leaving it more vulnerable to a challenge from the Republicans in 1936. Berle argued that liberal Republicans Philip LaFollette and Fiorello LaGuardia, along with "Sidney Hillman of the Labor crowd, have got to carry the ball" for Roosevelt's reelection.

By launching LNPL, Hillman and Lewis scotched a growing sentiment among labor activists that the new CIO should spearhead the development of a labor party. To overcome resistance among left-wing unionists to voting for the corrupt Tammany Hall party bosses in New York, the LNPL invented the independent-sounding "American Labor Party" to surreptitiously channel working-class votes to Roosevelt and other pro–New Deal candidates. The LNPL raised more than $750,000 for FDR's reelection, 80 percent of it from the new CIO unions. The league produced a pamphlet, "He Fights for Labor," which offered an "embarrassingly roseate" view of FDR's labor policies. League leaders pioneered the tried-and-true tactic of lesser-evil campaigning for the Democrats: predicting catastrophe if the Republicans were elected. In defending his decision to support Roosevelt against his own union's support for independent labor politics, Hillman warned "the defeat of Roosevelt [resulting] in a real Fascist administration . . . is going to make the work of organizations that are interested in building a labor movement impossible."[28] Despite the alarmist rhetoric of those like Hillman, Roosevelt won more that 60 percent of the vote and carried every state except Maine and Vermont. The number of Republicans in the Senate was reduced to nineteen and the number of Republicans in the House was reduced to 107—the lowest totals in the twentieth century.

Yet only one year after the 1936 election, the CIO was losing steam and New Deal domestic reforms had ground to a halt. The Democratic Party had provided the vehicle through which the labor movement was incorporated into national policy making. But labor had joined as a junior partner to the business interests that still controlled the Democrats. Hillman had predicted that a Roosevelt defeat would send the labor movement into reverse. Roosevelt had won, yet the labor movement by late 1937 was going backward. Indeed, as the economy again fell into recession in 1937, Roosevelt turned his back on the labor movement.

In that year, a group of virulently anti-union steel manufacturers, known as "Little Steel," pledged to halt the forward momentum of organized labor when their workers went on strike for union recognition. With millions of dollars worth of arms and ammunition at their disposal, the steel employers' private strikebreakers joined forces with the National Guard to attack picket lines and ransack workers' homes. All told, eighteen workers were killed during the steel strike, including ten whom Chicago police shot in the back during a peaceful rally on Memorial Day. Yet despite appeals from CIO leaders, Roosevelt's only statement came after the strike was over, when he condemned both sides, quoting Shakespeare's *Romeo and Juliet*: "A plague on both your houses!"[29]

The tide was clearly turning against labor. Republicans and Southern Democrats strengthened their "conservative coalition" in Congress.[30] Courts ruled that sit-down strikes for union recognition were illegal in 1938. With war on the horizon, Roosevelt sought corporate support for a massive military buildup, further strengthening his ties to big business. Unemployment rose during this period, yet Roosevelt cut programs for the poor and unemployed in both 1938 and 1939. Meanwhile leaders of the rival CIO and AFL union federations turned on each other in a war over turf.

The New Deal left behind a set of programs that, although certainly an advance over the pre-Depression lack of social provision, fell far short of erecting a European-style "welfare state." The Social Security Act, passed in 1935 as the cornerstone of the "second New Deal," established a divide between "Social Security" and "welfare." Unemployment and old-age insurance would not be paid out immediately, but only after employer and employee taxes had been collected in federally managed funds for workers. A regressive payroll tax, capped at a fixed amount, ensured that workers would pay more to finance the system than would the rich—despite the fact that the rich also would be eligible to receive benefits from the old-age pension program. Nevertheless, the "universalism" of Social Security—on offer to every worker—accounts for its enduring and widespread support ever since.

Federal outlays for "welfare" or Aid to Dependent Children (later renamed Aid to Families with Dependent Children, or AFDC) were deliberately kept low. One-half to two-thirds of welfare financing was left to states, as well as the ability to set benefit and eligibility levels. Part of this concern to preserve state-level input in welfare policies reflected the Democratic Party's dependence on the "solid South," which guarded "states' rights" as a way to preserve Jim Crow segregation. Low welfare benefits also effectively subsidized low-wage employers. In addition, Social Security administrators curbed liberal states so that their benefit levels would not be so high as to make life on welfare anything other than a miserable and humiliating experience. By design, the New Deal set up a distinction between those who "deserved" old-age or disability benefits because they worked and the "undeserving poor" who were viewed as too lazy to work. Millionaire FDR himself called welfare "a narcotic, a subtle destroyer of the human spirit."[32]

The Dilemmas of Imperialist Reformism

The New Deal did not save the U.S. economy from the Great Depression, but the Second World War did. Between 1940 and 1945, the U.S. government spent more money than it had in the previous 150 years combined. A flood of government contracts lined the pockets of big business while wartime wage-and-price controls and the CIO's "no-strike pledge" held down workers' incomes. Two-thirds of the more than $175 billion the U.S. government spent between June 1940 and September 1944 went to only one hundred companies—and more than $50 billion of this went to just ten companies. Historian George Lipsitz explained, "The nation's largest businesses clearly reaped the greatest benefits from one of the largest welfare projects in history—wartime industrial expansion." The U.S. economy nearly doubled in size in the war years, with most of the benefits accruing to those "who already had the greatest share of the nation's wealth."[33]

Wartime industrial expansion, combined with the wartime destruction of the United States' main economic competitors in Japan, Germany, Britain, Russia, and France, left the U.S. economy in an unprecedented position of strength. At the war's end, half of world industrial production occurred inside the United States. The U.S. gross national product was twice that of Western Europe and Japan combined.[34] What was more, the Democratic administrations that led the United States through the war dictated the terms of peace, solidifying the United States' leading role in the world economy. The Bretton Woods treaties negotiated among the United States, Britain, and Russia in 1944 created the World Bank and the International Monetary Fund. Both institutions established the United States and its finance industry as the world's banker. The IMF would control fluctuations of member countries' currencies and the World Bank would provide capital for postwar reconstruction. But even as the postwar settlement dissolved in 1946 into the

Cold War between the United States and the USSR, the United States created the Marshall Plan to "contain communism" through economic reconstruction grants to Western European governments.

Holdover isolationists opposed the Marshall Plan, but Democratic President Harry Truman gained support for the plan—and for his anticommunist foreign policy—from leading Republican politicians, such as Senator Arthur Vandenberg of Michigan. The Marshall Plan succeeded in containing "communism" in Western Europe, firmly establishing U.S. hegemony over "the West." It also brought economic benefits for the domestic economy. "Among other things, the Marshall Plan provided a method of funneling U.S. tax dollars to American sellers with Europe as the conduit. These funds laid the basis for the prosperity that would characterize the 1950s, at home and abroad."[35]

Unlike all other previous war mobilizations in U.S. history, the post–Second World War period did not see a large-scale demobilization of the standing army or of arms spending. In 1947, Truman signed the National Defense Act, which created the Defense Department, the National Security Council, and the Central Intelligence Agency. A National Security Council memorandum prepared for Truman estimated that the United States would have to spend as much as 20 percent of its GNP to maintain the war machine necessary to fight the Soviet "design for world domination."[36] Democratic administrations (aided briefly in 1946–47 by a Republican Congress) created all these initiatives. The Democratic Party was the architect of the Cold War, and its "permanent arms economy" also contributed to postwar U.S. prosperity.[37]

From the 1940s to the early 1960s, military spending accounted for more than one-half of the federal budget and more than 9 percent of the U.S. GNP. Diane B. Kunz explains that

> military spending continually primed the pump of the American economy, ensuring a steady stream of federal dollars into the civilian economy. The aerospace, communications, and computer industries especially benefited from government appropriations. Equally important, the postwar expansion in the Pacific region's wealth and population owed much to its disproportionate share of defense contracts. The growth of military bases also fueled local economies in rural areas.[38]

Taken together, arms spending and U.S. dominance in the world economy produced the greatest economic boom capitalism has ever experienced—while making the "American Dream" of material comfort, home ownership, and a secure retirement attainable to millions of U.S. workers. But access to the American Dream came at a great social cost to union workers. Rising wages were offset by an assault on workers' rights. In 1947 Congress passed the Taft-Hartley Act, cracking down on rank-and-file solidarity—banning wildcat strikes, solidarity strikes, secondary boycotts, and mass picketing. In addition, Taft-Hartley required all union officials to sign affidavits that they did not belong to the Communist Party and had no relationship with any organization seeking the "overthrow of the United States government by force or by any illegal or unconstitutional means."[39] CIO leaders supported Truman in the 1948 election based on his campaign promise to repeal Taft-Hartley—which never materialized.

The "partnership" between United Steelworkers of America (USWA) president David McDonald and U.S. Steel chairman Benjamin Fairless exemplified the so-called "social compact" between labor and management that emerged in the postwar era. In 1953 McDonald and Fairless toured U.S. Steel plants, meeting workers and plant management. At each stop, Fairless spoke for labor-management cooperation while McDonald spoke out against wildcat strikes. At a union- and company-sponsored "Day for Dave" McDonald, New York mayor-elect Robert Wagner—son of the New Deal senator who authored the National Labor Relations Act of 1935—said:

> Mr. Fairless and Mr. McDonald are touring the steel plants together, discussing conditions, talking to the men and the plant superintendents, doing everything they can to see that the United States Steel Company and the United Steelworkers of America are partners in the task of building a greater and stronger and more prosperous America.[40]

The social compact had produced higher wages and benefits for steelworkers, but its real intent was "labor peace" for management. By 1962, McDonald even said that there was almost no need for a union at U.S. Steel, as steelworkers "had achieved just about everything a union could provide for them."[41] The views of McDonald, who often bragged about his connections with Democratic presidents, were typical of the generation of officials who led both the CIO and the AFL (and, after 1955, the AFL-CIO) in the period of the long postwar boom. As the first AFL-CIO president George Meany put it, "Our goals as trade unionists are modest for we do not seek to recast American society . . . we seek a rising standard of living."[42]

Both major parties committed themselves to a "guns and butter" economy. As Mike Davis summarized this mid-twentieth-century conjuncture,

> The reorganization of power within the core capitalist bloc cleared the way for the political accommodation of *weak* versions of collective bargaining and welfare expenditure. . . . For the next quarter century, all Republican presidential candidates (Dewey, Eisenhower, Nixon in 1960) adhered to the core program of corporate internationalism and critical toleration of New Deal reforms.[43]

And although Eisenhower made no effort to repeal the New Deal, neither did Democrats Truman, Kennedy, or Johnson make any serious effort to repeal the labor laws, like Taft-Hartley, that hamstrung unions. Postwar prosperity changed the dynamic of reformism in U.S. politics. While many Depression-era New Deal administrators accepted the need for some limited reforms, the movements from below forced a significant shift in the balance of class forces. The connection between struggle and social change was clear. The period of postwar prosperity broke that connection. Median incomes for workers more than doubled between 1947 and 1973, and income inequality actually decreased.[44] Class struggle did not disappear in the 1950s and 1960s, but many large corporations did accept unions in their workplaces. Union officials, acting as "labor statesmen" in their bargaining with corporations, won increased wages and improved conditions for unionized workers. Even nonunion workers benefited from union contract increases since their own wages rose.

While the degree of "labor peace" from the 1940s to the 1960s has often been exaggerated, the institutionalization of labor-management cooperation and postwar prosperity had their impact on the labor movement and the rank and file, as Sharon Smith explains:

> The resolve that typified early CIO picket lines was gradually replaced by passivity, as workers became accustomed to waiting out strikes, rather than playing any meaningful role. This was bound to have an effect on class consciousness of white workers, who formed a politically conservative bloc, with little sympathy for either the civil rights movement or the antiwar movement until the late 1960s.[45]

The postwar social compact with the bosses in the plants had its political counterpart in the role of labor as an interest group in the Democratic Party. Labor formed the backbone of liberalism in the Democratic Party. But in playing this role, union leaders' partisan commitment to the Democrats replaced any commitment to pro–working-class policies. "Pro-union" positions became simply identified with Democratic candidates' positions, whatever their intention. The unions could not stand for working-class politics inside the Democratic Party without provoking business opposition. Therefore they trimmed their demands so that they would be acceptable to pro-Democratic business forces. Expressing this dilemma in electoral terms, historian Melvyn Dubofsky captures the essence of the problem: "If Democrats gave labor leaders real positions of authority and power in the party or repealed Taft-Hartley, they would alienate masses of nonunion voters. If the labor movement, in the words of [United Auto Workers president] Walter Reuther, tried to capture the Democratic Party, it would destroy the only political institution through which it might influence policymaking at the level of the national state."[46] As Jack Kroll, head of the CIO's Political Action Committee (CIO-PAC) in the 1950s, put it, organized labor bargained with the Democrats "much as it would bargain with an employer."[47]

Through most of the 1950s, moderate Republican Dwight Eisenhower ruled in the White House while moderate Democrats like Senate majority leader Lyndon Johnson ruled in Congress—in league with Southern segregationists. Historian Kevin Boyle describes the period in which "Republican and Democratic parties had forged an informal consensus committed to the maintenance of the status quo, favorable to government aid to big business but hostile to government control of corporate decisions, supportive of the New Deal's fragmented welfare state but not its extension." This situation frustrated the most dedicated members of the labor-liberal alliance. In 1952 the UAW's Donald Montgomery wrote to the Democratic National Committee complaining, "How can we get out the vote and win in northern . . . states on a program sparked by champions of . . . tax loopholes, white supremacy, and union-busting?"[48]

Thus the Democratic Party's brand of liberalism—which formed the framework for labor's—was pretty mild stuff. First, it refused to countenance large-scale government intervention into labor markets or into the operation of the economy. Unlike European social democracy, American liberalism did not support nationalization of industries or "cradle-to-grave" social welfare policies. Liberals accepted that the paramount aim of American economic policy was to maintain conditions for corporate-led economic growth. Even in the New Deal's halcyon days, Democratic programs fell far short of working-class demands or welfare policies in other advanced capitalist countries. As one observer noted, "In 1949, after four full terms of Democratic Party rule, the United States ranked last among industrial capitalist states in social welfare expenditures."[49] For years, Democratic Party platforms called for the repeal of the anti-union Taft-Hartley Act and for the establishment of a universal national health insurance program. Yet, despite Democratic control of the presidency for thirty-two of forty-eight years between 1932 and 1980, and both houses of Congress for forty-six years during the same period, these programs were no closer to enactment at the end of this era than when they were added to the platform.

Second, liberals did not question the necessity of a massive military machine or the imperialist aims for which it was deployed. In fact, "Cold War liberalism" rested on expanding the Pentagon. Indeed, liberals accepted—and largely defined—the ideological limits of acceptable political debate. For that reason, liberals like the UAW's Reuther and Senator (later Vice President) Hubert Humphrey were often the most zealous anticommunist witch-hunters during the 1950s. Humphrey, the patron saint of postwar liberalism, actually proposed—in the 1954 Communist Control Act—to round up American communists and to place them in concentration camps![50]

Liberalism remained the postwar era's guiding economic and political ideology because it served the needs of an expanding capitalism. U.S. economic expansion depended on increased investment in technology (and on a technologically sophisticated workforce). Moreover, economic growth pulled larger numbers of workers on the margins of the U.S. labor market into paid labor. Displaced agricultural workers, including millions of African Americans, women, and immigrants, moved into paid labor in the generation after the Second World War. Liberal government policies worked to facilitate these changes that the postwar economy demanded. Federal programs like the GI Bill of Rights and the National Defense Education Act of 1958 subsidized an expansion of higher education and the creation of a technologically equipped workforce. These programs were justified on the basis of the Cold War need to "keep up with the Russians"—which only added to their appeal. Government programs such as Head Start, Medicare, Medicaid, and child nutrition programs added to the working class's "social wage" and underwrote the expansion of the postwar workforce. State funding of some functions traditionally performed by women in families—caring for the elderly, ensuring adequate nutrition for children—helped increase the numbers of women available to enter the paid labor force. Liberals championed and won these reforms—all of which aided U.S. capitalism.

At the high-water mark of what became known as the "liberal-labor" alliance in the Democratic Party, some observers argued that the Democrats could become a vehicle for reform along the lines of the British Labour Party of the postwar period. But the Democratic Party, representing the liberal wing of the U.S. capitalist class, had no such intention. Democratic administrations erected most of what in the United States passes for a welfare state—Social Security, Medicare, Head Start, and federal aid to cities. But the Democratic Party remained a self-consciously capitalist party throughout, responding to the needs of business rather than to the desires of its "constituents," from labor unions to reform groups. As one astute observer remarked, this factor explains why the Democratic Party

> left ordinary Americans alternately confused, perplexed, alarmed, or disgusted, as they tried to puzzle out why the party did so little to help unionize the South, protect the victims of McCarthyism, promote civil rights for blacks, women or Hispanics, or in the late 1970s, combat America's great "right turn" against the New Deal itself. To such people, it always remained a mystery why the Democrats so often betrayed the ideals of the New Deal. Little did they realize that, in fact, the party was only living up to them.[51]

JFK, LBJ, and the Failure of the Great Society

Of all the issues that faced the Democratic Party in its history, none was more contentious than the issue of civil rights for African Americans. In building the New Deal coalition, Roosevelt retained Black votes and support in the deep South by offering token gestures to Blacks while allowing segregationist "Dixiecrats" to block civil rights legislation. By the late 1940s this rotten arrangement was crumbling. The movement of large numbers of Blacks from the South to Northern ghettoes led Democratic urban machines to court the Black vote. And American government leaders (most of them Democrats), locked in the Cold War competition for Third World "hearts and minds," concluded that Jim Crow wasn't a great selling point for what the Cold Warriors called "the American way of life." These factors led to some reforms from above—including Truman's 1947 order ending segregation in the military, the

Democrats' 1948 endorsement of a civil rights plank in their platform, and a series of Supreme Court decisions culminating in *Brown v. Board of Education* (1954) outlawing school segregation.

Despite these steps the national party still leaned heavily on the Dixiecrats. Illinois governor Adlai Stevenson, the Democrats' sacrificial lamb against Eisenhower in the 1952 and 1956 elections, is remembered today as a great liberal. But in the 1950s he refused to speak out in favor of civil rights. In fact, Eisenhower won the largest percentage of the Black vote of any postwar Republican president.[52]

John F. Kennedy—elected with widespread Black, labor, and liberal support—promised in 1961 to end housing discrimination by executive order or, as he put it, "with the stroke of a pen." Yet for two years Kennedy refused to act, pandering to the Dixiecrats in Congress on whom he depended for passage of the rest of his administration's program. The militant civil rights movement, swelling since the February 1960 sit-in protests across the South, broke the legislative logjam. Kennedy pledged support for the civil rights bill only after racist attacks on movement demonstrations, such as the May–June 1963 Birmingham crisis, threatened "law and order"—not only in Birmingham but also across the county. As Ahmed Shawki explained, "Birmingham forced Kennedy to identify himself more strongly with the civil rights movement—and to attempt to co-opt and control its activities."[53] Kennedy, with the help of civil rights leaders including the Reverend Martin Luther King Jr., moved to undercut criticism of the administration's foot dragging at the August 1963 March on Washington. It was a textbook illustration of the way the Democratic Party has often operated in the face of a social movement that shakes its voting base: shifting from obstructing the movement to taking it over. Nevertheless, by 1963–64, it was clear that the Dixiecrats' days as Democrats were over. Chapter 5 will revisit this important period when the Democrats confronted the civil rights revolution.

Following Kennedy's 1963 assassination, elite opinion and business overwhelmingly endorsed Johnson's 1964 election against reactionary Republican Barry Goldwater. The Democrats won the White House and Congress with overwhelming majorities. The booming economy produced revenue that underwrote an expansion of social welfare spending. Increased welfare spending offered the Democrats the opportunity to throw the Dixiecrats overboard and reconfigure the party. Johnson's endorsement of the 1964 Civil Rights Act and the 1965 Voting Rights Act pushed the Dixiecrats further toward the Republicans. The administration needed a formula to accomplish two tasks simultaneously: replacing racist votes with Black votes and undercutting Black militants. Johnson's 1964–65 Great Society initiative seemed to offer the appropriate formula.

The Great Society's two most important initiatives were the creation of medical assistance programs for the elderly (Medicare) and the poor (Medicaid), and waging the "War on Poverty" under the Office of Economic Opportunity (OEO). Medicare and Medicaid aimed to fill gaps in health insurance coverage—without challenging privatized health insurance or the medical profession's right to set fees. Medicare and Medicaid served millions of new beneficiaries and Democratic voters. Government intervention in the health care market also created a huge windfall for the medical-industrial complex. Texas billionaire Ross Perot—who ran for president in 1992—made his first billion selling computer software to the largest state Medicaid programs.[54]

But for President Johnson's immediate political purposes, the "War on Poverty" was more significant. Through the "War on Poverty" programs, the Johnson administration hoped to cultivate a moderate Black political leadership, tied to the Democratic Party, that could pose as an alternative to civil rights activists and Black Power militants. The programs greatly expanded funding for a number of existing programs for youth jobs, neighborhood development, and community education projects. With federal money, the OEO set up urban "community action" projects organizing ghetto residents to pressure local, state, and federal governments to fund anti-poverty programs. "In many cities Great Society agencies became the base for new black political organizations whose rhetoric may have been thunderous but whose activities came to consist mainly of vying for position and patronage within the urban political system," wrote Frances Fox Piven and Richard A. Cloward.[55]

A similar process took place in the South. After the movement defeated the Dixiecrats in Mississippi, Great Society anti-poverty programs rebuilt the Democratic Party in the Delta. In Mississippi, the OEO used millions in Head Start funds to recruit and build a coalition composed of "New South" white businessmen and old-guard Black middle-class leaders, who had earlier distinguished themselves by their opposition to the civil rights activists who had organized the Mississippi Freedom Democratic Party (discussed further in chapter 5). These leaders realized that "control over millions of dollars of Head Start funds would give them political patronage and power, enhancing their position as a credible alternative to the Freedom Democratic Party."[56] Middle-class Black opportunists who had boycotted the civil rights movement's struggles emerged from the woodwork to collect the spoils from the recast state Democratic Party. Civil rights movement hero Fannie Lou Hamer described such developments in her native Sunflower County:

> Now, the ministers, they get a little money, are selling their church to the white folks so the CAP [OEO's Community Action Program] can run Head Start.... They're these middle-class Negroes, the ones that never had it as hard as the grassroots people in Mississippi. They'll sell their parents for a few dollars. Sometimes I get so disgusted I feel like getting my gun after some of these school teachers and chicken-eatin' preachers.[57]

Yet by 1966, LBJ was raiding the budgets of the war on poverty to fight the war in Vietnam. The Vietnam-fueled spending binge pushed an overheated economy into an inflationary spiral. The ruling-class consensus that underpinned the "welfare-warfare" state began to splinter. By 1968, it was clear even to Wall Street that the Vietnam War was "un-winnable" and was causing major damage to the U.S. economy. Johnson's hope that the Great Society would buy allegiance from the poor blew up in his face. Instead, he faced disintegration in the U.S. Army, insurrectionary riots in all of the country's major cities, and widespread protest against the war in Vietnam. [58]

By the 1968 election, the Democratic Party was divided between those who wanted to continue—even to step up—the Vietnam War and those who favored withdrawal. The urban rebellions that swept U.S. cities—many of them launched against big-city Democratic machines—also splintered the Democrats. Conservative Republican Richard Nixon defeated the divided "majority" party with a mere 43 percent of the popular vote.

Nixon aimed to pull the country to the right. He abolished the War on Poverty programs and launched a racist "law and order" campaign. But the social movements of the day remained powerful enough to prevent the conservative Republican president from launching a full-scale dismantling of the Great Society programs. On the contrary, Nixon's administration actually increased food stamp funding, approved a 20 percent increase in Social Security payments, created Supplemental Security Income, and established a number of regulatory agencies, including the Environmental Protection Agency and the Occupational Safety and Health Administration. An Urban Institute study concluded that Nixon expanded domestic spending more than any Democratic president since FDR.[59]

Nixon also presided over the unraveling of the postwar economic order. Warfare and welfare spending pushed inflation rates from about one percent per year in 1960 to 7 percent annually in 1971. The dollar's value declined, but the Bretton Woods[60] system compelled foreigners to accept the dollar as payment for debts. Moreover, the United States could print as many dollars as it needed to pay its obligations. In effect, the United States "taxed its allies to pay for part of the costs of the Indochina War (and other commitments)," historian Charles Maier wrote.[61] Inflation also priced U.S. goods out of foreign markets at the same time that U.S. competitors Japan and Germany were beginning to make their presence felt in U.S. markets.

In 1971, for the first time since 1890, the United States imported more goods and services than it exported. To increase U.S. competitiveness in the world economy, the Nixon administration devalued the dollar in 1971 and tore up the Bretton Woods system. Treasury Secretary (and one-time Democratic Texas governor) John Connally explained the administration's reasoning: "Foreigners are out to screw us. Our job is to screw them first."[62] Despite Connally's braggadocio, the end of Bretton Woods was recognition that the United States no longer held its unchallenged position as world economic leader. That realization hit home for millions of Americans in the following years, when Middle Eastern "oil shocks" precipitated in 1974–75 the worst recession since the Depression.

Chapter Three

The Rise of
the New Democrats

For the historical period spanning roughly 1930 to 1980, the Democratic Party had been able to contain the demands of major social movements—including the labor movement in the 1930s and the civil rights movement in the 1960s. Living standards and social spending had risen steadily throughout the postwar economic boom, no matter which party occupied the White House. But the postwar boom came to an end in the mid-1970s, impelling the corporate class to collectively pursue a ruthless employers' offensive aimed at breaking the power of major industrial unions through open union-busting. The Conference Board, an organization of CEOs of the largest 350 corporations in the United States, aggressively pushed a new corporate agenda. Assembling in 1974 and 1975, in the midst of the worst recession since the Second World War, CEOs complained that the U.S. government had become "'too' democratic [and] had begun to overlook the central role that corporations and profits play in a capitalist economy."[1]

This was not a temporary shift in the balance of class forces, but a turning point marking the end of the New Deal era—a move to return class inequality to its pre-Depression levels. In 1978, UAW President Douglas Fraser called this corporate assault on labor a "one-sided class war," signaling the end of the postwar social compact with labor.[2] As former Republican strategist Kevin Phillips argued in *The Politics of Rich and Poor,*

> by the middle of Reagan's second term, official data had begun to show that America's broadly defined "rich"—the top half of 1 percent of the U.S. population—had never been richer. Federal policy favored the accumulation of wealth and rewarded financial assets, and the concentration of income that began in the mid-1970s was accelerating.... *No parallel upsurge of riches had been seen since the late nineteenth century, the era of the Vanderbilts, Morgans and Rockefellers.* [emphasis in original][3]

The employers' offensive did not end with the Reagan administration, however. It continued through the 1990s and accelerated again after 2001. The first decade of the twenty-first century has been one in which corporations rescinded long-standing pension and health care benefits won in union contracts decades earlier, while workers faced falling household incomes. As *Time* magazine reporters Donald L. Barlett and James B. Steele commented, "Corporate promises are often not worth the paper they're printed on. Businesses in one industry after another are revoking long-standing commitments to their workers. It's the equivalent of your bank telling you that it needs the money you put into your savings account more than you do—and then keeping it. Result: a wholesale downsizing of the American Dream."[4]

From its inception in the 1970s, the effort to restrict or eliminate welfare-state protections was an important part of the business mobilization against the working class. Francis Fox Piven and Richard Cloward explained:

> The expansion of the welfare state that was widely considered part of the class accord in the period immediately following World War II was once again interrupted by employer opposition, this time prompted by the economic convulsions of the 1970s. . . . It is clear that American business sought to reduce the impact of these instabilities with a renewed assault against the working class. Employers mobilized to cut wages, slash workplace protections, crush unions, and discredit the very possibility of worker power with an ideological campaign threatening capital flight if workers resisted the new demands.[5]

Reducing the "social wage" required an assault on liberalism, the main ideological prop to the postwar welfare state. Business lavished millions on think tanks like the Heritage Foundation and the American Enterprise Institute to revive the free market, laissez-faire capitalist ideology that had been discredited since the Great Depression. Big business revived the Republican Party—still reeling from the Watergate scandal—by converting it into the main vehicle for the corporate-backed conservative offensive.

The employers' offensive necessarily involved rolling back the gains won by the social struggles of the 1960s and early 1970s. This took two forms. On the economic front, attacking the gains of the 1960s and 1970s was also a way to attack any government programs that flowed from those gains, such as the War on Poverty programs. In this way, big business hoped to devalue the role of government in favor of free market nostrums, lower taxes, and general deregulation. On the cultural front, the Republican Party rebuilt its mass component through an appeal to segments of the population that rejected the social changes of the 1960s. The conservative "culture war" for "traditional values" was an indirect way to mount this attack. Opposition to abortion rights was one aspect of a rejection of the gains of the women's movement. Opposition to affirmative action and "forced busing" was another way to oppose the gains of the civil rights movement without appearing to defend Jim Crow segregation. And so on. When political ministers, including one-time segregationists like the Reverends Jerry Falwell and Pat Robertson, organized these various strands of backlash into a voting bloc, Republican Party politicians ended up courting it as another constituency that could offer thousands of foot soldiers for Election Day. The New Right was undeniably a Republican Party spin-off. But it could count on Democrats to play the role of willing enablers at key junctures.[6]

The Carter Debacle

The full impact of the business offensive wasn't felt until the 1977–81 Democratic administration of Jimmy Carter. As a former Georgia governor, Carter had crucial backing from leading corporations, including his hometown firm Coca-Cola, and a network of free traders in the Trilateral Commission.[7] Although his undistinguished record as governor did not excite the traditional New Deal constituencies of civil rights organizations and labor unions, they eventually rallied to Carter's side. When Carter assumed office, Democrats held large majorities in both houses of Congress and held the White House for the first time since 1969. Organized labor even anticipated the combination of the Carter White House and a Democratic Congress to produce a "resurgence of the kind of liberal legislation that marked the Kennedy-Johnson years."[8] But labor misread the way the political wind was blowing—and where Carter's loyalties lay.

Responding to business complaints that social programs had become unaffordable, Carter reversed the long period of increases in spending on domestic programs. Leaders of major African-American civil rights groups, meeting under the auspices of the Urban League in August 1977, denounced Carter for having "betrayed" them by practicing "callous neglect" toward African Americans.[9] Carter also supported and signed into law the Hyde Amendment, the 1976 measure barring the use of Medicaid funds for the performance of abortions. Its passage, one of the first major victories of the anti-abortion movement following the 1973 Supreme Court legalization of abortion, put the procedure out of reach for poor women who could not otherwise afford it. When President Carter was confronted with this inequity, he remarked: "There are many things in life that are not fair, that wealthy people can afford and poor people can't." It wasn't the federal government's place to make "opportunities exactly equal, particularly when there is a moral factor involved."[10]

Carter's 1978 tax plan anticipated what later became known as Reaganomics by cutting capital gains taxes for the wealthy while boosting Social Security taxes on workers. It was the first time since the 1930s that Congress—a Democratic-majority Congress at that—had passed an unambiguously regressive tax plan. In 1979 Carter negotiated a federal government "bailout" plan to rescue the Chrysler Corporation from bankruptcy, which opened the way to the subsequent 1980s wave of concessionary union contracts. And in the 1977–78 coal miners' strike, he resorted to the anti-union Taft-Hartley Act to force a settlement.[11] Carter's decision outraged labor leaders, but Carter was nonplussed. "Carter saw unions as just another interest group," said Stuart Eizenstadt, Carter's domestic policy adviser. "They did not have a special call on his heartstrings."[12]

Like Carter, congressional Democrats no longer felt beholden to their long-standing labor constituency. The AFL-CIO remarked that the ninety-fifth Congress left behind "not a monument to forward-looking legislation, but a tombstone." The AFL-CIO had proposed a package of mild labor law reforms that went down to defeat in 1977. One labor reform bill failed after eleven Democrats who had voted for it in 1975 switched their votes to oppose it in 1977. For their service to big business, these eleven Democrats gained more than $169,000 in business contributions to their reelection campaigns—more than compensating for the $69,000 they lost in AFL-CIO contributions. [13]

In light of Carter's post-presidential image as Nobel laureate and international peace envoy, it is worth recalling that Carter launched much of the military policy that Reagan later pursued with a vengeance. In 1980, in the wake of the Iranian Revolution, the Nicaraguan Revolution, and the Russian invasion of Afghanistan, Carter sharply increased the military budget, reinstated registration for the military draft, and created the Rapid Deployment Force for intervention in the Middle East. During the 1979–80 "hostage crisis" in Iran, Carter not only attempted to invade Iran, but also helped to whip up the racist anti-Iranian sentiment that helped bolster Reagan's 1987–88 policy of policing the Persian Gulf. In addition, Carter changed American nuclear weapons policy to make an American "first strike" in a "limited" nuclear war a real possibility. [14]

Liberals made one last stand to challenge the Democratic Party's conservative drift. In 1979 United Auto Workers president Douglas Fraser assembled the Progressive Alliance, a broad coalition of labor unions, the NAACP, the National Farmers' Union, the National Women's Political Caucus, and other liberal organizations. The Progressive Alliance formed the backbone of Senator Edward Kennedy's unsuccessful bid to unseat Carter as the Democratic nominee to run against Ronald Reagan in 1980. Running against an incumbent president who used all the power of his office to fend off the challenge, Kennedy lost the bid. The Progressive Alliance melted away: "Formed as much out of disgust with Carter and the Congress as disappointment in capital's new hostility, the fragments of the Progressive Alliance found themselves informally united behind Carter when he won the nomination. This alliance was on Carter's terms: more austerity." [15] But the Democrats lost the election and the Progressive Alliance dissolved.

Beginning with his 1981 budget, Republican president Ronald Reagan commenced a full-scale assault on the social gains of the 1960s. Judging from their failure to enact progressive reforms when Carter was in the White House, it should come as no surprise that the Democrats put up little resistance to Reagan's right-wing policies. The Senate Budget Committee unanimously endorsed Reagan's 1981 budget cuts that wiped out years of social welfare gains, while Democratic senators Daniel Patrick Moynihan (NY), Gary Hart (CO), Howard Metzenbaum (OH), and Donald Riegle (MI) all voted in favor. The forty-eight Democratic votes for the 1981 Reagan tax cut plan provided the margin of victory for its passage. Four years later, key Democrats—including liberal senators Edward Kennedy (MA) and Paul Simon (IL)—voted for the Gramm-Rudman-Hollings bill that imposed mandatory budget cuts.[16]

In the realm of foreign policy, the Democrats were quite willing to defend "U.S. interests" overseas. When Reagan ordered the 1983 invasion of Grenada, Democratic leaders in Congress lined up behind the president, agreeing that the invasion was needed to eliminate a "Cuban-Soviet" base in the Caribbean. In the summer of 1985 Democratic representatives pushed and passed a renewal of aid to UNITA, the South African backed thugs fighting to overthrow the Angolan government. One-time liberal Democratic House Armed Services Committee chairman Les Aspin (WI) became a leading advocate of aid to the Nicaraguan contras and development of the Midgetman missile, which he called "the Democrats' bomb." Democratic representatives David McCurdy (OK) and Marvin Leath (TX) worked to win House passage for a renewed effort to develop U.S. chemical warfare capabilities.[17]

"Special Interests" Launch the Democratic Leadership Council

The rightward shift in U.S. business used the revitalized Republican Party as its primary vehicle. But big business also found organized support among the Democrats. One month after Carter lost to Reagan, the Democratic National Committee appointed Los Angeles corporate lawyer Charles Manatt to regroup the party. (Manatt was a law partner of Warren Christopher, who was later appointed secretary of state by President Clinton.) He established the Democratic Business Council (DBC), an advisory group of leading CEOs, to develop a pro-business alternative to "Reaganism." These pro-business forces aimed to align the Democrats' official positions more closely with business's political agenda. "[Manatt's] program was perfectly straightforward. Like most other business Democrats, Manatt wanted to strengthen the party's ties with the business community, rather than those with Blacks, community organizations, or the poor. To that end, he and his allies deliberately sought out millionaires and other wealthy figures to run as candidates."[18]

In 1985, Manatt's successor, DNC chair Paul Kirk, saluted the DBC, calling it the "backbone of the Democratic Party's finances and its intellectual resources." But for some politicians and business Democrats, the DNC wasn't moving the party to the right fast enough. These politicians—including then–Arkansas governor Bill Clinton, then-senator Al Gore, then–Arizona governor Bruce Babbitt, and representative Richard Gephardt—launched the Democratic Leadership Council (DLC) to promote more conservative Democratic candidates and policies. Major corporations like RJ Reynolds Tobacco, Atlantic Richfield (oil), Georgia Pacific (wood and building products), Martin Marietta (military), and Prudential Bache (financial and insurance) bankrolled the DLC and its conservative policies, now dubbed "centrist."[19]

The twelve years of Republican presidential rule from 1981 to 1993 proved fabulously profitable for corporations and the rich. By the early 1990s, the corporate class had achieved many of its aims. The percentage of the workforce organized by trade unions declined from 22.3 percent in 1980 to 15.9 percent in 1989. The number of strikes dropped to post–Second World War lows. The ratio of profits to stockholder equity in manufacturing corporations jumped from 11.6 percent in 1975 to 16.1 percent in 1988 at the peak of the Republican recovery. Finally, the nearly two-trillion-dollar military buildup—proposed by Republican presidents and passed by Democratic Congresses—cracked the USSR's economy, leaving the United States the winner in the Cold War.[20]

But while the United States enjoyed its new hegemony as the world's sole remaining superpower, this did not prevent the economy from falling into recession in 1990—its most serious recession since the mid-1970s. The last Cold War president, George H. W. Bush, presided over the slowest economic growth since the administration of Herbert Hoover. Bush's popularity reached stratospheric levels following the 1991 Gulf War against Iraq. But it collapsed within a year. The recession triggered an ideological backlash against the right-wing policies that had shifted massive amounts of wealth from workers to the rich over the previous decade. In April 1992, after a jury acquitted four Los Angeles police officers who had beaten motorist Rodney King, the city erupted in a massive four-day riot. The Los Angeles rebellion—and the reaction to it across the country—highlighted the bitterness that millions of Americans felt. These factors—plus the loss of the "Soviet threat" as a campaign issue—favored a shift to the Democrats.

Meanwhile, the DLC positioned itself to take advantage of this opening:

> Fortune 500 corporate backers saw the DLC as a good investment. By 1990 major firms like AT&T and Philip Morris were important donors. Indeed, according to *Reinventing Democrats*, Kenneth S. Baer's history of the DLC, [DLC President] Al From used the organization's fundraising prowess as blandishment to attract an ambitious young Arkansas governor [Bill Clinton] to replace Senator Sam Nunn of Georgia as DLC chairman. Drawing heavily on internal memos written by From, Bruce Reed, and other DLCers, Baer says that the DLC offered Clinton not only a national platform for his presidential aspirations but "entree into the Washington and New York fundraising communities." Early in the 1992 primaries, writes Baer, "financially, Clinton's key Wall Street support was almost exclusively DLC-based," especially at firms like New York's Goldman Sachs.[21]

In light of this history, media critic Norman Solomon was more correct than he knew when he wrote in 1994 that "if Bill Clinton did not exist, it would have been necessary to invent someone like him. In a manner of speaking, he was invented: by his longtime backers in the Democratic Leadership Council. . . . They boosted Clinton in tandem with the news media that pronounced him the front-runner for the Democratic presidential nomination before a single vote was cast in the 1992 primaries."[22] Like many Democrats before him, Clinton made rhetorical nods to demands for "change" and reform. But he had no intention of carrying out any reforms that would alter the distribution of political power established by the corporate class since the mid-1970s.

As noted in chapter 1, the two-party system holds a built-in advantage for big business. If one corporate party can't be sold to voters (as the Republicans clearly couldn't be in 1992), there's always the other corporate party waiting in the wings. After twelve years of Republican rule, many liberals and Democratic interest groups were willing to accept anything from a new Democratic president. Into Bush's vacuum (and thanks to Texas billionaire Ross Perot's third-party run[23]) stepped Clinton, the most business-friendly Democratic president since Grover Cleveland.

From Reaganism to Clintonism

Clinton won the 1992 election, calling for change from Reagan-Bush's "twelve years of trickle-down economics." Yet in his first couple years as president, he pushed harder for passage of the corporate-backed North American Free Trade Agreement (NAFTA) than he did for any of the campaign promises that helped win him the election. The health care system overhaul that was supposed to be his signature achievement collapsed in 1994. Public disappointment ran so high that the 1994 election delivered control over Congress—a Democratic bastion for the previous sixty years—into the hands of conservative Republicans.

Within a year, Clinton figured out a modus operandi to deal with the Republican Congress and to recapture public support in the polls. Clinton adopted most of the GOP program, including its retrograde "welfare reform." At the same time, he staged high-profile battles with the Republicans to show that they were "going too far." This strategy, known as "triangulation," revived Clinton's presidency. In 1996 Clinton signed the Republican-sponsored Personal Responsibility and Work Opportunity Act, dismantling the hallmark welfare legislation enshrined in the New Deal. Bill Clinton won a second term in 1996—the first Democratic president to be reelected since Franklin Roosevelt in 1936.

But after regaining the initiative, Clinton immediately embraced "bipartisanship," signing off on a 1997 budget agreement that slashed billions from important programs like Medicare and Medicaid. Yet even this accommodation to the right-wing Congress won him few Republican allies. Indeed, Congress spent most of the next year trying to drive Clinton from office over his much-publicized affair with Monica Lewinsky, an intern.[24] The vigor with which Clinton and his surrogates fought off the Republican scandalmongers contrasted sharply with their failure to mount campaigns for health care reform, reproductive choice, or civil rights.

Clintonism may have appeared as nothing more than a series of poll-driven maneuvers intended to keep Clinton one step ahead of his political foes. But from the start the Clinton-Gore administration pursued a well-thought-out and deeply conservative political project. This "New Democrat" agenda emerged in the 1980s as the program of a faction of conservative Democrats determined to break the Democratic Party's identification with organized labor, civil rights, and other traditionally liberal causes. Embodied in the corporate-funded DLC, this faction succeeded in capturing the party machinery in 1992. It placed two of its chief leaders—Clinton and Gore—at the top of the Democratic ticket.

Four core ideas embodied Clintonism, according to journalist Ronald Brownstein, an open admirer of the "New Democrat" project: "opportunity and responsibility," "economic globalism," "fiscal discipline," and "government as catalyst."[25] Clinton-and-Gore-defined "opportunity and responsibility" embraced what Brownstein characterized as the "idea that government should both help those willing to help themselves and enforce common standards of behavior." Clinton put it more crudely in describing his plans to force welfare recipients to work for their benefits: "We will do with you. We will not do for you."[26]

"Economic globalism" involved the single-minded pursuit of free trade and free market policies around the world. The "fiscal discipline" of Clinton's economic policies generated record federal budget surpluses and the lowest level of government spending since the Eisenhower administration.[27] Finally, the Clinton-Gore manifestations of "government as catalyst" were a series of small-scale initiatives—from establishing a right to unpaid family medical leave to tax credits for college tuition. All these shared similar characteristics. They sounded like good reforms of a deeply flawed system, and sometimes they even addressed critical social needs. But they came nowhere near to filling the social need they were supposed to fill. What's more, they tended to stress private-sector initiatives, as when the administration marketed tax breaks for business as its anti-poverty program during its 1999 "poverty tour" of depressed areas.

Conservative David Frum, writing in the *Weekly Standard*, captured the essence of Clintonism better than many liberals could:

> Since 1994, Clinton has offered the Democratic Party a devilish bargain: Accept and defend policies you hate (welfare reform, the Defense of Marriage Act), condone and excuse crimes (perjury, campaign finance abuses) and I'll deliver you the executive branch of government. . . . He has assuaged the Left by continually proposing bold new programs—the expansion of Medicare to 55-year-olds, a national day-care program, the reversal of welfare reform, the hooking up of the Internet to every classroom, and now the socialization of the means of production via Social Security. And he has placated the Right by dropping every one of these programs as soon as he proposed it. Clinton makes speeches, Rubin and Greenspan make policy, the Left gets words, the Right gets deeds.[28]

Clintonomics: Boom for Whom?

"It's the economy, stupid" was the winning slogan coined by Clinton's 1992 campaign advisers. George H. W. Bush's approval ratings had plummeted as the country remained mired in recession during the early 1990s. Clinton took office promising to focus on the economy "like a laser beam." In keeping with his populist campaign themes, he pledged a "stimulus package" to create jobs and a "middle-class tax cut" to put money in ordinary people's pockets.[29] Although these two pledges proved popular during the campaign, Clinton failed on both measures within months of taking office. The stimulus package fell to a Republican filibuster in the Congress. But Clinton withdrew the tax-cut proposal of his own accord.

Indeed, Clinton's 1993 budget plan enshrined "deficit reduction" as the administration's chief domestic aim. The bill, which passed without a single Republican vote in Congress, raised taxes on the wealthiest Americans, expanded the earned income tax credit for the working poor, and increased a variety of regressive excise taxes, such as the federal gasoline tax. Abandoning his campaign proposals for "investments" in education and job training, Clinton's "deficit reduction plan" won support on Wall Street. "Clinton's willingness to raise taxes to close the deficit proved reassuring to a different kind of tradition-ally Republican constituency—the bond traders, who, initially at least, brought long-term interest rates down," wrote E. J. Dionne. "The bond sellers made Clinton's willingness to support some sort of levy on the middle class a test of his 'seriousness' about deficit reduction."[30]

The other major piece of economic legislation passed in 1993—ratification of NAFTA in October—added another fundamental plank to the Clinton-Gore economic program. Clinton and Gore went all out to win NAFTA, shunting aside protests from labor and environmentalists. If the 1993 budget plan enshrined "deficit reduction" as a domestic economic strategy, NAFTA established "free trade" as the holy writ of the Clinton-Gore foreign economic strategy. No modern administration was as aggressive in pushing deals for American business around the globe, as demonstrated by subsequent free-trade initiatives such as the 1994 ratification of the World Trade Organization (WTO) and the 2000 approval of "permanent normal trade relations" with China.

The administration's pro-business policies went further than simple "deficit reduction." Clinton and his treasury secretaries Lloyd Bentsen, Robert Rubin, and Larry Summers allowed conservative Federal Reserve chairman Alan Greenspan a free hand to jack up short-term interest rates at any hint of inflation, real or imagined. Although the Clinton Justice Department pursued a much-publicized antitrust action against the Microsoft Corporation, the administration meanwhile also actively encouraged deregulation and monopolization in the military (by encouraging outsourcing and defense-industry consolidation through successive Pentagon budgets), telecommunications (the Telecommunications Act of 1996), and finance (the Financial Services Modernization Act of 1999) industries.[31]

And despite the pro-environment rhetoric emanating regularly from the Clinton White House, big business had little to fear in the area of environmental regulation. "We just don't have unlimited resources to enforce all these measures and that can create a backlash [from corporations]," said Environmental Protection Agency administrator Carol Browner. "So we need to be realistic." For the Clinton-Gore administration, "being realistic" required sacrificing environmental protection at the first hint of any corporate objection. After fierce industry lobbying, the administration preserved sweetheart deals allowing the mining industry to pillage federal lands and the timber industry to clear-cut old-growth forests. In 1995 it opened some federal land holdings to oil drilling—a decision that enriched Occidental Petroleum and consequently Vice President Gore, an Occidental stockholder. Browner even allowed sugar growers and land developers—including a few Clinton-Gore campaign contributors—to dump polluted water into the Florida Everglades. The Clinton administration signed the 1997 Kyoto Agreement, a worldwide treaty aimed to limit global warming. But it never attempted to win treaty ratification in the U.S. Senate.[32]

By the time the GOP swept Congress in the 1994 elections, Clinton had already adopted "Republican-lite" economic policies. In the early 1990s, with the economy pulling out of recession, Clinton argued for "shared sacrifice" and budget austerity to "get our economic house in order."[33] Clinton embraced the goal of a balanced federal budget, and his "deficit reduction" policies produced the first federal budget surplus in a generation in 1998. Clinton's conversion to the balanced-budget religion ruled out any major government initiative to expand access to education, health care, or Social Security during his tenure.

Even with the budget running at a surplus, Clinton and Gore continued to tout the need for austerity. Gore ruled out deficit spending to stimulate the economy even in the face of a future recession. Instead,

Gore said, a recession "should be viewed as an opportunity to [down-size government further] before any other options are considered." Nobel Prize–winning economist Robert Solow responded that Gore "should wash his mouth out with soap" for echoing Republican President Herbert Hoover's approach to the Great Depression.[34] From Wall Street's point of view, Clinton's eight years in office were viewed as a smashing success. When he took office, the New York Stock Exchange's Dow Jones Industrial Average stood at 3,300—and rose to more than 10,000 before he left the White House. Inflation dropped to imperceptible levels and, in May 2000, unemployment hit a thirty-year low of 3.9 percent. Between 1992 and 1997, corporate profits grew by an average of 15 percent annually.[35] The United States had clearly zoomed ahead as the world's leading economy.[36]

Yet all that glittered in the "miracle economy" wasn't gold. Of the 22.5 million jobs the administration took credit for creating between 1993 and 2001, roughly half paid less than seven dollars an hour.[37] Low unemployment boosted wages, but in inflation-adjusted terms, they returned only to 1989 levels. To achieve even that standard of living, Americans worked six weeks longer per year than they did in the 1970s. Even with the tax increases in Clinton's 1993 budget plan, the wealthy paid a substantially lower percentage of their income in taxes than they did in 1977.[38]

Meanwhile, thirty-one million Americans remained poor according to the government's own statistics.[39] This growing gap between rich and poor was no accident. It followed directly from the Clinton-Gore economic program. Whenever Clinton faced a choice between economic policies favoring Wall Street or those that might help Main Street, "in almost every instance, [Clinton] took the route favored by Wall Street, business executives and conventional economists, not the ones that ordinary people might have favored and that almost certainly would have been easier to defend politically."[40]

Undoing the New Deal

Of all the Clinton-Gore administration's actions over the course of its eight years, none had a more far-reaching—and destructive—impact than Clinton's signing of the 1996 welfare repeal bill. Indeed, Clinton's 1992 campaign pledge to "end welfare as we know it" was one election promise Clinton didn't break. Welfare repeal ended the sixty-one-year-old guarantee of some income for the poorest Americans. It eliminated federal standards for welfare benefits. It imposed a five-year lifetime limit and a two-year continuous limit on benefits. It barred immigrants from receiving welfare and cut twenty-four billion dollars from the federal food-stamp program. It marked the first time that a piece of the 1935 Social Security Act was repealed. Peter Edelman, a Health and Human Services official who resigned in protest, called the bill "the worst thing Bill Clinton has done."[41]

Clinton's own Health and Human Services Department estimated that the bill would throw at least 1.1 million children into poverty. Other experts produced estimates three times higher. Despite these terrible consequences, Clinton encountered very little organized opposition to welfare repeal. Edelman conceded that "so many of those who would have shouted their opposition from the rooftops if a Republican president had done this were boxed in by their desire to see the president re-elected and in some cases by their own votes for the bill."[42]

Clinton didn't sign the bill because a Republican Congress forced him to. With no chance of losing to Senator Robert Dole in the 1996 elections, he didn't even have the excuse of political expediency. He signed it because he supported it. "Welfare reform" had always topped the New Democrat agenda.

The late 1990s economic expansion forestalled the full impact of welfare repeal when Clinton was in office. Five-year limits on benefits kicked in when Clinton was tending to his presidential library in 2002. But millions of poor people felt the cuts as the welfare caseload dropped from five million families in 1994 to around 2.5 million at the end of Clinton's presidency. Almost half a million children who, before welfare repeal would have been lifted out of poverty remained in poverty, according to one 1999 study.[43] Federal and state governments spent $10.6 billion less in 1999 than they did in 1994, while most states pocketed federal welfare block-grant money rather than making it available to poor people.[44]

Few would have predicted that "welfare repeal" would stand as the Clinton-Gore administration's most far-reaching change to social policy. Clinton arrived in office promising to enact a system of universal health care. But by seeking a "New Democrat" solution that preserved the central role of the biggest insurance companies in managing the health care system, he handcuffed himself from the start. As soon as small insurance companies mounted an attack on his 1994 proposal, Republicans and many congressional Democrats lined up to oppose it as well. With every attack on health care reform, Clinton retreated. In the end, health care reform wasn't so much defeated as it was compromised away, piece by piece, until there was nothing left. The bill never even came to a vote in Congress.

Clinton often took credit for defending Medicare and Social Security against Republican efforts to slash and burn both. But when the administration completed the 1997 Balanced Budget Agreement (BBA) with the congressional Republican leadership, it endorsed the GOP's long-term goal of gutting spending on "entitlements" like Medicare and Medicaid. The BBA imposed draconian spending "caps" on "discretionary" programs from home heating assistance to legal services.[45] These austerity measures accounted for the first-ever annual decline in Medicare spending in 1999. Between 1997 and 1998, the number of sick and elderly receiving Medicare-financed home health care services fell an astounding 45 percent, with six hundred thousand fewer people receiving care.[46] Under the BBA, Clinton literally abandoned millions of poor, sick, elderly, and disabled Americans.

What's more, the Clinton-Gore agreement with the GOP laid the groundwork for moving Medicare from a system guaranteeing a set of minimum benefits for all to one that allows patients who can afford it to opt out and buy their own insurance. This free-market solution reintroduced all the worst aspects of for-profit health care that Medicare was created to mitigate. At the same time, while denouncing Republican attempts to privatize Social Security, Clinton and Gore's proposal to invest some Social Security money in the stock market started down the same road of privatization.[47]

Kicking Labor in the Teeth

In 1992 Clinton won labor support with promises to ban permanent replacements for workers on strike and to fight for a minimum wage increase. Instead, he spent most of his political capital on legislation that organized labor opposed. Clinton twisted arms and passed the pork barrel to whip up support for NAFTA's passage in 1993. At the time, he even denounced labor for using "real roughshod, muscle-bound tactics" to oppose the free trade deal.[48] But when congressional Democrats introduced the anti-scab bill in 1994, Clinton barely lifted a finger as the bill fell to a Republican Senate filibuster. When the Democrats controlled Congress during Clinton's first term, Clinton did not mention the minimum wage once in any public statement. But as soon as the Republicans again dominated Congress in 1995, raising the minimum wage became a potent issue to use against the "Republican revolution" declared by House Speaker Newt Gingrich. The administration managed to push a minimum wage increase through the right-wing Congress, shoring up labor support for the 1996 and 1998 elections.

Despite owing Democratic congressional gains in 1996 and 1998 to labor unions' get-out-the-vote drives, the Clinton administration had no qualms about tossing labor aside when it could score points with big business. In February 1997 Clinton used the 1926 Railway Labor Act to outlaw an American Airlines pilots' strike. "Everyone understands that [American Airlines CEO] Bob Crandall's latest coup is getting Bill Clinton to side with management over labor," the Clinton-hating *Wall Street Journal* editorialized.[49] During the Clinton era, the number of Occupational Safety and Health Administration (OSHA) workplace inspections sunk to a new low, while the percentage of serious charges against corporations OSHA dismissed rose to its highest since Congress created the agency in 1973. Yet Clinton's "reinventing OSHA" initiative stressed "partnership" with business and "voluntary" compliance with regulations rather than enforcement.[50]

Despite Clinton's numerous betrayals, the labor movement maintained its loyalty. Labor leaders wanted the White House to take them seriously as "partners," but they knew the White House wouldn't return the favor. Still the AFL-CIO was willing to go to extraordinary lengths to prove its loyalty to the New Democrats. In the lead-up to the 1999 WTO summit in Seattle, AFL-CIO president John Sweeney joined with a dozen major corporate CEOs to endorse Clinton's free-trade policy. But no amount of loyalty earned the labor movement reciprocation from Clinton. Sweeney's signature had hardly dried on the pro-WTO declaration when the White House announced its intention to flout labor and environmental standards in a trade deal with China. Labor exacted some measure of revenge in the streets of Seattle during the 1999 WTO protests, but its demands were ignored.[51]

Likewise, Sweeney engineered an early AFL-CIO endorsement of Gore for president in 1999—a year before the election. Labor ignored the fact that Gore, as the official in charge of the administration's "reinventing government" program, had slashed the federal workforce by 17 percent (377,000 workers).[52] Only a few months later the AFL-CIO and Gore found themselves again on opposite sides of the vote for permanent normal trading status with China. Yet the federation remained firmly in Gore's camp.

Feeding the Prison-Industrial Complex

While Clinton and Gore presided over a retreat of government responsibility to meet human needs, the administration continuously expanded the government's policing of every aspect of life. Two-thirds of congressional Democrats supported Clinton-Gore's 1994 Omnibus Crime Control Act. This thirty-three-billion-dollar monstrosity expanded the use of the federal death penalty to sixty crimes, appropriated ten billion dollars for a vast expansion of prison building, and offered money to localities to hire one hundred thousand additional police officers. In 1996, Clinton's Anti-Terrorism and Effective Death Penalty Act greatly curtailed death row prisoners' habeas corpus appeals and established arbitrary time limits on death row appeals. On Clinton's watch, the U.S. prison population grew from about 1.3 million to nearly two million and the number of executions jumped to ninety-eight in 1999, its highest level in four decades.[53]

With Clinton's full support, a spate of bills supposedly directed at fighting terrorism took away ordinary people's civil rights, years before George W. Bush took office. The 1996 "antiterrorism" legislation allowed the U.S. government to prosecute Americans for raising money for any organization the government labeled as "terrorist"—setting the stage for the USA PATRIOT Act, passed shortly after the September 11, 2001, terrorist attacks. During the Clinton era, hundreds of legal immigrants who had lived in the United States since childhood were arrested and deported because immigration officials found that they had been convicted of petty crimes, often decades earlier. These immigrants were arrested, charged, and convicted on the grounds of secret testimony that the defendants' lawyers could not challenge, presaging the barbaric treatment of thousands of Arabs and Muslims rounded up as "suspected terrorists" after 9/11.[54]

The Clinton agenda reeked of an authoritarian moralism that meted out punishment to ordinary people who didn't conform to the administration's approved standards of "personal responsibility." Clinton's Housing and Urban Development Department in 1995 announced a "one strike and you're out" policy of expelling whole families from public housing on the mere suspicion that one family member was using drugs. The 1996 welfare reform law required women to disclose the identity of their children's fathers under penalty of losing benefits. This dovetailed nicely with the Clinton-Gore crusade against "deadbeat" dads. Clinton punctuated his 1996 reelection campaign with behavior-policing proposals the Christian right could endorse: V-chips in televisions to limit access to violent programming, teenage sexual abstinence programs, and school uniforms. Twice Clinton signed bills censoring content on the Internet and cable television. Both times the Supreme Court overturned them. All this from a man who told his impeachment inquisitors to keep their noses out of his personal life.[55]

Civil Rights: Lots of "Dialogue," Little Action

It hardly needs to be said that the Clinton-Gore administration's law-and-order policies—and their crusades for "personal responsibility"—fell the heaviest on African Americans, Latinos, and other racially oppressed populations. This was no accident, because abandoning the notion of government action to correct racial injustice was central to New Democrat politics from the start. In fact, the conservative Democrats who launched the DLC saw it largely as a vehicle to counter Jesse Jackson's Rainbow Coalition, the liberal lobby and political organization that grew out of Jackson's 1980s presidential campaigns. At best the Clinton-Gore administration promoted a "race-neutral" approach to social policy that simply tried to avoid issues of racial discrimination. At worst it pandered to racism by scapegoating African-American welfare recipients as lacking "personal responsibility" and Latino immigrants as deportable "criminals."

Clinton signaled his retreat on civil rights early when he abandoned African-American liberal Lani Guinier, his original choice to head the Justice Department's Civil Rights Division, in the face of a hysterical right-wing campaign branding Guinier a "quota queen." When conservatives and the Supreme Court attacked affirmative action programs, Clinton-Gore again retreated. While claiming a posture of wanting to "mend" rather than "end" affirmative action, Clinton ordered the end of dozens of federal affirmative action "set-aside" programs. "I've done more to eliminate programs—affirmative action programs—I didn't think were fair," Clinton boasted in one of the 1996 presidential debates, "and to tighten others up than my predecessors have since affirmative action's been around."[56] Clinton operatives actually sabotaged the 1996 campaign against an anti–affirmative action California ballot initiative. If Clinton's Democrats took a strong stand against the initiative, they argued, it would only energize conservative voters, whose turnout could jeopardize Clinton's reelection support in California.[57] In reality, support for hapless GOP candidate Robert Dole got nowhere near Clinton's in California in 1996.

While refusing to take any risks to oppose racism, the Clinton-Gore administration acted consciously to perpetuate racism in other cases. The administration pressed the Congressional Black Caucus to drop from the 1994 crime bill a "Racial Justice Act" that required assurances that the death penalty wouldn't be administered in a racially discriminatory way. And the administration refused to change federal drug sentencing laws on crack cocaine that overwhelmingly discriminated against African-American offenders. In light of this sorry record, it was hard to take seriously Clinton's 1997 "Presidential Initiative on Race." Clinton established a commission of respected individuals who could have used their positions to call for a national commitment to fight racism. When the commission finally issued its report in 1998, few specific proposals were included. The administration had hoped for such an outcome, as one commission member, former New Jersey governor Thomas Kean—a Republican—pointed out: "Race is very divisive. As the year wore on, people became—not the board, but the people in the Administration—became concerned. We were not encouraged to be bold. My recommendation was much bolder than anything contained in this report."[58]

Clinton and Gore's record on issues of civil rights for other oppressed groups was comparably weak. To win support from women's organizations, Clinton had pledged to appoint a significant number of women to top-ranking positions in his cabinet. When women's groups pressed Clinton to appoint more women than he initially announced in 1993, Clinton attacked them as "bean counters" who were "playing quota games."[59] On the election trail Clinton had pledged to pass a "Freedom of Choice Act" to guarantee the right to abortion. But after his election, he barely mentioned it again. Clinton twice vetoed congressional bans on so-called partial-birth abortions, yet he allowed congressionally imposed restrictions on abortion for federal employees, District of Columbia residents, and Medicaid recipients to pass.[60] In 1998 he proposed a twenty-two-billion-dollar expansion of child care benefits. When the GOP Congress voted it down, he stopped talking about expanding child care. In a larger context, all the attacks Clinton imposed on working people—from welfare "reform" to Medicare cuts—affected women disproportionately.

Clinton's approach to gay and lesbian rights likewise fell far short of activists' expectations. Clinton didn't answer to the Christian right, and he appointed a few openly gay advisers. But on most of the main issues on which the Human Rights Campaign (HRC) and the National Gay and Lesbian Task Force lobbied, the Clinton administration was on the other side. Clinton's 1993 "don't ask, don't tell" surrender to Pentagon bigots led to a 70 percent increase in discharges of gay service members from the Bush administration's final year in 1992.[61] In 1996, Clinton signed the GOP-inspired Defense of Marriage Act, barring states from approving same-sex marriage. He then touted his support for the bill in ads on Christian radio stations during his 1996 reelection campaign. Despite this, the HRC, considering Clinton the lesser evil to the open homophobes in the GOP, made Clinton the honored guest at its annual 1997 dinner.[62]

The Dead End of Lesser Evilism

Politically, the employers' offensive that began in the mid-1970s expressed itself first in a reinvigorated conservative ideology that captured and remade the Republican Party; and second in the rise of the "New Democrats" in the 1990s. As the party whose presidential administration presided over the 1990s boom, the Democrats were transformed. Although perhaps a bit overdrawn, Republican-turned-populist analyst Kevin Phillips's 2004 description of "the underlying partial transformation of the Democrats into a party of a wealthy cultural and technological elite, indeed one whose fortunes and supporting middle-class numbers in parts of the North matched those of the GOP" holds a lot of truth. Phillips continues:

> Holding office during a boom for which it got much of the credit, the Democratic Party of the '90s steered clear of indicting the wealth and income distributions that heyday capitalism had brought. As the first decade of the new century began to unfold with a Republican [George W. Bush] in the White House, some of those Democratic inhibitions fell away, but a substantial underlying party transformation remained.[63]

This transformation helps to explain why the Democrats appeared so disorganized when facing a concerted Republican onslaught after 2001. Indeed, congressional Democrats enabled *all* of Bush's post-9/11 legislation to pass handily. The economic agenda of Democratic leaders differed only in shades from the GOP's, so the Democrats' standard complaint about Bush's tax cuts, for example, centered largely on their impact on the budget deficit. Liberal John R. McArthur lamented that:

> The simplest (and potentially most popular) proposals—an increase in the minimum wage, for example—lie dormant within a Democratic Party that raises money from most of the same sources as the Republicans. Wal-Mart likes its hired help cheap and Wall Street likes Wal-Mart to be happy; they both pay the campaign bills, on both sides of the aisle.
> Thus, the leaders of the "popular" party do their best to appear unpopular, by allowing some of their members to support the administration's drive to eliminate the estate tax, an enormous, regressive windfall for America's already obese plutocracy.[64]

Abetting the shift to the right in the Democratic Party was the atrophy and decay of the popular constituencies that made up the New Deal and Great Society coalitions. Organized labor's continued decline (with the unionized workforce falling to only 13 percent of workers, compared with one out of four workers in the 1970s) has left it without significant influence on the Democratic political agenda. As a result, in the early twenty-first century, the Democrats leaned more heavily on labor to get out the vote, while labor's interests held even less clout inside the party than they did twenty years earlier. Organized labor, preoccupied with short-term maneuvers to maintain its own viability, has failed to project a vision that could galvanize large numbers of workers. The AFL-CIO's 2002 annual Labor Day survey, taken in the wake of the Enron collapse and other corporate scandals, recorded the highest-ever percentage of nonunion workers (50 percent) saying they wanted to join a union. Yet AFL-CIO president John Sweeney's main initiative at the time was a demonstration on Wall Street on behalf of swindled investors and in support of "socially responsible" companies. The same kind of decay in vision and mobilizing power seen among the unions also took hold of the civil rights and women's rights organizations.

As a result, conservatism held sway in official politics, even when it didn't hold majority support in the population. Anis Shivani wrote:

> A case can be made that in a period of voter disillusionment and apathy, it is conservative issues that hold the spotlight. This is not to say that the electorate is necessarily becoming more conservative, but that when voters don't see the political system able to handle large problems they vote conservatively. To the extent that the parties continue to be perceived as ineffective in articulating and solving the larger issues of the day, a conservative agenda—independent of which party holds power—will continue to dominate.[65]

As the Clinton-Gore administration headed into its final year, journalist William Greider recounted:

> [Clinton's] accomplishments, when the sentimental gestures are set aside, are indistinguishable from George [H. W.] Bush's. Like Bush, Clinton increased the top income tax rate a bit, raised the minimum wage modestly and expanded tax credits for the working poor. He reduced military spending somewhat but, like Bush, failed to restructure the military for post–Cold War realities. He got tough on crime, especially drug offenders, and built many more prisons. He championed educational reform. He completed the North American Free Trade Agreement, which was mainly negotiated by the Bush administration. On these and other matters, one can fairly say that Clinton completed Bush's agenda. It is not obvious that a Democratic successor in the White House would be much different.[66]

Greider's criticisms may have made liberals blanch, but he was right. The Clinton-Gore administration pushed through conservative policies—like ending welfare and running a balanced budget—that Republicans could never have won. No less than Alan Greenspan, the conservative chairman of the Federal Reserve from 1987 to 2006, agreed. "Bill Clinton," Greenspan told the *Wall Street Journal*, "was the best Republican president we've had in a while."[67]

The "New Democrat" overhaul of the Democratic Party had succeeded so well that, by the twenty-first century, hardly any leading Democrat challenged its central precepts. When the Democratic Leadership Council dissolved in 2011, DLC founder Al From wrote, "Our nation and our politics have changed significantly since 1985. The DLC has accomplished much of what we first set out to achieve."[68] Leaving From's self-congratulations aside, just how captive the Democrats had become to pro-business "centrism" would be brought into bold relief when the administration of President Barack Obama took power during the worst economic crisis since the Great Depression.

Chapter Four

From "Hope" to Hopeless: The Democrats in the Obama Era

On the eve of President Barack Obama's inauguration in January 2009, Obama's popularity reached 80 percent, and large numbers of Americans had high expectations for his administration. A *USA Today*/Gallup Poll found "stratospheric expectations for the incoming president that his own supporters acknowledge may be unrealistic. A majority of those surveyed say Obama will be able to achieve every one of 10 major campaign promises, from doubling the production of alternative energy to ensuring that all children have health insurance coverage."[1] The *USA Today* poll showed that seven of ten people believed the country would be better off after Obama's first term. After two straight national elections in which the Republicans took a beating, the largest Democratic majority since the 1970s looked set to shift American mainstream politics away from three decades of conservative domination. The American right looked small, irrelevant to the concerns of most Americans, and appeared ready to spend years in the political "wilderness."

Two years later, the formerly discredited and out-of-touch Republican Party scored a historic landslide in the 2010 midterm election. In the largest congressional midterm shift since 1938, the Republicans captured sixty-three seats, ending the four-year Democratic majority in the House of Representatives. As expected, the GOP failed to gain the U.S. Senate. But that was the only consolation for the Democrats.

The Republican sweep was so broad that the GOP took control of nineteen state legislatures outright, twenty-nine governorships, and the largest percentage of state legislative seats since 1928.[2] Ironically, as a result of the worst recession since the Great Depression, the Republicans emerged from the 2010 election with more power at the state level since before the Black Friday crash of 1929.

As the 2012 election season got underway, national polls gave Obama *at best* an even-money chance of winning reelection. But even if he did manage to best the GOP, he was likely to end up with a Republican Congress who would be dedicated to thwarting his policies. In sum, Barack Obama—the first African-American president, elected in 2008 with the largest Democratic vote since 1964—faced the real prospect of joining Jimmy Carter, George H.W. Bush, and Herbert Hoover in the ranks of one-term failed presidents. This chapter aims to explain how Obama fell from the heights of 2008—when many liberals envisioned him leading an FDR-style reorientation of government—to a weak incumbent fighting to keep his job.

The Obama Era Arrives

The election of Barack Obama in a November 2008 Democratic Party sweep was, to many, the main indication of the arrival of a new era in American politics. Obama's election set off jubilant multiracial celebrations in cities across the country, as millions looked forward to Obama's and the Democrats' promises to reverse George W. Bush's disastrous reign. The Obama-Biden ticket defeated the Republican McCain-Palin ticket by more than seven percentage points (52.9 percent to 45.6 percent) and by nearly ten million votes (69.5 million for Obama, 59.9 million for McCain). Obama became the first Democrat since Jimmy Carter, and only the second since Franklin Roosevelt to win an outright majority (i.e., more than 50 percent of the electorate). The Democrats won states like Indiana, North Carolina, and Virginia that had been solidly GOP states for most of the last generation. At the same time, Obama arrived in Washington with the largest Democratic majority in the House of Representatives since 1992 and the largest Democratic majority in the Senate since 1977.

The Democrats' win seemed to put an end to the type of politics that had dominated mainstream U.S. elections for a generation. The

Republican emergence from the late 1960s as the main presidential party hinged on the "Southern strategy" of coded racist appeals that served to make the post-civil rights movement South the GOP's base. This political appeal to opponents of the social change of the 1960s and 1970s merged with a revived free-market ideology that became the reigning orthodoxy of the last four decades. Perhaps there can be no greater repudiation of "Southern strategy" politics than the election of the first African-American president. Although exit polls showed that McCain still won the majority of white voters, Obama did better among whites than any Democrat since Carter. As public opinion expert Andrew Kohut explained:

> Obama did better among [whites] than Kerry by a modest three percentage points. However, when you unpack the white vote, you find that Obama made large gains among young whites, well-educated whites and affluent whites.... When we unpack the data further, we do find that the very least tolerant groups—older white working class voters and older white Southerners—gave McCain somewhat more support than they gave Bush 4 years ago.
>
> In sum, race was certainly a factor in the vote, but on balance more of a positive than a negative for Obama. Black turnout (13% of the electorate) was considerably higher than it was in 2004 (11%). That 20% increase in black turnout is attributable to first-time voters. Overall, 19% of African American voters were first time voters compared with 8% of white voters who went to the polls for the first time. The increased turnout combined with the near universal support for Obama among black voters alone was responsible for adding a couple of percentage points to his overall popular vote take.[3]

Obama's election coincided with the near collapse of the neoliberal economic system, a fact that served to dislodge entrenched attitudes on a whole range of questions. For millions who were losing their jobs, their homes, and their retirement savings, the economic system had already undermined the mantra of deregulation, tax cuts, free trade, and marketization of everything that accompanied the neoliberalism of the last generation. What is more, the fact that the conservative Bush administration took a number of what formerly would have been considered unthinkable actions—nationalizing the world's largest insurance company, spending billions to buy stock in major banks, intervening to guarantee the security of money market accounts and the commercial paper market—put paid to the knee-jerk right-wing praise of the free market and denigration of government intervention.

At the same time, the idea that "big government" is the problem, rather than part of a solution to the economic crisis, fell by the wayside.

The exit polls showed that 51 percent of the voters said they wanted government "to do more" rather than less, and 76 percent of that group voted for Obama. In contrast, 43 percent said it thought that government was doing "too much," and 71 percent of them voted for McCain. A Democracy Corps poll conducted after the 2008 election found that voters most consistently chose the more progressive of the two choices when they were given a "liberal" and a "conservative" description of a problem and solution on issues like trade, health care, and Social Security. When asked to list in order of priority a list of policies, voters put ones like repealing the Bush tax cuts for the rich, providing affordable health care, and ending the war in Iraq at the top of their lists.

Despite the fact that the two parties of American business can be ideologically flexible, the contest between McCain and Obama also took on some ideological tones. Obama was fond of saying that his election would be the "final verdict" on a failed conservative philosophy. In his 2008 Democratic convention acceptance speech, Obama mocked the Republicans' "ownership society" idea as a cover for telling working people that "you're on your own." On the other side, McCain tried to rally his base by warning against Obama's "redistributionist" ideas—even calling Obama's proposals "socialist." McCain's attacks on Obama, which were based on grotesque exaggerations and fabrications, still didn't do him any good. When the votes were tallied—even in supposed "red" states like Indiana and North Carolina—it appeared that the public chose the "socialist" Obama over the tax-cutting, anti-redistributionist McCain.

On the eve of the inauguration, Obama's popularity approached 80 percent, far outstripping similar numbers for the last two presidents. While having the backing of the majority of the public, Obama also had significant support from within the U.S. ruling class to enact a program to stave off the economic crisis. The *Wall Street Journal's* Gerald F. Seib observed:

> One thing is certain: Traditional thinking about relations between a Democratic administration and the business community needs to be thrown out. This is a new era.
>
> For starters, in many ways the government now is the business community, or at least a part of it. When the government is a direct stakeholder in the nation's auto and financial industries, and is becoming the life-support system for the housing industry, it seems almost anachronistic to talk about a divide between government and business.[4]

American business largely supported Obama's proposed eight-hundred-billion-dollar stimulus package, and significant players in the financial industry supported Obama's calls for reregulation of financial markets.[5]

Within a year, the impulse for "change" seemed to be spent, and the public appeared to be turning against the administration. Almost a year to the day after Obama's inauguration, a formerly unknown Republican state senator named Scott Brown won a special election to replace the late senator Ted Kennedy in the U.S. Senate—in one-party Democratic Massachusetts. Brown had pledged to be the "forty-first vote" to defeat Obama's plan for health insurance reform. Polls showed that Brown captured about one in five Obama voters from 2008, while taking advantage of widespread demoralization among Obama supporters.[6] In and of itself, Brown's election didn't much change the political dynamic in Washington. But it set off alarm bells among liberals. The liberal pundit E. J. Dionne put it in stark terms on February 18: "If you want to be honest, face these facts: At this moment, President Obama is losing, Democrats are losing and liberals are losing. Who's winning? Republicans, conservatives, the practitioners of obstruction, and the Tea Party."[7] Given the confluence of forces in early 2009, how could the administration and the Democratic majority have squandered their mandate so completely in less than a year?

It's tempting to answer that question with a reference to all of the standard Washington explanations: the bad economy, an uncooperative Congress, a fickle public, weak advisers and strategies, and all of the rest. While each of these may play a part in the explanation, they avoid a more fundamental point that lies at the heart of this book's case about the nature and role of the Democratic Party—especially in a time of systemic crisis such as the United States faced in 2008. Political scientist Sheldon Wolin noted that inflection points in American history produce calls from the elite for "change" that could be "mitigative" or "paradigmatic." Whereas the former opts to trim around the edges to restore a fundamentally sound system, the latter attempts to recast political and economic relationships in more fundamental ways.[8] In many ways, the Obama administration's failures could be tied to this distinction. Millions voted for Obama hoping for a decisive (or, using Wolin's term, a "paradigmatic") shift in Washington politics and policy. But Obama and his elite backers were more interested in restoring the capital to its pre-2008 "business as usual." The gap between expectation and reality sapped Obama of mass support.

The challenge for the elites who had benefited so much from the neoliberal era was to support a change in U.S. politics that would address the parts of these crises that impinged on their ability to reap profit and power, while containing popular demands for reforms to health care, workplace rights, or military spending that would challenge them. That is where the Democratic Party proves its usefulness to the people who run the United States. The Bush-era Republican Party—saddled with responsibility for unpopular policies, mired in corruption, and having demonstrated its incompetence in managing the affairs of state—had run its course as a vehicle for carrying out, and winning support for, big business's agenda. In the language of Madison Avenue, the Republican "brand" was damaged. And business knows when it's time to pull a bad brand from the shelf.[9] Business's alternative was *Advertising Age's* 2008 "Brand of the Year": Barack Obama, Inc.

The Myths of Campaign 2008

In the hagiographic accounts of Obama's campaign and rise to the White House, the picture of an outsider candidate, running a grassroots campaign, raised to the highest office on the shoulders of millions of ordinary people's donations and electoral work, predominated. But like much else in what radical Obama critic Noam Chomsky calls "personalized electoral extravaganzas," this image obscured reality more than it illuminated it. For anyone looking behind the hype, it was clear that Obama was the same cautious *status quo* politician he was before he found that calls for "hope" and "change" moved crowds during his 2008 primary and general election campaigns. Despite his campaign's positioning as the outsider against the Democratic "establishment's" first choice (Hillary Clinton), Obama was and is a figure tightly bound to big business forces in the Democratic Party.[10]

As noted in chapter 1, Obama out-fundraised and outspent the Republicans and John McCain, even edging out the GOP in contributions from the financial sector. Throughout the primary season, Obama and Clinton each regularly raised more money than any single Republican candidate. Of the thirteen leading industrial sectors whose political contributions the Center for Responsive Politics tracks, the

Republicans led the Democrats in only three (agribusiness, energy, and construction).[11] Even the corporate doyen of neoliberal economics, Walmart, shifted its contributions from almost 95 percent for Republicans to a near fifty-fifty split between the parties.[12]

Investigative journalist Ken Silverstein documented the creation of Obama's money and political machine a few months before Obama announced his intention to run for president: "On condition of anonymity, one Washington lobbyist I spoke with was willing to point out the obvious: that big [Wall Street] donors would not be helping out Obama if they didn't see him as a 'player.' The lobbyist added: 'What's the dollar value of a starry-eyed idealist?'"[13]

Although Obama and the media made much of his development of a grassroots network of small contributors, the big money that funded Obama's campaign came from corporate "bundlers" who rounded up $2,300-maximum contributions from as many of their management colleagues as possible. Under pressure from the *New York Times*, Obama disclosed in July 2008 that more than five hundred individuals had committed to raising at least fifty thousand dollars for him, with 178 of them committed to raising at least two hundred thousand dollars each.[14] A post-election analysis of the Obama money machine showed that only 26 percent of its money came from people who donated two hundred dollars or less—*about the same percentage of small donors who contributed to George W. Bush in 2004.*[15] The flood of money from corporations and the rich assured that Obama's agenda wouldn't stray too far from economic orthodoxy.

None of this could deny the historic nature of Obama's candidacy. As the first African American to win a majority of voters in a country founded on slavery, he lifted the hopes of millions of people. Obama's win was to be another piece of evidence supporting the proposition that the United States is a more racially tolerant and multicultural society than it has ever been. Yet his primary campaign, which subtly played on its historic character, was much more a triumph of style over substance. His rhetoric in the Democratic primaries—crafted with the more liberal Democratic primary voter in mind—evoked images of mass movements for social change throughout U.S. history. He sought, very skillfully and consciously, to cloak himself in the legitimacy of struggles for the right to vote, the eight-hour day, and civil rights for the oppressed:

I believe change does not happen from the top down. It happens from the bottom up. Dr. King understood that.

It was those women who were willing to walk instead of ride the bus, union workers who are willing to take on violence and intimidation to get the right to organize. It was women who decided, "I'm as smart as my husband. I'd better get the right to vote." Them arguing, mobilizing, agitating, and ultimately forcing elected officials to be accountable. I think that's the key.[16]

But when one looked beyond his inspirational rhetoric, it was often hard to pin down exactly where Obama stood on crucial questions. In many ways, Obama remained as Ezra Klein, writing in the *American Prospect* in late 2006, described him, "a cipher, an easy repository for the hopes and dreams of liberals everywhere."[17]

Despite Obama's nods to social protest movements, he advocated few policies that broke with any of the accepted orthodoxy in Washington. During the primary campaign against Clinton and Senator John Edwards, Obama often took stands on economic issues that placed him to the right of Clinton's and Edwards's fake populism. When Clinton flogged John McCain's proposal for a temporary cut in the excise tax on gasoline, Obama brushed it aside as a gimmick. For refusing to back the gas tax holiday, Obama won the seal of approval from one of the deans of neoliberal punditry, the *New York Times*'s Thomas Friedman: "Good for Barack Obama for resisting this shameful pandering."[18]

As the scale of the housing crisis began to force its way into the primary campaign, Obama held back from support for a moratorium on foreclosures and for government aid to strapped homeowners, when Edwards and Clinton advocated both. Instead, Obama called for making mortgage fraud a federal crime and for a small federal tax credit. By summer, after clinching the nomination, Obama recognized the untenability of maintaining this "above the fray" attitude to the housing crisis; he (and free-market McCain, for that matter) voted for the multibillion-dollar housing bill that passed the Senate. But it was telling that his first inclination on addressing the housing crisis was to take the position least offensive to financial interests and to neoliberal dogma.

Obama tapped "centrist," pro-free-market economists like the University of Chicago's Austan Goolsbee and Walmart defender Jason Furman as his top economic advisers. Other informal Obama advisers included such mainstream figures as billionaire investor Warren Buffett, former Federal Reserve chairman Paul Volcker, and former Bush treasury secretary Paul O'Neill. At a July 2008 economic summit involving those figures and other corporate and Republican leaders, Obama highlighted a "bipartisan" approach to the economy that, although deliberately vague, seemed to countenance limited government intervention while emphasizing a reduction of the federal deficit and aid to the private sector—in essence, a rehash of 1990s Clintonomics. "If you can attract senior Republican figures to an economic summit in the July before an election, then you are sending a strong message of bipartisan credibility. It is really doubtful Senator McCain could emulate this," Obama adviser and former Clinton economic official Gene Sperling told the *Financial Times*.[19]

Aside from his skill as a politician and the fact that he had the backing of leading Democratic politicians and fundraisers to finance his bid, Obama probably owed his victory over Hillary Clinton to his opposition to the Iraq War. Clinton's refusal to concede that she was mistaken to vote to authorize the war played into Obama's self-narrative as someone who would not sacrifice judgment or principle for political expediency. In fact, his opposition to the war was far more conditional than he later claimed, and his votes on war-related matters were virtually identical to those of the hawkish Clinton.[20] But Obama managed to tap the mood of Democratic voters fed up with the war and politicians who supported it. One of his campaign's greatest applause lines was this: "I don't want to just end the war, but I want to end the mindset that got us into the war in the first place. That's the kind of leadership that I think we need from the next president of the United States. That's what I intend to provide."

In reality, Obama's foreign policy turned out to be conventional, even hawkish, as chapter 6 will detail. This was another piece of Obama's stance that shouldn't have come as a surprise to his supporters. He told the *New York Times*'s David Brooks: "I have enormous sympathy for the foreign policy of George H. W. Bush. I don't have a lot of complaints about their handling of Desert Storm [i.e., the 1991 war against Iraq]."[21] In a 2007 *Foreign Affairs* article, "Renewing American Leadership," Obama proposed to regain the leadership of the world that George W. Bush's reckless and dumb foreign policy had squandered. "In the wake of Iraq and Abu Ghraib, the world has lost trust in our purposes and our principles," Obama wrote. "We must lead the world, by deed and by example."[22]

There was no disputing that the United States was more widely hated during the Bush administration than before, and Obama's message recognized that. And it's not surprising that Obama would urge "renewing American leadership," because "leading the world" has been the overriding U.S. foreign policy aim since at least the end of the Second World War. Obama's pitch for reinvigorating alliances with European powers and engaging countries such as Iran drew support from the European establishment after years of Bush administration disdain toward multilateral action and insults hurled at "Old Europe." And the U.S. political and foreign policy establishment preferred their president to draw crowds of thousands waving American flags than to draw demonstrations of millions who view the president as a pariah.

As Obama neared the fall election, he adopted a posture of "president-in-waiting," while making a number of political moves that disappointed his most ardent supporters. For example, after first announcing he would filibuster a bill to grant immunity to telecommunications companies that collaborated with the government's warrantless wiretap program, he flipped and announced his support for the bill. Thousands of Obama supporters filled his campaign's interactive website with protests of his sellout on the FISA bill, and other prominent supporters expressed unease in editorials in various liberal publications. One group of prominent Obama supporters issued "An Open Letter to Barack Obama" in the pages of the liberal *Nation*. After congratulating Obama for his campaign's "tremendous achievements" that have "inspired a wave of political enthusiasm like nothing seen in this country for decades," the letter goes on to raise concern: "There have been troubling signs that you are moving away from the core commitments shared by many who have supported your campaign, toward a more cautious and centrist stance." It outlined a list of policies—including withdrawal from Iraq on a fixed timetable and universal health care—that the signatories considered a minimum program for Obama to pursue. It concluded, in part: "If you win in November, we will work to support your stands when we agree with you and to challenge them when we don't. We look forward to an ongoing and constructive dialogue with you when you are elected President."[23]

In the light of these indications of unease among his liberal supporters, Obama felt compelled to note the displeasure among "my friends on the left," only to slap them down again: "Look, let me talk about the broader issue, this whole notion that I am shifting to the center," Obama told a crowd in Georgia in July 2008:

> The people who say this apparently haven't been listening to me. I believe in a whole lot of things that make me progressive and put me squarely in the Democratic camp. . . . I believe in personal responsibility; I also believe in faith. . . . That's not something new; I've been talking about that for years. So the notion that this is me trying to look centrist is not true."[24]

Despite signs of discomfort with Obama in the liberal camp, many leading progressives went to extraordinary lengths to consider Obama—already a member of one of the world's most exclusive clubs, with campaign coffers stuffed with millions in corporate cash—as one of them.

Typical of this willful suspension of disbelief was the founding statement of "Progressives for Obama," issued in March 2008 under the signatures of prominent progressives Tom Hayden, Bill Fletcher Jr., Danny Glover, and Barbara Ehrenreich. The letter opened by proclaiming, "All American progressives should unite for Barack Obama." The statement's key idea was that the support for Obama generated in the Democratic primaries—heavy voter turnouts and decisive support from African Americans and young people—constituted a social movement that stood in the traditions of the great American social movements of the past, like the labor movement of the 1930s or the civil rights and Black Power movements of the 1960s. "We intend to join and engage with our brothers and sisters in the vast rainbow of social movements to come together in support of Obama's unprecedented campaign and candidacy. Even though it is candidate-centered, there is no doubt that the campaign is a social movement, one greater than the candidate himself ever imagined." Although the statement conceded that Obama "openly defines himself as a centrist," its writers regarded this as reason for the "formation of a progressive force within his coalition."[25]

Obama's campaign—or at least its incarnation during the Democratic primaries—mobilized first-time voters and raised hopes for "change" among millions. But declaring Obama's campaign a social movement was an exercise in sophistry at best, and self-delusion at worst. To confuse voting in a Democratic primary with militant struggle against the state or employers is to lose any realistic way to assess what is actually needed to win real social change. If activists subsume their own means and ends to those of a mainstream electoral campaign, they risk settling for a lot less than what they can attain through mobilization that puts pressure on all of the politicians. That was the real lesson of the 1930s and 1960s: what will determine the direction of social and political change in the United States will be grassroots movements on the ground, not tallies at the ballot box. Progressives for Obama would most likely agree with that point, but they, as Glen Ford of *Black Agenda Report* put it, lent their names and reputations to an effort "to allow Obama to 'pass' for what he is not: a progressive."[26] It wouldn't take long for Obama's actions in office to confirm Ford's point.

From Capitalist Crisis to Business as Usual

The September 2008 financial meltdown that seized the world economy when the investment bank Lehman Brothers went bankrupt arguably clinched the election of Obama that November. By the time of Obama's election, the U.S. economy had already been in recession for almost a year, and on Inauguration Day, employers were laying off workers at a rate of eight hundred thousand a month. As a result, the "Great Recession," which most acknowledged stemmed from the bursting of a Wall Street–engineered credit bubble, dominated every aspect of politics and popular consciousness through most of Obama's term. The administration would rise or fall on how it dealt with the economic crisis.

Obama's first response to the crisis was the promotion and passage, in February 2009, of the American Recovery and Reinvestment Act. The giant stimulus bill, which clocked in at $787 billion, reflected the administration's view that the economy needed a jolt of temporary stimulus to break the free fall. The administration assumed, against much evidence from previous credit bubble-induced recessions, that increased government spending would push the economy back onto its pre-recession path, after which the administration could tackle the country's long-term deficit.

Desiring to signal fiscal rectitude, Obama and his administration kept their economic stimulus bill to less than eight hundred billion dollars. Then, the administration trimmed it further to attract more conservative votes. At that time, independent economists, and even some of the administration's own economists, were calling for a stimulus measure in excess of one trillion dollars, focused primarily on creating jobs. Instead, to win more bipartisan support, the administration limited the amount of money allocated to jobs creation and explicitly ruled out direct government jobs programs modeled on the 1930s-era Works Progress Administration. It dedicated far too much of the stimulus, upwards of 40 percent of the total, to a variety of tax cuts and credits to individuals and business that were useless in creating jobs. These concessions won the votes of three Republican senators and no Republicans in the House, but they further limited the bill's impact.

When the administration pushed for the stimulus bill, it released studies claiming that it would push the unemployment rate down to 7 percent by 2010. In reality, the unemployment rate increased to more than 10 percent. When it was clear that a greater and more job-focused stimulus was needed, Obama *himself* ruled it out on two grounds: one, the need to show "fiscal responsibility," and two, because he couldn't (or wouldn't) push Congress, with its overwhelming Democratic majorities, to enact one.[27] The Obama administration was left with the worst of all possible worlds. The stimulus bill may have helped avert a plunge into depression, but it failed to reduce unemployment in any noticeable way. Nevertheless, as the *Washington Post's* Ezra Klein described,

> the administration insisted on optimism. There was talk of "green shoots" and the "recovery summer." Events in Greece and in oil markets were chalked up to bad luck rather than the predictable aftershocks of a financial crisis. The promised recovery was always just around the corner, but it never quite came. Eventually, the American people stopped listening. A September poll showed that 50 percent of Americans thought Obama's policies had hurt the economy.[28]

Perhaps all of this wasn't surprising, given that Obama appointed an economic team staffed almost completely with Clinton administration retreads. Almost all of them were acolytes of Clinton treasury secretary Robert Rubin, who championed balanced budgets, deregulation of financial markets, free trade, and the rest of the "New Democrat" neoliberal economic playbook. Sitting in the most prominent position was Obama's treasury secretary Timothy Geithner, who, as president of the New York Fed during the Bush administration, had helped to engineer many of the government-funded bailouts and forced mergers of banks into "too big to fail" behemoths. Geithner was also implicated in the scandalous 2008 multibillion-dollar payoff of AIG debts that made AIG's creditors (most prominently Goldman Sachs and Deutsche Bank) whole, while still preserving AIG executives' bonuses.

One might have thought that the near-meltdown of the world economy would have caused some of the Clintonites whom Obama hired to reconsider their pro-business agenda of the 1990s. Instead, the crisis provided them with the opportunity to spend a vast amount of money—more than Clinton ever did—without really changing their neoliberal policy assumptions. In a sort of "Keynesian neoliberalism," the administration put trillions of taxpayer dollars at the disposal of private business, trying to "incentivize" it to carry out social policy. It didn't work—either in the bailout of the banks or in several failed Treasury attempts to stem the mortgage and housing crisis.[29] The banks and big corporations were happy to take the money, but they didn't commit to lending money, saving homes, or hiring workers. By 2010, corporate America had piled up a surplus of cash approaching two trillion dollars.

Typical of the administration's kid-gloves approach to Wall Street was a March 2009 meeting at the White House between Obama, Geithner, and the CEOs of the largest thirteen banks in the United States. News reports quoted Obama lecturing the CEOs, telling them that "my administration is the only thing between you and pitchforks."[30] But the main result of the meeting was the administration's reassurance to the bankers that it had no intention of forcing a change in the way Wall Street did business. Journalist Ron Suskind quoted one of the CEOs who attended:

> The sense of everyone after the big meeting was relief. . . . The president had us at a moment of real vulnerability. At that point, he could have ordered us to do just about anything, and we would have rolled over. But he didn't—he mostly wanted to help us out, to quell the mob. And the guy we figured we had to thank for that was [Geithner]. He was our man in Washington.[31]

No wonder more and more Americans came to see the Obama administration as a bankers' administration—in the same way that they viewed the Bush-Cheney regime as an "oil and gas" administration. A September 2009 Economic Policy Institute poll asked a national sample of registered voters to say who they thought had "been helped a lot or some" from the policies that the administration had enacted. The result: thirteen percent said "the average working person," 64 percent identified "large banks," and 54 percent fingered "Wall Street investment companies."[32]

By 2010, the financial sector, kept alive with taxpayers' money, was in open revolt against the administration's initiatives for financial regulatory reform. Prominent Wall Streeters were expressing their disappointment with Obama and pledging to support Republicans in the 2010 midterms. Meanwhile, a virtual army of financial sector lobbyists was doing its utmost to neuter Obama's regulatory proposals, including the creation of a new financial consumer protection agency. It wasn't that any of the reforms themselves were truly onerous to the banks. In fact, experts noted that the administration-supported Dodd-Frank financial reform bill failed to address many of the issues that led to the crash, while at the same time "the very regulators who dropped the ball in the current crisis have garnered more, not less, authority."[33] On the contrary, the banks moved to gut financial reform *because they could*. As Suskind wryly noted, "The princes of New York had sized [Obama] up. He'd already been shorted by the Street."[34]

The contrast between the administration's handling of Wall Street and the auto industry—both industries operating under effective government ownership—was striking. While the banks were allowed to pay back their bailout funds quickly and to resume business as usual, the government used its leverage to restructure Chrysler and General Motors with mass layoffs and to gut wages and benefits won over generations of struggle. In Michigan, the state hardest hit by the auto industry's collapse—and whose union households voted for Obama two to one over Republican McCain—the disparate treatment was a slap in the face. Brian Fredline, president of UAW Local 602 near Lansing, Michigan, noted:

> It's the age-old Wall Street vs. Main Street smackdown again. You have all kinds of funding available to banks that are apparently too big to fail, but they're also too big to be responsible. . . . But when it comes to auto manufacturing and middle-class jobs and people that don't matter on Wall Street, there are certainly different standards that we have to meet—higher standards—than the financials. That is a double standard that exists, and it's unfair.[35]

The double standard was clear to see. Yet it would seem to contradict the notion, traditionally held in civics textbooks and popular lore, that the Democrats represent "the people" while the Republicans represent big business. With unionized workers an important group in the Democratic "base," it would seem that Democrats were acting against their own best interests. This conception assumes that the Democrats simply reflect the interests and aspirations of the people who vote for them. But this is actually the wrong way to look at the Democratic Party, which is one of the two corporate parties that manage the American state. One of the long-term goals of the U.S. corporate elite is to rebuild the nation's industrial base as a low-wage competitor to "emerging markets" like China, as the Obama-appointed President's Council on Jobs and Competitiveness envisions.[36]

As Obama's support fell, the political media filled with analyses purporting to explain this. It was said that Obama was "too far to the left" of the country, or that he was too "high-minded" to play hardball politics, or that the dysfunctional Senate was impeding the administration. All of these shallow explanations missed the most obvious point. As radical journalist Arun Gupta put it: "Far from failures or mistakes, these episodes illustrate how Team Obama, which surfed a tsunami of corporate money and savvy branding to victory, is doing exactly what it was elected to do: redistribute money upwards."[37] The Obama administration was, as a Hillary Clinton administration would have been, a "center-right" regime that tended first and foremost to the interests of capital, with a heavy emphasis on catering to finance capital.[38] Obama told Senate Democrats:

> We've got to be the party of business, small business and large business, because they produce jobs. We've got to be in favor of competition and exports and trade. We've got to be non-ideological about our approach to these things. We've got to make sure that our party understands that, like it or not, we have to have a financial system that is healthy and functioning, so we can't be demonizing every bank out there.[39]

Obama's attitude pervaded the entire Democratic leadership in Congress as well.[40]

The "Inglorious" Road to Obamacare

The administration's chief domestic policy achievement was the passage of the Patient Protection and Affordable Care Act of 2010, a far-reaching health insurance reform bill that its opponents soon labeled "Obamacare." Yet as the reform legislation in Congress limped to what National Nurses United president Rose Ann DeMoro called an "inglorious end," it was remarkable how few liberals felt enthusiastic about a bill that was supposed to represent a crowning achievement for them. Aside from a few policy wonks, many (if not most) liberals felt that the health care legislation was insufficient—and, in parts, harmful to ordinary people's health care. Supporters of genuine health care reform knew that the "compromise" bill was a huge gift to the insurance industry. At the same time, they felt that Democrats got far less than they could or should have, in large part because they didn't even try.[41] The administration made this result inevitable when it adopted an approach to the health insurance and health provider industries that paralleled its approach to the banks. The health care case also illustrated the ways in which the modern Democratic Party corrals its most ardent supporters and forces them to accept "compromises" that will delay, if not impede, a solution to a crisis that faces nearly every non-rich American.

Few doubt that the U.S. health care system faces a crisis. Although the health care sector accounts for more than one-sixth of the U.S. GDP, more than fifty million Americans lack health insurance coverage. The bloated, for-profit nature of the health care industry leaves the U.S. system the most expensive of all industrial nations' while simultaneously failing to provide coverage for all U.S. residents. A true solution to this crisis would be a government-run "single-payer" health care system like those operated in countries such as Canada, Britain, or Taiwan. Compared to the United States' non-system, single-payer systems in other countries are less costly, more efficient, and universal. When Obama was preparing to mount a run for the U.S. Senate in 2003, he seemed to acknowledge all of these points:

> I happen to be a proponent of a single-payer universal health care program. I see no reason why the United States of America, the wealthiest country in the history of the world, spending 14 percent of its Gross National Product on health care, cannot provide basic health insurance to everybody. . . . A single-payer health care plan, a universal health care plan. And that's what I'd like to see. But as all of you know, we may not get there immediately. Because first we have to take back the White House, we have to take back the Senate, and we have to take back the House.[42]

Five years later, with the Democrats holding sixty votes in the Senate and the White House, Obama appointed as his chief health care adviser Nancy Ann DeParle, a Clinton-era Medicare administrator who spent more than a decade out of government working for for-profit health industry firms like Medco Health Solutions, Cerner, Boston Scientific, DaVita, and Triad Hospitals. In the highly choreographed March 2009 White House health care summit called to launch the president's health care reform effort, advocates of the single-payer solution had to mount a furious campaign to win a token invitation for two of their supporters to join the politicians, health industry lobbyists, and neoliberal policy wonks who formed the core of the White House guest list.[43]

Seeking to head off an industry-sponsored campaign to defeat the bill like the one that finished off the Clinton health care reform plan in the 1990s, the White House pursued a strategy of involving industry "stakeholders" in writing the legislation. As a result, the proposals that emerged contained a number of unpopular provisions, including a mandate for all people to buy health insurance, taxing health care benefits for those with good benefits packages, and cutting five hundred billion dollars from Medicare to finance the plan. In fact, the outlines of the Obama health reform program were actually those of the conservative Republican alternative to the 1993–94 Clinton plan.[44] Because of the concessions to industry and conservatives, all offered as the cost of continuing to do business with the medical-industrial complex, the finished product will be unlikely to fulfill the lofty promises that Obama made on its behalf.

Every now and again, the administration launched rhetorical broadsides against the health insurers. But the health insurance industry remained "on board" because it knew it stood to make billions from Obamacare:

> What people in Washington tend not to discuss, at least on the record, is the open secret that insurers are minimizing their forecasts of the eventual windfall they will enjoy from expanded coverage for Americans. UnitedHealth has given certain key members of Congress details about its finances and tax liability— both historical numbers and figures projected under various cost-sharing scenarios. But some on Capitol Hill are skeptical. "The bottom line," says an aide to the Senate Finance Committee, "is that health reform would lead to increased revenues and profits [for the insurance industry]. . . . There will be [added] costs [to the companies], but we're not sure the revenues and profits will be as low as they say."[45]

This might suggest that Obama's and the Democrats' good intentions simply fell victim to a multimillion-dollar medical industry lobbying campaign. But that's the opposite of reality. For one thing, Obama himself was intimately involved in behind-the-scenes negotiations with lobbyists, and ten of the thirteen Democrats on the crucial Senate Finance Committee were connected to at least twenty different former staff members who became health industry lobbyists.[46] The poison fruit of one of those deals, according to a secret memo the *Huffington Post* obtained, was a commitment from the White House to the main pharmaceutical industry lobby that it wouldn't press for any more than the eighty billion dollars in savings that the industry pledged to implement over ten years. Off the table, therefore, was Obama's oft-made promise (usually a sure applause-getter during his campaign) to end the Bush administration's stupid policy of preventing Medicare from negotiating for lower drug prices with the pharmaceutical manufacturers. In exchange for the deal, Big Pharma committed $150 million to rally support for the bill.[47]

Another casualty of the administration's deals with the insurance industry was the liberal-supported "public option," or government-provided health insurance. Instead of eliminating the role of private insurance, as a "single-payer" system would do, the public option would have provided government-provided health insurance as an alternative to private health insurance in the health insurance "exchanges" Obamacare envisioned. Even though the public option represented a huge retreat from a single-payer system and a concession to the logic of market competition in health insurance, liberals clung to it as a means, however inadequate, of controlling costs and increasing access. Despite mouthing words favorable to the public option, the Obama administration did all it could to keep it out of the final legislation. Liberals excoriated Obama for caving to the pressure of the insurance industry or to conservative opponents like Senator Joseph Lieberman (I-CT). But the record showed that Obama's alleged support for the public option was always more rhetorical than real. "The evidence was overwhelming from the start that the White House was not only indifferent, but opposed, to the provisions most important to progressives," *Salon's* Glenn Greenwald concluded. "The administration is getting the bill which they, more or less, wanted from the start—the one that is a huge boon to the health insurance and pharmaceutical industry."[48]

The demise of the public option was also a study in the fecklessness of progressive Democrats when faced with a challenge from their "centrist" president. In 2009, the House Progressive Caucus threatened to vote as a bloc against any legislation that didn't include a public option. Almost all of them ended up voting for the bill without the public option in 2010. What happened to all the brave announcements of "lines in the sand" and "standing up for real reform"? The logic of lesser-evilism and careerism took over. House speaker Nancy Pelosi was willing to give a few Progressive Caucus members a "free vote" to oppose the bill. But she knew that if progressive opposition stood in the way of the bill's passage, the progressives would fold and vote for it. Former DNC chair Howard Dean opined that stripped of a public option the bill "wasn't worth voting for." But after warnings from the White House that suggested his future as a Democratic wise man was in doubt if he opposed the bill, Dean flip-flopped as well. As *Newsweek's* Suzy Khimm pointed out, "In the end, Dean wants to be at the negotiating table—not cast outside it—and he probably decided to adjust accordingly."[49]

But the most pathetic collapse occurred among leading Democratic progressives, such as representatives John Conyers (D-MI) and Dennis Kucinich (D-OH), who were longtime proponents of a "single-payer" government-run health care plan. When Pelosi pressured single-payer advocates to withdraw a single-payer bill from consideration, representatives Conyers and Kucinich issued a letter supporting the climbdown. It read, in part:

> Many progressives in Congress, ourselves included, feel that calling for a vote tomorrow for single-payer would be tantamount to driving the movement over a cliff. . . . We are now asking you to join us in suggesting to congressional leaders that this is not the right time to call the roll on a stand-alone single-payer bill. That time will come.

Pelosi claimed that allowing a single-payer amendment would have opened the floodgates to other amendments, like those banning abortion. So what happened? The single-payer amendment was withdrawn, and representative Bart Stupak (D-MI) introduced his, banning coverage for abortion. The bill, with the Stupak amendment included, passed the House. Kucinich subsequently voted for the full plan, after Obama made him a personal appeal (or threat) in a one-on-one conversation on Air Force One.

No doubt Democratic leaders like Obama and Pelosi used the threat of the defeat of health insurance reform at the hands of charged-up conservatives to force progressives' hands. By late 2009, older conservatives, organized by industry-backed lobbying organizations into "Tea Parties," had disrupted scores of congressional town hall meetings.[50] Support for health care reform was already dwindling, and conservative senator Jim DeMint (R-SC) issued a call to defeat health care reform to force Obama's "Waterloo." Faced with the choice of passing a half-measure loaded with corporate giveaways or seeing "Obamacare" go down in flames, the liberals decided to accept "half a loaf." As always, the liberals played loyal soldiers for an administration that showed itself to be much more interested in winning the support of industry "stakeholders" and conservatives like senators Ben Nelson (D-NE) and Lieberman than in fighting for any genuine health reform.

In fact, this sort of "lesser-evil" choice was embedded in the entire process of developing the bill. The insurance and provider lobbies played both sides of the health care reform debate. On the inside, they worked with the Obama administration to craft the legislation. On the outside, they (or their associates, like the U.S. Chamber of Commerce) funded many of the anti-reform and Tea Party organizations. Industry used the "Astroturf" (i.e., fake grassroots) pressure of rank-and-file right-wingers to create an atmosphere in which their insiders could more effectively bend White House and congressional ears to accept more "realistic" goals. In fact, one might even describe this as bipartisanship in action: while industry front groups provided the GOP with its talking points, industry lobbies supplied congressional Democrats with theirs. The result was a big win for the health care industry, as ordinary Americans were left to wonder what was in it for them. An Associated Press poll taken about six months after passage of the Affordable Care Act found that four in ten adults said they didn't think Obama's health reform went far enough.[51]

Embracing Austerity

The historic defeat that Democrats sustained in November 2010 launched the Obama administration on a new and even more disastrous course. In the lead-up to the election, the Obama administration, from the president on down, sent out two contradictory messages. On the one hand, Obama and White House spokesman Robert Gibbs attacked the Democrats' core supporters for, essentially, expecting too much from 2008's Mr. Hope and Change. At the same time, Obama made nice with the Republicans, urging them yet again to reach across the aisle to find bipartisan solutions.

Obama the "centrist" was setting the stage for his own planned shift to the right to embrace the politics of austerity after the election. He was positioning himself—as Bill Clinton did in 1995 and 1996—as the sensible actor, working in a bipartisan fashion to enact policy over the objections of the Tea Party crazies and the "far left," as the media regularly describe the liberal wing of the Democratic Party. Obama did nothing to dispel this expectation with his post-election press conference, where he proclaimed himself "humbled" and willing to listen to Republican proposals on a range of topics.

The politics of austerity was the conservative and big business answer to the economic crisis. The massive transfer of wealth from taxpayers to the financial sector left a huge debt overhang. The recession also dampened tax receipts to their lowest level as a percentage of GDP in sixty years, while government spending on programs like unemployment insurance had ticked upward. Added to the unbudgeted cost of the 2001 and 2003 Bush tax cuts and two major wars, the government's budget deficits of more an a trillion dollars threatened United States' economic stability. Facing this budget gap, the U.S. ruling class, along with its global partners, "effectively declared that working class people and the poor will pay the cost of the global bank bailout."[52]

As if to underscore that austerity wouldn't proceed from the assumption of "shared sacrifice," Obama accepted the congressional Republican minority's demand to extend the deficit-swelling Bush-era tax cuts for an additional two years. This about-face from an early campaign promise to end the Bush tax cuts for the rich followed the Democrats' failure even to put the tax cuts to a vote when the party held massive congressional majorities. The administration then "pivoted" to an austerity agenda based, initially, on the 2010 report of the president's National Commission on Fiscal Responsibility and Reform. The commission, appointed jointly by Obama and the leaders of both parties in Congress, issued recommendations for four trillion dollars in cutbacks to social entitlement programs like Medicare and Social Security.[53]

The commission's proposals helped to set the stage for a debate on federal spending that dominated the first year of the 112th Congress where a Republican House majority cohabited with a bare Democratic majority in the Senate. Obama repeatedly said that "everything must be on the table," indicating that no program, including Social Security, would be considered safe from cutbacks. In embracing austerity, Obama and the Democrats ceded so much ideological ground that any sort of Clintonite triangulation amounted to meeting the Republicans halfway on *how much* to cut safety net programs, not whether to cut in the first place.

The disastrous move toward austerity hit its nadir in the August 2011 GOP-engineered confrontation over the federal debt ceiling. In exchange for providing a normally pro-forma vote for raising the federal government's borrowing limit, the Tea Party–infused congressional Republican caucuses forced an unprecedented series of cuts in federal spending, scheduled to begin in 2013. But putting the blame for the debt ceiling disaster on the ultra-conservative Tea Partiers, as liberals and the White House did, obscured the reality that Washington's commitment to austerity politics was thoroughly bipartisan. The Tea Party hostage-takers got what they wanted because Obama wanted to ransom the hostage.

In their negotiations with the White House, Republican house speaker John Boehner and Senate minority leader Mitch McConnell both publicly stated that they wouldn't allow a U.S. government default. In other words, they signaled that, rhetoric aside, they weren't willing to push the government to the brink. But rather than press them to stop the posturing, Obama upped the ante by putting a "grand bargain" of four trillion dollars in cuts on the table—including cuts in "entitlement" spending—not once, but twice. Obama may have been an inept negotiator, but he is also part of a political establishment that has wanted to cut entitlement programs like Social Security for decades. In fact, even while assembling the early 2009 fiscal stimulus program, Obama administration officials spoke of a "grand bargain" involving increased taxes and cuts in entitlement programs as their long-term "bipartisan" strategy to fix the U.S. government budget.[54]

In the end, Obama's attempt to project himself as "the adult in the room," navigating between the far-right Tea Partiers and the Democratic base, left him politically wounded. Even the AFL-CIO, the Democrats' chief institutional mechanism for get-out-the-vote operations, threatened to withhold support for Obama in 2012. Yet only a few weeks later, in September 2011, Obama used an address to a joint session of Congress to introduce an "American Jobs Act," a legislative package that had almost no chance to pass an austerity-addled Congress. Polls showed that Obama's jobs package and proposed increased taxes on the rich were far more popular than any austerity measures.[55] But while Obama's plans may have been popular, they were also too little and too late.

Where was all the concern about jobs and ending tax breaks for the rich back during the first two years of the Obama administration, when

Democrats held large majorities in Congress and presumably could have passed real legislation to create jobs? Even after realizing that the 2009 stimulus measure didn't bring down unemployment to the extent the administration had hoped, it never seriously considered a 1930s-style jobs program. Even if the White House underestimated the depth of the jobs crisis, that couldn't excuse its jettisoning a central promise of its 2008 campaign: ending the Bush tax cuts for the wealthy. Nor could it offer an alibi for the gutlessness of Democrats in Congress who refused to even consider raising taxes on the rich despite the over-whelming popularity of that idea. In the wake of the debt ceiling fiasco, public esteem of the Congress, both major parties, and the president sunk to new lows.

The Base and the Veal Pen

To say that liberals' and Democratic partisans' high hopes in Obama were dashed was an understatement. Patricia Elizondo, president of a Milwaukee International Association of Machinists local, told the *New York Times* that the union had trouble motivating its members to get out the vote for the Democrats in the 2010 midterm elections. "People have been unemployed for two years, and they're unhappy that the health care bill was not as good as they expected," she said. "Two years ago, I had many members going door-to-door to campaign. Now they're saying, 'Why should I? We supported that candidate, but he didn't follow through.'"[56]

Repeated across the country, this sentiment produced what poll-sters and pundits referred to as the "enthusiasm gap" between conservative voters who couldn't wait to throw the Democratic bums out and the traditional Democratic "base" groups (such as youth, African Americans, and trade unionists) who showed much less interest in the election then they did in 2008. ABC's polling expert Gary Langer calculated that twenty-nine million Obama voters in 2008 stayed home during the midterms, compared to 19.5 million McCain voters.[57] As a result, the electorate that turned up in 2010 was much more white, wealthy, old, and conservative than either the 2008 electorate or the U.S. population as a whole. By late 2010, CNN estimated that about one-quarter of the people expressing disapproval of Obama were people who said he "hasn't been liberal enough."[58]

The White House reaped what it sowed, because the administration seemed to go out of its way to alienate its most ardent supporters. Consider the administration's actions in relation to three key Democratic "base" groups, all of whom contributed heavily to his 2008 victory: African Americans and civil rights advocates, environmentalists, and Latinos and immigrant rights activists.

Obama and Race

As the first African-America president, Obama, who regularly paid homage to the civil rights movement in his rhetoric, would have seemed well-positioned to tackle the United States' racial inequalities. Yet, Obama insisted on presenting himself as a "post-racial" president, acting as if issues of racial discrimination were relics of the 1960s. He persisted with this stance even after it became clear that much of the right-wing opposition to him stemmed from the racial animus of older white conservatives who wanted "their country back."[59]

Loath to be accused of favoring African Americans, Obama did virtually nothing for Black America. When, in 2009, he criticized Cambridge, Massachusetts, police for arresting African-American Harvard professor Henry Louis Gates Jr. as an intruder at his own house, he faced a firestorm of criticism. He ended up backing down, apologizing to the police, and hosting a silly "beer summit" at the White House with Gates and the arresting officer. In another incident, the White House ordered the firing of African-American Agriculture Department official Shirley Sherrod when right-wing media, using a selectively edited recording, appeared to "expose" Sherrod for animosity to white farmers. Exactly the opposite was the truth, but the Obama administration insisted on firing her before even finding out. The White House subsequently offered to rehire Sherrod, but she declined in 2011. The Gates and Sherrod incidents illustrated how the White House's "post-racialism" actually led to capitulations to racism. Morever, in their zeal to show "tough love" to African Americans when appearing before Black audiences, Barack Obama often criticized Black men for failing as fathers, and first lady Michelle Obama lectured Black families for subsisting on junk food.[60]

While laying down these cultural markers, the Obama White House shied away from championing policies that would help racial minorities and the poor. The administration has refused to end the "War on Drugs," the single greatest contributor to the nation's catastrophic African-American incarceration rates. In fact, the Obama administration increased punishment for drug possession (from the Bush administration) and slashed Department of Education funding for drug treatment.[61] The failures of the administration's housing policies hit Black and Latino communities, where the foreclosure crisis was concentrated, the hardest. The White House's jump on the austerity bandwagon not only sacrificed the poor, but it also imperiled the jobs, wages, and benefits of the federal workforce, a redoubt for the Black middle class. At the height of Washington's anti-deficit mania, popular Black talk show host Tavis Smiley and Princeton University professor Cornel West mounted a twelve-city "poverty tour" to bring attention to the plight of the poor—and to criticize Obama's seeming indifference to them. Smiley told reporters: "I think too often [Obama] compromises, too often he capitulates. I think the Republicans know that. I think they laugh when he's not around. . . . [The underclass] want him to fight for them and I think they're tired of seeing the Republicans clean his clock."[62] When confronting criticism like this, the White House and its supporters attacked the messengers. Speaking to the Congressional Black Caucus after the debt-ceiling debacle, Obama chastised the CBC: "Take off your bedroom slippers, put on your marching shoes. Shake it off. Stop complaining, stop grumbling, stop crying."[63]

Obama and the Environment

After the Bush regime that harbored climate-change deniers and allowed industry lobbyists to write its environmental regulations, the Obama administration came as a relief to many environmentalists. Obama and Energy Secretary Steven Chu even talked boldly about moving the nation to renewable energy and creating millions of "green" jobs. But as with many other of the administration's initiatives, lofty rhetoric covered for a thoroughly status quo–oriented approach. The administration supported "market-based" policies, such as "cap-and-trade" for greenhouse emissions and "clean coal," that most environmentalists considered non-solutions at best, disasters at worst.[64] It considered nuclear power a "clean" technology, and pledged thirty-six billion dollars in loan guarantees for the construction of nuclear power plants—almost twice the amount the George W. Bush administration proposed.[65] The administration caved to a right-wing smear campaign against Van Jones, the administration's appointed "green jobs czar." After Jones resigned in 2009, the administration seemed to stop talking about green jobs.

For environmentalists, it was hard to say which was the Obama administration's greatest betrayal. In 2009, the administration, in its role as representative of American business on the world stage, actively sabotaged the United Nations climate summit in Copenhagen, Denmark. It succeeded in removing from the summit's final communiqué any concrete developed nation commitment to lower emissions in the twenty-first century. Obama endorsed the GOP's "drill, baby, drill" solution to offshore oil drilling—only a few weeks before one of those offshore oil rigs (the Transocean Deepwater Horizon) caused the worst environmental disaster in U.S. history in 2010. And in 2011, as part of its "outreach" to business, the administration shelved Environmental Protection Agency regulations establishing stricter restrictions on ozone in the atmosphere. In this case, the Obama administration did not simply fail to improve on the Bush EPA, which at least had promulgated weak improvements to air pollution regulations. Its action was actually *worse* than the Bush administration's.[66] Even in the face of catastrophe—like the 2010 Deepwater Horizon disaster or the 2011 Fukushima, Japan, nuclear plant meltdowns—the administration remained as committed to offshore drilling and nuclear power as ever. This despite the revelations that twenty-three aging U.S. nuclear facilities were built using similar designs to the reactors at Fukushima—four of them in California near earthquake fault lines.[67] As the radical environmentalist Jeffrey St. Clair drew up the balance in 2011: "On the environment, the transition between Bush and Obama has been disturbingly smooth when it should have been decisively abrupt."[68]

Obama and Immigration

On the campaign trail in 2008, Obama promised the National Council of La Raza: "I will be a president who will stand with you, who will fight for you, who will walk with you every step of the way."[69] Under President Obama, those words seem like a distant memory to immigrant rights activists or to the more than eleven million undocumented workers in the United States. As in virtually every other area involving "homeland security," the Obama administration intensified

Bush-initiated plans. Shaun Harkin and Nicole Colson wrote:

> The Obama White House's multi-pronged approach to immigration enforcement includes expanding the federal 287(g) programs, which allow state and local law enforcement to enforce immigration law; extension and expansion of the E-Verify database system targeting undocumented workers; and implementation of the "Secure Communities Initiative" that lets participating cities and towns access federal immigration and criminal databases to check the status of people detained in local jails.[70]

Under the Department of Homeland Security's "Secure Communities" program, local police agencies forward the fingerprints of all apprehended people to Immigration and Customs Enforcement (ICE). The government then orders the deportation of any undocumented arrestees with criminal records. In 2010, the Obama administration increased these "removals" by 71 percent over Bush's final year in office. Under Obama, the number of local agencies participating in Secure Communities has skyrocketed from fourteen to more than 1,300. In August 2010 Obama signed a six-hundred-million-dollar "border security bill" that includes adding 1,500 more Border Patrol agents, customs inspectors, and other law enforcement officers at the border, as well as more unmanned aerial "drones." By September 2011, the Obama administration had deported more than one million undocumented people, compared to the 1.57 million the Bush administration deported in its full eight-year term.[71]

While mouthing the rhetoric of support for "comprehensive immigration reform," the Democrats' actions spoke louder than their words. Congress and the Obama administration excluded undocumented immigrants from coverage under the health insurance reform bill. The Democrats never seriously attempted to pass a comprehensive immigration reform bill. They held off attempting to pass the DREAM Act, a bill that would grant undocumented youth a path to citizenship, until December 2010, during the lame duck session before the Republicans took over the House of Representatives. Even then, the Democrats couldn't muster the votes to break a GOP filibuster to pass the act. In an attempt to quell outrage among Latinos and other supporters of immigrants' rights, the Obama administration announced a shift in its deportation policies in August 2011. It would prioritize deportations of "criminals" over deportations of those like DREAM Act campaigners, whose only "crime" was being undocumented. Press reports treated the administration's action as a major concession, but one immigrant rights supporter called it "a cynical and aggressive strategy that bolsters ICE and delegitimizes anyone who continues to oppose the president's deportation policies."[72]

Obama and the Democratic "Base"

The White House's courting of corporate and "bipartisan" support eroded its standing with its base of support and provided openings to the political right. Findings from an AFL-CIO poll of voters in the 2010 Massachusetts special U.S. Senate election found that union members divided their votes equally between Republican Scott Brown and Democratic candidate Martha Coakley—in a state where the Democratic candidate normally wins two-thirds or more of union votes. Pollsters found evidence that union workers were concerned about the so-called "Cadillac benefits" tax of generous health plans included in Obamacare. AFL-CIO spokesperson Karen Ackerman went so far as to call the union vote for Brown a "working-class revolt." She continued: "What happened in Massachusetts is that working families did not see the Democratic candidate as being on their side."[73]

One element that could have changed this dynamic was a popular movement to pressure the government to act to face the crisis of unemployment, health care, and cuts in public services—or to fight for rights for the oppressed. But until the labor uprising in Wisconsin and the eruption of the "Occupy" movement in 2011, that sort of pressure from below was lacking. There were two fundamental reasons for this. First, a time of economic insecurity and high unemployment does not, in the first instance, produce confident, mass social movements. The number of strikes of more than a thousand workers fell to its lowest level since the 1947.[74] While this no doubt reflected the level of disintegration in organized labor, it also underscored a lack of confidence or willingness to fight among union members.

Second, organizations that claim to have mass constituencies dedicated to progressive causes remain largely captive to the Democratic Party. It's difficult even to consider many of these organizations as anything other than appendages to the Democratic Party, as their political activity revolves largely around fundraising and GOTV ("get out the vote") operations for Democratic politicians. With a few notable exceptions,[75] they did not agitate to put pressure on the Democrats.

The Obama White House even institutionalized subservience to its agenda with the weekly "Common Purpose" meetings with liberal interest groups that "exist to form a solid left flank and keep the White House immune from liberal criticism."[76] The liberal blogger Jane Hamsher has accurately characterized these meetings as the "veal pen" for progressives.

For much of Obama's term, the leading liberal organizations—like the AFL-CIO, the NAACP, and the Human Rights Campaign—played "good soldiers" in trying to carry out the White House's agenda. As a result, there was no sustained national effort to give voice to the millions facing economic devastation. *Nation* editor Katrina vanden Heuvel accurately summed up the liberals' plight in late 2011:

> The biggest liberal groups in the country lined up to help pass his agenda. They stayed loyal even as [Obama's] aides cut deals they found deplorable (sustaining the ban on Medicare negotiating bulk discounts on prescription drugs; abandoning the public option; buying off big oil, King Coal and virtually every energy lobby; opposing restructuring of the big banks). He faced unified Republican obstruction, not liberal opposition. Powerful corporate lobbies were able to purchase sufficient conservative Democrats—Blue Dogs, New Dems—to dilute, delay and sometimes defeat reform. Progressives in Congress criticized the limitations, but produced votes when it was time to get something passed.[77]

It was bad enough that the Tea Party right seemed to capture the "populist" tenor of the times, but popular organizations that should have been mobilizing to push the administration were instead pressed into service as the last line of defense for a corporate party that disdains them.[78]

To organized labor, one of the biggest failures of Obama's first term was the abandonment of the Employee Free Choice Act (EFCA), a measure that would made organizing unions easier. EFCA allows workers who want to join unions to simply sign up for them (a procedure known as "card check"). But the story of EFCA's defeat was not just one of White House indifference. It also illustrated all of the pitfalls Democratic constituencies face when they put their trust in politicians they help to elect. Despite the key role that labor union mobilization for Obama played in his election,

> once [Obama] was elected, labor leaders made a fateful decision. Originally, they had planned to keep in place their extensive network of field organizers, who had just worked to elect Democratic candidates, and ask them to build pressure on lawmakers to vote for card check.

Instead, they changed course. The labor groups scaled back, partly to give Obama time to get his bearings amid the deepening economic crisis. Business groups, meanwhile, had started work well before the election and did not stop.[79]

The result of this decision was the defeat of EFCA without its even coming to a vote in Congress.

During the 2010 midterm election, the Democrats decried the millions in secret corporate money that flooded into the elections industry following the Supreme Court's 2010 *Citizens United* decision. But they didn't point out that *Citizens United* also freed union treasuries to spend unlimited sums on the Democrats. As a result of this loophole, the *Wall Street Journal* was delighted to report that a last minute contribution to the Democrats from the American Federation of State, County and Municipal Employees (AFSCME) actually made AFSCME—not the Chamber of Commerce—the largest contributor in the 2010 election cycle. "We're the big dog," AFSCME's Larry Scanlon told the *Journal.* "But we don't like to brag." But this big dog ended up with its tail between its legs. After threatening for months to punish Democrats who opposed labor priorities like the Employee Free Choice Act and the "public option" for health care reform, AFSCME backed conservative Democratic incumbents like Ohio's Zack Space.

"We know he has been bad on the issues, but the point is, if you don't elect the Zack Spaces of the world, then you end up with Speaker Boehner," said Scanlon.[80] Unfortunately for working people, the sums of money that unions threw away on corporate America's second favorite party took away from other more important tasks, like organizing or mobilizing for jobs. Zack Space lost by fourteen percentage points, and the country ended up with Speaker Boehner.

FDR or Hoover?

Throughout most of the period of unified Democratic control of the government, Obama baffled and demoralized his main supporters, including the millions who were moved to political action during his campaign, by the fact that most of his problems appeared to be self-inflicted. Clinton's "triangulation" appeared to be a defensive adaptation to an unfavorable environment. Clinton never won the votes of more than 50 percent of the electorate, and for most of his term he coexisted with a hostile Republican Congress that even tried to throw him out of office. But armed with a strong public mandate and a large Democratic majority, Obama continued on the "centrist" path that Clinton charted. The question is why. The explanation has everything to do with the profile of the Democratic Party in the neoliberal era. While the Democrats have always been a big-business party, they are more openly so today than in heyday of the "labor-liberal-civil rights" era of the 1940s to 1960s. Commenting on the seeming inability of the Democratic congressional majority to push through fundamental reforms, Harvard University social policy expert Theda Skocpol explained: "Even in the majority, Democrats still have many ties to business interests and quietly look for excuses to avoid doing things that offend them. Not being able to act without sixty votes is a ready excuse."[81]

What about Obama? Obama failed to "lead" in the direction of a liberal future because he is committed to what writer Kevin Baker, in a very astute *Harper's* article, called "business liberalism," President Clinton's formula. In the article, Baker compared Obama not to FDR but to the man FDR routed in 1932, Republican president Herbert Hoover. The New Democrats' "business liberalism" is

> a chimera, every bit as much a capitulation to powerful and selfish interests as was Hoover's 1920s progressivism. . . . [It] espous[es] a "pragmatism" that is not really pragmatism at all, just surrender to the usual corporate interests.
> The common thread running through all of Obama's major proposals right now is that they are labyrinthine solutions designed mainly to avoid conflict. The bank bailout, cap-and-trade on carbon emissions, health-care pools—all of these ideas are, like Hillary Clinton's ill-fated 1993 health plan, simultaneously too complicated to draw a constituency and too threatening for Congress to shape and pass as Obama would like. They bear the seeds of their own defeat.

Moreover, much like Hoover, "Barack Obama is a man attempting to realize a stirring new vision of his society without cutting himself free from the dogmas of the past—without accepting the inevitable conflict. Like Hoover, he is bound to fail." Obama's penchant to reach for compromise and "bipartisanship" was exactly the opposite of what the dire situation he inherited required—and what the American populace was ready for. Obama's first term, Baker wrote, offered "one of those rare moments in history when the radical becomes pragmatic, when deliberation and compromise foster disaster."[82] In the wake of the 2011 debt-ceiling debacle, how can one conclude otherwise?

Assuming power as the economic crisis hit with full ferocity, the Democrats were destined to face a difficult situation. Since Democrats "owned" Washington, they were certain to be first in line to receive blame from voters looking for help from rising unemployment, poverty, and foreclosures. The voters perceived that "the government" wasn't doing enough, and "the government" was run by Democrats. So they paid the political price. But if the Democrats were perceived as trying to help ordinary people while the Republicans stonewalled any relief, wouldn't the public at least give the Democrats credit for trying? If they launched a bold jobs program or proposed a genuine national health program, they would have at least provided an answer to critics who charge them with ignoring the public's needs. But this would have presupposed a Democratic Party that was willing to use its governmental power to reorder the status quo of the last generation, rather than just giving the status quo a new lease on life.

Using the evidence of the Democrats' failure to confront economic power, the radical sociologist Stanley Aronowitz characterized today's Democratic Party as "the party of finance capital":

> That mantle once belonged to the Republicans—the fabled party of the rich and wealthy. But the GOP has sunk into a right-wing party of opposition and no longer pretends to be a party of government. Its cast, begun as far back as the Goldwater takeover in 1964, is anti-internationalist, narrowly ideological and administratively incompetent. Meanwhile, the Democrats live a glaring contradiction: on the one hand, they rely on labor and the new social movements of feminism, ecology and black freedom both for votes and for a large portion of their political cadres. On the other, they need hundreds of millions of dollars to oil the party apparatus and run 535 national election campaigns. Aside from the unions, most of this money comes from corporate sponsors and wealthy individuals. . . . Obama is the perfect manifestation of the contradiction that rips across the Democratic Party bow.[83]

Obama tried to straddle this contradiction with a stance that appealed to "bipartisanship" and a reasonable approach to national problems. While this may soothe elements of the Washington establishment, it's exactly the opposite of what the climate of economic and political polarization demanded. The attempt to hew to a "centrist" course in the midst of a crisis that demanded radical solutions ended up pleasing no one.

In September 2011, a protest of a few hundred people in New York ignited the "Occupy" movement that spread across the country. For the first time since the recession took hold, a mass movement targeting the banks and corporations and placing the issue of income inequality on the national agenda had erupted. In a few short weeks, the class politics of solidarity—of standing with the 99 percent working majority—replaced the plutocratic politics of austerity in national consciousness. As he prepared to run for reelection in 2012, Obama grasped this. Obama and the Democrats sensed that their only hope to survive a tough reelection fight was to activate working people, youth, African Americans, and others whom the Occupy movement had engaged. So it was no surprise when Obama, in his December 2011 speech in Osawatomie, Kansas, spoke of overcoming income inequality as "the defining issue of our time" and gave rhetorical nods to the "people who have been occupying the streets of New York and other cities" and "99 percent values." Obama's shameless attempt to co-opt Occupy's themes covered for a reality in which dozens of Democratic mayors, in a campaign that *Obama's* federal Homeland Security forces coordinated, launched military-style raids to rout Occupy encampments.[84]

So who was the real Barack Obama? The one who wanted to seek bipartisan and "reasonable" cuts in the social safety net during the debt-ceiling fiasco of July–August 2011, or the "fighter for the middle class" who emerged in the fall of that year, as he geared up for reelection? It would be facile to say that Obama is both things. Four years of experience suggest that the real Obama is the Obama of the "grand bargain"—while "fighter for the middle class" is a costume Obama pulls out of his closet when elections roll around.

Rolling Stone's Matt Taibbi confessed that he couldn't bear to listen to Obama's speeches anymore:

> Hearing Obama talk about jobs and shared prosperity . . . reminded me that we are back in campaign mode, and Barack Obama has started doing again what he does best—play the part of a progressive. He's good at it. It sounds like he has a natural affinity for union workers and ordinary people when he makes these speeches. But his policies are crafted by representatives of corporate/financial America, who happen to entirely make up his inner circle.[85]

Obama was reaching for the 2008 playbook—trying to appeal to ordinary Americans' grievances and presenting himself as a vehicle for their aspirations. As the election year of 2012 dawned, it remained to be seen whether President Obama—with a record of disappointment for his most ardent 2008 supporters—could succeed. Nevertheless, it was clear that if the Republicans managed to nominate a candidate who wasn't up to beating Obama in 2012, corporate America would know that it would have little to fear—and probably much to look forward to—in a second Obama term.

Chapter Five

Social Movements and the "Party of the People"

The official version of U.S. history reads as the gradual extension of democratic rights and government benefits to ever-wider layers of the population. But although the Declaration of Independence famously declared that "all men are created equal," the Constitution excluded large sectors of the population from exercising the most basic democratic and civil rights. Indeed, the Constitution codified the system of chattel slavery and counted disfranchised slaves as three-fifths of a person in apportioning representation—providing slaveholding states systematic overrepresentation in the House of Representatives.[1]

As abolitionist leader Frederick Douglass argued, "If there is no struggle, there is no progress."[2] Struggle has been a defining, recurring feature of U.S. history. Slavery itself was finally abolished only by the Civil War, after some 250 years of struggle by slaves and abolitionists. Nearly every important gain—including women's right to vote, workers' right to form unions, abortion rights, affirmative action, and gay rights—has come about not because political leaders offered reforms willingly but as a result of struggle. On the other side, the U.S. ruling class has proven itself historically to be one of the most class-conscious and aggressively combative in the world. The level of violence and militarization of labor relations in the United States in the nineteenth and early twentieth centuries far exceeded that of its Western European counterparts, and yet the U.S. working class has never won anything approaching the social welfare provisions established by European social democracies in the mid-twentieth century.[3]

But repression is only part of the explanation for the failure of U.S. social movements to achieve more or to build a lasting political alternative to the corporate domination of politics. In this regard we must focus not only on the "stick" of repression, but also on the "carrot" of political representation through the two-party system that has served as one of the bulwarks of American political stability. Historically, the two-party system has played the role of shock absorber, trying to head off or co-opt restive segments of the electorate. It aims to manage political change so that change occurs at a pace that big business can accept. For most of the last century the Democratic Party has been the most successful at playing this shock-absorber role.

Writing in 1972, radical scholar G. William Domhoff eloquently outlined the role the Democratic Party plays in accommodating the oppressed and exploited to the mainstream political system:

> Despite the social and economic hardships suffered by hundreds of millions of Americans over the past one hundred years, the power elite have been able to contain demands for a steady job, fair wages, good pensions, and effective health care within very modest limits compared to other highly developed Western countries. One of the most important factors in maintaining those limits has been the Democratic Party. The party dominates the left alternative in this country, and the sophisticated rich want to keep it that way. Democrats are not only attractive to the working man, but vital to the wealthy, too, precisely because they are the branch of the Property Party that to some extent *accommodates* [emphasis in original] labor, blacks, and liberals, but at the same time hinders genuine economic solutions to age-old problems.[4]

The Democrats didn't always play this role. Republicans like Presidents Abraham Lincoln, Theodore Roosevelt, and Wisconsin progressive senator Robert LaFollette stood for liberal reforms in their days. Nevertheless, over most of the last one hundred years— and especially since the New Deal era—the Democrats have been the party to which progressive social movements have looked for support. But this support has come with strings attached—and without the movements' best interests at heart. This history of Democratic co-optation and betrayal begins with what might be a considered a "dress rehearsal" for the twentieth century—the collision between the Democrats and the Populists.

The Democrats and the Populists

Emerging from the Jacksonian and Civil War periods, the Democrats remained very much a party of urban machines and rural county notables. The only mass support the party could claim was from its downscale voters and its patronage workers. Unlike many European social democratic parties that emerged at this time, the Democrats had no genuine mass membership. Party leaders were committed to low tariffs, white supremacy, and the spoils system. At the time when the Democrats were reestablishing themselves as the dominant party in the South, however, a mass popular movement of farmers, Black and white, shook the system to its core.

The local elites that ran the Democratic Party in the South were overwhelmingly representatives of the landlord class that had reestablished its control after the defeat of Reconstruction in 1876. Through the 1880s, small farmers became increasingly indebted and impoverished, sparking a protest movement that "united yeomen and tenants across state and racial lines" and constituted itself into the Farmers' Alliance.[5] The Farmers' Alliance presented a threat to the local landlords as long as it targeted them for responsibility for the farmers' plight. As it did so, it threatened to undermine the local base of the planter class, which depended on at least passive support at the ballot box from white farmers.[6] In the period up to 1891, the Farmers' Alliance acted as a protest organization that organized small farmers to challenge aspects of the existing tenancy system. It also dabbled in local electoral experiments, creating or supporting campaigns and demanding a combination of reforms ranging from the expansion of paper money (greenbackism) to legal equality of labor and capital, independent of the two major parties.

In 1891, activists within the alliance pushed for the formation of an independent People's Party (the Populists) that included representatives of the Knights of Labor and the Colored Farmers' Alliance. Only a year earlier, hundreds of politicians had been elected to state legislatures across the South on pledges to support the Farmers' Alliance's demands of public ownership of railroads and support for a publicly financed "subtreasury" to finance crop loans. However, many of these politicians—almost all of them Democrats—were happy to accept the alliance's support but uninterested in fulfilling the alliance's demands. So by the time the Populists came on the scene, the alliance rank and file was fed up and open to a political alternative. Historian Robert C. McMath Jr., explained the movement's crossroads:

> The real question was whether, once reform through the Democratic Party had failed, the great mass of southern voters could be persuaded by the logic of insurgency: *if* Alliance principles took precedence over partisan loyalty and the Democratic Party rejected those principles, *then* [italics in original] men of integrity must leave the party of their fathers. . . . To bring Alliance voters to such a drastic step and to enfold them in an alternative culture of American politics called for an unprecedented campaign of political education.[7]

McMath neatly sums up a choice that all fighters for social justice have debated when confronted with a two-party duopoly that ignores their demands.

Without a doubt the Populists scored major successes in the early 1890s, electing Populists to state legislatures and to Congress. They appeared to be on the verge of either making the United States a three-party political system or even displacing one of the two major parties. As an electoral phenomenon, the Populists gained support between 1892 and 1896. Populist presidential candidate James Weaver took more than one million votes, winning twenty-two electoral votes and five states.[8] At the same time the Democrats, who had won the presidency and the Congress in 1892 for the first time since the Civil War, were suffering the hammer blows of the most severe economic depression in the second half of the nineteenth century. With the Democrats weakened from the impact of the 1892–93 economic panic, the time seemed ripe for a third-party challenge from the Populists. At its founding convention, held in 1892 in Omaha, Nebraska, a confident People's Party announced a radical program of a progressive income tax, public ownership of railways and utilities, and support for labor organization.

But just when the Populists appeared to be on the verge of remaking national politics, two things happened. First, the Democrats changed their rhetoric to weaken the Populists' appeal. "Anything you can do to soft-soap the Alliance will go down to your interest," said a leading Democratic contender for the Kentucky gubernatorial nomination. The Democratic nominee pledged to "get tough" on the Louisville and Nashville Railroad.[9] Second, with the Democratic Party facing extinction in whole swaths of the country, some Democratic politicians decided that regaining political footing required that they co-opt some of the Populist program. And for this they chose to advocate the most innocuous part of the Populist program, the demand for free coinage of silver. Legions of "silver Democrats" were born.[10]

With the movement's organization in decline and the Democrats seemingly open to Populist issues, the argument inside the party of the "fusionists," those who advocated Populist alliances with the major parties, gained momentum. The argument in favor of fusion wasn't based on the strength of the movement from below demanding that the major parties support Populist positions. Rather, it was based on a decline in the confidence of the movement in its ability to win on its own. The Populist politicians elected in the early 1890s formed the main fusionist constituency:

> At bottom, the third party's internal struggle was a contest between a cooperating group of political office-seekers on the one hand and the Populist movement on the other. The politicians had short-run objectives—winning the next election. In contrast, the agrarian movement, both as shaped by the Alliance organizers who had recruited the party's mass base of partisans and as shaped by the recruits themselves, had long-term goals, fashioned during the years of cooperative struggle and expressed politically in the planks of the Omaha Platform. While the movement itself had a mass following, the only popular support that the office-seekers could muster within the third party itself was centered in those regions of the country that the cooperative crusade had never been able to penetrate successfully.[11]

The weakening of the Populists' farmer-labor base and the transformation of the party into a more conventional electoral machine resulted in a watering-down of the party's radical 1892 Omaha program. Initially intended as the electoral expression of a movement organized around the demands of its class base, the People's Party increasingly gravitated to the lowest common denominator: "free silver," a late nineteenth-century panacea of middle-class reformers. Perhaps not coincidentally, the only major Democrat to withstand his party's smashing defeat in the 1894 midterm elections (when it lost 113 seats in Congress) was Nebraska representative William Jennings Bryan. Bryan forged a winning coalition of Democrats and Populists in Nebraska, and his championing of free silver won him not only Populist support but also that of silver mining interests, which mounted a two-year campaign to take over the Democratic Party for "free silver."

When the Democrats met to choose a candidate to run in the 1896 presidential election, Bryan managed to steal the nomination from the widely unpopular conservative sitting president, the "Gold Democrat" Grover Cleveland. From the outside this appeared to be a triumph of popular opinion over an unpopular president. From the inside it was clear that the silver lobby had helped to engineer Cleveland's overthrow. And while silver interests were reshaping the Democrats to their will, they were also funneling money to the fusionists in the Populist Party, who used it to organize pro-fusion state delegations to the national convention. When the Populists met in convention after the Democrats had nominated the ticket of Bryan and conservative banker James Sewall, the fusionists pulled out all stops—exploiting every advantage of their hold on the party machine and convention operations they could—to win an endorsement for Bryan over the objection of much of the party's rank and file. "Given Bryan's commitment to silver, the income tax, and other reforms, and given the close working relationship he had developed with Populists in Nebraska, the Populists felt compelled to give him their nomination, but tried to maintain their independence by naming a Populist [Tom Watson] for vice president."[12]

In the end, the Populist old-timers who wanted to build an alternative to the two-party duopoly knew the convention sounded the death knell of their party. Illinois liberal reformer and Populist Henry Demarest Lloyd summed up the party's dilemma: "If we fuse [i.e., endorse Bryan], we are sunk. If we don't fuse, all the silver men we have will leave us for the more powerful Democrats."[13] Lloyd was quite prescient. The election of 1896 turned out to be the one that ushered in a generation of Republican rule. The Democrats were consigned to almost forty years of minority party status. And the Populists, who had folded into the Democrats in 1896, never recovered as an independent party. Howard Zinn explained this denouement: "It was a time, as election times have often been in the United States, to consolidate the system after years of protest and rebellion. . . . Where a threatening mass movement developed, the two-party system stood ready to send out one of its columns to surround that movement and drain it of vitality."[14]

The tragedy of Populism's defeat was felt in many ways, most sharply in the South, where it destroyed the most powerful interracial movement in U.S. history up to that point. When white supremacist Democrats swept subsequent elections and pushed through legislation disenfranchising Blacks and poor whites, there was no movement from below to challenge them. Worse, some former Populists, despairing of the possibility of social change in the business-dominated Gilded Age, accommodated to the politics of their former enemies. Most dramatically, Tom Watson, "who had dropped out of politics after the defeat of 1896, reemerged a virulent racist and anti-Semite in 1904."[15] The Southern ruling class's defeat of Populism helped it, through the Democratic Party machines, to cement its hold over the "solid South." And while Democratic control in the South was complete, the party dwindled as a national force. The Democrats wouldn't be revived as a majority party until the Great Depression, when they would harness the power of another social movement—the movement for industrial unions.

Labor Remakes the Democrats, the Democrats Return the Favor

The Great Depression marked the greatest crisis U.S. capitalism had faced since the Civil War. Political and business leaders worried that the country was ripe for upheaval—perhaps even for revolution. "I say to you, gentlemen, advisedly, that if something is not done and starvation is going to continue, the doors to revolt in this country are going to be thrown open," an American Federation of Labor (AFL) official told Congress in 1932.[16] Powerful movements of industrial workers grew up over the next few years, culminating in the formation of the Congress of Industrial Organizations (CIO) in 1935 and a massive strike wave in 1936 and 1937.

Franklin Delano Roosevelt had not taken office in 1933 with the intention of championing workers' rights or of creating a welfare state. For much of his campaign against President Herbert Hoover, he attacked Hoover for "reckless" spending and pledged to balance the budget by cutting federal spending by 25 percent.[17] The 1932 Democratic platform affirmed the call for a balanced budget, a 25 percent cut in federal spending, and a call for the states to follow suit. In words familiar to free-market capitalists, it also called for "the removal of government from all fields of private enterprise except where necessary to develop public works and natural resources in the common interest." What is perhaps more amazing is the fact that the platform said nothing about labor issues and did not even include the word "union."[18] By encouraging business collusion through the National Industrial Recovery Act (NIRA), Roosevelt's first tentative steps toward addressing the crisis in the economy bore a number of similarities to initiatives the discredited Hoover administration had taken. Historians John Braeman, Robert H. Bremner, and David Brody argue that the idea of a sharp break in the attitude to business between the Hoover administration and the Roosevelt administration is "exaggerated" because the "shift was not from laissez-faire to a managed economy, but rather from one attempt at management, that through informal business-government cooperation, to another more formal and coercive attempt."[19]

But circumstances forced Roosevelt's hand. As discussed in chapter 2, the inclusion of Clause 7a in the NIRA had the unintended consequence (at least from the government's point of view) of spurring an explosion of union organizing. "There was a virtual uprising of workers for union membership," the American Federation of Labor executive council reported to the AFL's 1934 convention. "Workers held mass meetings and sent word they wanted to be organized." Unions organized hundreds of locals within weeks. Existing unions tripled, quadrupled, or quintupled in size. New unions seemed be created overnight.[20] Between 1933 and 1937, the number of workers who were union members jumped from 2.7 million to more than seven million. Driving these numbers upward was a quantitative and qualitative leap in the class struggle, as the number of strikes—a large number of them demanding union recognition against employers who refused to follow Clause 7a's recognition of collective bargaining—jumped from 1,856 in 1934 to a peak of 4,740 in 1937, with the number of strikers involved leaping from 1.12 million to 1.86 million in the same period.[21] Many of these strikes, especially the three 1934 general strikes in Toledo, San Francisco, and Minneapolis, took on a near-insurrectionary character.[22] Between 1934 and 1936, eighty-eight workers were killed on the picket line.[23]

Roosevelt responded to the pressure of the rising class struggle by legalizing collective bargaining rights for workers who were using the strike weapon to demand them. But he didn't do so enthusiastically. Liberal Democratic senator Robert Wagner introduced what became the National Labor Relations Act in 1934. The bill aimed to create a permanent labor relations machinery that would make union recognition and labor relations a matter regulated by the government instead of one fought out on the shop floor between workers and bosses. Industry opposition to the bill made FDR withhold his support, causing Wagner's bill to stall in Congress. But the 1934 strike wave "confirmed Senator Wagner in his conviction that the nation needed a new labor policy."[24] Wagner reintroduced the bill, which won overwhelming support in Congress in 1935. David M. Kennedy describes Roosevelt's reaction to the Wagner Act:

> Roosevelt only belatedly threw his support behind it in 1935, and then largely because he saw it as a way to increase workers' consuming power, as well as a means to suppress the repeated labor disturbances that, as the act claimed, were "burdening and obstructing commerce." Small wonder, then, that the administration found itself bamboozled and irritated by the labor eruptions of Roosevelt's first term and that it moved only hesitantly and ineffectively to channel the accelerating momentum of labor militancy.[25]

To be sure, the Roosevelt administration often found itself at odds with the rabidly anti-union corporate class during this tumultuous period. These New Deal haters rallied around the American Liberty League, founded in 1934 to organize capitalists against the New Deal. The League was the brainchild of conservative Democrats, including Al Smith and John W. Davis (the 1928 and 1924 Democratic candidates for president, respectively) and John Jacob Raskob (insurance mogul and former Democratic National Committee member), before it inducted Republican capitalists like the Du Ponts. The Liberty League, "devoted to defeating Roosevelt, trade unions, liberal Democrats in Congress, 'communism' and assorted social welfare causes," backed Republican Alf Landon for president in 1936.[26] In the heat of the 1936 campaign, Liberty League spokesperson Jouett Shouse charged that "the New Deal represents the attempt in America to set up a totalitarian government, one which recognizes no sphere of individual or business life as immune from governmental authority and which submerges the welfare of the individual to that of the government."[27]

But however much animosity corporate leaders expressed against Roosevelt, his pro–working-class legislation served a larger purpose in salvaging the capitalist system during this enormous crisis by ensuring that the system would not be forced to concede more than was absolutely necessary to contain the class struggle. A remade Democratic Party was the vehicle Roosevelt used to absorb the rising labor movement within the confines of the existing political establishment. Socialist Dan La Botz explained FDR's calculations:

> Roosevelt realized that if he was to succeed in reforming and reconstructing American capitalism, he would have to broaden the social base of the Democratic Party. The Democratic Party that had elected him in 1932 had been based on the corrupt political machines of big cities like Chicago and New York, on the white votes of the Solid South, on the American Federation of Labor, and on financiers like Bernard Baruch who reportedly "owned" sixty congressmen whose campaigns he had financed. That base was simply too narrow to deal with the upheavals in the industrial cities of the Great Lakes region and among the farmers of the Midwest.[28]

By supporting the creation of Social Security and of the National Labor Relations Act in 1935, Roosevelt laid the groundwork for capturing the labor movement vote for the Democrats in the 1936 election and beyond. Roosevelt's legacy has meant that many generations later, millions of working Americans still regard the Democrats as the party that speaks to working-class interests. Ever since the Great Depression, organized labor has provided crucial financial and organizational support for Democratic candidates, however little labor receives in return.

Roosevelt's capture of the labor movement wasn't a one-way proposition. He had willing collaborators among labor leaders whose vision for organized labor offered them a "seat at the table" alongside the nation's policymakers. Even before the formation of the CIO, Sidney Hillman of the Amalgamated Clothing Workers was "a labor statesman in waiting, waiting for a movement to represent and a regime to accept that representation," according to his biographer.[29] This observation doesn't take away from the initiative and courage that top CIO leaders like Hillman and John L. Lewis of the United Mine Workers of America (UMWA) exhibited when launching the CIO. But it does make clear what they, or at least what New Deal loyalists like Hillman, ultimately wanted from the industrial union movement. Rather than seeing it as a means by which workers could organize an independent voice to win their demands, they saw it as a means to give labor leverage in the halls of power.

The leadership of the CIO was "connected by a thousand threads to a newly emergent managerial and political elite, an elite which in collaboration with the CIO would foster a permanent change not only in the national political economy but in the internal political chemistry of the Democratic Party and in the prevailing politics of production in basic industry," commented labor historian Stephen Fraser.[30] It wasn't long before these leaders' commitment to remain credible in the halls of power rendered them opponents to rank-and-file initiatives. Roosevelt shrewdly used his power to cement the loyalty of the trade union officialdom to the New Deal and to the Democratic Party. Mine Workers leader Lewis, who later broke with Roosevelt, complained about the difficulty of organizing a labor-based opposition to the administration:

> [FDR] has been carefully selecting my key lieutenants and appointing them to honorary posts in various of his multitudinous, grandiose commissions. He has his lackeys fawning upon and wining and dining many of my people. . . . In a quiet, confidential way he approaches one of my lieutenants, weans his loyalty away, overpowers him with the dazzling glory of the White House, and appoints him to a federal post under such circumstances that his prime loyalty shall be to the President and only a secondary, residual one to the working-class movement from which he came.[31]

Rank-and-file union activists—especially those on the front lines of the class struggle—were far less loyal to the Democrats or even to Roosevelt. By 1933, pressure began to mount among unionists for the creation of labor's own party to end unions' collaboration with both Democrats and Republicans. Calls for a labor party reflected a newly confident working class's desire to fight on its own. But they also reflected a response to the strikebreaking tactics that unionists had faced under even the most liberal, pro–New Deal Democratic Party state and local governments. In 1935 alone, twenty states' militias, the majority of them called up under Democratic governors, were turned against strikers in seventy-three disputes.[32]

There is no question that the creation of a mass labor or social democratic party would have marked a great step forward for the American working class—toward political action independent of the capitalist parties. Several state-level labor federations experimented with support for "farmer-labor" parties in this period. In Washington and Oregon, the Cooperative Commonwealth Federation, modeled on a similar organization in Canada that was the organizing center for what eventually became the New Democratic Party, won state and congressional seats in this period. In Minnesota the Farmer-Labor Party won the governorship and five House seats. In Wisconsin the Progressive Party, with the backing of the Socialist Party, played a significant role in politics in that state.[33] And 21 percent of those questioned in a 1937 Gallup poll agreed that a labor party should be formed.[34] This pro–labor party sentiment threatened Roosevelt's plan to incorporate the labor movement into the New Deal coalition by channeling class struggle into the New Deal labor-relations machinery.

CIO leaders Lewis and Hillman made a priority of garnering CIO support for Roosevelt in the 1936 election. But in order to do so, CIO leaders had to squelch pro–labor party sentiment among CIO members. This meant sabotaging unionists' own initiatives independent of the Democrats. When the newly formed United Auto Workers voted in 1936 to support the creation of a national Farmer-Labor Party, CIO leaders threatened to remove funding for organizing the rest of the auto industry if the UAW didn't rescind the vote and back Roosevelt. The delegates capitulated at this crucial turning point. Sharon Smith notes:

> CIO leaders faced a serious dilemma: having promised to deliver union support for Roosevelt, they now faced the possibility of a mutiny within the ranks of one of the fastest-growing unions in a key industry. That the UAW delegates had already voted, however, did not stop CIO leaders from taking quick action to ensure the union's support for Roosevelt.[35]

In places where strong-arm tactics like these didn't work, CIO leaders used more devious methods to win workers' votes for Roosevelt. In New York, Hillman backed the formation of the "American Labor Party" to provide a more palatable ballot line for socialists in New York labor circles, who voted for this "labor" party—that in fact channeled votes to Roosevelt. In 1936 the CIO created Labor's Non-Partisan League (LNPL), which worked to provide FDR with money and votes for the 1936 election.

Union leaders thus plowed the CIO's resources into Roosevelt's and other New Deal Democrats' reelection campaigns, solidifying the alliance between labor and the Democrats. Though there were subsequent demands for the formation of a labor party, the 1936 election and its immediate aftermath represented a watershed for Roosevelt—squandering the tremendous opportunity for political independence from capitalist politicians that existed for the labor movement.

In forming CIO-PAC (Political Action Committee) in 1943, the CIO ratified its refusal to form a labor party. CIO-PAC functioned as one of many competing interest groups within the Democratic Party in pledging money to Democratic candidates. One historian explained the political rationale behind CIO-PAC: "In launching the new Political Action Committee, the CIO leadership specifically rejected any 'ultra-liberal party in the name of the working man.' Instead, they sought to discipline the unruly left wing by channeling its energy into a firmly controlled political action group that could function safely within the two-party system."[36]

The CIO's hybrid nature as both a trade union organizing center and a recruiting sergeant for the New Deal Democratic coalition limited its historic potential. Socialist historian Art Preis summed up the CIO's legacy this way:

> The history of the CIO was to constantly appear as an admixture of two elements. On the one hand, mass organization of the industrial workers was to lead to titanic strike battles, most often initiated by the militant ranks despite the leadership. On the other, the workers were to be cheated of many gains they might have won because of the intervention of the government, which had the backing of the CIO leadership themselves. Unwilling to "embarrass" the Democratic administration . . . the CIO leaders kept one arm of the CIO—its political arm—tied behind its back.[37]

Thus the Depression-era labor movement failed to achieve some important goals. First, the U.S. labor movement, unlike those in other industrial countries, did not develop its own political party, however radical its members were on the industrial front. Second, it failed to organize large sections of the working class in the South and the West, which remained conservative, anti-union strongholds. Both of these shortcomings had damaging, long-term impacts on the labor movement. And both of them are directly attributable to CIO leaders' failure to break with the Democratic Party at this critical juncture in U.S. history.

The United States' entry into the Second World War should have shattered any illusions that unions had friends in the Democratic Party. Twice in 1941—before the United States officially entered the war—the government, including the military, intervened to break major strikes at the Allis-Chalmers agricultural implements factory in West Allis, Wisconsin, and at the North American Aviation plant in Inglewood, California. In the second of these, Roosevelt ordered federal troops to take over the plant.[38] When the United States entered the war, union leaders agreed to the wartime "no strike" pledge in exchange for the dues check-off system. Thus, union treasuries swelled while workers' living standards eroded. As Smith notes, "Rapid union dues growth—without the expense of depleted strike funds—allowed the CIO to buy an enormous office building in Washington, D.C., in 1942 . . . and to hire a staff to fill it."[39] Despite the CIO's loyalty to the Democrats, the Democrats showed little concern for the rights of labor. In 1943, the Democratic Congress passed the Smith-Connally Act, empowering the president to break strikes in war industries. Of the 219 Democrats who voted for the act, 191 had received CIO-PAC support.[40]

Business Unionism Triumphant: The Truman Years

The United States emerged from the Second World War as the preeminent world power. Large sections of American business broke with the Republicans' traditional high-tariff policies to support successive Democratic governments' "free trade" policies. "Free trade" and the restructuring of the world banking system under U.S. tutelage became the pillars of the Democrats' "interventionist" foreign policy in what became the longest expansion in capitalism's history.[41] Meanwhile, wartime inflation had driven workers' living standards back to pre-war levels. Demonstrations of unemployed workers, many of them newly returned soldiers, mounted around the country in 1945 and 1946. After the war, U.S. workers erupted in a massive strike wave, exceeding even 1937's level. More than five million workers went on strike in the year after Japan's surrender in August 1945. To Art Preis, the number of workers involved and their weight in U.S. industry meant that "the 1945–46 strike wave in the U.S. surpassed anything of its kind in any capitalist country, including the British General Strike of 1926."[42]

The postwar explosion in working-class militancy stretched the close relationship between union leaders and the Democratic Party. Harry Truman, inaugurated as president upon Roosevelt's death in April 1945, reacted to the strike wave by taking the employers' side, using wartime powers to break strikes. When a nationwide railroad strike shut down passenger and freight traffic for more than a month, Truman announced he would seize the railroads and draft strikers into the army. In May 1946, as Truman was on Capitol Hill requesting authority from Congress for the authority to break the strike, word came that the railroad union leaders had accepted Truman's terms to end the strike. Truman announced the union's capitulation to thunderous applause in the Democratic-controlled Congress.[43] To the employers' dismay, pressure for an independent labor party swelled once again. Railway union leader A. F. Whitney pledged his entire union treasury to defeat Truman in 1948. Other unions passed resolutions pledging support for third-party efforts or political action independent of the Democrats.[44] International Ladies' Garment Workers' Union leader David Dubinsky called for the formation of a labor party because unions "cannot satisfy themselves with a party that includes the Southern reactionaries or the industrialists in the Republican Party."[45] The potential of a labor party or a third political party with significant labor backing threatened not only Truman but also the union leaders who had worked so hard to solidify their role in the Democratic Party.

Following the 1946 elections—in which Republicans took over Congress largely due to workers' discontent with the Democrats—Truman cut a deal with union leaders that enabled him to pull workers behind the Democratic Party once again. In return for labor's support for his reelection, Truman pledged to veto the Taft-Hartley anti-union bill after it passed in 1947. The bill, sponsored by Republican senator Robert Taft and Republican representative Fred A. Hartley, codified a collection of anti-union measures that had been proposed in Congress for years: outlawing sympathy strikes or "secondary boycotts" of one union in solidarity with another; allowing states to outlaw the "closed shop," the requirement that all members of a workforce in a company with a union contract be members of the union; requiring all unions and union leaders seeking redress from the National Labor Relations Board to swear that they were not members of the Communist Party or supporters of any organization seeking the overthrow of the U.S. government "by force of arms," and giving the president the right to force a sixty-day "cooling off period" in any strike deemed threatening to the national interest.[46] Truman vetoed the bill, knowing that Congress—with Democrats casting the key votes—would override his veto.

"[CIO and Steelworkers president Philip] Murray, [AFL leader William] Green, [UAW president Walter] Reuther, Whitney, and other labor leaders promptly hailed Truman, forgetting his virulent anti-labor record. Truman's veto action was to prove a vital factor in rallying labor support for his reelection in 1948, although he was to use the Taft-Hartley Act against labor more zealously than a Republican might have dared."[47] Nevertheless, the trade union leadership poured millions through the CIO-PAC and the AFL's League for Political Education into Truman's 1948 campaign.

The old New Deal coalition, and a few trade-union dissidents—most of them connected with the Communist Party—rallied to the third-party challenge of former vice president Henry Wallace. Wallace's Progressive Party challenged the anticommunist focus of Truman's foreign policy and its retreat across the board from domestic reform. Initial enthusiasm for Wallace—the presumed inheritor of labor's 1946 discontent with Truman—was snuffed out after CIO and AFL leaders determined that Truman would be a "lesser evil" than the election of a Republican president in 1948. UAW president Walter Reuther, a one-time admirer of Wallace who had toyed with the idea of backing a labor-supported third party, did a quick about-face as soon as Wallace's 1948 candidacy became a reality. "As soon as Wallace announced his candidacy, the Reutherites rushed back into the Democratic fold, turning on the Progressive Party with a furious barrage of red baiting."[48]

In explaining his come-from-behind victory in the 1948 election, Truman is supposed to have said, "Labor did it."[49] Organized labor certainly expended a tremendous amount of resources for Truman, highlighted by a Labor Day rally for the president in Detroit that drew an estimated one million workers. And Truman had campaigned for a "Fair Deal," a much more liberal program than he had previously endorsed, and for the immediate repeal of Taft-Hartley. The "Fair Deal" was deliberately calculated to steal thunder from Wallace and to get labor on board Truman's campaign. Truman aide Clark Clifford, the architect of Truman's 1948 campaign strategy, later said:

> Labor at the time, inclined toward the Democratic Party and President Truman, but you will recall we had had some very fierce battles with labor . . . although labor would be inclined to vote for the Democratic Party, and I did not think under any circumstances they could be for the Republican nominee, yet that was not good enough. What we needed was an active, militant support of labor if we were going to have any chance to win.[50]

The Truman victory was heralded as a massive step forward for labor at both the AFL and CIO conventions. But Truman's promise to repeal Taft-Hartley was soon forgotten, as was the union leaders' promised fightback. "Labor's friend" Truman invoked the Taft-Hartley Act to break strikes twelve times in the first year of his second term.[51] As part of the campaign to line up organized labor behind Truman's Cold War foreign policy, a variety of union leaders and Truman worked closely to weed out socialists, communists, and other dissidents from the unions between 1947 and 1950. In fact, Truman's 1947 Executive Order 9835, requiring loyalty oaths for federal employees, opened the floodgates for a wave of political repression that later became synonymous with one of its most zealous promoters, Republican Wisconsin senator Joseph McCarthy.[52] The CIO followed suit. Complying with the Taft-Hartley anticommunist regulations allowed union leaders to use trumped-up charges and union-sponsored "raids" on the memberships of whole unions to drive out radicals who had helped build the unions in the 1930s.[53] Elimination of these "troublemakers" allowed liberal, anticommunist union leaders to consolidate their hold on the unions, relegating the unions themselves to second-class status in the corporate-dominated Democratic coalition. Ellen Schrecker, a historian of McCarthyism, concluded that organized labor was "the most important institutional victim of the Cold War red scare," because many labor leaders tied to Democrats "collaborated with the witch-hunt. . . . McCarthyism weakened the entire labor movement, damaging Communists and anticommunists alike."[54] In 1952, during the Korean War, Truman went so far as to nationalize the steel mills in an unsuccessful attempt to break the steelworkers' union.[55] Yet at no point was the CIO's loyalty to Truman ever questioned.

The Defeat of Operation Dixie

From its origins as the party of slavery, the Democratic Party had been a Southern- and rural-based party. The New Deal had challenged this. In providing the vehicle by which the national party remade itself, the New Deal also made the Democrats a more urban, Northern-based party with a large working-class voting base. The small-town bankers, merchants, farmers, and business owners who formed the backbone of the post-Reconstruction, Southern-based Democratic Party found this "situation was different—and more difficult to deal with, more threatening, more subversive. In the past, threats to their power had come from the Republicans and from the Populists. They had been able to draw themselves securely into their party, the party of the South, the party of white supremacy, the Democratic party—and to fight off the attacks. Now, however, the threat came from within that very party."[56] Even though the Southern segregationist Democrats perceived this threat, they continued to hold a strong influence over the national party. Southern Democratic parties, which enforced disenfranchisement of Black voters inside their states, were until 1948 the most reliably Democratic states in presidential elections. Yet their leaders maintained their positions by nurturing a low-wage, "union-free" economy that led their congressional representatives into an alliance with conservative Republicans. As a result, the Southern reactionaries remained a permanent hamper to any attempt to enact reforms at a national level. As labor historian Nelson Lichtenstein explained, "because of the vital role the South still played in national Democratic Party politics, even those liberals elected from solidly pro-labor constituencies were drawn into compromise and coalition with the right."[57] If anything would break this right-wing logjam, breaching the South's anti-union bastions would do it.

Unfortunately, one disastrous outcome of the CIO's longstanding commitment to the Democratic Party was the defeat of "Operation Dixie," launched in 1946 as a major effort to organize the Deep South. The CIO allotted a million-dollar budget and hired four hundred organizers with high expectations for Operation Dixie. But two years later union leaders cancelled the entire effort, bowing to hostility from segregationist Dixiecrats who joined forces with anti-union employers to crush the union drive. The Dixiecrats received a boost when the national Democratic Party under Truman stepped up repression of "communists" in conjunction with the Cold War against the Soviet Union. As Michael K. Honey explained,

> [the CIO's] allies in the Democratic Party began moving to the right, as demagogic anticommunists began to take control of Congress and the media. In the South, the accelerating anticommunist rhetoric had the effect of cloaking segregationist and anti-union appeals with a new degree of patriotic respectability. Backed by the accusations of HUAC [the House Un-American Activities Committee, the main investigative body in Congress], and the news media, segregationists could argue more convincingly than ever before that groups organizing for labor and civil rights were subversive and that persecuting them furthered American interests in the Cold War with the Soviet Union. Anticommunism and Cold War patriotism in effect gave segregation a new lease on life.[58]

The CIO leadership was forced to choose between organizing the South and maintaining the labor-Democratic alliance. As Art Preis explained their dilemma, "It was impossible to support the Democratic Party and not reinforce its Southern wing, the chief prop of the Jim Crow system and the one-party dictatorship in the South. The CIO leaders refused to wage political war against the Southern ruling class because that would undermine the whole Democratic Party and put an end to the Democratic Party–labor coalition."[59]

The labor movement never returned to the project of organizing the Deep South, which remains a nonunion stronghold in the twenty-first century. Companies in the North have used the availability of this large nonunion Southern workforce to their advantage ever since—by threatening to move to the Sunbelt if workers did not accept pay cuts and other concessions. A weakened labor movement is the living legacy of Operation Dixie's failure.

The events of the immediate postwar era—the short-circuiting of the militant postwar struggles, the purging of radicals from the labor movement, and union leaders' unconditional loyalty to the Democratic Party—are the roots of the crisis in the labor movement today. As union leaders came to rely more on winning acceptance in the Democratic Party for their roles as "labor statesmen," shop-floor organization and organizing drives suffered.

In each election victory following 1948, the AFL and CIO (and after their 1955 merger, the AFL-CIO) could claim credit for providing the key organizational, financial, and electoral support for the Democrats. In 1952, when CIO-PAC evaluated its own progress, it concluded that none of the pro-labor policies it had pressed had been won. Rather than concluding that tying CIO-PAC to the Democratic Party was a dead end and breaking the affiliation, CIO leaders decided to continue CIO-PAC's ineffectual role in the Democratic Party.[60]

As a result, the alliance between organized labor and the Democratic Party solidified throughout the next twenty years while the coalition of Southern Democrats and Republicans passed restriction after restriction on labor unions. In addition to the Taft-Hartley Act described earlier, the Communist Control Act (1954) allowed the government to remove elected union leaderships by fiat and to deny collective bargaining rights to "communist" unions. The Landrum-Griffin Act (1959) allowed union leaders to use "trusteeships" against militants and allowed the government to take over unions. It is no overstatement to say that the United States currently possesses the most tightly controlled union movement outside of countries run under forms of authoritarian rule or dictatorship.[61]

By the 1940s the full shape of the postwar compact among labor, the Democratic Party, and management had established itself. Although it provided labor with sought-after political representation, it limited the potential of the U.S. working class to win more.

Meanwhile, as the Democrats leaned more heavily on labor to get out the vote, labor increasingly identified its agenda with Democratic electoral victories. As one observer noted, "the pattern of union participation [in Democratic elections] underwent a subtle change in which a partisan orientation to the Democratic Party gradually replaced the working-class orientation of the 1930s."[62] Mike Davis's observation on the "barren marriage" between labor and the Democratic Party is apt:

> The New Deal capture of the labor movement broadened the base of the Democratic Party, but it scarcely transformed it into an analogue of European laborism or social democracy. Indeed, what has been more striking than the discrepancy between labor's role in electoral mobilization and finance, and the meager legislative rewards it has received in return? The survival of Taft-Hartley and the stunting of the welfare state in America are among the most eloquent monuments to labor's failure to "functionalize" its most day-to-day interests through the Democratic Party.[63]

The Democrats and the Civil Rights Revolution

African Americans today are one of the Democratic Party's most solid blocs of supporters. The explanation for this is simple. In the 1960s and early 1970s, the Democrats succeeded in absorbing key sections of the civil rights and Black Power movements in a way similar to that in which they captured the labor movement. Initially this met with resistance from the party's traditional base, the Southern racist Dixiecrats. But by the 1970s, the party establishment recognized that losing the Dixiecrats was a small price to pay to incorporate a layer of Black politicians and Black voters into the party machine.

Several factors explained the weakening of the Dixiecrats' hold on the Democratic Party. Blacks' migrations from the rural South to Northern cities during the First and Second World Wars boosted the impact of Black votes on Northern urban party machines. In addition, the impact of voting rights legislation made Southern Black voters a constituency to be cultivated. Most importantly, Democratic Party electoralism acted as the chief method by which the system pulled thousands of Blacks radicalized in the 1968–74 period back into its fold.

Until 1936 Blacks had been a solidly Republican voting constituency. Only the New Deal pulled large numbers of Black voters into the Democratic Party, despite its segregationist wing. Black support for the Democrats, however, was no guarantee of Democratic support for Black demands. In one of many examples, civil rights leader A. Philip Randolph had to threaten a mass march on Washington in 1941 to win President Roosevelt's executive order barring discrimination in the war industries.

Kennedy and King

When the mass civil rights movement erupted in the late 1950s, a new day seemed to be at hand. In the 1960 presidential campaign, the Southern Christian Leadership Conference (SCLC), led by Reverend Martin Luther King Jr., refused to endorse either Democrat John F. Kennedy or Republican Richard Nixon, planning instead to demonstrate for civil rights legislation at both party conventions. However, Kennedy's telephone call to King as King sat in a Georgia jail cell earned Kennedy a liberal, pro–civil rights reputation and the tacit endorsement of civil rights movement leaders.

But for most of its time in office, the Kennedy administration did little to justify the civil rights movement's expectations of it. At a secret meeting between King's and attorney general Robert Kennedy's staffs, held only a few months after the Kennedy administration arrived in Washington, Robert Kennedy and his staff claimed they were limited in what they could do about Jim Crow. But, they said, the Justice Department had much more ability to intervene in the states to protect voting rights.[64] The message was clear: the Kennedy administration preferred that civil rights groups pursue voting rights through a legal strategy, rather than take direct action against segregation. During the 1961 "Freedom Rides," in which civil rights workers rode buses through the South to force integration, Robert Kennedy denounced the Freedom Riders for providing "good propaganda for America's enemies" in the Cold War.[65] But on further reflection, Kennedy's Justice Department decided that it was better to approach the new civil rights militants with a carrot of federal aid than with the stick of public criticism. The

Kennedy administration established, with foundation money, the Voter Education Project (VEP). Attorney General Kennedy explained the VEP's main purpose to Congress on Racial Equality (CORE) leader James Farmer in stark, crude terms: "If you cut out this freedom rider and sitting-in stuff and concentrate on voter registration, I'll get you a tax exemption."[66] At the same time, Kennedy's Justice Department was unwilling to pledge full protection from racist attacks to the freedom riders and the FBI was conducting a slander campaign against King.

The Kennedy administration hoped the VEP would divert attention from the undeniable fact that it had done nothing for civil rights in office. Having promised during his presidential campaign to eliminate housing discrimination by executive order "with the stroke of a pen," President Kennedy shelved the plan. For him it was more important to pander to the Southern Dixiecrats, whose leadership of key congressional committees would determine the fate of his legislative agenda. The Kennedy administration preferred to handle civil rights matters from an office in the Justice Department. But the movement kept forcing itself and civil rights back onto JFK's agenda. The most serious crisis that forced the administration's hand was the Birmingham, Alabama, events of May–June 1963. A mass civil disobedience campaign to desegregate downtown businesses had been met with attacks from the likes of Police Commissioner Bull Conner, with the support of Alabama's Dixiecrat governor George Wallace. Conner's use of dogs and fire hoses on children provoked the Black community of Birmingham to riot. At the White House, President Kennedy feared the situation would scuttle an agreement among conservative civil rights leaders, the Justice Department, and Birmingham elites to allow phased desegregation. Kennedy's Justice Department aide Burke Marshall warned the president, "If that agreement blows up, the Negroes will be, uh…." "Uncontrollable," Kennedy said. Marshall added, "And I think not only in Birmingham."[67] Fearing this threat to "law and order" nationwide, Kennedy announced federal troop movements to enforce the agreement. A few weeks later, he took to the federal airwaves to announce his support for the Civil Rights Act in Congress.

When leaders of the main civil rights groups, including King's SCLC and the more conservative NAACP and Urban League, called for a march on Washington to take place in August 1963, Kennedy responded by attempting as much as possible to shape the march's content. Having endorsed the Civil Rights Act in June 1963, Kennedy and the administration worked side by side with movement organizers to ensure that speakers would not criticize the administration's previous foot-dragging. The day before the march on Washington, the Kennedy administration's Burke Marshall and moderate civil rights leaders, including Bayard Rustin, forced Student Non-Violent Coordinating Committee (SNCC) leader John Lewis to change his prepared speech. Lewis, arriving in Washington from the South, where he had faced dozens of arrests and beatings at racist Dixiecrats' hands, planned to condemn the administration's initiative as "too little, too late," and to exhort marchers to "burn Jim Crow to the ground."[68] Lewis bowed to the pressure, but even his watered-down speech included these questions: "Where is our party? Where is the party that will make it unnecessary for us to march on Washington? Where is the political party that will make it unnecessary to march in the streets of Birmingham?[69] The Kennedy administration's shift—from treating civil rights issues as an annoyance to using them as another means to co-opt interest groups into the Democratic Party— served to echo Lewis's point.

LBJ and the Mississippi Freedom Democratic Party

As the powerful civil rights movement was cracking segregation in the South, the Democrats belatedly attempted to put themselves at the head of the movement. President Lyndon B. Johnson used the phrase "we shall overcome" in a speech endorsing the 1964 Civil Rights Act, as if he had been a long-time advocate. In reality, the Civil Rights Act of 1964 and the Voting Rights Act of 1965, important reforms though they were, simply ratified in law what Blacks had already won in struggle. In endorsing the two bills, LBJ was willing to countenance some disaffection among Southern segregationists. But he was unwilling to alienate the racists from his party completely. The 1964 example of the Mississippi Freedom Democratic Party (MFDP) provides the best illustration of LBJ's duplicity.

The 1960s Southern struggle for Blacks' right to vote—a fundamental democratic right that segregationist legislatures and racist violence had denied for more than six decades—required much more than simply pulling a lever for a candidate. In many areas of the rural South, it required setting up political institutions outside the control of the Jim Crow Democratic Party that ran the Southern governments. In Mississippi, civil rights workers created their own nonsegregated political party, the Mississippi Freedom Democratic Party. Within weeks of its founding, the MFDP signed up sixty thousand voters and nominated a delegation to represent it at the 1964 Democratic Party convention in Atlantic City, New Jersey. The MFDP planned a floor fight in order to be seated in place of the all-white Jim Crow Mississippi Democratic delegation on the grounds that MFDP was the only freely elected delegation in which all of the state's citizens could vote.

But LBJ wished to avoid a floor battle that might damage the televised image of party "unity" he wanted to project. More importantly, however, LBJ feared the defection of the "white South" to his opponent, Republican senator Barry Goldwater, who, in a bid to attract Southern support, opposed the Civil Rights Act. As Democratic Texas governor John Connally put it to Johnson, "If you seat those Black buggers, the whole South will walk out."[70] Not wanting to appear to be working on behalf of the Connallys of the party, Johnson turned to Democratic liberals and supposed friends of civil rights to do his dirty work. Minnesota senator Hubert Humphrey, who gave his support in exchange for a vice-presidential spot on Johnson's ticket, cajoled the MFDP with pledges to support its general agenda while warning them against the disaster of a Goldwater presidency. UAW president Walter Reuther threatened to fire MFDP lawyer Joseph Rauh—who was also the UAW's lawyer—if Rauh didn't get the MFDP to back down. Reuther, whose union provided hundreds of thousands of dollars to what was then known as the "labor-liberal-civil rights" coalition, also threatened Martin Luther King Jr.: "Your funding is on the line. . . . The kind of money you got from us in Birmingham is there again for Mississippi, but you've got to help us and we've got to help Johnson."[71] King ended up supporting the "compromise" that Humphrey's protégé, Minnesota attorney general Walter Mondale, foisted on the MFDP. Under this deal, the MFDP would receive only two delegates—to be chosen by the convention's Credentials Committee. With several major civil rights leaders, including King, Rustin, and MFDP founder Aaron Henry throwing their weight behind Humphrey's sellout, the Credentials Committee voted to seat the Jim Crow delegation. The MFDP delegation voted down the compromise overwhelmingly, calling it a "back-of-the-bus" agreement. It staged a protest in the convention hall, seizing the Mississippi delegation's seats until the Democratic leaders called in security guards and police to eject them from the convention center.[72] As it turned out, the Jim Crow delegation returned to Mississippi from the Atlantic City convention and endorsed Goldwater!

So while the Democratic Party machine was trying to accommodate the racists in the party, its liberal wing was trying to figure out how to corral the civil rights movement into the Democratic fold. The party's liberals performed their tried-and-true role: endorsing some reforms to win movement support while simultaneously trying to undermine the movement's independence and radicalism. In November 1964 an internal report of the liberal Americans for Democratic Action (ADA), whose board included Humphrey, Reuther, and Rauh, urged ADA to push for a voting rights act because "quick granting of voting rights will mean quick recruitment by the Democratic Party, which will mean quick scuttling of the Freedom Democratic Parties and SNCC control." The report also endorsed "a quick freeze of funds on these projects which have a Freedom Democratic Party orientation."[73] It would be tough to find a better example than the MFDP episode at the 1964 convention to illustrate the treacherous role that Democratic Party liberals—who continue to claim the Civil Rights and Voting Rights Acts among their greatest triumphs—have played in the face of real, living movements on the ground.

Safely reelected with an overwhelming Democratic majority in 1964, LBJ proceeded to enact the Great Society programs that he dubbed the "War on Poverty." These programs provided jobs, educational assistance, and economic advancement opportunities to the urban and rural poor. But they also provided a side benefit for the Democrats in their encounters with the civil rights and Black Power movements: a method to co-opt and at the same time derail these powerful movements. August Meier and Elliott Rudwick called attention to the impact of the Great Society's Community Action Programs (CAP) in blunting the militant edge of the Congress of Racial Equality (CORE), the civil rights organization:

> Participation in the War on Poverty was in several respects dysfunctional for CORE as an organization. Leaders who accepted the well-paying positions with CAP programs found it difficult to maintain active connections with their local affiliates, and since they were generally the most experienced chapter members,

the loss was substantial. . . . People on [CORE's National Action Committee] even began to complain that the anti-poverty program "has been used to buy off militant civil rights leaders." Equally important, CORE's efforts with the CAP projects absorbed CORE projects. . . . On both counts the War on Poverty proved to be a significant contributing factor in the decline of chapter activity.[74]

From Black Power to the New Black Vote

The experience of facing racist violence in the South, along with being disillusioned by sellouts from Democratic politicians, radicalized a generation of Black activists who took up the banner of "Black Power" after 1965. For SNCC activists, Atlantic City had marked a turning point that

> completed SNCC's alienation from the mainstream of the movement and its estrangement from the federal government and the Democratic Party. . . . The treatment of the Freedom Democrats snapped the frayed ties that bound SNCC to liberal values, to integration and nonviolence, and to seeking solutions through the political process. The time had come for SNCC to formulate new goals and methods. To its battered and bloody field troops, the American dilemma had become irreconcilable and the American dream a nightmare. "Things could never be the same again," SNCC's Cleveland Sellers wrote later. "Never again were we lulled into believing that our task was exposing injustices so that the 'good' people of America could eliminate them. After Atlantic City, our struggle was not for civil rights, but for liberation."[75]

Perhaps the revolutionary Malcolm X spoke first for this generation of activists. Malcolm expressed more clearly than other movement leaders the racist nature of the Democratic Party. "When you keep the Democrats in power," Malcolm said in a 1964 speech to the Cleveland CORE chapter, "you're keeping the Dixiecrats in power. . . . A vote for a Democrat is a vote for the Dixiecrats . . . it's time for you and me to become more politically mature and realize what the ballot is for; what we're supposed to get when we cast a ballot; and that if we don't cast a ballot, it's going to end up in a situation where we're going to have to cast a bullet. It's either the ballot or a bullet."[76] Malcolm praised the MFDP activists' courage. Nevertheless, he argued that much more radical action—a "Mau Mau," in his words[77]—was needed.

Thousands of Black radicals realized the need to break from the Democrats in this period, identifying their political outlook with radical groups like the Black Panther Party for Self-Defense (BPP). The BPP, formed by Bobby Seale and Huey Newton in Oakland, California, in

1966, began as a small group of activists who challenged police brutality by dispatching armed patrols to monitor police behavior in Oakland's Black neighborhoods. The party received international attention after it staged an armed demonstration against pending gun control legislation inside the California Assembly in Sacramento. The image of armed Black people standing up for their rights electrified Black America. Within three years, polls showed that 25 percent of the Black population had great respect for the BPP, including 43 percent of Blacks under twenty-one years of age.[78] What was more, the BPP's revolutionary nationalist and socialist ideology—a mélange of Maoism, Third World nationalism, and American radicalism—posed a challenge to the established, moderate civil rights leaders, and to their allies in the Democratic Party.[79] In many inner cities, the Panthers provided essential services like school breakfasts and drug treatment—programs that were victims of chronic underfunding from federal, state, and local authorities.

A different type of challenge from Black radicalism grew up in the heart of another liberal institution tied to the Democratic Party—the United Auto Workers union. The Dodge Revolutionary Union Movement (DRUM), formed in the Hamtramck Assembly Chrysler plant in Detroit in 1968, represented a fusion of radical nationalist and socialist politics with the power of the industrial working class. Launched with a wildcat strike against speedups in the plants, DRUM quickly challenged both management and the union leadership that had denied opportunities to Blacks. DRUM's example spread to other auto plants and to other industries, culminating in the formation of the short-lived Revolutionary Union Movement (1969–72). Socialist Martin Glaberman pointed out the significance of these developments in an article written shortly after DRUM's founding: "Whatever the future course of events what has already happened is of tremendous importance for revolutionary developments in the United States. When talk and action about the white power structure moves from local sheriffs and city administrations to General Motors, Ford and Chrysler, there is not much further to go."[80]

Glaberman's expectations were validated in 1970 when U.S. postal workers, led in many cities by Black workers, mounted an illegal wildcat strike involving 210,000 workers. The postal workers won a 14 percent wage increase, received collective bargaining rights, and forced the reorganization of the postal service—despite the fact that the Nixon administration called up the National Guard to deliver the mail.[81]

These challenges to the bipartisan status quo became even more serious when they were combined with the urban rebellions that "swept across almost every major US city in the Northeast, Middle West and California . . . . Combining the total weight of socio-economic destruction, the ghetto rebellions from 1964 to 1972 led to 250 deaths, 10,000 serious injuries and 60,000 arrests."[82] The urban rebellions swelled the ranks of the Black Panther Party, leading FBI director J. Edgar Hoover to declare it the "greatest threat to the internal security of the United States." And the 1967 uprising in Detroit clearly influenced the founding of DRUM.[83]

The Democratic establishment responded to this challenge in tried-and-true fashion: with the carrot of reform and the stick of repression. Repression led the way in the immediate aftermath of the uprisings. The federal government, under the Democratic Johnson administration, launched the Counter-Intelligence Program (COINTEL-PRO) of disruption and repression against radicals, of which the BPP was a top target. In Democratic-dominated Chicago, "as the [Panthers'] free-meal program expanded throughout the city, feeding hundreds of poor children, mainly through churches, the Chicago police and the FBI grew more intent on quashing them."[84] In December 1969, a joint task force of the Chicago Police and the Cook County (IL) state attorney's office—Democratic through and through—raided the Black Panther headquarters in Chicago and murdered its key leaders, Fred Hampton and Mark Clark.

Liberal union leaders confronted the revolutionary union movement with hostility as well. In the first challenge to the UAW hierarchy, DRUM supported a candidate for election to executive board of the Dodge Main local in 1968. UAW president Reuther responded by rigging the election to make sure the DRUM candidate lost and by appointing the first African American to hold the post of regional director in Detroit.[85] The wildcat strikes DRUM inspired continued to challenge UAW–Big Three relations into the early 1970s, when Black militants in plants forged working relationships with white, Arab, and other workers. The firing of a white radical at the Mack Avenue Chrysler plant led to a wildcat strike in August 1973. The union—represented mainly by

Chrysler division head Douglas Fraser—worked with the local police to have the instigator arrested and removed from the plant. When workers showed up the next day to protest and to continue the wildcat, "they were confronted by [UAW top officers] Doug Fraser, Irving Bluestone, Emil Mazey and other top UAW executives backed up by a force of nearly 2,000 older or retired UAW loyalists. There was some fighting with local militants, but the sheer size of the union force guaranteed that the strike was over." The police thanked Fraser, remarking that it was great to be on the same side with the union.[86]

In both cases, institutions strongly allied with, or under the direct control of, the Democratic Party were not merely determined to stamp out radicalism for its own sake. They were also aiming to eliminate rivals who challenged the Democrats' political hold on their constituency. The Chicago machine's concern about the BPP's influence has already been noted. In the UAW in the late 1960s, writes historian Kevin Boyle:

> Black workers generally had sought a share of power and a measure of opportunity within a political structure dominated by whites, while both black and white workers had believed that the Democratic Party's liberals best defended both their economic positions and their social values. That identification had been shattered for many workers in the mid-1960s. The UAW's appeals therefore seemed somewhat shopworn in late 1968, more a relic of a fading era than a representation of political reality.[87]

By the 1970s powerful forces were working against Black radicalism. First, as the 1970s wore on, the postwar economic boom slowed. It crashed into recession in 1974–75. As the government cut back on social spending, reforms became much harder to win. As the movement saw its opportunities to win concrete gains contract, its goals contracted as well. Thus the goal of transforming society from below gave way to the "realism" of the Democratic Party.

Second, as many of the 1960s movement activists looked back to the Democratic Party, an increasing core of middle-class Black politicians arose to offer activists "concrete" and "realistic" roads to reform. These politicians, often using militant-sounding rhetoric, associated "Black Power" with their own electoral success. From 1967 to 1973, Black politicians gained increasing prominence with the elections of mayors Carl Stokes (Cleveland), Richard Hatcher (Gary, IN), Kenneth Gibson (Newark, NJ), Maynard Jackson (Atlanta), Coleman

Young (Detroit), and Tom Bradley (Los Angeles). Many activists joined these campaigns.

The 1967 urban rebellions and the prospects of more militant activity prodded the Democratic Party machines, particularly in Northern urban centers, to make concessions to Black sentiment. Radical commentator Robert L. Allen explained in 1969 that "from the liberal point of view, some concessions must be made if future disruptions such as the 1967 riot are to be avoided." The election of Black politicians would not change the conditions of Black people's lives in their jurisdictions, yet "Black people were supposed to get the impression that progress was being made, that they were finally being let in the front door. . . . The intention is to create an impression of real movement while actual movement is too limited to be significant."[88]

The Democratic strategy of co-optation succeeded. Not only did Black electoralism serve its purpose for the predominantly white ruling class—that of demobilizing the Black movement—but it coincided with the interests of Black middle-class politicians and their Black business backers. Between 1964 and 1986, the number of Black elected U.S. officials grew from 103 to 6,424. But at the same time, conditions for the mass of the Black population—workers and the poor—grew increasingly desperate. In fact by the 1980s, a range of indices suggested that living conditions, job opportunities, and poverty levels for Black America were worse than they were before the civil rights movement.[89] Often, Black electoral victories proved hollow. Assuming the reins of cities and counties facing fiscal crisis, Black Democratic politicians were able to deliver little more than austerity to their Black working-class constituents. And in certain circumstances the new Black mayors and officials found themselves in open conflict with their Black constituents. In 1973 Maynard Jackson, the first Black mayor of Atlanta, found himself winning praise from the business establishment but condemnation from Black supporters for crushing a strike by a predominantly Black union of sanitation workers. Only a few months earlier, the sanitation workers' union had worked hard for Jackson's election.[90] In an even more ghastly demonstration of these elected officials' fealty to the establishment, Philadelphia mayor Wilson Goode, the first African American to hold that post, ordered a 1985 firebombing of an apartment where members of the Black radical group MOVE lived. In addition to incinerating the

MOVE apartment, the incendiary device razed an entire city block, leaving eleven MOVE members—including five children—dead and leaving hundreds homeless.[91]

The Graveyard of Social Movements

Following the model of the civil rights movement, other oppressed groups organized themselves to demand respect and recognition of longstanding social claims. The scope of the radicalization of the 1960s and 1970s and the demands for social reforms that it produced had a widespread impact on American society. Women, gays and lesbians, Chicanos, and Native Americans were a few of the oppressed groups who launched new movements to fight for their rights. At the same time, the experience of the anti–Vietnam War movement encouraged other sorts of citizen activism, in which ordinary people organized to pressure the government to respond to demands to address environmental degradation or corporate abuse of consumers. Developing during a period of widespread social agitation, these new social movements faced many of the same choices that the civil rights and anti–Vietnam War movements faced. These choices were manifested by divisions within these movements between militant grassroots campaigns and those that were more oriented toward lobbying and electoral activity. The latter group inevitably found itself feeling the gravitational pull of the Democratic Party. A brief consideration of the movements for women's liberation and for gay/lesbian/bisexual/transgender (LGBT) liberation will illustrate this.

From Women's Liberation to Power Feminism

In 1950 approximately 33 percent of women worked outside the home. By 1970 the figure was 44 percent, and by 1985 it was nearly 55 percent.[92] Moreover, with the need for managers and skilled professionals rising, the doors to higher education finally opened to women on a large scale—and middle-class women began to flock to universities across the country. Expectations soared, particularly for middle-class women, that university educations would lead to high-status professional careers. But most of these expectations were unfulfilled; female college graduates entered the corporate world only to find new doors slammed in their faces, as they faced sexist attitudes and limited opportunities for women professionals.

In the midst of the social upheaval of the 1960s, the women's movement began to emerge as middle-class women started to look for a way to raise demands for equal opportunity. To this end, the National Organization for Women (NOW) was formed in 1966. By 1974, NOW's membership totaled more than forty thousand nationally. On college campuses, a more radical version of the women's movement took hold, organized initially by activists from the civil rights and antiwar movements. Consciously imitating the Black liberation movement, young female students organized around the demand for women's liberation. The new women's liberation groups began meeting in 1967. By 1969, groups had been established in more than forty cities across the United States.

The women's movement never reached the massive size of the civil rights movement. But at times it organized protests that involved many thousands. On August 26, 1970, the women's movement called the Women's Strike for Equality, bringing out more than fifty thousand women to demonstrate for women's rights across the country. These demonstrations also called for free abortion on demand. Literally hundreds of local protests took place between 1969 and 1973 in favor of legal abortion.

But more important than the actual numbers drawn into the movement itself, the ideas of women's liberation found a much larger audience in the population at large. The effects of the women's movement were far-reaching in changing the consciousness and expectations of millions of women, especially those in the workforce. It brought the issues of equal pay, child care, and abortion rights into the national spotlight. By 1976, a Harris survey reported that 65 percent of American women supported "efforts to strengthen and change women's status in society."[93] The movement reached its high point in 1973 when the U.S. Supreme Court legalized abortion.

Although most of the new women's movement organizations applauded the legalization of abortion, it was particularly a victory for the more militant wings of the movement. The main women's organization of the day (and of today) deliberately rejected radicalism as an approach to winning equality for women. For much of the late 1960s and the 1970s, NOW's main focus was on passage of the Equal Rights Amendment (ERA). The ERA was a straightforward amendment guaranteeing "equal rights under the law" for women. During this period of social upheaval, the ERA seemed quite mild and destined to be ratified as a constitutional amendment.

Despite majority support for the ERA across the country, a concerted conservative effort to stop its ratification in the required thirty-eight states by 1982—the ten-year deadline for its ratification—succeeded in burying it. The ERA's fate was clearly tied up with the strength of the women's liberation movement, which peaked around the time the ratification for ERA began. But NOW's strategy of downplaying activism in favor of "respectable" lobbying for pro-ERA politicians contributed to the debacle as well. As the activism in the women's movement dwindled, so did momentum for the passage of ERA. NOW's leaders did not renew a commitment to activism in the face of its losing battles. Instead, as time wore on, NOW's strategies became more conservative in the hopes of winning more friends among state legislators. NOW leaders banned lesbian and radical contingents at pro-ERA marches. NOW president Eleanor Smeal urged lawyers appealing the constitutionality of the federal ban on Medicaid funding for abortion not to link their claim to the Fourteenth Amendment's equal protection clause so as not to alienate pro-ERA legislators who were anti-abortion.[94] Increasingly, the nominally nonpartisan NOW shifted its attention to campaigning for pro-ERA and pro-choice politicians, usually Democrats.

At the close of the 1970s, a rapidly growing anti-abortion and conservative movement faced a women's movement that was declining and growing more conservative in its aims and methods. Yet over the course of the Reagan-Bush years, as the women's vote became more important to the Democrats[95] and women's organizations like NOW and the National Abortion Rights Action League (NARAL) devoted more of their resources to electing Democratic candidates, women's rights continued to slide backward. Feminist Martha Burk reviewed the period:

> Women in Congress fared no better with their colleagues. During the past twelve years Congress has grown accustomed to trading away the rights of women as bargaining chips in the larger game of "scratch my back" politics. Democratic majorities approved caps on damages for women in the 1991 Civil Rights Act, confirmed the Souter and Thomas nominations to the Supreme Court, agreed to exclude gender from hate-crimes legislation and went along with numerous funding cuts in women's programs. Even though Democrats have held a majority in both houses since 1987, that was not enough to override actual or threatened presidential vetoes on legislation of concern to

women. This situation served some armchair feminists well, allowing them to declare their support for women but to plead that their hands were tied. Congressional leaders could also decline to bring legislation to the floor without an assured two-thirds majority, as they did with the Freedom of Choice Act before the 1992 elections—conveniently sparing members a recorded vote.[96]

Despite the disappointing record of the Democratic Clinton administration noted in chapter 3, middle-class feminist organizations like NOW and NARAL (now known as NARAL/Pro-Choice America) became fixtures among Democratic power brokers. But as rank-and-file mobilization organizations they have atrophied. In the late 1980s and early 1990s, NOW-organized demonstrations against GOP-sponsored attacks on abortion rights brought hundreds of thousands to the capital. Eight years of a nominally pro-choice Democratic administration sapped NOW. It failed to mount a strong activist campaign against the erosion of abortion rights, which accelerated during the Clinton years. NOW became little more than a Democratic Party caucus, and its active membership declined throughout the 1990s. By the late 1990s and early 2000s, as Democratic politicians had shifted to a position of defending the legality of the general right to abortion while discouraging the exercise of that right—and even supporting "common-sense" restrictions to the right to abortion—leading feminist organizations played along. In 2005, when then–Democratic senator Hillary Rodham Clinton described abortion as a "tragedy," Eleanor Smeal of the Feminist Majority Foundation found little to criticize: "In many ways, [Clinton] said that if you're interested in reducing the number of abortions, you should be with us."[97]

It was ironic that, a generation after legalized abortion stood as one of the women's movement's main achievements, leading feminists were retreating from its defense. But it was, in part, a reflection of a worldview shaped less by the needs of ordinary women than by the needs of Democratic politicians accommodating to a more conservative environment.

Out of the Streets and Into Congress

Three days of riots in protest of a June 1969 police raid on the Stonewall Inn, a gay bar in New York's Greenwich Village, sparked an upsurge of gay organizing and activism. For this reason, the 1969 Stonewall Rebellion is considered the beginning of the modern gay and lesbian liberation movement. The period immediately after Stonewall spawned the short-lived Gay Liberation Front (GLF), an activist group that saw itself as part of the New Left political movements of the day. One group of activists, concluding that it was more interested in reforming the system than in overthrowing it, split in 1971 to form the Gay Activists Alliance (GAA), the first of several gay lobbying organizations and the forerunner of today's Human Rights Campaign (HRC). The remaining GLF radicals divided themselves between "organized leninist [sic] party supporters and the diffused forces of an alternative society," one activist wrote. "This division between what might be termed 'actionists' and 'life-stylers' is clearly evident in the history and theory of the GLF, and its Manifesto."[98]

As the activist movement of the 1970s declined, the lifestyle politics of "personal autonomy" and separatism (between gay men and lesbians, between Black gays and white gays, etc.) took hold of the radical wing of the movement. While some of these politics had a rebirth during the 1980s AIDS crisis in the form of organizations like the AIDS Coalition to Unleash Power (ACT UP) and Queer Nation, they proved not to have the organizational staying power of the more openly reformist wing of the movement, whose first foray into presidential politics came via the 1972 presidential campaign of liberal Democratic senator George McGovern.

Democratic presidential contender Jimmy Carter subsequently became the first presidential hopeful to declare his support for outlawing discrimination on the basis of sexual orientation. But Carter began backing away from his rhetorical support for equal rights as soon as he established a clear lead among Democrats and turned to the right in the general election, where he wanted to appeal to the "center."[99] During Carter's term, Congress overhauled the federal civil service code but still failed to incorporate the Employment Non-Discrimination Act (ENDA).

To those committed to the Washington insider and lobbying strategy for LGBT rights, the answer to this failure to win more substantive gains was to elect more pro-gay politicians. For this purpose, a group of liberal gay activists formed the Human Rights Campaign (HRC) in 1980. Unlike other activist organizations, the HRC has never claimed to be anything but a Washington political action committee (PAC) and lobby representing a predominantly affluent constituency. Today, the HRC is one of the top fifty PACs in Washington and its annual black-tie dinner has become a standard stop on the

Washington political circuit.[100]

Although officially nonpartisan, HRC has become a virtual satellite of the Democratic Party. However, it doesn't always endorse Democrats. For instance, in 1998, convinced that Republicans would hold the congressional majority for the foreseeable future, the HRC endorsed for reelection senator Alphonse D'Amato (R-NY), one of the sleaziest and most conservative members of Congress at the time. Despite his consistent 75 percent positive ratings from the Christian Coalition, D'Amato's vote for ENDA was good enough for HRC. In the end, D'Amato lost his election to representative Charles Schumer, a Democrat.

HRC's willingness to settle for so little with D'Amato was only because it became used to accepting hollow rhetoric from the Clinton administration during the 1990s. On the campaign trail Clinton had pledged to end discrimination against gays in the military. And he became the first presidential candidate to give a major speech on AIDS. The HRC and the National Gay and Lesbian Task Force (NGLTF) regularly described the Clinton administration as the most "gay friendly" ever. "History will always connect Clinton and the gay and lesbian movement," said NGLTF's former executive director Torie Osborne. "He has stood up for us when others would not. No matter what happens, we can't forget what he has done for us."[101] But former NGLTF Policy Institute director Urvashi Vaid was more honest in assessing the history of the LBGT alliance with the Democrats:

> These meetings did in the 1970s exactly what Bill Clinton's third White House meeting with the gay and lesbian community did in 1993: they demonstrated the administration's symbolic willingness to listen backed by an intransigent refusal to act. The major difference in sixteen years seems to be that we have graduated from meeting with senior staffers to meeting directly with the president. But measured in action, the difference is negligible.[103]

In the sense that it appointed more openly gay advisers than earlier administrations, Clinton's administration may very well have been "gay friendly." But on issues that mattered to ordinary gays and lesbians, Clinton surrendered. Nevertheless, the leading LGBT lobbying organizations continue to form a major institutional support for Democratic Party candidates. And some Democratic politicians, realizing that popular opinion in the twenty-first century has shifted in a much more gay-friendly direction, are willing to support LGBT issues. But when they do, they have to be careful not to step beyond where the Democratic

Party establishment wants them to be, as Democratic San Francisco mayor Gavin Newsom found in 2004 when he announced that he would grant marriage licenses to gays and lesbians from City Hall. For a brief period in early 2004, Newsom's action electrified activists and prompted thousands to flock to San Francisco to tie the knot. The movement for marriage equality had the potential to spark a movement in defense of elementary LGBT civil rights. But establishment Democratic politicians, including gay and lesbian ones like Massachusetts representative Barney Frank, drew back, worried that Newsom's action would embolden the right. They particularly feared the prospect of an energized Christian right mobilizing against the 2004 Democratic presidential candidate, senator John Kerry. Yet by running scared from the issue of gay marriage, the Democrats and liberals simply helped the right make the argument that there was something wrong about defending equal rights for LGBT people.

During the 2004 presidential election, conservatives—in concert with the Bush campaign—supported referenda in eleven states intended to ban same-sex marriage. This tactic to drive up conservative turnout at the polls put Kerry and the Democrats on the defensive. Hoping to take the issue "off the table," Kerry continued to insist that he, too, opposed same sex marriage. But this simply left the field open to the right. An LGBT activist in the crucial swing state of Ohio complained that Democrats deserted the campaign against an anti-gay initiative there: "When we were trying to keep this off the ballot, we were given everything short of . . . help."[102] While the Democrats were refusing to lift a finger to defeat the anti–gay marriage initiatives, they actively worked to shut down the grassroots activism on behalf of equal marriage that exploded after Newsom began issuing marriage licenses to same-sex couples. So on the issue of gay marriage, as on many others, the mainstream parties closed ranks around similar positions, and the left largely fell behind Kerry, who opposed equal marriage. Therefore, it wasn't surprising that conservative politics won the day. Exit polls showed that 60 percent of the 2004 electorate supported either gay marriage or civil unions for gays and lesbians—a position that was itself considered "controversial" only four years before when the Vermont Supreme Court forced then-governor Howard Dean to implement civil unions. Yet with few Democratic politicians willing to champion equal marriage rights, this popular sentiment remained largely untapped.

By the time that President Obama occupied the White House, support for equal marriage had become a majority opinion in the United States. Eight in ten Americans supported the ending of the military's "don't ask, don't tell" policy.[103] This sea change in Americans' attitudes owed to many things: general liberalization of attitudes, experience with equal marriage laws in the few states where they were in effect, shortages of military personnel during two long wars, and the committed activism of the LGBT grassroots. In October 2009, a grassroots coalition brought more than two hundred thousand people to Washington to petition for equal rights for LGBT people in the National Equality March. It was one of the few grassroots efforts to push the Obama administration to the left.

Yet in the face of overwhelming support for pro-LGBT policies, the "progressive" Obama administration dragged its feet, outraging many of its LGBT supporters. Only after the Pentagon urged dropping "don't ask, don't tell" did the administration and congressional supporters push through its repeal—during the "lame duck" session after the 2010 midterm election. In 2011, as the president looked to spark the Democratic base in preparation for his reelection, Obama's Justice Department announced it would not enforce the Clinton-era Defense of Marriage Act. While these were certainly steps in the right direction, they were no profile in courage. But they had the desired payoff for Obama, particularly in the community of wealthy LGBT Democratic donors. "It's ironic—a year ago there was no constituency more unhappy. There was a sea change," David Mixner, formerly Clinton's liaison with the LGBT community, told *Politico*. "You not only will see a united community that will contribute to Obama, but they will work their asses off."[104]

The Democrats and Social Movements

The social movements considered here span more than a century and involve widely disparate constituencies with widely disparate impacts on the society of their times. But one constant unites them: the presence and role of the Democratic Party as the chief national political institution with which they had to contend. The Democratic Party, as the quote from Domhoff at the beginning of this chapter noted, is one of the main conduits through which various "out" groups in U.S. society have been integrated into the mainstream political process. This has had the effect of blunting and co-opting the social movements that were the vehicles by which these out groups had made their voices heard. As leading Populists, labor activists, civil rights activists, and others have learned the hard way over the years, the Democratic Party doesn't simply seek to represent these groups. It seeks to corral them and to ensure that they don't strike out on an independent political path. And rather than championing the demands of the social movements in the broader political system, movement organizations with a Democratic Party orientation often end up making alibis for Democratic politicians or agreeing to trim their sails so as not to alienate their Democratic "friends." In fact it was this quest for friends in high places that placed leaders of United for Peace and Justice (UFPJ), the largest organization opposing the early 2000s war in Iraq, in the position of urging support for congressional and presidential candidates (nearly all Democrats), fully admitting that almost none of them was committed to UFPJ's central demand of ending the Iraq War. Although UFPJ called this "engaging in the 2008 electoral season to project a peace and justice agenda," it had the effect of fueling a sense of futility in a movement that potentially represented three-quarters of the American population.[105] Based on their research of the antiwar movement in this period, political scientists Michael T. Heaney and Fabio Rojas argued that "the relationship between the Democratic Party and the antiwar movement was essential in accounting for the demobilization of the antiwar movement between 2007 and 2009."[106]

It should be stressed that this process doesn't just run one way, with the Democrats co-opting restive movements that resist the Democrats' embrace. In fact there are plenty of constituencies inside social movements that view an orientation toward the Democrats as both logical and necessary. Leaving aside the very real material incentives the Democrats can use to corrupt and buy off social movements, the political rationales for allying with the Democrats have become familiar refrains: "We need politicians who will vote with us, instead of against us." "We can't let the perfect be the enemy of the good." "The Democrats depend on us for their elections, so they should listen to us." And always: "The Democrats may not be so great, but they're better than the Republicans."

While these arguments for reform through the Democratic Party sound reasonable, they suffer from a critical flaw at their heart. This "paradox of social democracy," as Robert Brenner has called it, has afflicted every mass movement for social change since the beginnings of mass reformist or social democratic parties in the 1800s. And while the Democratic Party is in no sense a social democratic party, it has often presented itself as the reformist alternative in the mainstream American political system. Brenner explains the paradox:

> On the one hand, [reformism's] rise has depended upon tumultuous mass working-class struggles, the same struggles which have provided the muscle to win major reforms which have provided the basis for the emergence of far left political organizations and ideology. . . . On the other hand, to the extent that social democracy has been able to consolidate itself organizationally, its core representatives—drawn from the ranks of trade union officials, the parliamentary politicians, and petty bourgeois leaderships of the mass organizations of the oppressed—have invariably sought to implement policies reflecting their own distinctive social positions and interest—positions which are separate from and interests which are, in fundamental ways, opposed to those of the working class. . . .
>   . . . . The paradoxical consequence has been that, to the extent that the official representatives of reformism . . . have been freed to implement their characteristic worldviews, strategies, and tactics, they have systematically undermined the basis for their own continuing existence, paving the way for their dissolution.[107]

In other words, the power that social movements exert—through protests, strikes, and disruption of business as usual—is what forces the political establishment to address their demands and to recognize their leaders. This has been the case historically whether Democrats or Republicans occupy the White House, despite the fact that the Democrats have promoted themselves as the party that represents the interests of workers and the oppressed. But as this chapter has shown, the Democratic Party expects movement leaders to rein in their movements, thereby undercutting the potential for struggle from below. That is the deal with the devil that any movement activist makes when entering into an alliance with the Democratic Party, whose institutional loyalties lie with its corporate funders—not its working-class and movement supporters.

A perfect example of this process in microcosm occurred in Wisconsin in early 2011. There, newly elected Republican governor Scott Walker introduced a "budget repair" bill that, in addition to cutting millions from health and education services, would gut collective bargaining rights for public employees in the state. Walker's action pre-

cipitated a mass mobilization of workers, students, and their supporters to occupy the state capitol in Madison to prevent the legislation's
passage. The state's largest teachers' unions struck in opposition to the
bill. The mass mobilization forced fourteen Democratic state senators
to flee the state to deny Walker a quorum. The local labor federation
even supported a call for a general strike against the Walker bill. As
long as workers held the initiative and thousands occupied the capitol,
Walker was checked. But Walker regained the initiative after Wisconsin
authorities managed to clear the capitol and, *crucially*, leading labor
unions and their Democratic Party allies shifted the mobilization into
recall campaigns against Republican state senators who voted for the
union-stripping bill.

The Democrats tried to capitalize on the explosion in working-class
anger to carry them to victory. But as they shifted the movement on to
the multimillion-dollar terrain of electoral politics, they also started to
downplay the class issues that had touched off the mobilization. Apparently, their pollsters had convinced them that they already had the most
passionate labor supporters in their camp, so they should soften their
message to win over "centrist" voters. The recall campaign succeeded in
recalling two Republicans, but it fell short of its goal of retaking the
state senate for the Democrats. And while Democratic partisans spun
this result as a "victory," labor union members knew better. After all of
the millions spent and votes cast, Walker's bill remained law and tens of
thousands of public-sector workers in Wisconsin lost their rights to bargain. One activist summed it up: "The Democrats channeled the movement's best energies into electoral politics with the aim of increasing
their own power. By abandoning the collective bargaining issue, the Democrats showed their true colors, and proved once again that the Democratic Party exists solely to elect Democrats." [108]

The late Peter Miguel Camejo, who joined Ralph Nader on an independent left-wing presidential ticket running against Kerry and
Bush in 2004, understood this well:

> One important value of the Democratic Party to the corporate world is that it
> makes the Republican Party possible through the maintenance of the stability
> that is essential for "business as usual." It does this by preventing a genuine
> mass opposition from developing. Together the two parties offer one of the
> best frameworks possible with which to rule a people that otherwise would
> begin to move society toward the rule of the people (i.e., democracy). [109]

If the Democrats and Republicans have this relationship in domestic politics, their bipartisan modus operandi is even more pronounced in their joint conduct of U.S. foreign policy, to which we turn in the next chapter.

Chapter Six

Defenders of the Empire

One of the enduring truisms of American politics since the 1960s is the notion that Republicans are "strong on national defense" while Democrats are "weak." In 2004, largely on this basis, George W. Bush, who hid out in the Texas National Guard to avoid service in Vietnam, defeated Democratic senator John Kerry, a decorated Vietnam veteran who emphasized his military service at every turn.

Like many of the truisms about American politics, this one is largely a myth. One undeniable truth is that Democratic presidents led the United States into every major war of the twentieth century. The First World War (Wilson), the Second World War (Roosevelt), the Korean War (Truman), and the Vietnam War (Kennedy) were "Democratic" wars. Truman is the only government leader to have authorized the use of atomic weapons. Kennedy brought the world the closest it came to a global holocaust in the 1962 Cuban missile crisis between the United States and the USSR.

The reason behind these facts is simple: the Democrats are as committed as the Republicans to upholding the United States' right to police the world. Truman's "Doctrine," announced in 1947, asserted the U.S. government's intention to intervene anywhere to uphold U.S. interests in the name of fighting "communism."[1] In 1960 Kennedy campaigned on a foreign policy platform more conservative than

Nixon's, chiding the Eisenhower administration for falling behind the Soviet Union in its development and deployment of missiles, satellites, and nuclear weapons. This "missile gap" was later discovered to be nonexistent.[2] In 1984 Walter Mondale called for a quarantine of Nicaragua, a position farther to the right than Reagan's support for the *contras*, the mercenary force fighting to overthrow the democratically elected Sandinista government.[3] And in the wake of the September 11, 2001, attacks, Democrats and Republicans competed to show who was tougher in the "War on Terror."

The Parties and Foreign Policy: A Case of Political Kabuki

Given the fairly minimal differences between the Republicans and Democrats on U.S. foreign policy, it's amazing that the image of sharp polarization between the parties exists. It's particularly curious since this is the one main policy area in which the idea of "bipartisanship" extends the farthest. One of the oldest clichés in American politics holds that "politics stops at the water's edge"—i.e., that partisan disputes aren't supposed to interfere with the conduct of American foreign policy. On the biggest, guiding questions of American foreign policy, this is certainly the case. During the Cold War, for instance, no mainstream candidate ever ran a campaign challenging the United States' anticommunist "containment" policy against the USSR. After September 11, 2001, nearly every Democrat or Republican running for office has claimed to have the best strategy for fighting "terrorism."

But within these wider agreements on goals and aims there is room for disagreement on the particulars. This is especially true during election season, when candidates and parties accentuate even miniscule differences in order to appeal to their respective voting bases. As foreign policy analyst Andrew Bacevich explained, "Through tacit agreement, the two major parties approach the contest for the presidency less as an opportunity for assessing U.S. policies abroad than for striking poses—a hallowed and inviolable bit of political kabuki."[4] During the 2000 election, Gore foreign policy adviser Richard Holbrooke maintained an agreement with Bush adviser Paul Wolfowitz—who gained notoriety soon thereafter as the intellectual author of the Bush Doctrine of preemptive war—to keep discussion of U.S. policy toward Indonesia and East Timor out of the presidential fray. As Holbrooke put it, "Paul and I have been in frequent touch to make sure we keep East Timor out of the presidential campaign, where it would do no good for American or Indonesian interests."[5]

When he was a presidential candidate in 1992, Bill Clinton ridiculed George H. W. Bush for "coddling" dictators in his policy toward China.[6] He said of Bush's policy of forcibly returning refugees escaping from Haiti's military dictatorship, "I am appalled by the decision of the Bush administration to pick up fleeing Haitians on the high seas and forcibly return them to Haiti before considering their claim to political asylum."[7] He slammed Bush for being too slow to intervene militarily in Bosnia.[8] Once in office he reversed himself on both Haiti and China, adopting Bush's policies on these questions. In the case of Haiti, Clinton didn't even wait until his inauguration to announce that he would maintain Bush's policy of locking up Haitian refugees in the Guantánamo Bay camp (that in 2001–2002 became a gulag for accused terrorists). Clinton lifted any human rights considerations regarding trade with China as part of his policy of adopting China as a "strategic partner" with the United States. By the end of his term, Clinton faced fire from right-wing Republicans who denounced his China policy in terms that resembled Clinton's own criticism of Bush. In Bosnia, Clinton eventually made good on his plans for military intervention, but only after following George H. W. Bush's policy for nearly three years.

Likewise, during the 2000 election campaign, George W. Bush blasted Clinton for promoting "nation building" in places like the Balkans, for overextending the deployment of the armed forces, and for taking too soft a posture toward China, among other points. Future national security adviser Condoleezza Rice even hinted that the United States would pull its forces out of the Balkans, telling the *New York Times* in 2000, "We really don't need to have the 82nd Airborne escorting kids to kindergarten."[9] After Rice's trial balloon caused outcry in Europe and in the U.S. media, Bush said he had no intention of pulling out of the Balkans. Despite its stated hostility to "nation building," the Bush administration became bogged down in exactly such an endeavor in Afghanistan and Iraq. And with roughly half the combat power of the U.S. armed forces deployed around the world, the military under Bush was stretched thinner than it ever was under Clinton. Finally, even before Bush decided to count China as an ally in the "War on Terror," he was backing away from his earlier bellicose rhetoric. When Chinese pilots shot down a U.S. spy plane in April 2001, Bush made a few saber-rattling noises. The administration then decided to trade U.S. crewmembers for an apology to China, leaving Bush's cheerleaders in the conservative press to denounce him for producing "a national humiliation" in China.[10]

These examples show that when it comes to foreign policy, there is much more continuity between the administrations of both political parties than there is difference between them. As Bacevich noted, most disagreements between Democratic and Republican administrations emerge on the margins of the main questions of U.S. foreign policy. This reality makes it harder to explain the widely shared—almost automatic—perception that Democrats are "weak on defense" (or, put more positively from a liberal point of view, "committed to peace") and that the Republicans are both "stronger" and "more professional" in their approach to foreign affairs. It omits the fact that Democratic administrations were the architects of the Cold War national security state and the policy of containment toward the USSR. FDR and his administration set up the International Monetary Fund, the World Bank, and the United Nations—ongoing tools of American imperialism. After Truman ordered atomic bombs dropped on Japan, he went on to create the National Security Council, the CIA, and the Defense Department. The Truman Doctrine authorized U.S. troops to intervene anywhere to "defend free enterprise" against "communism." The myth-makers laud Kennedy for creating the Peace Corps, while ignoring that he also created the Green Berets.[11]

The Birth of American Imperialism

The Spanish-American War marked the entrance of the United States into the worldwide scramble for colonies among the advanced powers. In April 1898 the United States went to war with Cuba's colonial over-lord, Spain, under the pretext of retaliating for the sinking of the USS *Maine*, anchored in Havana, Cuba. By the end of December, the United States had routed Europe's weakest colonial power and made off with all of Spain's colonial possessions in Latin America and Asia, seizing control of Cuba, Puerto Rico, Guam, and the Philippines.[12] Novelist Mark Twain made no bones about the imperialist nature of this war:

How our hearts burned with indignation against the atrocious Spaniards. . . . But when the smoke was over, the dead buried and the cost of the war came back to the people in an increase in the price of commodities and rent—that is, when we sobered up from our patriotic spree—it suddenly dawned on us that the cause of the Spanish-American war was the price of sugar . . . that the lives, blood, and money of the American people were used to protect the interests of American capitalists.[13]

Ambassador John Hay wrote to congratulate assistant naval secretary Theodore Roosevelt on this "splendid little war," engineered by the Republican administration of William McKinley. Theodore Roosevelt, who later assumed the presidency upon McKinley's assassination, declared the United States' right to intervene as "an international police power" throughout the Western Hemisphere in a speech before Congress in December 1904.[14]

No Democrat put a presidential stamp on U.S. empire until Woodrow Wilson became president in 1913. Wilson ordered military interventions in more countries and stationed troops for longer periods than either Roosevelt or Roosevelt's Republican successor, William Howard Taft. In particular, Wilson turned the Caribbean Sea into a virtual American lake. In the years before U.S. intervention in the First World War, Wilson dispatched the Marines to Mexico, Haiti, the Dominican Republic, Cuba, Panama, Honduras, and Guatemala. In 1914 U.S. troops landed in Port-au-Prince, Haiti, on a mission to collect from Haitian customhouses a debt owed to National City Bank. When the Haitians rose up against this attack on their sovereignty, the United States launched a full-scale occupation that lasted until 1934. When the United States finally withdrew from Haiti, it left behind a U.S.-trained military whose successors continued to terrorize the Haitian population for the rest of the century.[15]

Wilson's actions in Haiti and the rest of the Americas followed logically from his understanding of the role U.S. foreign policy should play in the twentieth century. Writing as a Princeton political scientist more than a decade before he was elected president, he concluded that the "flag followed commerce":

Since trade ignores national boundaries and the manufacturer insists on having the world as a market, the flag of his nation must follow him, and the doors of the nations which are closed against him must be battered down. Concessions obtained by financiers must be safeguarded by ministers of state, *even if the sovereignty of unwilling nations be outraged in the process.* [Emphasis added.] Colonies must be obtained or planted, in order that no useful corner of the world may be overlooked or left unused.[16]

Despite his nakedly imperialist point of view, Wilson is remembered as a great humanitarian who pioneered the notion that U.S. foreign policy should serve loftier goals, promoting democracy and defending the self-determination of small nations. These hallmarks of what international relations specialists describe as a foreign policy of "idealism" are often interchangeably referred to as "Wilsonian."[17] Wilson's idealistic reputation is a legacy based first on his decision to launch the United States into the First World War on the grounds of fighting to "make the world safe for democracy"; and second on his failed effort to win the U.S. Senate's ratification of the Treaty of Versailles, the Wilson-spearheaded settlement of the First World War that included such planks as the creation of the League of Nations.

In 1916 Wilson ran for reelection by tapping into mass antiwar sentiment, using the slogan "He Kept Us Out of War." Only months after winning his second term, however, Wilson declared war on Germany in April 1917. Even during his first term, Wilson's protestations of neutrality in the European conflict barely concealed his support for the side of allies Britain and France against Germany. American bankers and manufacturers, who were making millions from supplying the Allies with arms, foodstuffs, and money, pressed the government to move away from its stated neutrality. As the American economy became more entwined with the Allied side and therefore more committed to Allied victory, pressure built on Wilson to commit U.S. troops to assure victory over Germany. When in 1916 the U.S. government announced it would not act against U.S. banks that openly loaned money to the Allied belligerents, it was setting itself on the path to war. In fact, German submarine attacks on U.S. ships—the ostensible reason for U.S. entry into the war—increased in response to the U.S. decision to allow the House of Morgan banks to lend to the Allies. Forces inside the German general staff knew this action would likely draw the United States into the war, but they preferred to fight the United States as an open belligerent rather than as a supporter of the Allies.[18] In 1919 testimony before the Senate, Wilson admitted that Germany's actions were secondary to the U.S. decision to enter the war:

Senator McCumber: Do you think if Germany had committed no act of war or no act of injustice against our citizens that we would have gotten into this war?

The President: I do think so.

Senator McCumber: You do think we would have gotten in anyway?

The President: I do.[19]

Once committed to entering the war on the Allied side, Wilson wanted to make sure that the United States would have a part in the conflict's final settlement.

With the Allied homelands devastated and their economies in shambles at the end of the First World War, the United States emerged globally as an ascending industrial and economic power. The United States might have depended solely on its economic might to assert its place at the top of world affairs. But the Russian Revolution of 1917 had introduced another variable into the equation. Not only were the Allies competing to defeat Germany, but they were also competing to maintain their own legitimacy in the eyes of war-weary populations, which looked with hope to the workers' revolution that ended Russia's participation in the war on the Allied side. Wilson's "Fourteen Points," his declared war aims, including lofty-sounding goals of a "just peace" and "self-determination of peoples," were promulgated to keep the new Russian revolutionary government from pulling out of the war.[20] While Wilson tried to combat the Bolshevik revolution ideologically, he also authorized open support to the counterrevolutionary White Armies in 1918–20. The United States dispatched an invasion force to Siberia in 1918.

As the socialist historian Sidney Lens put it, the period of "peace" after the First World War "was to be a continuation of war by other means."[21] Not only did this mean the United States flexing its economic muscles, it also meant the attempt to put a "Wilsonian" stamp on the world through the League of Nations. Promoted as an international organization to preserve international peace through "collective security," the league left socialists of the day skeptical. Russian revolutionary Leon Trotsky explained its role this way:

Under the League of Nations flag, the United States made an attempt to extend to the other side of the ocean its experience with a federated unification of large, multinational masses—an attempt to chain to its chariot of gold the peoples of Europe and other parts of the world, and bring them under

Washington's rule. In essence the League of Nations was intended to be a world monopoly corporation, "Yankee and Co."[22]

Wilson could not convince the U.S. Senate to ratify the treaty ending the First World War, largely because of opposition to the League of Nations. But isolationist senators opposed the treaty for very different reasons than Trotsky did. By the time the Democrats made their play as the architects of U.S. imperialism, the Republican Party had become dominated by "America First" isolationism. This position held that U.S. foreign policy should be concerned only with the military defense of U.S. territory and should eschew overseas intervention or other U.S. involvement in other regions' affairs. Isolationist Republicans in the Senate successfully defeated President Wilson's attempt to join the League of Nations.

As the radical historian William Appleman Williams argued, it would be

> misleading to employ the terms isolationist and internationalist when analyzing the refusal of the Senate to approve the League Treaty. The votes that defeated President Wilson's "only possible program for peace" were cast by men of widely different purposes and motivations. Some were empire builders on a world scale; others were continentalists, who argued that the United States could control the balance of world power as soon as the Western Hemisphere was brought under more direct control and organization by Washington. Some were progressive, or even radical; while others were conservative or reactionary. But perhaps most significant of all was the manner in which they reacted to the movements of social and colonial revolution that seemed to be typified in the Bolshevik Revolution. For while President Wilson saw in the League Treaty an instrument which could prevent future upheavals of that character, his opponents thought his proposal either too liberal or too conservative, and so opposed it for those reasons.[23]

The United Nations, a global organization of nation-states modeled on the League of Nations, would emerge after the Second World War, this time with the United States' blessing. And the man who served as Wilson's assistant naval secretary, Franklin Delano Roosevelt, would be its main sponsor.

Liberals and the "Good War"

The First World War left the United States as the world's leading economic power. The Second World War would leave the United States as the world's leading military power. In the period between the wars, the

United States concentrated on leveraging its economic power to enlarge its empire—to win with economic power what the European powers had won with the open imperialism of colonies and viceroys. Under the Republican administrations of the 1920s—and even more explicitly under the Democratic Roosevelt administration as of 1933—the United States pressed its advantages by means of the "open door," forcing weaker economies into competition with the United States through "free trade" and "open commerce." The Great Depression, which began in 1929, simultaneously made the U.S. strategy more difficult and more necessary. In a remarkably prescient statement written while in exile from Stalin's Russia in 1934, Trotsky explained:

> The gigantic economic superiority of the United States over Europe, and, consequently, over the world allowed the bourgeoisie of the United States to appear in the first postwar period as a dispassionate "conciliator," defender of "freedom of the seas" and the "open door." The industrial and business crisis revealed, however, with terrific force the disturbance of the old economic equilibrium, which had found sufficient support on the internal market. This road is completely exhausted.
>
> Of course, the economic superiority of the United States has not disappeared; on the contrary, it has even grown potentially, due to the further disintegration of Europe. . . . The superiority of the United States must find its expression in new forms, the way to which can be opened only by war.
>
> . . . U.S. capitalism is up against the same problems that pushed Germany in 1914 on the path of war. The world is divided? It must be redivided. For Germany it was a question of "organizing Europe." The United States must "organize" the world. History is bringing humanity face to face with the volcanic eruption of American imperialism.[24]

Trotsky identified the dynamics that would push the United States into the Second World War seven years later. In both major theaters where the United States ultimately fought, the Pacific and Europe, it faced economic rivals for whom the "open door" meant subordination to the United States. Rejecting that choice, Japan in the East and Germany in the West embarked on military campaigns to enlarge their economic spheres of influence. After Japan conquered Manchuria in 1937, the State Department worried that "Japanese superiority in the Far East would definitely mean the closing of the Open Door."[25] A German conquest of Europe would have created an economic super-state that would have blocked what Trotsky characterized as the United States' own desire to organize the world. Defying his own campaign promises to stay out of "foreign wars," FDR positioned the United States to join the conflict.

The Japanese bombing of Pearl Harbor gave Roosevelt the license he needed to launch the United States into the Second World War. Only the time and place of the Japanese attack took the Roosevelt administration by surprise. For years beforehand it was clear that the president was preparing the nation, through a massive arms buildup, for its eventual entry into the war. In 1940, knowing that his actions would lead to Japanese expansionism in Asia, Roosevelt cut off supplies of oil, iron, and aircraft fuel to Japan. By late 1941 FDR's advisers were meeting to discuss how they could maneuver Japan into "firing the first shot" for the war they planned to fight.[26] In the West—throwing out all pretense of maintaining "neutrality" toward the belligerents—the United States used the 1941 Lend-Lease Act to arm Britain, France, and other allies in their war with Nazi Germany. With these tactics FDR cannily created an air of inevitability about the United States' eventual entry into the war.[27]

For Roosevelt and secretary of state Cordell Hull, U.S. war aims were simple and consistent for the four years of U.S. participation in the war. They envisioned a reinforcement of the U.S. "open door" policy. In Asia, this meant defeating Japan's attempt to create an Asian "Co-Prosperity Sphere." In Europe, this meant not only defeating Nazi Germany's attempt to subjugate the continent, but also liquidating the British Empire. Toward this latter goal, Hull and Roosevelt insisted that Britain give up its "imperial preference" system in exchange for Lend-Lease aid. In other words, in order to receive U.S. aid in the war against Germany, Britain had to commit to eliminating the special trading preferences that it as the "mother country" maintained with its own colonies. For the United States to truly attain the "open door" policy it wanted, it had be able to trade with the British Commonwealth on an even status with Britain—in effect breaking down the economic glue that held the British Empire together. To Hull, this "internationalism" anticipated the United States dominating the international system that would emerge from the war: "Leadership toward a new system of international relationships in trade and other economic affairs will devolve very largely upon the United States because of our great economic strength. We should assume this leadership, and the responsibility that goes with it, primarily for reasons of pure national self-interest."[28]

While Hull consistently enunciated these war aims, Roosevelt couched U.S. goals in terms of the "Four Freedoms": freedom of speech and expression, freedom of worship, freedom from want, and freedom from fear.[29] These cast U.S. and Allied goals in Wilsonian terms as a fight for democracy against dictatorship and militarism. But U.S domestic policies belied this high-minded rhetoric of freedom and democracy. These included FDR's executive order interning Japanese Americans and continued segregation in the U.S. armed forces. His reluctant decision to ban racial discrimination in wartime hiring was forced only when Brotherhood of Sleeping Car Porters union leader A. Philip Randolph threatened a massive march on Washington that promised to expose the United States' racist hypocrisy in 1941.[30]

Even the ultimate justification of combating Hitler's genocidal anti-Semitism was tainted by the administration's refusal to lift immigration restrictions that prevented potentially millions of Jews from seeking refuge from the Holocaust in the United States. The most celebrated case was that of the USS *St. Louis* in 1939, when the U.S. Coast Guard turned away a ship carrying nearly one thousand Jewish refugees desperate to immigrate to the United States.[31] The point here is not that FDR and the Democrats were merely hypocrites or that the administration did not believe in the high-minded principles it was pronouncing. It is that those high-minded principles always took a backseat to the imperial war aims of which Hull was the administration's most consistent proponent.

The radical historian Richard Hofstadter pointed out this contradiction in his discussion of wartime U.S. opposition to old-fashioned colonial imperialism:

> Roosevelt's opposition to the colonial empires was not simply altruistic; American commercial interests—for instance, the vast oil concessions that had been made to American companies in Saudi Arabia—were much in his mind. Although he believed that "imperialists"—he used the word as an epithet— had been short-sighted in taking a purely exploitative view of the colonies and that much greater potentialities lay in them if the welfare of the colonial peoples was taken into account, he was also aware of the possibilities for American trade in an economic revivification of the colonial areas under American encouragement.[32]

Humanitarian ideals, real or artificial, certainly did not carry over to the way the "good war" was fought. The "arsenal of democracy," as the U.S. military-industrial complex came to be called during the Second World War, produced weapons that killed armies and civilian populations in the tens and hundreds of thousands. As many as thirty-five thousand perished in Allied firebombing of Dresden, Germany—a horror immortalized in Kurt Vonnegut's *Slaughterhouse Five*—and Tokyo and other major Japanese cities were reduced to cinders even before the United States planned an invasion. The war for the Pacific took on the character of what historian John W. Dower called a "race war" against the Japanese. Admiral William Halsey, commander of the South Pacific Force, described U.S. war plans in the East as "Kill Japs, kill Japs, kill Japs." Elliott Roosevelt, the president's brother, advocated killing one-half of the Japanese population.[33] In this climate it was understandable that Roosevelt's successor, Harry Truman, had no qualms about ordering the dropping of atomic bombs on Hiroshima and Nagasaki—despite the fact that military leaders, including future Republican president Dwight Eisenhower, considered the bombings unnecessary to securing Japan's surrender.[34] Owing to what he characterized as "direct orders to commit 'indiscriminate murder,'" an Indian judge at the postwar International Tribunal for the Far East argued that the Allies' decision to use the atomic bombs was the greatest atrocity committed during the war in Asia.[35]

Architects of the Cold War

As U.S. troops swept across Europe and the Pacific, the highest officials in the Roosevelt and, after FDR's death in April 1945, the Truman administrations drew up plans to establish a global U.S. empire after the Second World War. As the only major wartime belligerent that escaped large-scale destruction of its home territory and infrastructure, the United States accounted for nearly 60 percent of the total production of the seven largest capitalist countries. By the war's end, the U.S. military literally covered the globe, with troops stationed in more than 1,100 bases in all regions of the world.[36] For a brief period after the Second World War, the United States possessed a monopoly on the most destructive weapon ever produced—the atomic bomb. With its economic and military power at their height, the United States aimed to shape the world in its own interests.

As its first task, the new U.S. empire constructed an international economic system designed to promote U.S. dominance in the world market. Official statements from government officials praised "free trade" as a means to break down barriers between nations. But behind the rhetoric lay the reality of U.S. economic dominance. To stabilize the world financial system after the war, the United States pushed for the creation of the International Monetary Fund (IMF). To revive the economies of its European allies (and former enemies Germany and Japan), it sponsored the creation of the World Bank. "The United States could not passively sanction the employment of capital raised within the United States for ends contrary to our major policies or interests," said the State Department's Herbert Feis in 1944. "Capital is a form of power."[37] U.S. strategic interests were also at stake. As political scientist Diane B. Kunz explained,

> American officials worried about the leftward turn in European politics, from the pervasive socialist influence throughout Europe to the heavy communist inroads in France and Italy. No one in Washington in May 1947 feared the imminent arrival of Soviet tanks in Paris or Rome. But, as George Kennan's Policy Planning Staff had pointed out, "economic maladjustment . . . makes European society vulnerable to exploitation by any and all totalitarian movements." In other words, a hungry, suffering electorate might vote communist governments into power.[38]

To back up economic clout with military muscle, the United States built military alliances spanning the globe. The most important of these alliances, the North Atlantic Treaty Organization (NATO), founded in 1949, served to involve the United States permanently in European affairs. Ostensibly formed to present a common European defense against a Soviet invasion of the West, its real aim was, to paraphrase the first NATO General Secretary, Britain's Lord Ismay, to keep the United States in Europe, to keep Russia out, and to keep Germany tied down.[39] George Kennan, the U.S. State Department's architect of anticommunist "containment," nevertheless ridiculed NATO as a "military defense against an attack no one is planning." He added that NATO "added depth and recalcitrance to the division of the continent and virtually forced individual countries to choose sides."[40] But forcing countries to choose sides between the United States–led Western bloc and the USSR–led Eastern bloc was what the Cold War was all about.

Postwar institutions such as NATO, the Association of South East Asian Nations (ASEAN), the IMF, the World Bank, and the rest served more than simply anti-USSR aims. NSC 68, the 1950 State Department paper that outlined the pillars of the strategy of containment of the USSR, advocated U.S. military superiority as "a policy which the United

States would probably pursue even if there were no Soviet threat."[41] Not only was the United States geared up to confront the Soviet Union, but it also aimed to ensure that Germany and Japan would not present a military threat to U.S. dominance again. To assure this, the United States greatly restricted Germany and Japan from rebuilding their militaries. To discourage the two countries from developing nuclear weapons, the United States offered them "protection" under its nuclear umbrella. Finally, the United States encouraged the revival of the Japanese and German economies and promoted a global "free trade" regime to preserve the Western alliance under U.S. economic domination.

The United States maintained a monopoly on nuclear weapons until 1949, when the USSR exploded an atomic bomb. Russia's acquisition of nuclear weapons touched off a superpower arms race. By 1980 the two superpowers possessed nearly twenty thousand warheads—each of them hundreds of times more powerful than the bombs dropped on Japan in 1945—aimed at each other's major cities. With both superpowers armed with weapons that could destroy all life on the planet, the Cold War fostered a set of military doctrines that a reasonable person would consider insane. The policy of "mutually assured destruction" (known by the appropriate acronym "MAD") guided the use of the U.S. nuclear arsenal. The MAD policy assumed that neither the United States nor the USSR would launch a nuclear strike against the other because each knew a retaliatory strike would destroy it as well. Despite this deterrent, the United States provoked several nuclear confrontations with the Russians. The most serious of these, the 1962 Cuban Missile Crisis, held the world hostage for nearly two weeks before Khrushchev agreed to remove nuclear missiles from Cuba.

This nuclear stalemate imposed a certain amount of stability on the bipolar world created by the Cold War. Any direct confrontation between the superpowers threatened to spiral toward nuclear annihilation. So the main arena for "hot wars" that flowed out of the U.S.-USSR confrontation took place in the system's periphery, the Third World. The Cold War's unwritten rules allowed the United States and the USSR free rein within their respective "backyards." So, despite issuing tirades against Soviet oppression, the United States never seriously considered aiding the Hungarian Revolution of 1956 or the Czechoslovakian Prague Spring of 1968. It acquiesced to the 1981 military coup that smashed Poland's Solidarity movement.

Meanwhile, Western communist parties devolved into tame reformist organizations that did more to sabotage movements such as the May 1968 French general strike than to help them. A successful revolution in either half of divided Europe was not in the interests of either Washington or Moscow.[42]

To maintain political, military, and economic dominance, the United States needed to establish its willingness to intervene anywhere to police its empire. The Truman Doctrine, announced in 1947, asserted the United States' right "to support free peoples who are resisting attempted subjugation by armed minorities."[43] Announced as a justification for aiding the Greek government in its civil war against communist-led insurgents, it put the United States permanently on the side of all forces resisting change throughout the world. The United States became the chief underwriter of counterrevolution and backer of right-wing dictators and despots. Yet if governments showed inclinations to challenge the United States, Washington had no problem sponsoring "armed minorities" against them. The CIA, another 1947 creation of the Cold War, mounted numerous operations against regimes that refused to follow U.S. dictates.

Intervention to prevent defections from the free-enterprise system seemed a crude rationale for policy. So U.S. officials simply harped on the alleged dangers of "communism." As a Truman adviser told the president, "The only way we can sell the public on our new policy is by emphasizing . . . Communism vs. democracy" as the "major theme."[44] Any dictatorial regime was accepted as part of the "Free World" as long as it traded with the Western bloc, allowed Western investment, and supported the West in the Cold War. As a result, the Free World included such exemplars of democracy as the apartheid regime in South Africa, the shah's Iran, and the medieval dictatorship of Emperor Haile Selassie in Ethiopia. Under the pretext of defending the Free World, U.S. forces intervened dozens of times in countries around the world between 1947 and 1990. The longest and most costly of these took place in Asia, where the United States fought full-scale wars in Korea and Vietnam.

Camelot Goes to War

The legacies of poverty and colonialism in Asia made the region ripe for nationalist unrest and superpower meddling. The fall of the corrupt pro-Western Chinese regime to Chinese communists in 1949 set off alarm bells in Washington. When North Korea, backed by Russia and China, overran the U.S.-backed puppet state in South Korea in 1950, the United States rushed thousands of troops to defend its interests in Korea. Presented as a UN "police action," the 1950–53 Korean War cost the lives of thirty-three thousand Americans and two million Koreans, most of them civilians. Despite the carnage, the Korean War solved nothing. It simply redrew the partition line between the Stalinist state in the North and the pro-Western military regime in the South.

The United States intervened in Korea because a shift in the balance of power on the Korean peninsula threatened to disrupt its post–Second World War designs in Asia. Strengthening a non-militarized Japan as a bulwark of capitalist stability in Asia formed the policy's core. In order to rehabilitate and reintegrate Japan into an American-dominated world, the United States had to preserve Japan's access to markets and trading partners in the region. U.S. Cold Warriors feared the collapse of one pro-Western regime after another—which they feared could isolate Japan and other U.S. allies and lead to their eventual collapse. U.S. leaders called this scenario the "domino theory." After the Korea stalemate, the focus of U.S. efforts in Asia shifted to Vietnam:

> The U.S. regarded Indochina as a firewall needed to prevent the more economically vital parts of the region—especially Malaya and Indonesia—from falling under communist control. Washington's concern was that the economic repercussions of toppling dominoes would have geopolitical consequences: if Japan were cut off from Southeast Asia, the resulting economic hardship might cause domestic instability in Japan and result in Tokyo drifting out of the U.S. orbit.[45]

The communist-led Vietminh national independence movement drove France, Vietnam's colonial overlord, out of the country in 1954. The United States sent military and economic aid to the corrupt South Vietnamese state, a creation of French colonialism, and propped up a series of hated South Vietnamese regimes to fight pro-independence forces from "communist" North Vietnam.

Perhaps there is no greater myth in U.S. politics than the idea, promoted by popular films like Oliver Stone's *JFK*, that the Kennedy administration had planned to wind down the Vietnam War at the time of Kennedy's assassination in 1963. In this mythology the sainted JFK would have avoided the disaster into which his benighted successor,

Lyndon Johnson, led the U.S. military and foreign policy establishment. But the record shows otherwise. In 1961 Kennedy's top adviser, McGeorge Bundy, told the State Department that Kennedy "was really very eager indeed that [Vietnam] should have the highest priority for rapid and energetic action."[46] When Washington's chosen puppet in South Vietnam, Ngo Dinh Diem (whom Johnson once touted as "the Winston Churchill of Southeast Asia"), refused U.S. pressure to defuse anti-government demonstrations in 1963, Kennedy authorized a CIA-led military coup that resulted in Diem's assassination. Three weeks after Diem's fall, Kennedy was assassinated. "We had a hand in killing [Diem]," Johnson told new vice president Hubert Humphrey. "Now it's happening here." Kennedy raised the number of U.S. military "advisers" in Vietnam from eight hundred when he took office to 16,700 in 1962.[47] The effect—and indeed the intent—of Kennedy's policy committed the United States to a wider role in Vietnam.

In one of his first major statements on Vietnam as president, Johnson claimed, "We are not about to send American boys 9,000 or 10,000 miles away from home to do what Asian boys ought to be doing for themselves."[48] Yet Johnson had been one of the administration's Vietnam hawks. Only four days after assuming the presidency, he signed off on a secret memo, NSAM 273, that authorized U.S. attacks against North Vietnam.[49] These covert operations were meant to goad North Vietnam into retaliations that would justify further and more open escalations of U.S. military force. Despite campaigning as a "peace" candidate in the 1964 election against Republican archconservative Barry Goldwater, LBJ followed through on his plans to escalate the conflict. To stave off the collapse of the new puppet regime in South Vietnam, the United States sent twenty-five thousand troops to Vietnam in 1965. It then escalated the conflict, stationing more than 540,000 U.S. troops in Vietnam by 1969. A key to winning this commitment of lives and treasure to Vietnam was the Gulf of Tonkin Resolution, passed through Congress in 1964 with only two dissenting votes. The resolution authorized the president to "take all necessary steps," including using military force against North Vietnamese "aggression." All serious studies and revelations from leaks of top-secret government documents proved that the "aggression" in the Gulf of Tonkin, to which the resolution was supposed to have responded, was largely a fabrication of the Pentagon and the Johnson administration.[50]

Despite a horrifying campaign of mass murder against the Vietnamese—carpet bombing, napalm, chemical warfare, assassination, and torture—the United States could not crush the movement for national liberation. The Vietnamese struggle, antiwar protest in the U.S. and other countries, and resistance to the war among U.S. troops in Vietnam forced Washington to give up. It withdrew troops and let the South Vietnamese state fend for itself. South Vietnam collapsed in the face of a two-month offensive by South Vietnamese guerrillas and North Vietnamese regulars in 1975. At the cost of two million Vietnamese lives and fifty-eight thousand American lives, U.S. imperialism suffered its greatest defeat.[51]

The Vietnam debacle left the U.S. military in disarray and its political leaders averse to another overseas adventure involving large numbers of U.S. troops. The defeat caused a "Vietnam syndrome," a subsequent reluctance of American leaders to dispatch ground troops around the world. The sense of defeat and drift among the U.S. political elite, reinforced when a Republican favorite, Richard Nixon, was forced to resign the presidency in disgrace in 1974, opened the door to the Democratic "outsider" Jimmy Carter in 1976.

Mr. Carter and His Doctrine

In 2002 the Nobel Prize Committee awarded Jimmy Carter the Nobel Peace Prize in recognition of work by his foundation, the Carter Center, in observing elections and mediating conflicts around the world. That Carter would win the Peace Prize for work *after* he left the presidency conveniently overlooks the fact that he helped bring the world closer to war when he was president. Nobel laureate Carter reinstituted the military draft in 1979, requiring all males of draft age to register. But Carter's care and feeding of the U.S. war machine went far beyond bringing back the draft, whose abolition represented a victory of the movement against the Vietnam War. Carter increased the U.S. military budget at a rate of 4 percent above inflation annually.[52] In fact, he launched the Pentagon buildup that Ronald Reagan would take to then-unprecedented heights. Toward that end, in 1980, Carter signed Presidential Directive 59, establishing plans for fighting a "limited" nuclear war, including a first-strike policy.[53]

"Human rights" played a big role in Carter's rhetoric about U.S.

foreign policy, but not its practice. As historian Howard Zinn summarized: "Under Carter, the United States continued to support, all over the world, regimes that engaged in imprisonment of dissenters, torture, and mass murder: in the Philippines, in Iran, in Nicaragua, and in Indonesia, where the inhabitants of East Timor were being annihilated in a campaign bordering on genocide."[54]

The biggest gap between word and deed came in Washington's unconditional support for the shah of Iran, Mohammad Reza Pahlavi, the brutal dictator who acted as a U.S. strongman in the Gulf. In 1977, during a state visit to Iran, Carter toasted the shah as an "enlightened monarch who enjoys his people's total confidence."[55] Less than two years later, the Iranian people overthrew the shah. Another Carter favorite was Romanian dictator Nicolai Ceausescu, who won praise and Western aid for abiding by Carter's boycott of the 1980 Moscow Olympics. In 1989, Ceausescu and his hideous regime met the same fate that the shah's did.

To many, Carter's greatest achievement for "peace" was brokering the 1978 Camp David Accords that resulted in Egypt's recognition of Israel. In fact the United States designed the Camp David Accords to bolster Israel by removing Egypt as a military challenger. Israeli hawks openly admit that the peace treaty with Egypt allowed Israel to concentrate its forces for its 1978 and 1982 wars in Lebanon.[56] No thought of justice for the Palestinians entered into Carter's considerations. One year after Camp David, Carter fired UN ambassador Andrew Young for meeting with a member of the Palestine Liberation Organization.[57]

The 1979 Russian invasion of Afghanistan marked a turning point for Carter's shift to a Cold War confrontation with the USSR. Years later, national security adviser Zbigniew Brzezinski admitted the Carter administration had armed Afghan insurgents to provoke a Soviet invasion.[58] In other words, the New Cold War whipped up in 1979–80 was based on a lie from someone who made a campaign pledge to a Watergate-weary electorate that "I will never lie to you."[59] In his 1980 State of the Union address, Carter asserted openly what all U.S. administrations since the 1940s had believed: "An attempt by any outside force to gain control of the Persian Gulf region will be regarded as an assault on the vital interests of the United States of America, and any such assault will be repelled by any means necessary, including military force."[60]

The United States didn't seriously believe the Soviet Union was using Afghanistan as a staging area for a thrust into the Persian Gulf. The "Soviet threat" justified a new policy of direct U.S. intervention in the Persian Gulf after the 1979 Iranian Revolution had eliminated the main U.S. ally in the region. To enforce this "Carter Doctrine," the United States created the Rapid Deployment Force, later renamed the U.S. Central Command (CENTCOM). CENTCOM oversaw U.S. efforts to "pre-position" tons of U.S. military hardware and thousands of troops in friendly states around the Gulf. This deployment in the Gulf gave the United States the power to respond immediately to any crisis that threatened its access to oil and to "hold" the situation until a more substantial U.S. force could be assembled for war. Operation Desert Storm, the U.S.-led war in Iraq in 1991, represented the culmination of the Carter Doctrine and CENTCOM's mission.[61]

In the years since he left the White House, Carter has constructed a public persona calculated to airbrush his disastrous presidency from history. Winning the Nobel Prize is the ultimate recognition of just how successful he has been in making millions forget that he helped rekindle the Cold War and lay the groundwork for future U.S. wars in the Middle East.

Cold War Lite

The Carter-Reagan military buildup helped to break the Russian economy. No longer able to sustain its European empire, Moscow moved to disengage from Eastern Europe. The Russian pullback set off a chain reaction in 1989, sparking political revolutions in one after another of its satellites. Within two years the entire postwar setup underlying the Cold War in Europe—a superpower USSR with pro-Moscow satellites and a Germany divided between East and West—collapsed. The Cold War ended, changing the structure of global politics fundamentally. There was no more "evil empire," as Reagan once described the USSR and its Eastern Bloc satellites, to justify U.S. intervention around the world.

In 1993 the Clinton administration inherited a favorable position for the United States as an imperial power. Two years after the disappearance of its chief military rival, the Soviet Union, the United States stood unchallenged as the world's lone superpower. As the only military power with a global reach, it spent more on intelligence serv-

ices alone than most countries spent on their entire military apparatuses. The United States and its allies accounted for 80 percent of
world military spending.[62] The time was ripe for a "peace dividend," a
major cut in military spending that would free up resources for spending on health care, education, and other social needs that had taken a
backseat during the Cold War. Instead Clinton took the opposite
course. Clinton's plan for the post–Cold War military adopted most of
the outgoing Bush administration's assumptions. It preserved a Cold
War–sized military after the Cold War was over. Under Clinton, the
United States spent about 85 percent of what it had at the height of the
Cold War to maintain a military with the power to intervene anywhere
in the world. In 1998 Clinton announced a six-year boost to the military budget of $112 billion, including a go-ahead to the Pentagon's
biggest boondoggle, a "national missile defense" system. Ironically, the
$112 billion figure corresponded almost exactly to a 1996 General Ac-
counting Office estimate of the cost to make decrepit U.S. public
school buildings functional for the nation's schoolchildren.[63]

    In 2000, when presidential candidate George W. Bush's advisers
attacked the Clinton-Gore administration for presiding over a decline
in military "readiness," Reagan-era Pentagon official Lawrence Korb
rose to Clinton-Gore's defense. Korb noted that military budgets
under Clinton and Gore were larger than President George H. W. Bush
had planned, had he won the 1992 election. The budget for training,
readiness, and maintenance was actually 40 percent higher per person
in uniform than it was under Bush, Korb pointed out.[64] Six of Clinton's eight budgets called for increases in military spending.

    Clinton and Gore dispatched troops around the world far more
frequently than any other modern administration. Before launching
the 1999 war against Yugoslavia, Clinton had sent U.S. forces into
combat situations forty-six times. This compared to only twenty-six
times for Presidents Ford (4), Carter (1), Reagan (14), and H. W. Bush
(7) combined.[65] Clinton, the one-time anti–Vietnam War protester,
continued Bush's 1992 invasion of Somalia, invaded Haiti in 1994,
bombed Serbia in 1995 and 1999, Sudan and Afghanistan in 1997, and
Iraq almost continuously throughout his administration. To force
North Korea into negotiations, Clinton threatened a 1994 war that
could have provoked a nuclear conflict. In 1995 the United States
aided its Croatian ally in the ethnic cleansing of more than 170,000

Serbs. And it remained the main enforcer of genocidal sanctions on Iraq that killed more than a million Iraqis throughout the 1990s. In 1996, when CBS reporter Lesley Stahl asked then-UN ambassador (and later secretary of state) Madeleine Albright, "We have heard that half a million children have died. I mean, that's more children than died in Hiroshima. And you know, is the price worth it?," Albright replied, "I think this is a very hard choice, but the price—we think the price is worth it."[66] In another case where the administration aided the violation of the human rights of millions, the administration won congressional approval for $1.3 billion in aid to the Colombian military in 2000.[67]

The administration's support for sanctions in Iraq and for the death squads in Colombia belied all its talk about establishing a foreign policy based on human rights. But this had been clear from the start. After denouncing the Bush administration for ordering the forcible repatriation of Haitians fleeing persecution from their country, Clinton did an about-face. Bush's policy became Clinton's policy. Blasting Bush for "coddling dictators" in China, in 1994 Clinton removed any human rights considerations from U.S.-China trade. Clinton supported the Suharto dictatorship in Indonesia to the bitter end in 1998. And his administration in 1997 lifted the ban on weapons sales to Latin American governments, including present and future military regimes. Given this record, it should come as no surprise that Clinton's "humanitarian" war against Yugoslavia in 1999 produced a catastrophe for ordinary Serbs and Kosovar Albanians alike. "If there is a Clinton Doctrine—an innovation by the present administration in the conduct of foreign policy—it is this: punishing the innocent in order to express indignation at the guilty," wrote one establishment critic of the NATO war.[68]

This critic was only partially correct, because Clinton—and especially his administration's interventions in the Balkans—played a key role in helping to rehabilitate American imperialism *ideologically.* Down the line, the people who led the war over Kosovo represented the liberal or social democratic parties of their countries. The traditional right-wing "warmongers" like Bush, Reagan, Thatcher, and Kohl were in retirement—with Clinton, Britain's Tony Blair, Germany's Gerhard Schroeder, and France's Lionel Jospin filling their shoes. For them, leading NATO's war represented a collective final step from the left side of the political spectrum to the "center" of capitalist politics. They had built their careers on playing to the aspirations of ordinary people while working hard to convince big business that they would be respectable custodians of the status quo. Blair and Clinton showed big business their willingness to cut social welfare programs. The Kosovo war gave them the opportunity to show the military establishment that they could win a major war and, at the same time, to sell it as a humanitarian gesture.

In February 1999 Clinton announced plans for U.S. military power:

> It's easy . . . to say that we really have no interest in who lives in this or that valley in Bosnia, or who owns a strip of brushland in the Horn of Africa, or some pieces of parched earth by the Jordan River. But our true interests lie not in how small or distant these places are, or in whether we have trouble pronouncing their names. The question we must ask is, what are the consequences to our security of letting conflicts fester and spread. We cannot, indeed, we should not, do everything or be everywhere. But where our values and our interests are at stake, and where we can make a difference, we must be prepared to do so.[69]

Military analyst Michael T. Klare wrote, "No American president in recent times has articulated as ambitious a far-reaching policy."[70] No president, that is, until George W. Bush, who ran at full speed down a trail that Clinton had blazed for him.

The Bush Doctrine, the Democrats, and American Imperialism

In the wake of the September 11, 2001, attacks, American foreign policy took a sharp and dangerous turn to a more aggressive, militarist posture. The George W. Bush administration seized on the September 11 attacks to push what Bush defense secretary Donald Rumsfeld called a "forward-leaning" policy—using military intervention in every part of the world to advance U.S. political and economic interests. Neoconservative ideologues like Rumsfeld, his deputy Paul Wolfowitz, and others took advantage of the post–September 11 climate to push through a program that had been considered untenable only a decade before.[71] At its core was the "Bush Doctrine," the unilateral declaration that the United States had the right to force "regime change" on enemy states—a policy implemented in full with the October 2001 invasion of Afghanistan and the March 2003 invasion of Iraq. The administration pushed up the level of military spending from about $290 billion annually to more than four hundred billion dollars annually in three years, accomplishing in those three years the increase in military spending that Vice President Al Gore's 2000 presidential campaign pledged to accomplish in ten years.

In the face of this challenge, the Democrats in Congress wilted. In the 2002 midterm elections, the Democrats insisted that they would run on a critique of Bush's domestic agenda and avoid a battle with the president over the conduct of foreign policy. This was at a time when Bush deliberately pushed the congressional resolution authorizing war in Iraq in order to shape the midterm elections around "his" issue—the war on terrorism. The Democratic non-strategy, unsurprisingly, turned out to be a loser. As liberal foreign policy commentator William Hartung explained,

> As for the Democrats, their leadership badly misplayed what admittedly was a difficult hand. The notion that granting the President his war resolution would somehow take the war issue off the table and clear the way for discussion of domestic issues, which were considered the Democratic party's strong suit, was a colossal miscalculation. Not only did it give voters concerned about the war nowhere to turn on election day—depressing turnout in the process—but the national Democratic party never even bothered to craft an alternative domestic agenda. Not only was there no equivalent of the ten-point "Contract With America" that helped Republicans seize control of the house in the 1994 midterm elections, there was no plan at all.[72]

The Democrats ended up with the worst of both worlds. Those who supported Bush's call to war—including 2004 presidential candidates Senator John Kerry, Senator Joe Lieberman, and Representative Richard Gephardt—found themselves lending legitimacy to a war policy that most rank-and-file Democrats opposed. Those who fell silent on the war in order to campaign on prescription drug benefits and the like had nothing to offer millions who were then besieging congressional offices with letters, emails, and phone calls opposing the war. As a result, discouraged Democratic voters stayed home and Bush claimed a major victory for his "war on terrorism" policy. Given their pathetic showings—on both foreign and domestic agendas—the Democrats were lucky to have confined their losses to only five House seats and two Senate seats.

To truly understand what happened in this clash over the direction of U.S. foreign policy after September 11, it was essential to pay attention to the players' records more than their election campaign rhetoric. From this point of view, a different understanding of the differences between Democrats and Republicans emerged. The Bush Doctrine indeed represented a departure in U.S. foreign policy. But it didn't represent the sharp and radical break with the past that liberal Democrats imagined. If anything, the more aggressive U.S. imperial policy under Bush represented an amplification of trends in U.S. policy that the Clinton administration had set into motion.

Many Democratic supporters willingly forgot this because the Clinton-Gore administration labeled its militarist policies as "humanitarian" efforts, while the post-9/11 Bush administration made no such claim. Contrasting the fear and loathing Bush inspired in Europe with the "mourning for Clinton" in European public opinion, Perry Anderson commented in 2002:

> Where the rhetoric of the Clinton regime spoke of the cause of international justice and the construction of a democratic peace, the Bush administration has hoisted the banner of the war on terrorism. These are not incompatible motifs, but the order of emphasis assigned to each has altered. The result is a sharp contrast of atmospherics. The war on terrorism orchestrated by Cheney and Rumsfeld is a far more strident, if also brittle, rallying cry than the cloying pieties of the Clinton–Albright years. The immediate political yield of each has also differed. The new and sharper line from Washington has gone down badly in Europe, where human-rights discourse was and is especially prized. Here the earlier line was clearly superior as a hegemonic idiom.[73]

As Anderson noted, the Clinton administration was diplomatically adept at cloaking its agenda of American domination in idealistic claptrap about the "international community." But it also spoke incessantly of the United States as the world's "indispensable nation." Its rhetoric may not have been as "unilateralist" as Bush's, but its actions set many of the precedents that Bush ended up flaunting. To force a settlement in Bosnia, the United States launched NATO air strikes on Bosnian Serb positions in 1995. In using NATO in this way, the United States openly flouted the UN Security Council, which had been the forum for U.S. and European Balkans policy up to that point. The United States simply asserted NATO's right to act as an arm of the UN Security Council. Four years later the United States junked even that pretext. Knowing it would face a Security Council veto from Russia and/or China, the United States didn't even bother to seek a UN sanction for the 1999 NATO war in Kosovo. Economically, the United States exercised its might as well. When the 1997 economic crisis spread through Asia, the United States strong-armed

Japan out of its offer to organize the bailout of major Southeast Asian countries. The United States insisted that only the IMF could organize the bailout. More than at any time in modern history, the United States used its influence in world organizations like the IMF and the World Bank to force free-market, U.S.-friendly policies on countries around the world.

Although George W. Bush would never credit his predecessor, his administration took full advantage of policies Clinton had enacted years earlier. Rumsfeld would not have been in the position to play "New Europe" against "Old Europe" had Clinton not pushed through NATO expansion in 1996 or pursued an aggressive policy in the Balkans. The U.S. military would not have been able to topple the Taliban in a few months using air strikes and local militias had the Clinton administration not already tested this strategy in Kosovo in 1999.[74] Bush would not have been poised to press free-trade pacts on Central and Latin American countries had Clinton not fought for NAFTA in 1993.

The Clinton administration also pursued policies that presaged the world-dominating strategy of the Bush Doctrine. The watchword of the 1997 *Quadrennial Defense Review* (*QDR*), the main statement of an administration's military policies, was "shaping the international security environment in ways that promote and protect U.S. national interests." In other words, using the military in "forward-leaning" ways to alter the political and economic configuration of the world to conform to U.S. interests. The *QDR* asserted that "preventing the emergence of a hostile regional coalition or hegemon" was a chief U.S. national security goal. And the Clinton administration did not shrink from even more expansive definitions of U.S. goals. The Pentagon under Clinton sponsored Joint Vision 2020, a task force promoting the idea that the United States should strive for "full-spectrum dominance" of all possible theaters of war, from the oceans to space. Clinton authorized the key weapon in this plan for global domination: the national missile defense system, a long-time goal of neoconservatives.[75]

Of all mainstream commentators, Andrew Bacevich was the most clear-sighted among those analyzing the continuity of Clinton and Bush policies. Writing a review of the national security strategy document that announced the Bush Doctrine, he explained:

> Throughout the Clinton era, U.S. military forces marched hither and yon, intervening in a wider variety of places, for a wider variety of purposes than at

any time in our history. More often than not, once the troops arrived, they stayed. As a result, by the time that Clinton left office in 2001, the defining fact of international politics—albeit one vigorously denied by the outgoing administration—had become not openness and not globalization but the emergence of a Pax Americana.

The Bush administration didn't share the Clinton administration's "ambivalence" about using military force, he wrote. It wanted to lead with its mailed fist. Nevertheless,

> the Bush administration's grand strategy reeks of hubris. Yet one may also detect in its saber-rattling occasional notes of desperation. America today is, by any measure, the most powerful nation on earth, enjoying a level of mastery that may exceed that of any great power or any previous empire in all of history. Yet to judge by this extraordinary document, we cannot rest easy, we cannot guarantee our freedom or our prosperity until we have solved every problem everywhere, relying chiefly on armed force to do so. In the end, we have little real choice—as the similarities between this new strategy and the Clinton strategy that Republicans once denounced with such gusto attest. In truth, whatever their party affiliation or ideological disposition, members of the so-called foreign policy elite cannot conceive of an alternative to "global leadership"—the preferred euphemism for global empire.[76]

The Neocons' Democratic Origins

In the years following the 9/11 attacks, it became fashionable in liberal circles to assert that a small "cabal" of Republican neoconservatives had hijacked an otherwise sound bipartisan American foreign policy.[77] Yet a brief account of the origins of these neoconservatives shows that they—and their project—did not emerge from the netherworld. In fact, a large number of the neocons emerged from a wing of the Democratic Party. Their story begins in the late 1960s in the battle inside the foreign policy establishment over the fate of the Vietnam War. After the 1968 Tet Offensive made clear that the war was unwinnable, not only public opinion but also leading business executives and sectors of the military and intelligence establishments turned against it. This growing "antiwar camp" concealed differences between those who opposed the war in principle and those who thought cutting its losses in Vietnam would help the United States to advance its business and political interests elsewhere. In 1972 Democratic presidential candidate George McGovern, backed by a segment of business executives including cosmetics boss Max Factor III and the CEOs of Xerox and

Continental Grain, pursued a conscious strategy of "co-opting the left" by recruiting antiwar activists into his campaign.[78]

The bulk of U.S. business wasn't willing to follow the McGovern backers. Neither were powerful forces inside the Democratic Party that had become accustomed to playing their assigned roles in the setup of Cold War liberalism. The State Department had long corrupted the AFL-CIO, funneling millions in government money to a cadre of trade union activists (many of them ex-leftists) who used it to build anti-communist unions and parties throughout the Third World.[79] Because of its strong identification with Cold War anticommunists, the mainstream labor movement refused to back McGovern. Cold War liberal politicians, who combined liberal positions on social welfare issues with strong support for Cold War military spending, formed another piece of the Democratic establishment that rebelled against McGovern. The most prominent among these was U.S. senator Henry "Scoop" Jackson of Washington, who mounted presidential runs in 1972 and 1976 based on his "strong on defense" positions. Having abandoned McGovern, these sections of the Democratic establishment contributed to his landslide defeat in 1972—a defeat that solidified the image of the Democrats as being "soft on defense."

All this history is important for understanding the peculiar character of the foreign policy architects of the George W. Bush administration. Nearly all the leading figures among twenty-first century neocons emerged from the "Scoop" Jackson wing of the Democratic Party. They found a home in the Reaganite Republican Party that made a huge military buildup against the USSR and Third World "communism" central to its project in the 1980s.

Richard Perle, a member of the Bush-appointed Defense Policy Board who was the leading advocate of the 2003 Iraq War, began his Washington career on "Scoop" Jackson's staff. The *Weekly Standard*'s Bill Kristol, co-author of *The War Over Iraq: Saddam's Tyranny and America's Mission*, is the son of Irving Kristol, one-time Trotskyist and editor of the once-liberal *Commentary*, and Gertrude Himmelfarb, another former liberal turned "virtuecrat." Defense Policy Board member R. James Woolsey III, a Washington lawyer who served in the Carter administration and spent two years as Bill Clinton's first CIA director, was a fanatical supporter of a theory that Iraq was behind the 9/11 attacks. Former Iran-Contra criminal Elliott Abrams, the Bush administration's director of Middle East policy, is a former staffer for Jackson and a former member of Social Democrats USA,[80] the organization that supplied much of the cadre for the anticommunist trade-union activities in the Third World. Paul Wolfowitz received his introduction to Washington as a graduate assistant to defense intellectual (and former Trotskyist) Albert Wohlstetter, who served as an adviser to Jackson.[81] The neocon hawks first roosted in the Committee for the Present Danger (CPD), a Washington lobby formed in the 1970s to urge an end to U.S. détente with the Soviet Union in favor of a huge increase in military spending. CPD founders Paul Nitze and Eugene V. Rostow were both Democrats who supported Reagan in 1980. Nitze, who later joined the Reagan administration, was hardly a fringe player. He was the chief author of NSC 68, the 1950 blueprint for U.S. Cold War policy produced for the Democratic Truman administration.

Another letterhead organization emerging from the "Scoop" Jackson wing of the Democratic Party, the Coalition for a Democratic Majority (CDM), included among its members major figures in the Clinton-Gore administration: Les Aspin, Clinton's first defense secretary; Woolsey; former New Mexico governor Bill Richardson, Clinton's energy secretary and UN ambassador; Henry Cisneros, Clinton's housing secretary, and Lloyd Bentsen, Clinton's first treasury secretary. The CDM joined these Clintonites with such Reaganites as former UN ambassador Jeane Kirkpatrick and Contra promoter Penn Kemble.[82] The neocons found kindred spirits in longtime Republican hawks like vice president Dick Cheney and defense secretary Donald Rumsfeld. These labyrinthine, bipartisan interconnections indicate that there is nothing inherently "Republican" about the neoconservatives, who many argued had hijacked U.S. foreign policy after 2001. Building and expanding the U.S. empire is and has been a bipartisan project, with its ideological warriors accepted in both major parties.

The Iraq War: Neoconservatism's Waterloo?

For a short period of time—roughly between September 11, 2001, and May 1, 2003 (the day Bush declared "Mission Accomplished" in Iraq from the deck of the USS *Lincoln*)—the neocons and the Bush administration appeared to have won the day. But quickly thereafter the war turned sour, as a resistance movement the administration hadn't anticipated began launching attacks on U.S. forces.

The Iraq debacle divided the U.S. ruling class over the strategy to move forward. On one side were those who wanted to join with Bush to push on to "victory" in Iraq. On the other were those who believed that salvaging the United States' reputation or preventing a breakdown in the military required a change of course in Iraq. To be sure, these divisions were already appearing during the 2004 election campaign, when a slim majority of U.S. newspapers endorsed John Kerry and establishment organs like *Foreign Affairs* published critiques of the neocons' Iraq strategy.[83]

But in 2005 and 2006, as the situation in Iraq steadily worsened, both public and elite opinion turned against the U.S. adventure. Leakers inside the Pentagon and intelligence agencies determined to undermine the administration's "stay the course" rhetoric in Iraq found willing accomplices in a national media that had only recently served as a Bush administration palace guard. A turning point came in November 2005 when Representative John Murtha (D-PA), a member of Congress with close ties to the Pentagon, called for "redeployment" of U.S. forces from Iraq. The United States "cannot accomplish anything further in Iraq militarily," Murtha said. "It is time to bring them home."[84]

Over the next year, as the news from Iraq became more dire, more establishment figures called for a change of course. A Bush-appointed committee of "wise men," led by former secretary of state James Baker and former Representative Lee Hamilton, convened to devise a strategy to disengage from Iraq while preserving U.S. influence in the Middle East. Judging from 2006 donations, sections of big business and the rich appeared to conclude that a Democratic-led Congress was the only way to force a change on the Bush administration. Whether campaign donors were trying to push the GOP out or simply to assure themselves a "seat at the table" in a Democratic Congress, they were quite generous to the Democrats in 2006.[85] With so many forces lining up to force a change in Washington, the only real question before Election Day was whether the Democrats would win both the House and the Senate.

But were the Democrats prepared to deliver on a clear mandate to wind down the war? Within a few months in office they were already tamping down public expectations, for several reasons. First, although Democrats and much of the American establishment rejected the

Bush administration's head-in-the-sand, "stay the course" approach in Iraq, they were no more committed to pulling up stakes in Iraq than Bush. Democrats campaigned against Bush's bungling of the war, not against the war itself. They looked to Baker and Hamilton's Iraq Study Group to provide them with a strategy to change course in Iraq *in order to salvage U.S. credibility and influence in the Middle East.*

If Democrats were dedicated to doing what their most committed supporters wanted them to do—that is, to ending the war in Iraq—they could have used their newfound power over financing the war to force Bush's hand. However, through their first year in the congressional majority, they repeatedly refused to use their "power of the purse" to force a change in Iraq. The Democratic leadership faced a Waterloo of its own in May 2007, when it caved into Bush's threats and voted for more than $120 billion in "supplemental" funding for the wars in Iraq and Afghanistan. The Democrats even agreed to spend more money than Bush had requested. As a "responsible" party that expected to win the White House and to inherit the wars in Iraq and Afghanistan after the 2008 presidential election, they were already trying to position themselves. One indication of the shift in Democrats' thinking was the decision by all the leading 2008 presidential contenders, including eventual nominee Senator Barack Obama, to refuse to pledge to pull all troops out of Iraq during their first presidential term (through 2013!).

Plus ça Change . . . Más de lo Mismo

George W. Bush departed the White House as one of the most despised political figures in the world. Barack Obama, on the other hand, rode a wave of worldwide goodwill that was evident even in the summer before his election as president, when hundreds of thousands of Germans greeted him like a rock star at a Berlin rally. The Nobel Foundation confirmed the hopes for a shift in U.S. foreign policy when it awarded Obama, barely eight months into his term, a Peace Prize "for his extraordinary efforts to strengthen international diplomacy and cooperation between peoples".[86] With the exception of the obvious fact that he was not George W. Bush, it was hard to see what Obama had accomplished to qualify him for a Peace Prize. Nevertheless, the American establishment had to have been pleased, because it realized that the

United States needed a makeover on the international stage. As the socialist and Middle East expert Gilbert Achcar put it, "The interests of American imperialism obviously find their ultimate guarantee in military supremacy, but a politico-ideological facelift is a necessary and useful complement. Under Bush, the arrogance and right-wing shift went so far that it seems imperative for the 'enlightened' fraction of the American establishment to steer 'to the left,' at least in words. This is where someone like Barack Obama can be useful."[87]

It soon became clear that the "change" Obama brought to foreign policy was one of style, rather than of substance. Obama signaled his commitment to continuity with the Bush administration early on when he reappointed Bush's defense secretary, Robert Gates. Later, Obama promoted General David Petraeus, architect of Bush's 2007–2008 "surge" strategy in Afghanistan, first to commander of the international force in Afghanistan, and later, in 2011, to Central Intelligence Agency director. And his choice of Hillary Clinton as secretary of state affirmed that the differences on the Iraq War they had aired during the 2008 Democratic presidential nominating campaign were forgotten.

The continuity of personnel underscored the continuity of goals and policies between the Bush administration and the Obama administration. The lack of any "progressive" content in Obama's foreign policy could be seen clearly in the administration's relations with Latin America, a region that had experienced a "pink tide" of reformist governments throughout the Bush years. Rather than embrace this demand for change in the Americas, Obama—like Bush before him—stood apart from it, when not trying to undermine it. When the Honduran military overthrew reformist Honduran president Manuel Zelaya in 2009, the Obama administration made noises about the coup being "illegal," but then did nothing to support Zelaya or to speak out on repression in the country. In the standard weasel words of diplomacy, it called for "a negotiated solution" and for "both sides" to agree. By failing to stand firmly against the coup, the Obama administration sided with the coup-makers. International negotiations ultimately secured the return of Zelaya in 2011, but in the meantime, the United States won international recognition for the coup regime and the demobilization of the grassroots resistance to the coup. If U.S. support for the Honduran military harkened back to the old days when the Pentagon trained repressive Central American militaries at the School of the Americas, Obama's economic policies built on the "free trade" agreements of his predecessors. In 2011, Obama couldn't muster congressional support for a jobs bill, but he had no trouble pushing through "free trade" agreements with Colombia, Panama, and South Korea.[88] Manuel Perez-Rocha drew this balance sheet of Obama's policy in Latin America: "In spite of catchy new phrases for cooperation and engagement with Latin America and rhetoric about the importance of equal partnerships with the countries in the region, Obama's trip to Latin America promised more of the same—*más de lo mismo*—for the countries of the region, which in the end tastes like the imperialism of the past."[89]

Obama's continuation of U.S. domination in Latin America was a minor concession to conventional wisdom compared to his embrace of the Bush administration's "War on Terror." In one of his first acts as president, Obama signed an executive order to close the prison in Guantánamo Bay, Cuba. At "Gitmo," hundreds of "War on Terror" prisoners had spent years held without charges or trials—violating international law and drawing condemnation from the U.S. Supreme Court. Yet within a few months of signing the executive order—in the face of opposition from members of Congress, including most members of his own party—Obama began to back away from his pledge to close the camp. By mid-2009, the Obama administration announced its position on many of Bush's most controversial "War on Terror" policies, accepting many of the Bush administration's policies—military tribunals to try detainees and indefinite detention on presidential fiat among them—as its own. Coupled with his double-speak on torture—that he repudiated the Bush policies as illegal, but would not actually prosecute anyone who executed them—Obama served to legitimize many of the practices that he had criticized as a candidate for president. By the one-year anniversary of the executive order, when the closure of Guantámamo Bay was supposed to be completed, it was clear that Obama's executive order was a dead letter. One could even ask if Obama ever had a real plan to close the prison in Cuba; at most he planned to move it to a prison in Illinois before Congress refused to fund the transfer. The administration gave up trying to find a way to shut the prison that had crystallized so much worldwide hatred of the Bush regime. In a separate executive order issued in March 2011, Obama codified the Bush policies of indefinite detention and military tribunals.[90]

The capitulation on Guantánamo put into relief the role in the conduct of U.S. foreign policy that the Obama administration adopted for itself. Rather than fundamentally changing course away from many of the Bush administration's most repressive policies, the Obama administration helped to sanitize them. This was completely predictable, because the power of the U.S. presidency is cumulative. Once one chief executive seizes power for himself, his predecessors will not give it up willingly. What liberals and Democrats considered to be heinous and extreme policies when Bush enacted them became, with Obama's help, part of the bipartisan consensus of American foreign policy.

During the 2008 election campaign, Obama consistently contrasted Bush's war in Iraq with the war in Afghanistan. The Iraq War, he often said, was the "wrong war at the wrong time" that diverted attention and resources from the real front in the fight against "terrorism": Afghanistan. Obama pledged to refocus U.S. policy and to reinforce the war in Afghanistan. This was one campaign promise that Obama kept. In 2009, he announced the deployment of an additional thirty thousand troops to Afghanistan, bringing the total number of U.S. troops there to more than a hundred thousand by mid-2011, on the eve of the war's tenth anniversary. At the same time, Obama stepped up the use of unmanned aerial vehicles (i.e., drones) to attack supposed "militant" targets in Afghanistan and in Pakistan. These moves escalated the war in Central Asia beyond even the Bush administration's limits. In his first twenty-one months in office, Obama had already authorized 120 drone attacks on Islamist targets in Pakistan—an ostensible ally in the Afghan war. This amounted to twice as many attacks as Bush authorized *in eight years.*

In fact, Obama expanded this use of remote-control warfare from Afghanistan and Pakistan to Yemen, where, in 2011, a drone carried out Obama's order to assassinate American-born Islamist cleric Anwar al-Awlaki. As constititutional lawyer and commentator Glenn Greenwald pointed out, not even Bush had ventured to assert the U.S. president's right to order the extrajudicial killing of an American citizen without any semblance of due process.[91] Obama had proven to be a more ruthless, and in some senses, more extreme conservator of his predecessor's legacy, as two writers for the German newspaper *Der Spiegel* noted:

> Today, Obama's CIA no longer carries out kidnappings—it carries out killings. This means that the CIA can assume a military role and wage a war

unconstrained by international law or the laws of war. It is waging that war in Afghanistan, but also in Pakistan and Yemen, where officially there is no war.

The advantage of the CIA's new approach is simple. Prisoners have to be released at some point, or at least put on trial. Prisoners mean the possibility of facing investigations or having to address journalists' questions. Killing is easier.

Obama's CIA decides who lives and who dies.[92]

As with all American presidents in the post–Second World War era, Obama's overall policy goals hinged heavily on the United States' relationship with the Middle East, the most strategically important region of the world. Having inherited an unpopular, disastrous, and costly (at more than a trillion dollars) war of choice in Iraq, Obama was expected to encourage a less belligerent posture than Bush. Obama won praise from across the political spectrum for his widely touted June 2009 speech in Cairo, Egypt, designed to signal a "new beginning" in relations between the United States and the Islamic world. But Obama's rhetorical nods toward dialogue, democracy and openness carried little change in U.S. policy toward the region.[93]

One indication of this was the Obama administration's continued devotion to supporting the most rejectionist policies of its main ally in the region, Israel. Unlike Bush and Cheney, Obama and Biden criticized Israel's policy of continued settlement in the West Bank and East Jerusalem. But like Bush and Cheney, Obama and Biden did nothing about it. On multiple occasions when Israel's actions brought worldwide condemnation, the Obama administration stood alone in Israel's defense. In 2010, when Israeli commandoes attacked a flotilla bringing humanitarian aid to Gaza, killing nine unarmed civilians, the Obama administration worked overtime to water down the United Nations' condemnation of the raid.[94] When the Palestinian Authority petitioned to the United Nations to be recognized as the government of an independent state in 2011, the United States and Israel, virtually alone, led the opposition to it.

Perhaps even more indicative of the Obama administration's commitment to the status quo in the Middle East was its reaction to popular movements for democracy in the region. In 2011, when movements for democracy erupted across the Middle East and North Africa, the administration stayed loyal to U.S.-allied dictators like Egyptian president Hosni Mubarak almost to the bitter end. Meanwhile, it supported Saudi Arabia's invasion of Bahrain to suppress a popular movement for democracy there. It subsequently dispatched Secretary of State Clinton to Bahrain, the headquarters of the U.S. Fifth Fleet, to offer an increase in arms sales to the kingdom.[95]

Nevertheless, the Obama administration's most audacious action during the Arab Spring was to support (and bankroll) a UN-sanctioned NATO intervention in the civil war in Libya. In so doing, Obama rehabilitated the concept of "humanitarian intervention," last embraced during Clinton's 1999 Kosovo adventure. Despite their rhetorical differences, the "liberal interventionists" in Obama's administration behaved almost identically to the discredited neoconservatives of the Bush regime, foreign policy expert Stephen M. Walt argued. "So if you're baffled by how Mr. 'Change You Can Believe In' morphed into Mr. 'More of the Same,' you shouldn't really be surprised. . . . Most of the US foreign policy establishment has become addicted to empire, it seems, and it doesn't really matter which party happens to be occupying Pennsylvania Avenue."[96] NATO intervention tipped the balance in favor of rebels who overthrew the Libyan dictator (and one-time U.S. ally) Moammar Qaddafi. But at the moment of triumph, it was unclear whether the Libyan opposition would be able to forge a truly independent country, or if NATO intervention had made the new Libya safe for Western oil companies, popular aspirations be damned.[97]

As the U.S./Western intervention in North Africa reached its goal of toppling Qaddafi, Obama dispatched a hundred U.S. Special Forces to Uganda on the premise that they would help the Ugandan government to defeat the Lord's Resistance Army, a fanatical sect of a few hundred. But like the intervention in Libya, the intervention in Uganda was part of a longer campaign, accelerated under Obama, of militarizing U.S. foreign policy toward Africa with the aim of challenging China's increasing influence in the region.[98]

What became of the Iraq War, opposition to which was one of the main launching points for Obama's candidacy for president? In October 2011, Obama announced that all U.S. combat troops would be pulled out of Iraq. While this announcement appeared to fulfill liberals' hopes, it was also coupled with a clear sense that the U.S. was merely refocusing its efforts in the region. The withdrawal still left the world's largest U.S. embassy and tens of thousands of private mercenaries, who operated outside the boundaries of U.S. military law, in Iraq. Moreover, the

Obama administration executed what amounted to a redeployment of U.S. forces to reactionary Gulf monarchies like Kuwait and Saudi Arabia that stood out as bulwarks of the status quo against the Arab Spring. While redeployed, U.S. troops would be kept at the ready for any future military action in the region, including against the new U.S. bogeyman, Iran. The U.S. envisioned a stronger and more formal military alliance with the Gulf Cooperation Council, developing further the alliance that Republican presidents Ronald Reagan and George H. W. Bush had initiated. "We are kind of thinking of going back to the way it was before we had a big 'boots on the ground' presence," Major General Karl R. Horst, Central Command's chief of staff, said. "I think it is healthy. I think it is efficient. I think it is practical."[99] Ironically, Obama won election in repudiation of George W. Bush, only to reestablish the foreign policy of George H.W. Bush.

Chapter Seven

Can the Left Take Over the Democratic Party?

Since at least the time of the New Deal, when organized labor gained a solid institutional foothold in the Democratic Party, liberals and activists have proposed that popular forces or "the left" can democratically take over the Democratic Party. If the left could accomplish this, the argument goes, it could transform the Democrats into a vehicle for progressive social change. This is very much on the agenda of a present-day embodiment of this idea, the Progressive Democrats of America (PDA).

Formed in 2004, PDA proclaims its strategy of fighting for progressive causes inside the Democratic Party:

> Progressive Democrats of America was founded in 2004 to transform the Democratic Party and our country. We seek to build a party and government controlled by citizens, not corporate elites—with policies that serve the broad public interest, not just private interests. As a grassroots PAC operating inside the Democratic Party, and outside in movements for peace and justice, PDA played a key role in the stunning electoral victory of November 2006. Our inside/outside strategy is guided by the belief that a lasting majority will require a revitalized Democratic Party built on firm progressive principles.
>
> For over two decades, the party declined as its leadership listened more to the voices of Wall Street than those of Main Street. PDA strives to rebuild the Democratic Party from the bottom up—from every Congressional District to statewide party structures to the corridors of power in Washington, where we work arm in arm with the Congressional Progressive Caucus. In just a couple

of years, PDA and its allies have shaken up the political status quo—on issues from the Iraq War to voter rights to economic justice.[1]

There is a certain logic to this argument. In most places, the Democratic Party—at least as an activist organization—is a shell. The notion that a dedicated group of activists could reclaim the "party of the people" for the people seems to be attainable.[2] And with a social force of millions behind them, as with the labor or civil rights movement, the idea that activists could shift the Democrats to the left—or even take over the party—would appear to be within reach.

In fact, decades before the PDA was formed, at a time when the influence of the labor movement and the liberal coalition was at its height, an influential group of Socialist Party members developed a similar perspective.[3] These socialists, who held influence in leading labor unions, civil rights organizations, and in cultural and literary circles, concluded, in the words of one of their leading spokespeople, Michael Harrington, that

> American socialism must concentrate its efforts on the battle for political realignment, for the creation of a real second party that will unite labor, liberals, Negroes, and provide them with an instrument for principled debate and effective action. Such a party as the Democratic Party will be when the Southern racists and certain other corruptive elements have been forced out of it. Political realignment is a precondition for the resurgence of a meaningful Socialist politics in America; it is also a precondition for meaningful and progressive social welfare, labor, and civil rights legislation.[4]

Harrington wrote these words in 1960, when the civil rights movement was activating millions and pushing the political climate to the left. At the same time, the Democrats under John F. Kennedy were preparing to take control of the White House and the national agenda. Harrington himself later published a best-selling exposé on American poverty, *The Other America*, which won him a hearing in the "War on Poverty" programs that the Kennedy/Johnson administrations developed and enacted. Indeed, one measure of how far the current parameters of politics have shifted in a conservative direction is the difference between Harrington's end goal ("American socialism") and that of the present-day PDA (of "working *inside* the Democratic Party to return it to its roots as the party that represents the workers and the less fortunate").[5] Even Harrington's present-day heirs in the Democratic Socialists of America don't officially embrace the "realignment" thesis of the 1950s and 1960s, but they still remain committed to working within the Democratic Party to push it to the left.[6] Yet the question to be posed to activists in the DSA and PDA remains: Can the left or popular forces take over and transform the Democratic Party? To answer this question, we will consider the PDA's recent record and then take a look at a far more substantial attempt to mount an internal challenge to the Democrats, the Reverend Jesse Jackson's Rainbow Coalition campaigns of the 1980s.

PDA and the "Inside-Outside" Strategy

The Progressive Democrats of America described itself as "a large group of progressive grassroots activists from across the country who want to support other progressive grassroots activists locally." It self-consciously styled itself as a grassroots organization that wanted to reclaim the Democrats from the clutches of the right-wing DLCers. While the denizens of the DLC insisted the Democrats must move further to the right, appease anti-abortion zealots, and demonstrate their own zeal in fighting "terrorism," the PDA wanted to challenge the Democrats to champion working people, national health care, and an exit from Iraq.

The PDA traced its roots to the 2004 presidential campaign of liberal Democratic representative Dennis Kucinich and, to a lesser extent, to the failed campaigns of former Vermont governor Howard Dean and Reverend Al Sharpton. As PDA founder Kevin Spidel told liberal journalist William Rivers Pitt, PDA was a fusion between Progressive Vote, activists in the Kucinich campaign, and more liberal politicians and congressional aides:

> Progressive Vote was an organization that I and my wife, Michele White, created basically on the phone and in the living room of our house. We combined the skill sets of folks from the Kucinich campaign—Web and technical experts, accounting, etc.—to build the organization and infrastructure of Progressive Vote. We created an organization where the grassroots were our advisory council. They drove our initiatives. It was truly reflective and reactive to the grassroots. We took our lead from them, provided for their needs, and facilitated their movement to establish these caucuses, to see that those caucuses were recognized within the Democratic Party.
>
> Early on, when I pitched the idea of Progressive Vote to Tim Carpenter, who was Deputy Campaign Manager for Kucinich, we intended this whole idea to be one organization we would work on together. Because I left [the] campaign

sooner than Carpenter, and needed an organizational structure to carry this idea forward, Progressive Vote came into being. Carpenter and his allies on Capitol Hill, the relationships he has fostered for 30 years—Rainbow PUSH, the Congressional Black Caucus, leaders like Rep. Conyers and Barbara Lee, people like Tom Hayden—those are contacts Carpenter came to the table with. We needed to be progressive "Democrats" to provide cover to strong progressive Democratic allies. At [the] same time, we wanted Progressive Vote's inside-outside strategy to be representative of the entire progressive community.

The structure of Progressive Vote—caucus-oriented and driven by the grassroots—needed to remain intact. We basically brought Progressive Vote into Progressive Democrats of America, and Progressive Democrats of America became a new name. Political allies in Congress, people like Reverend Jackson and Tom Hayden is what PDA brought to the table. PDA is actually Progressive Vote with a new name and more political allies. That merger and the launch of PDA took place in Roxbury, Massachusetts, at the Progressive Democratic convention, which took place during the Democratic National Convention last summer.[7]

This long, albeit partisan, account of the PDA's formation should establish two main points that are worth keeping in mind when considering PDA's project. First, despite all its talk about being "grassroots," it was still the creation of political operatives connected to the Democratic Party. Even more to the point, one of the speakers at the PDA founding conference in Boston was John Norris, national field director of the Kerry-Edwards campaign. "Warmly if not enthusiastically received by a crowd toting a bobbing sea of the same anti–war in Iraq and single-payer health care signs [that the Kerry-Edwards campaign] had banned from the floor of the Fleet Center [i.e., the Democratic Convention], Norris encouraged those assembled to commit to working with the Kerry effort to oust Bush—and promising that this time a grassroots infrastructure would be left behind," reported a pro-PDA account of the meeting.[8]

Second, the PDA's strategy was not a new one. It was the latest in a series of vehicles, including Tom Hayden's Campaign for Democracy in California and Jesse Jackson's Rainbow Coalition in the 1980s, to attempt an "inside/outside" strategy to shift the Democrats in a more liberal direction. The "outside" aspect comes in two parts: first, a willingness to combine traditional lobbying with more public forms of pressure like press conferences, rallies, and teach-ins; second, and more importantly, a desire to bring into its "big tent" members of the Green Party and other projects aimed at building an alternative on the left to the Democrats. That's why Code Pink leader and Green Party member Medea Benjamin; Nader's 2000 vice-presidential running mate, Winona LaDuke; and David Cobb, the Green Party's 2004 candidate for president, were featured prominently at PDA events.

Throwing a Lifeline to the Democrats

By 2005, PDA claimed dozens of chapters and thousands of members in thirty-six states. Since its founding it had taken up one campaign after another. In the immediate period between its founding conference and the November 2004 election, the PDA network worked to get out the vote for Kerry and other Democratic candidates. A crucial part of this effort was aimed at ensuring that the most left-reaching section of the Democratic electorate wouldn't stray into the independent presidential campaign of Ralph Nader and running mate Peter Camejo. In the immediate aftermath of the election, PDA worked with the Reverend Jesse Jackson and David Cobb to protest election irregularities in Ohio. The November election and the Ohio battle formed the backdrop of PDA's second national meeting, held on inauguration weekend in January 2005. PDA also worked for liberal and antiwar Democrats in the 2006 congressional elections.

Measured by the standard tallies of electoral politics—monies raised, elections won, voters registered—the PDA's record was modest. Yet its most important role lay elsewhere: that is, its creation of a political space to pull activists who might otherwise be drawn to building a left-wing political alternative to the Democratic Party back into the Democratic "big tent." What's more, the existence of PDA (and other organizations that share its politics, like the Independent Progressive Politics Network) helped lend credence to the idea that activists can win issues like national health care or an end to the war in Iraq by working within the Democratic Party. Admittedly, it did this in a more activist-friendly way than organizations like the liberal Campaign for America's Future, whose starting point is a rejection of activity outside the Democratic Party. PDA leaders said the organization would in certain circumstances support Greens, socialists, or other third-party candidates. But this was window-dressing at best.[9] One of the political analyses underpinning PDA was the assessment that the votes of almost three million people for Ralph Nader in 2000, rather than representing a positive declaration of independence from the two corporate parties, represented a disastrous split among progressives that allowed Bush to steal the White House. The official press release announcing PDA's founding included this quote from Lu Bauer, a Maine Democratic Party leader:

> While there are some efforts to win those voters back, they have not emerged from within the anti-war, progressive camp. This time around, it will take former Nader voters to win over real progressives and help defeat Bush. Kerry can't do it, because his position on the war remains out of sync with most progressive voters, let alone with early and strong opponents of the invasion of Iraq.[10]

This helped to explain the prominence of leading Greens at PDA events throughout the 2004 election season. David Cobb, whose campaign was largely invisible through the 2004 election, thrust himself into the center of the controversy in Ohio. Medea Benjamin, the Green Party's candidate for U.S. Senate in California in 2000 and a leading advocate for Cobb in 2004, made fundraising appeals for PDA. Clearly there was a symbiotic relationship between the organizers of PDA, who wanted to pull Green-leaning activists and voters into the Democratic Party, and the "fusion" current in the Green Party that believes the party should be little more than a pressure group on the Democrats. Benjamin tried to have it both ways. After Kerry went down in flames, she wrote in the *Nation* that:

> Many of us in the Green Party made a tremendous compromise by campaigning in swing states for such a miserable standard-bearer for the progressive movement as John Kerry. Well, I've had it. As George Bush says, "Fool me once, shame on you. Fool me—you can't get fooled again."
>
> For those of you willing to keep wading in the muddy waters of the Democratic Party, all power to you. I plan to work with the Greens to get more Green candidates elected to local office.[11]

But by March 2005, Benjamin had put her wading boots back on, issuing a fundraising appeal for PDA urging support for the PDA's effort to "take over and transform the Democratic Party." She squared this circle by claiming that PDA is not really the Democratic Party. But as Peter Camejo, a Green who dedicated his life to building an alternative to the Democrats, responded:

> In the fund appeal for the PDA she says the PDA is not the Democratic Party. It is like saying the Panama Canal is not Panama. I'd have to say it's still in Panama. The Progressive DEMOCRATS of America are not the Democratic Party but they're in the Democratic Party. In fact they are the front line fight-

ing to prevent an independent force from developing against the two parties and clearly in competition with the Green Party. Part of their goal is to co-opt the Green Party back into the Democratic Party.[12]

Camejo was completely correct—not only about Benjamin's double-talk, but also about PDA's intentions. As PDA founder Kevin Spidel told William Rivers Pitt:

> The most important thing we do is that inside-outside strategy: Pulling together members of the Green Party, the Independent Progressive Politics Network, the hip-hop community, the civil rights community, our allies in Congress, the anti-war community. We are bringing together all the social movements within the Democratic Party under one effective tent, and we will do it better if people can contribute to our cause.[13]

None of PDA's leading "election reformers" denounced the Democrat-funded campaign to force Nader-Camejo off 2004 ballots. Nor did PDA invite Nader or Camejo to speak at any of its events—despite the fact that they received five times as many votes as Cobb did in the 2004 election.

Getting Lost under the "Big Tent"

The PDA's "big tent" perspective sounded like a more "realistic" and achievable objective for the left than building a party completely independent of the corporate Democrats. But one only has to look at the experience of the 2004 election, when almost the entire left crowded under the Democrats' tent, to see how wrong this logic was. Was George W. Bush with his conservative agenda destined to win the 2004 election in the face of an unpopular war, huge job losses, and pessimism about the direction of the country? To many progressives the answer was "yes," because they believed that the United States is an irredeemably conservative country. But did the 2004 elections give working people the opportunity to vote against the occupation of Iraq, for national health care, or against attacks on civil rights? The pro-war, pro-business, anti–civil liberties Kerry-Edwards ticket didn't.

The Nader-Camejo independent presidential campaign did offer left-wing alternatives on all the key issues. But it was marginalized from the outset by an "anybody but Bush" drumbeat promoted by many leading progressive intellectuals and activists, including many of the current leaders and allies of PDA. The result of these political choices in 2004 was a disaster: the complete marginalization of any progressive ideas, the suspension of antiwar organizing for the better part of a year, and a possibly fatal blow to the Green Party as an independent force—all in the service of a strategy that failed on its own terms (i.e., electing Kerry). When elections roll around, Democratic politicians operate on the assumption that the left "has nowhere else to go." So they spend much of their time courting the "center" of ostensible "swing voters" unable to decide between voting Democrat or Republican, as the party continues moving to the right. As long as the left doesn't build an alternative, the Democrats will continue to take it for granted, just as it takes the Democratic "base" (women, Blacks, labor, and so on) for granted. As long as progressives' threat to leave the Democratic Party is empty, they will always be forced to back "lesser evil" Democratic candidates. One has to look back no further than 2004 to the failed presidential campaign of Dennis Kucinich to see how this process works.

Kucinich remained in the race long after Kerry had locked up the nomination. He pledged to bring his delegates to the Democratic convention to fight for progressive issues like ending the war in Iraq and for single-payer health care. Instead, the Kerry-controlled Democratic platform and convention committees compelled the Kucinich forces to recant their positions. The Kerry forces could have simply outvoted the Kucinich forces. Instead, they demanded unconditional surrender, and Kucinich gave it to them. "Unless we have a firm and unshakeable resolve for John Kerry, we will have no opportunity to take America in a new direction," Kucinich said in urging his supporters to back Kerry.[14]

Yet Kucinich made it quite clear that he had no intention of leaving the Democratic Party over any of the principles that had defined his own presidential campaign. At one point during the campaign he said, "The Democratic Party created third parties by running to the middle. What I'm trying to do is to go back to the big tent so that everyone who felt alienated could come back through my candidacy."[15] And so Kucinich endorsed and campaigned for—and urged his supporters to support and campaign for—Kerry, a candidate who ran "to the middle." Kucinich campaigned against the USA PATRIOT Act, yet he urged his supporters to work to elect a man who voted for it. He acted likewise on a host of other issues, from the No Child Left Behind Act to the war in Iraq. Kucinich told his supporters that the only responsible thing they could do in November 2004 was to elect a man who stood closer to Bush on these issues than he did to progressives. The Kucinich candidacy vividly illustrates the ultimate tragedy of reducing elections to party loyalty to the lesser evil.

The Democrats therefore feel no pressure to support progressive policies. But the situation worsens when the left performs somersaults to justify its subservience to the Democrats. For instance, during John Kerry's challenge to George W. Bush in 2004, Bush dared Kerry: "My opponent hasn't answered the question of whether, knowing what we know now, he would have supported going into Iraq." Despite the fact that millions of Americans had already concluded that Bush had sold the war based on a false threat from Iraq's nonexistent "weapons of mass destruction," Kerry responded: "Yes, I would have voted for the authority. I believe it was the right authority for a president to have."[16] With those few words, Kerry outraged millions of people who opposed the war—and threw away his best argument for dumping Bush. If there ever was a better argument for the necessity of a party independent of the twin parties of capitalism and war, Kerry's statement made it. But PDA board member Joe Libertelli, acknowledging that Kerry's "curious" statement had "infuriate[d]" progressives and opponents of the war, nevertheless called for progressives to stick with Kerry:

> But the truth is, merely demanding that John Kerry change his position will get us almost nowhere. Progressives have been making similar demands for years. And threatening to support Ralph Nader or the Greens will only alienate those who, at our founding conference, Rep. John Conyers (D-MI) called "future progressives." That's worse than going nowhere, that's going backward—at least if we harbor any hope of ever reaching a truly progressive voting majority in this country.[17]

Libertelli's statement went on to argue that Kerry's statement reflected not merely Kerry's opinion but the Democratic Party's wholesale commitment to militarism and "imperialism." This is certainly true, but it hardly helped make a convincing case for shifting the party leftward. Nevertheless, Libertelli continued, that was why progressives must change the Democratic Party from within: "Think of the PDA as a stem cell injection!"[18]

Progressives got their chance in 2006 and 2008, when two "wave" elections, driven on opposition to the Iraq War and to the Bush administration generally, installed the largest Democratic majorities in Congress in decades. Prominent progressive Democrats and PDA favorites—like Conyers—assumed powerful positions as committee and subcommittee chairs. But just as the Democrats attained the positions that presumably would have allowed them to make good on all of their progressive rhetoric, they seemed to forget all of their bold pronouncements. Conyers, who had promised to consider articles of impeachment against Bush and Cheney as chairman of the House Judiciary Committee, dropped his pledge under pressure from a Democratic leadership that wanted to "look forward, not back."

As Democrats in Congress marked the anniversary of their retaking of Congress in the 2006 midterm election, many wondered what the election really had changed. Throughout 2007 the Democrats proffered a series of proposals for "redeployment" of troops and "timetables for withdrawal" from Iraq. But none of them attained the veto-proof majorities they needed to force a change on Bush. So the Democratic leadership retreated. And in May 2007 the Democratic majority in both houses of Congress voted to hand Bush $120 billion in supplemental funds to continue the wars in Afghanistan and Iraq.

The May betrayal prompted antiwar activist Cindy Sheehan to resign from the Democratic Party and to issue a public letter explaining why. She wrote:

Dear Democratic Congress,

Hello, my name is Cindy Sheehan and my son Casey Sheehan was killed on April 04, 2004 in Sadr City, Baghdad, Iraq. He was killed when the Republicans still were in control of Congress. Naively, I set off on my tireless campaign calling on Congress to rescind George's authority to wage his war of terror while asking him "for what noble cause" did Casey and thousands of other have to die. Now, with Democrats in control of Congress, I have lost my optimistic naiveté and have become cynically pessimistic as I see you all caving into "Mr. 28%."

. . . The Camp Casey Peace Institute is calling all citizens who are as disgusted as we are with you all to join us in Philadelphia on July 4th to try and figure a way out of this "two" party system that is bought and paid for by the war machine which has a stranglehold on every aspect of our lives. As for myself, I am leaving the Democratic Party. You have completely failed those who put you in power to change the direction our country is heading. We did not elect you to help sink our ship of state but to guide it to safe harbor.

We do not condone our government's violent meddling in sovereign countries and we condemn the continued murderous occupation of Iraq.

We gave you a chance, you betrayed us."[19]

In the face of such criticism, leading Democratic politicians told their supporters to wait—again. In a meeting with frustrated antiwar activists, Representative Jim Moran (D-VA) put up this defense to the activists' criticism of the Democrats' caving on the war: "I know that, but in all fairness, until we get a Democratic president, until we get a president who is committed to ending the war."[20] Having disappointed supporters after the election of 2006, the Democrats were asking for another chance—this time in 2008.

Following the 2008 election, when Democrats controlled both the Congress and the White House, progressive Democrats again demonstrated their haplessness. As discussed in chapter 4, House Progressive Caucus members folded on their pledges to support a "public option" in a health care reform bill. And single-payer advocates Conyers and Kucinich played key roles in rounding up support for Obama's flawed corporate-giveaway health care reform. As always, progressive Democrats (the "inside" of the inside/outside strategy) are Democrats first, and progressives second. For example, elected Democrats made little protest when Obama announced his intention to cut entitlement programs during the 2011 debt ceiling negotiation. In fact, 173 members of the Democratic caucus, including every member of the Progressive Caucus, voted for the final deal that set up a congressional "supercommittee" tasked with slashing federal spending, including that for vital social programs. As Obama critic Glenn Greenwald noted:

> Therein lies one of the most enduring attributes of Obama's legacy: in many crucial areas, he has done more to subvert and weaken the left's political agenda than a GOP president could have dreamed of achieving. So potent, so overarching, are tribal loyalties in American politics that partisans will support, or at least tolerate, any and all policies their party's leader endorses—even if those policies are ones they long claimed to loathe.[21]

Liberal blogger Jane Hamsher was even more scathing in her denunciation of progressive "enablers," whose vote for the debt ceiling bill legitimized cuts to Medicare and Social Security:

> New leadership will not emerge until you make room for them by taking out the old, corrupt order. And that job starts with the enablers. The ones who will be rolling out any minute now to placate liberal outrage and whitewash the piece of shit they voted for . . . The ones who will wrap themselves in the flag and mewl that they "had to do it for the country."[22]

The question remains: Can progressives take over the Democratic Party, perhaps using a different strategy? To answer that, one has to consider that the Democratic Party really represents one of two parties of corporate rule in the United States. Despite its name, it is not a democratic organization whose members control it. So any activist or trade union or popular attempt to take it over always faces a counterattack by the people who really control it—big business interests, who will use every underhanded trick in the book to maintain their hold. They may tolerate the party's left tail, but only insofar as it helps sweep in more voters.

Consider how the DLC-dominated Democratic establishment torpedoed the 2004 candidacy of Howard Dean, who was hardly the progressive that the media made him out to be. When it appeared on the eve of the 2004 Iowa caucus that the "insurgent" Dean was running away with the Democratic race, DLC-connected financiers, organized by the sleazy ex-senator Robert Torricelli (D-NJ), mounted a vicious ad campaign against him. Among other things, the ads—taking a page out of the Bush playbook—used an image of Osama bin Laden to argue that Dean didn't have the experience to take on terrorists.[23] These ads played a major role in Dean's collapse in Iowa and New Hampshire.

If a few hundred thousand dollars could end an internal party challenge from someone who wasn't even a progressive, what would big business do if it faced a challenge from a popular movement supporting genuine reforms? In 1934 the radical novelist Upton Sinclair actually won the Democratic primary for the governorship in California on a progressive platform to "End Poverty in California" during the Depression decade. Sinclair proposed for the state to take over idle factories and farmland and to turn them over to cooperatives. He also proposed to levy a state income tax on corporations. Did the Democratic establishment, including President Franklin Roosevelt, show loyalty to the Democrats' democratically elected candidate? No. Democratic big business money shifted to the Republican candidate, formed a one-time third party to siphon votes away from Sinclair, and financed a red-baiting scare campaign. As a result the Democratic Party helped to guarantee the reelection of Republican Frank Merriam with only 48 percent of the vote, compared to the 37 percent that Sinclair received. And this took place at the height of the social upheaval that included the 1934 San Francisco general strike.[24]

The kinds of shenanigans that defeated Sinclair are the stock-in-trade of Democratic Party politicians when they are determined to prevent the expression of democracy inside the Democratic Party. At times this even extends to organizations outside the Democratic Party. In the late 1950s in Chicago, the South Side chapter of the National Association for the Advancement of Colored People (NAACP) elected as its president UAW official Willoughby Abner. Abner immediately became a thorn in the side of the Democratic machine of Mayor Richard J. Daley and the Black "submachine" run by Representative William Dawson.[25] Abner denounced Dawson for failing to speak out in the 1955 lynching death of Chicago teen Emmett Till.[26] A resurgent NAACP looked set to challenge Daley across the board on the city's record of school and housing segregation. While Dawson regularly dismissed Abner and the NAACP,

> privately, he was plotting political retribution. The Chicago [NAACP] chapter was scheduled to hold its election of officers on December 17, 1957. Precisely thirty days before the election, the submachine took out memberships for between four hundred and six hundred of its precinct captains and patronage workers. It was the last day that an applicant could join and be eligible to vote, which meant that when Abner and his supporters learned that the chapter's membership rolls had been flooded, it was too late to respond in kind. On the appointed night, the submachine's troops turned out in force. A parade of Dawson and Daley loyalists rose to denounce Abner. . . . In the end, the chapter's members voted to replace Abner with Theodore Jones, an executive with the Supreme Liberty Life Insurance Company who could be counted on to take a more moderate course. Dawson never denied that he played a role in ousting Abner and his fellow civil rights activists. "I'm not interested in controlling the NAACP or its policy making body," Dawson later told historian Dempsey Travis. "However, I do want to see the 'right man' as president."[27]

These cases are examples of strong-arm tactics that establishment Democrats use when they perceive a threat. Civil rights leader Jesse Jackson's 1980s attempt to mount a challenge to the party from within provides another example. Jackson's Rainbow Coalition campaigns for president in 1984 and 1988 excited millions of voters who were looking for some way to express opposition to Reaganism. Even strong left-wing critics of the Democratic Party agree that Jackson's campaigns represented "the last coherent left populist campaign in America mounted within the framework of the Democratic Party."[28] The fate of the Rainbow Coalition illustrates the way that the Democrats can also muffle opposition by co-opting it—as long as that "opposition" is willing to be co-opted.

Jesse Jackson and the Rainbow Coalition

Many sincere activists and antiracists looking for a way to respond to Reaganite retrenchment were drawn to the Reverend Jesse Jackson's 1984 and 1988 presidential campaigns as well as to other "insurgent" local campaigns, such as the one that elected Harold Washington as Chicago's first African-American mayor in 1983. Some on the left argued that the National Rainbow Coalition (NRC) posed a solution to the failure of the 1960s civil rights and Black Power movements to consolidate their gains because of "the separation of the social movements from electoral politics."[29] Others argued that the Rainbow Coalition assembled a "coalition of the rejected" that, if mobilized in the electoral arena, would push American politics to the left. Still others claimed that the Rainbow Coalition offered a way to reinvigorate the movements of the 1960s.

To many Rainbow supporters, the NRC's electoralism was secondary to its potential as a "political movement," a description in the NRC's founding document that appeared to reach beyond electoral politics. The Rainbow Coalition held the potential to mobilize thousands of the poor and oppressed for progressive ends, Rainbow supporters argued. Rainbow politicians' electoral ambitions were seen as secondary to the "mass movement," which would provide the push for real reform struggles. What's more, they argued, activists could use Jackson's rhetoric and his access to the media to build "grassroots" struggles, like the movement against apartheid in South Africa.

The 1984 Jackson campaign took about 21 percent of the votes in Democratic primaries as well as several key Southern states. Nevertheless, Democratic Party rules limited the number of Jackson's convention delegates so that Jackson could count on the support of only 11 percent of delegates. Thus, former vice president Walter Mondale exacted Jackson's endorsement. In the process Mondale dismissed all of the Rainbow Coalition's platform proposals, which included only two of seven proposals that comprised a minimum Black political agenda, according to two Jackson advisers.[30]

Nevertheless, some on the left, including organizations like the National Committee for Independent Political Action (NCIPA), viewed the Rainbow Coalition as offering a "mass base" of the oppressed that could form a possible third party. But a Rainbow Coalition break from the Democrats was a highly unlikely proposition, no matter how disdainfully the party treated Jackson and the NRC. As Jackson explained at the 1986 conference that transformed Jackson's campaign into an ongoing organization, "We have too much invested in the Democratic Party. When you have money in the bank you don't walk away from it."[31] In essence, the NRC's strategy was that of a liberal caucus in a Democratic Party moving rapidly rightward.

Jackson's defense of an electoral strategy within the confines of the Democratic Party was fully in character with his career. Jackson was never a radical. He stood, for example, on the right wing of the mainstream civil rights movement. As one of the Reverend Martin Luther King's lieutenants in the Southern Christian Leadership Conference, Jackson distinguished himself as an able fundraiser. Politically, however, he represented the SCLC's right wing that opposed King's emphasis in the 1968 Poor Peoples' Campaign on demanding social-democratic measures to address widespread poverty. Jackson supported a version of Black capitalism. Years later, Jackson summed up his differences with King in words that sound as if they could have come from a free-market Republican: "[King's] experience of the private sector was not substantial. He believed that the government was more likely to do what it had done before. But I believed we had to build a private-sector body of allies."[32]

At the same time Jackson acted to undercut the efforts of Black militants to build a political alternative independent of the capitalist parties. In 1972, when more than eight thousand Blacks from every part of the political spectrum gathered for the National Black Political Convention in Gary, Indiana, Jackson worked to sabotage militant leaders' attempts to create an all-Black radical party. The convention passed a Black Political Agenda that condemned both the American system and the Democratic and Republican parties for ignoring Black demands. Jackson repudiated the agenda, insisting to the conservative, heavily Democratic Michigan delegation that it was only a draft. Jackson accused delegates who opposed the convention leadership's electoralism of undermining Black "unity." Jackson later abandoned any pretense of supporting an independent Black initiative by joining up with Senator George McGovern's 1972 Democratic presidential campaign. Jackson backed Jimmy Carter in 1976. In 1980, after Carter had alienated Blacks with his conservative policies, Jackson said that Blacks "had the responsibility" to listen to appeals from both major parties, implying that Ronald Reagan could offer something positive to Black America.[33]

After giving the Democratic establishment a little discomfort in 1984, the Jackson campaign took a different tack in 1988. Jackson opened the race with much greater support. Rather than running an "insurgent" campaign, Jackson ran a deliberately mainstream race that rested on the support of the Black Democratic establishment. One writer's description of the 1988 February New Hampshire primary illustrated the difference: "In contrast to 1984, when elected officials and community leaders virtually ignored Jackson, the campaign boasts an impressive list of mainstream endorsements, including Chamber of Commerce officials, four state legislators . . . and the state president of the Association for the Elderly, among others."[34] Noting Jackson's appeal among their constituents, many Black Democratic politicians who had opposed Jackson in 1984—like Atlanta mayor Andrew Young and U.S. representative Mickey Leland (D-TX)—either backed Jackson or at least did not back any of his opponents.

In November 1987 Jackson appointed Black California Assembly Speaker Willie Brown, one of the most powerful politicians in California, to be chairman of his campaign. At the same time he named Gerald Austin, manager for winning campaigns of Governor Richard Celeste (D-OH), as his campaign manager. Brown said the Jackson campaign would not "appeal excessively to so-called Black concerns." Austin pledged to run a "centrist" campaign.[35] With experienced Democratic hands in charge of the campaign, it was more difficult than ever to distinguish Jackson's "movement" from any other mainstream Democratic campaign.

From the start Jackson opted to run a "respectable" campaign. His October 10, 1987, announcement speech resonated with patriotic, anti-drug themes. He fudged on key issues: instead of calling for an end to the 1987–88 U.S. Navy's reflagging and escort of oil tankers through the Persian Gulf, he called for a greater sense of purpose in the operation and for moral support to U.S. troops no matter their location.[36] Jackson made clear efforts to distance himself from other "extreme" positions. Only after the primaries ended in June 1988 did he mention the inequity of the Democratic presidential selection process, which had been the centerpiece of his campaign in 1984. In March 1988, in a bid for Zionist support, he said he would not meet with Palestine Liberation Organization chairman Yasser Arafat until the PLO recognized Israel and renounced "terrorism." This position represented an acceptance of the standard American foreign policy formulas for the Middle East.[37]

At the same time, Jackson kept an arm's distance from real fights against racism—attempting to avoid the appearance of running a "Black" campaign. Thus, when campaigning in the New York primary, he avoided commenting on a spate of police killings of Blacks and Latinos in New York City. For this reason, New York's leading Black newspaper at the time, the *City Sun*, refused to endorse him in the April primary.

After his victory in the 1988 Michigan primary, Jackson dropped references in his campaign speeches to his "poor campaign with a rich message." This was because his campaign began to attract support from rich donors and business. Figures released in April 1988 showed that the Jackson camp pulled in some two million dollars in March, only four hundred thousand dollars short of Democratic presidential nominee Governor Michael Dukakis's campaign contributions. Jackson received the backing of former Carter budget director Bert Lance and a virtual "Who's Who of prominent Black businessmen."[38] Another important Jackson adviser was Felix Rohatyn, the Lazard Frères investment banker who supervised massive budget cuts and union-busting in the mid-1970s New York City financial "bailout."

What Happened to the Rainbow?

Despite appearances to the contrary, the 1988 Jackson campaign was not a grassroots effort. If it had been, the NRC would have built independently of the Jackson presidential campaign. This was not the case, and the NRC withered as all its resources were plowed into the Jackson campaign. Activists who joined the Rainbow Coalition with the aim of building an "independent" Rainbow distinct from Jackson's campaign found their hopes dashed.

When all was said and done, the Democratic Party's candidate for 1988 was Massachusetts governor Michael Dukakis, a dull technocrat. Big victories in the June 1988 California and New Jersey primaries gave Dukakis more than the 2,081 delegates he needed for the Democratic nomination at the July convention in Atlanta. With more than six hundred "superdelegates," party officials and politicians chosen by party officials and politicians to assure selection of an "electable" candidate, committed to Dukakis, the Massachusetts governor wrapped up the Democratic nomination on the first ballot.

The choice of Texas senator Lloyd Bentsen as Dukakis's running mate confirmed the Democrats' acceptance of Reaganite policies. Bentsen had the distinction of being the most "pro-Reagan" Democrat in the 1981 Congress that passed Reagan's reactionary program, according to *Congressional Quarterly*. Bentsen, backed with millions in contributions from Texas big business, supported aid to the Contras, the death penalty, the B-1 bomber and the MX missile, mandatory school prayer, denial of public funds for abortion, and mandatory AIDS testing. It's little wonder that Bentsen's rating by the liberal lobbying group Americans for Democratic Action equaled the ratings of three Republican senators.[39]

Jackson's forces arrived at the Atlanta convention with much fanfare. But within days of the convention's opening, Jackson pledged his delegates' backing for the Dukakis-Bentsen ticket in exchange for representation of several of his advisers (including his son) on the Democratic National Committee and in the Dukakis campaign. Any hope that he would bring a progressive influence to the party platform was quashed for the sake of party "unity." Jackson agreed to withdraw or water down his delegation's progressive platform planks. For example, Jackson's initial call to double education spending was watered down to a call to "significantly increase" education spending. Dukakis accepted the symbolic labeling of South Africa as a terrorist state, a decision that two years after the Republican-dominated Senate had voted for sanctions against South Africa hardly represented a breakthrough for the left. Dukakis forces soundly defeated three other Jackson minority planks calling for increased taxes on the rich, for "no first use" of nuclear weapons, and for a vague form of Palestinian self-determination. Jackson's forces actually agreed to withdraw the proposal on

Palestinian self-determination rather than forcing the convention to take a "divisive" vote.[40]

There should never have been any doubt that Jackson would deliver his supporters to Dukakis in the end. That was the whole aim of the operation: Jackson traded his delegates for his own acceptance into the party's inner circle. A comment from one of Jackson's advisers summed it up: "We could come in to sack and ruin, particularly with the number of delegates we have. But we're not doing that. We've agreed to disagree [with Dukakis], but that in itself is a form of agreement."[41] In the spirit of party unity, Jackson's address to the convention endorsed the demands of party conservatives: "Conservatives and progressives, when you fight for what you believe, you are right—but your patch isn't big enough."[42]

But Rainbow supporters were faced with the prospect of voting for Dukakis, an uninspiring policy wonk who, facing attacks for his "liberalism" from the GOP attack machine, tried to claim "I am, in some respects, more conservative . . . than that crowd in the White House." He compared his record of slashing programs to balance the budget in Massachusetts with Reagan's multibillion-dollar deficit, asking, "Who's the conservative and who's the liberal?"[43]

Activists who had given so much energy to nominate Jesse Jackson then faced the choice of voting for the conservative ticket Jackson endorsed. Such was a stark illustration of the ultimate problem with the Rainbow Coalition strategy. From the start, the NRC only succeeded in binding activists to the big business interests that really control the Democratic Party. As such, the Rainbow Coalition was one more detour away from building a true alternative, independent of the capitalist parties.

Where Real Change Comes From

"We are the only 'advanced' country without a solid liberal-left bloc. It makes us bleed. Without a left, liberalism loses its spine," wrote 1960s activist-turned-Democratic-politician Tom Hayden in a fall 2004 letter on behalf of PDA.[44] There is some truth to what Hayden wrote, but he had the wrong aim. He backed PDA because he wanted to build the left-liberal bloc *inside* the Democratic Party. Unfortunately, that perspective sees social change upside down. Hayden seemed to have forgotten the lessons of the 1960s: that social movements in the streets, from the civil rights and Black Power movements to the anti-war, women's liberation, and gay liberation movements, forced the pace of change. The Democratic Party (and the Republican Party, for that matter) was then forced to confront these movements and their demands—and adapt leftward. But the crucial point is this: social movements set out to organize people on the ground to confront racism, the war, and sexual oppression. They did not set out with the intention of creating a caucus in the Democratic Party. The move of the left into electoralism attended the *decline* of the social movements in the 1970s and 1980s.

The inside-outside strategy, and the willingness of well-known activists to sign onto it, consciously attempts to blur the distinctions between movement-building and an orientation on the Democratic Party. The idea that there is no contradiction between the two seems obvious to most people. But one has to remember the concession captured well in Libertelli's letter exhorting the antiwar movement to get behind the pro-war Kerry. The antiwar movement virtually disappeared during 2004 as most of its leaders buried themselves in Kerry's election campaign. In short, when it counted, those claiming to be running a strategy to push the party leftward were in fact providing a left cover for a candidate who reflected the party's shift rightward. Could anyone say after the wreckage of the 2004 presidential election that the left or the antiwar movement was better off for it?

Partisans of the inside-outside strategy might reply that voting only takes a few minutes, and activists can spend the rest of their time building movements for social change. But if you're serious about believing that elections offer the hope of social change, then a "few minutes on Election Day" isn't enough. Each election year the leading unions spend millions to get out the vote for the Democratic candidate. Those millions could be spent, for example, organizing Walmart workers into unions—which would have far greater impact on advancing organized labor's agenda. So this strategy of working for the Democrats diverts resources away from the real fights that need to be waged outside the party. And what if movement goals contradict the Democrats' electoral strategies? Often, Democrats ask that public shows of support from more progressive groups be put on hold, so as not to antagonize conservative voters. The Democratic establishment regularly asked this of the civil rights movement in the 1960s. But when movements or the left accept this framework, it weakens them. They get used to lowering their sights and putting their issues on the back burner.

Mark Kamleiter, former co-chair of the Florida Green Party and supporter of building an independent Green challenge to the Democrats, asked:

> What if the "fundis" [i.e., those who advocate a Green Party independent of the Democrats] are actually very politically savvy? What if they have great clarity about the American bipolar corporate political system? What if they already have years of futile experience trying to work with and accommodate liberal Democrats? What if they are not "fundis," in the pejorative sense, but are, in fact, intelligent, rational, political individuals, who make political decisions based upon experience, maturity, and a clear sense of what must happen to effectively change American politics? What if they are absolutely and logically convinced that the Democratic Party, and its perpetually recycling liberal/progressive wing, must be challenged by a steadfast, firmly independent, value-based third party?
>
> What if the "realos" [those who advocate the PDA strategy inside the Green Party] are in reality not so politically clever? What if in the depths of their beings, they simply do not really believe that the Green Party can actually break open the bipolar corporate party system? What if they are, therefore, very content to ride on the present popular progressive movement, without fundamentally challenging the existing political power structures? What if they are so eager to be next to the "power" that they will compromise Green Party independence and the dream of Greens across the country?[45]

It's said that one definition of insanity is doing the same thing over and over and expecting a different result each time. If that's true, the partisans of such "realistic" strategies of fusing with the Democrats or of "taking over" the Democratic Party—both of which have failed generations of progressives—are really the ones who are out of touch with reality.

The many efforts at the inside-outside strategy, from the Rainbow Coalition to the PDA, have not pushed the Democratic Party in a liberal direction. All liberal intra-party challenges, from Jackson's to Kucinich's, ended with their leaders delivering their supporters over to the more conservative Democrats against whom they had mounted their challenges in the first place. Indeed, for politicians committed to Democrats like Jackson and Kucinich, this was the effective aim of their campaigns. Although they may at times flirt with the rhetoric of breaking with the Democrats, their clear commitment is to bring into, or back into, the Democratic orbit people who are disenchanted with the Democratic Party and have moved to the left. The real impact of these inside-outside challenges is, to paraphrase Jackson, to "keep hope alive" in the Democratic Party. These campaigns help to extinguish third-party movements. For those who want to build a genuine and credible left in the United States, there is no substitute for the slow and painstaking work of building movements on the ground, *and of building a political alternative to the Democrats.*

Chapter Eight

Why Is There No Alternative?

Each election day seems to confront Americans with a Hobson's choice of one pro-business party that pretends to represent the interests of working people (the Democrats) and another pro-business party that doesn't even bother to pretend (the Republicans). Facing the uninspiring choice in the 1996 presidential elections between Democrat Bill Clinton and Republican Bob Dole, *New York Times* columnist Russell Baker—hardly a radical—complained, "We can only conclude that a 'New Democrat' is just another Gingrich Republican, except of course for lacking the Republicans' philosophical consistency. . . . Except that [Clinton] makes a nicer speech than Dole, what difference is there between them?"[1] Is it any wonder, then, that the United States regularly leads among advanced Western countries in rates of voter abstention?

Both the Democrats and Republicans have worked hard to protect their corporate duopoly, which allows these two pro-business parties to share power between them. America's elites can thus rest assured that whichever party wins a given election, their interests will dictate government policy. A review of the last century of U.S. history finds many attempts to build alternatives to the left of the Democratic Party. Yet the U.S. ruling class has been unique in its ability to squash attempts to forge mass labor or social democratic parties such as those that exist in nearly every other advanced industrial society. Because Democratic and Republican parties collude to design the most arcane regulations for gaining ballot access, third parties face practically insurmountable obstacles just to get on the ballot. For a statewide candidate to get on the ballot in New York, for example, the candidate must collect fifteen thousand valid signatures, including one hundred signatures from each of half of the state's congressional districts. An individual voter's signature cannot count for more than one statewide candidate, and signatures can be invalidated if the voter reports his or her city or town incorrectly. Finally, all this must be done in a period of thirty-eight days. Rules like this prompted the Illinois Supreme Court, in a 1979 ruling involving the Socialist Workers Party's attempt to get on the ballot, to conclude that "by limiting the choices available to voters, the State impairs the voters' ability to express their political preferences."[2]

Despite these obstacles, third-party efforts have gained significant support at various points in history. In 1886 the Central Labor Union of New York formed an Independent Labor Party (ILP) and ran Henry George for mayor in a challenge to the corrupt Tammany Hall Democrats. George officially received sixty-eight thousand votes, one-third of the total—despite reports of widespread intimidation and fraud by local Democrats, including statements that "containers holding votes for Henry George were cast into the East River."[3]

Furthermore, the notion that U.S. workers have been too enamored with capitalism to support left-wing parties is not based in history. During the first two decades of the twentieth century, socialist candidates pulled hundreds of thousands of votes nationally and were elected as mayors, city council members, and state legislators across the country. In 1912 the Socialist Party's candidate for president, Eugene V. Debs, won 6 percent of the vote, and 1,200 SP members held elected office in 340 municipalities.[4]

The late 1930s was a period of great radicalization in the working class, as the militant factory occupations that built the CIO attested. It is estimated that by 1938 the Communist Party claimed eighty-two thousand members, while by 1937 its members led or held substantial influence in 40 percent of the CIO internationals.[5]

But the Democratic Party has been able to emerge unscathed after every attempt to forge a lasting break to its left. The Democrats have been able to absorb dissenting movements into its fold ever since the first challenge by the Populist movement in the 1890s. This was even the case during the mass working-class radicalization in the 1930s. Even as UAW delegates voted in 1936 to endorse the formation of a national farmer-labor party, the Communist Party acceded in that election to Roosevelt's and the union leaders' capture of the CIO for the Democratic Party—ensuring Roosevelt's landslide reelection rather than attempting to weld workers into a third-party force.[6]

This pattern unfortunately repeated itself in recent decades, following the emergence of the "New Left" in the 1960s.

The 1960s New Left and the Democrats

The 1950s anticommunist witch-hunts in the unions severed the link between socialist ideas and the working class that had flourished in the 1930s. But the 1960s civil rights movement, followed by the student movement and the emerging movement against the U.S. war in Vietnam, revived the left's fortunes. Throughout the 1960s and early 1970s, millions were swept into political activity. By the end of the 1960s thousands of radicals had joined new organizations of the revolutionary left. Despite this radicalization, the New Left's political weaknesses accounted for the fact that the upsurge produced no lasting third-party organizations of significant size or influence. On the contrary, many of the "generation of '68" campaign today for Democratic candidates, however conservative their platforms.

The New Left represented an amalgam of all sorts of political perspectives—liberal, anarchist, and revolutionary. Students for a Democratic Society (SDS), the main New Left organization, which claimed eighty thousand to one hundred thousand members by 1968, was founded as an offshoot of the liberal League for Industrial Democracy (LID) in 1960. SDS held initially to LID's liberal politics.[7] In 1964 this translated into support for the Democratic campaign of President Lyndon B. Johnson.

Johnson's opponent that year was reactionary Republican senator Barry Goldwater. Johnson campaigned as the "peace candidate" against "extremist" Goldwater. When Congress in August 1964 passed the Gulf of Tonkin Resolution, Johnson promised, "We seek no wider war." The resolution provided Johnson the blank check he sought to escalate the war. Johnson had actually prepared the resolution long before the Tonkin Gulf incident and had waited for an opportune time to use it.[8] Johnson signaled his intentions when in late 1963 he told a meeting of the Joint Chiefs of Staff: "Just let me get elected and then you can have your war."[9]

The threat of a Goldwater victory frightened SDS, which adopted the slogan "Half the Way with LBJ." This slogan meant support for Johnson against Goldwater—predominantly on the strength of his liberal "Great Society" domestic programs—without a wholesale endorsement of the Democrats. Many SDS activists flocked to Johnson's campaign, registering voters and getting out the vote on Election Day. Johnson won in a landslide, taking 61 percent of the popular vote.

Ironically, the left need not have worried about Goldwater's election. First, all public opinion polls showed huge majorities opposed to his election. Second, even most of big business found Goldwater too "extreme" for its tastes. Sixty percent of members of the Business Council, an extremely influential Washington advisory group composed of chief executives of the largest and most important U.S. companies, backed Johnson. And LBJ won the lion's share of corporate contributions to the presidential candidates.[10]

Within months of his inauguration Johnson showed his cards. In 1965 Johnson dispatched the Marines to install a pro-U.S. government in the Dominican Republic. In March 1965 he asked Congress for a massive escalation of the Vietnam War effort. By the decade's end, more than 550,000 troops would be sent to fight in Vietnam. More than fifty-eight thousand Americans and two million Vietnamese would die in the Vietnam War. As the war effort impinged on the government's ability to spend on the "War on Poverty," even the promise of liberal reform at home was undercut. A leading radical explained the lessons of the 1964 election:

> In 1964, you know all the people who convinced themselves that Lyndon Johnson was the lesser evil as against Goldwater. . . . Many of them have realized that the spiked shoe was on the other foot; and they lacerate themselves with the thought that the man they voted for "actually carried out Goldwater's policy." . . . Who was really the Lesser Evil in 1964? The point is that it is the question which is a disaster, not the answer. In setups in which the choice is between one capitalist politician and another, the defeat comes in accepting the limitation to this choice.[11]

Fueled by the escalation of the Vietnam War, the student and antiwar movements shifted rapidly to the left in reaction to Johnson's betrayals. By 1968 much of the radical movement identified the Democratic Party as "the enemy." For those radicals who rejected electoralism altogether, 1968 is remembered for the Chicago police riot against the young radicals who picketed the Democratic convention held there. Unfortunately, the revolutionary left was unable to offer a strong alternative for those radicals who rejected the Democratic Party.

The dominant politics of the revolutionary left, which modeled itself on "Third World" nationalist guerrilla movements (e.g., Cuba, Vietnam, China), gave little guidance to those fed up with the system at home. Revolutionary organizations like the Black Panther Party proposed action, such as urban guerrilla warfare, inappropriate to the American context.[12] Other revolutionaries engendered a sense of impending revolution when there was little evidence to support it. Max Elbaum, historian of the "new communist movement" of Maoist- and Stalinist-influenced groups, notes that revolutionaries of that era made an analogy between the 1970s United States and the period of 1905–17 in Russia:

> The "dress rehearsal for revolution" framework pressed relentlessly toward an assessment that the system was in big trouble, that reform openings were more superficial than real, that new popular upsurges were right around the corner, and that the vast bulk of the working class was on the verge of moving decisively to the left. . . .
>
> . . . The 1970s did see major economic and other shocks—but the resulting shift in the country's politics was to the right, not the left.[13]

Those revolutionaries who had viewed Mao's China as a model of a new society and a leader of anti-imperialist fights were disoriented when in 1972 Mao himself made peace with Nixon, the world's chief imperialist leader. With their hopes dashed, revolutionary organizations found their energies sapped. By the mid-1970s, movement struggle had declined. Significant revolutionary organizations, unable to readjust to the changed circumstances, simply dissolved. Many embittered ex-radicals rejected as "sectarian" attempts to build explicitly revolutionary organizations and drifted into Democratic electoral campaigns. A handful of ex-radicals, like former Chicago Eight defendant Tom Hayden, found new careers as Democratic Party politicians. But many others from the "generation of '68" became foot soldiers in the

Reverend Jesse Jackson's Rainbow Coalition, working to sign up voters for the Democratic Party they had once condemned as the party of Southern segregation and of the Vietnam War.

As the Carter administration moved American politics to the right—preparing the ground for the hard-right shift that emerged fully with the 1980 election of Ronald Reagan—the liberal establishment launched a series of initiatives to counter it. The leadership of the UAW launched a Progressive Alliance, and liberals rallied to Senator Edward Kennedy's 1980 primary challenge to Carter. This boomlet of liberal activity coincided with the revolutionary left's reevaluation of its past practices and its arrival at "a more realistic assessment of U.S. politics and realiz[ation] that revolutionary transformations were not on the horizon" in early 1980.[14] Elbaum explained the conjuncture:

> What was striking about this flurry of liberal energy (which turned out to be very brief) was how it shifted the center of gravity of strategic thinking among socialists strongly to the right. Activists who just a few years earlier had criticized involvement in Democratic Party politics as a violation of principle now immersed themselves in that arena, and in many cases without much concern for how they might maintain a measure of independent radical initiative in the process.[15]

One consequence of the shift of 1960s radicals into the political mainstream was the revival in the 1970s of projects to create a U.S. social democracy, an undertaking still represented today by the Democratic Socialists of America.

The "Left Wing of the Possible"

The Democratic Socialists of America (DSA) was formed in 1983 with the intent of participating "as part of the left wing of the Democratic Party, in order to change this party itself, to turn it into a new kind of mass party."[16] The DSA brought together the New American Movement, a former New Left group, with the Democratic Socialist Organizing Committee, a remnant of the old Socialist Party. Reflecting the influence of its leading intellectual Michael Harrington, an advocate of the "realignment" theory of transforming the Democratic Party, DSA viewed the Democratic Party as a coalition of popular voting blocs— women, labor, Blacks, and farmers—unbound by any principles. DSA believed it should work to strengthen the party's progressive elements and hoped that one day it could grasp the party's leadership, which would put DSA supporters in a position to enact a policy of social reform. In theory, "capturing" the party in this way would drive the conservatives out, leaving the realigned Democratic Party as something approximating a European-style labor party.[17]

In hindsight, the problems with this approach are clear. Above all, the DSA strategy was flawed because it was based on an incorrect assessment of the class character of the Democratic Party. The Democratic Party is fundamentally a capitalist party, which means that capitalist interests—and not "progressive" voting blocs—really set the party agenda. The big-business interests who finance the party have never allowed any serious attempts to implement party platform planks such as those calling for the repeal of Taft-Hartley or for the establishment of national health care. DSA's attempts to influence the party platform and to support progressive candidates committed (on paper, at least) to those policies often led activists to frustration.

DSA maintains a profile of what it calls the "left wing of the possible" in the Democratic Party. While this position appealed to a number of former 1960s radicals, it had a serious flaw because it "was in direct opposition to the proposition that a key task of the left is to *expand the boundaries of what is considered possible*," as 1960s veteran Elbaum noted [emphasis in original]. Adhering to the "left wing of the possible" means "tailing behind the fluctuations—to the right and to the left—of the liberal establishment."[18] In 1984 most DSA leaders backed former vice president Walter Mondale, despite the fact that Mondale ran one of the most conservative Democratic campaigns since the Second World War.

At the rank-and-file level, however, the DSA split three ways, with significant support within the organization for each of the major Democratic candidates—Mondale, Jesse Jackson, and Senator Gary Hart (D-CO). The same happened in 1987 when a poll of the organization showed 51 percent supported Jackson for the 1988 Democratic presidential nomination, 20 percent supported Senator Paul Simon (D-IL), and 15 percent supported no candidate. Instead of maintaining a "social democratic" pole within the party, the DSA reflected the divisions within the party itself.[19] Instead of DSA influencing the Democrats, the Democrats influenced the DSA.

The DSA's 1987 endorsement of Jackson highlighted another problem with its approach: explicitly socialist politics had always taken a back seat to its willingness to provide foot soldiers for Democratic election campaigns. DSA leaders, concerned that their choice for candidate could be red-baited for accepting DSA's support, approached Jackson and asked his permission for DSA to endorse him publicly. "We raised the problem with Jackson that we want to support you but we don't want to support you in a way that would harm you," said DSA co-chair Harrington at the time.[20] Jackson initially balked, but agreed to accept DSA's endorsement. DSA's timidity in publicizing its support for Jackson was certainly a strange way of implementing its minimum goal of moving the Democratic Party leftward—let alone its stated desire of popularizing the ideas of socialism in the United States.

DSA often cites prominent Democrats' and labor leaders' endorsements of its positions as indications of its "influence" in shaping the Democratic Party's policy debate. However, the willingness of politicians and labor leaders to endorse elements of the DSA program should not be confused with influence in the party or in the labor movement. As is more often the case, DSA attempts to rally support for whatever so-called progressive programs Democratic liberals concoct, however little they might change the status quo. What's more, one has only to view the records of some self-identified DSA endorsers to see that quite often their commitment to "socialism" flags when they are forced to transform their words into action.

One of the most prominent early supporters of DSA was William Winpisinger, president of the International Association of Machinists (IAM) during the Reagan era. Although a prominent critic of Reagan and the anticommunist foreign policy of the AFL-CIO, Winpisinger opposed efforts to increase rank-and-file democracy inside unions and urged machinists to accept widespread concessions in the airline industry. During the momentous 1981 Professional Air Traffic Controllers Organization (PATCO) strike—Reagan's first union-busting success— Winpisinger urged IAM members "to behave like good trade-unionists" rather than lead them onto picket lines in support of PATCO. If IAM members had struck, the PATCO strike would not have been the crushing defeat for labor that it was. Winpisinger often decried "Reaganism," but he failed to act in a case in which his leadership might have defeated one of "Reaganism's" first assaults against the working class.[21] AFL-CIO president John Sweeney was a leading DSA supporter, but few would argue that Sweeney advanced the cause of socialism during his tenure as AFL-CIO leader.

The establishment of the New Democrats' hegemony in the Democratic Party during the 1990s led the DSA to reconsider its strategic perspective. Globalized capitalism and a generation-long employers' offensive had weakened the liberal bases on which the DSA had formed its perspective. As increasingly conservative ideas and policies became "the possible" in the Democratic Party, the DSA moved away from the idea that its work would "realign" the Democratic Party. DSA described its political posture at the end of the twentieth century as follows: "If we once positioned ourselves as the left wing of the possible, there is now no 'possible' to be the left wing of."[22] But if this conclusion led DSA to be less sanguine about its prospects in the Democratic Party, it did not encourage an open break with the Democrats. Instead, it moved into the camp of the "inside-outside" strategy, nearly identical to the efforts discussed in chapter 7: "Democratic socialists reject an either-or approach to electoral coalition building, focused solely on a new party or on realignment within the Democratic Party."[23] While the revised perspective assigned the main task of democratic socialists to building "anti-corporate social movements," these are still largely conceived of in relation to their impact on the electoral arena:

> Since such social movements seek to influence state policy, they will intervene in electoral politics, whether through Democratic primaries, non-partisan local elections, or third-party efforts. Our electoral work aims at building majoritarian coalitions capable of not only electing public officials on the anti-corporate program of these movements, but also of holding officials accountable after they are elected.[24]

The nod toward "third-party" efforts only went so far. In 2000 the DSA's National Political Committee was divided between supporters of Green Party candidate Ralph Nader, Democrat Al Gore, and Socialist Party candidate David McReynolds. So the organization declined to make any endorsement in the 2000 presidential race.[25] Four years later, with much of the left convinced that it faced the "most important election of our lifetimes," DSA issued a grudging endorsement of John Kerry on July 23, 2004. "Kerry was hardly the first choice of our members. Most supported Dennis Kucinich or Howard Dean in the Democratic primary elections and would be very critical of Senator Kerry's voting record on trade issues, as well as his support for the resolution authorizing the use of force in Iraq; but the most important concern of our members now is to defeat Bush," said Frank Llewellyn, DSA's national director.[26] Unfortunately, DSA's action in 2004 was a familiar one for activists who seem fated every election year to "fight the good fight" during the primaries, then to unite behind the Democratic nominee, no matter how conservative.

In the summer of 2008, the organization predictably endorsed Obama over McCain, but hedged its support with calls to build a movement to pressure Obama and Democrats in Congress. At that time, DSA noted that the "November election can't be the end of a fight, but its beginning, and connections made on a local and national level leading up to November can position the Left to play a role in struggles to come."[27] But if anyone may have concluded that DSA wasn't sufficiently committed to an Obama victory, DSA honorary co-chair Bogdan Denitch made sure to disabuse them of that notion. In an election eve statement published in *Democratic Left*, Denitch wrote in a near-hysterical tone, reminding DSA supporters of the catastrophic consequences of a McCain-Palin presidency, concluding, "We are duty bound to do what we can to prevent this."[28] In the end, it seems, the argument always comes back to this. No matter how conservative or business-dominated the Democrats are, the Republicans are always "much worse," and socialists are "duty bound" to throw their support behind the lesser-evil capitalist party. In that way, DSA's reliance on the Democrats chains sincere activists—many of whom are attracted to the "socialist" in DSA's title because they want to see fundamental change in the system—to one of the most solid institutions of capitalist rule, the Democratic Party.

Taking a Dive for the Dems

In the wake of the collapse of Stalinism and the establishment of U.S.-led, globalized, neoliberal capitalism as the political-economic model of the early twenty-first century, radical and socialist projects appeared to suffer a death blow.[29] In the United States, these macro-trends had the effect of strengthening the two corporate parties and weakening what was left of a labor movement still caught in the grip of a long decline from its peak of influence in the 1940s.[30] The project of building a working-class political alternative to the two corporate parties could count on far weaker forces than it had possessed in a hundred years, while on the key questions of the day the political programs and social visions of the two major parties coincided more and more. Yet the convergence of the two neoliberal parties created a vacuum on the left side of the political spectrum into which an independent movement could flow.

The Green Party presidential campaign of consumer advocate Ralph Nader in 2000 illustrated this possibility. In an otherwise dismal election year, Ralph Nader's anti-corporate, pro-worker Green Party campaign provided the only genuine excitement. Packing professional sports arenas for "super rallies" and inspiring crowds across the country, Nader offered an alternative to the Tweedledee-Tweedledum choices for president. Describing the two-party duopoly as a "giant corporate party with two heads" on top of a political system that was "spoiled to the core," Nader's was the first mass presidential campaign in a generation to attract the support of millions to an openly left-of-center platform.[31] Placed in historical context, Nader's 2.7 percent of the vote exceeded the 2.5 percent that Henry Wallace's 1947 Progressive Party presidential campaign attracted. In fact, Nader's vote was the highest for an independent progressive candidate since Robert LaFollette's third-party run in 1924. Nader drew particularly well among young people and activists in the global justice movement born from the 1999 protests in Seattle against the World Trade Organization. Proportionally, trade unionists supported Nader at a rate similar to their support for Democratic candidate Al Gore.[32] Nader's campaign showed the potential to reach beyond liberal enclaves and university campuses, but it didn't make that breakthrough. But four years later, the leaders of the Green Party threw away whatever potential Nader had shown in 2000 by refusing to mount a serious challenge to the Democrats.

In the interim between the two elections, the political climate took a sharp turn to the right in the wake of the September 11, 2001, al-Qaeda attacks. The emboldened Bush administration had seized the initiative to push through a raft of repressive policies, along with starting wars in Afghanistan and Iraq. Although congressional Democrats had supported—or refused to oppose—the vast majority of these policies, by 2004 much of the U.S. left was lining up to support whatever Democratic candidate for president the party would pick. Global Exchange leader and Code Pink founder Medea Benjamin, who had run for U.S. Senate on the Green Party ticket in 2000, put it this way:

> The world is watching and waiting with bated breath to see if the U.S. people will reject the Bush agenda. When I was last in Iraq, Ghazwan Al-Mukhtar, an Iraqi engineer, said, "Saddam Hussein was a bastard, but this was not a democracy, and we didn't elect him. So his evil deeds were not done in our name. Can you say the same thing for George Bush?"
>
> We owe it to ourselves and to the global community to make sure that Bush is no longer allowed to speak in our name.

Benjamin concluded that the only way to accomplish this was to elect Democratic senator John Kerry, the Democrats' choice in 2004. In "An Open Letter to Progressives," Benjamin, actor Peter Coyote, antiwar activist (and *Pentagon Papers* whistleblower) Daniel Ellsberg, and other prominent figures made the case that "the only candidate who can win instead of Bush in November is John Kerry"—and urged a vote for Kerry in "swing states," where small numbers of popular votes could tip the state's Electoral College votes to Bush or Kerry.[33]

The Green Party itself accepted this "safe state" logic and nominated as its standard bearer the no-name lawyer David Cobb, who pledged to put it into effect. The impact of the "safe states strategy" was illustrated most absurdly when Cobb's running mate, Pat LaMarche, a Maine native, said in an interview that she might even vote against herself if the election looked close in Maine. "If Bush has got 11 percent of the vote in Maine come November 2, I can vote for whoever I want. If the race is close, I'll vote for Kerry. . . . I love my country . . . [and] if [Vice President] Cheney loved his country, he wouldn't be voting for himself."[34] Cobb's nomination marked the culmination of years of intraparty manuevering to marginalize Nader and any possibility that the Greens would mount an effective challenge to the Democrats in 2004. Not only did this opposition to Nader come from forces inside the Greens who were dedicated to a "fusion" strategy with liberal Democrats, but it also came from liberal Democrats outside the Greens who wanted to prevent any kind of challenge to the militaristic, hyper-cautious Kerry campaign.[35] By succumbing to this pressure, the Green Party surrendered its possibility of aggressively taking on Bush and Kerry on issues on which those two largely agreed: continuing the war and occupation in Iraq or the shredding of civil liberties under the USA PATRIOT Act. By pledging not to campaign, the Green ticket declared its own irrelevance to the national debate.

Nader and his running mate Peter Camejo, the Greens' candidate for California governor in the 2003 recall election and a longtime progressive, mounted an underfunded and understaffed independent campaign to offer a left alternative for people who wanted to vote against the war and occupation, against the USA PATRIOT Act, and for gay marriage and national health care. Despite vicious baiting from people on the left and a full-court press by Democrats determined to keep Nader off ballots around the country, the Nader-Camejo ticket won 465,150 votes nationwide compared to 119,856 for Cobb-LaMarche. Even the far-right Constitutional Party outpolled Cobb-Lamarche! Because of Cobb's non-campaign, the Greens lost their ballot status, including recognition as a political party, in at least seven states.[36] Only four years after Nader's campaign gave the Green Party an opening to millions, the organization's viability as an independent political force was put under question. Yet again, it appeared, another attempt to build an alternative to the two-party duopoly had succumbed to the siren call of lesser evilism. Surveying the damage, Green Party activist Howie Hawkins concluded,

> Popular Front, fusion, inside-outside, and safe states are all species of the same genus of lesser evilism. By relying on the liberal wing of the corporate power structure to defend us from its right wing, the left surrenders its own voice and very identity as an alternative to corporate domination. And history shows, when push comes to shove, that the corporate liberals ally with their conservative counterparts against the people.[37]

Conclusion

The U.S. left—confronted as it has been with a political system dominated by two firmly entrenched bourgeois parties—has found it very difficult to realize the potential for a popular party to the left of the Democrats. Chapter 4 recounted how the Democrats managed to defuse and derail the threat the Populists posed. And this chapter has explored more recent efforts, from the New Left to today's Green Party. Each of these efforts stalled for its own particular reasons, rooted in its own particular time. But one constant throughout has been the role—either direct or indirect—of the Democratic Party in heading off, disorganizing, or even destroying these political alternatives.

Conclusion

Is the Lesser Evil Good Enough?

Because voters typically face the uninspiring choice between two business parties each election year, those who decide to vote for the Democratic candidate often explain their decision by saying that they are picking the "lesser of two evils." Neither party represents what they really want, but the Democrats at least promise to do less harm than the Republicans do.

In 2008, a different dynamic seemed to be in place. Large numbers of people—from political pundits to ordinary people—looked forward to a national election that would produce a Democratic sweep from the White House to city halls. Unlike in earlier election years, millions viewed the election of Obama and a Democratic Congress with hope, rather than with resignation or dread. Yet, in reality, the Democrats assumed the role of shoring up the system, which led them to short-circuit ordinary people's demands. The "party of the people" pursued policies that produced some minimal reforms for workers and the oppressed, but only as a byproduct of its historic role: to save the capitalist system from its own excesses while preserving the political status quo.

Although both major parties in the United States have undergone major changes over the years of their existence, the Democratic Party is the ultimate chameleon in the two-party system. The party that spawned the Confederate States of America was, by 2008, the party of the first African-American president. For most of the last century it has served a particular role in the two-party system. It is the party that encourages the loyalty of oppressed and exploited groups in U.S. society—Blacks, union members, women, immigrants—only to contain and blunt their aspirations for a more fundamental reordering of capitalist priorities.

In times of great social crisis, such as that which confronted the Roosevelt administration in 1933, the Democrats can shift "left" to appeal to mass discontent with the system. Democratic politicians have introduced reforms, such as Social Security and unemployment insurance, which both stabilized the system and convinced millions to tie their hopes for a better future to continuously reelecting Democrats. Yet as an institution the Democratic Party has routinely used its control over government resources (patronage, social programs, etc.) to build a social and voting base for policies that are both pro-business and pro-imperialist. The Democrats' skill in using these means to co-opt labor unions and other social movements to its agenda remains one of the chief reasons why no labor or social democratic party exists in the United States.

Despite the reforms that some Democratic administrations have enacted, the essential character of the Democrats as a big business party hasn't changed. It represents an institution that corporate money funds and sustains—and increasingly so. Its bedrock loyalty to big business explains its history as a party that has championed intervention and "free trade" abroad while limiting the reforms it promotes within the U.S. capitalist consensus. The fact that the Democratic Party remains a party of American business explains why the American "welfare state" is so anemic as compared to the rest of the capitalist world. The conservative Republican dominance of U.S. politics over the last generation only obscures how from the 1930s through the 1960s the Democrats were the dominant party of U.S. capitalism. The Democrats are the party of Social Security and the Voting Rights Act. But, as this book has argued, the Democrats are equally the party of the World Bank, the CIA, and the Vietnam War.

The Republican ascendancy of the recent past fit with the worldwide triumph of neoliberal capitalism that displaced the previous Keynesian consensus. More recently, as neoliberalism is increasingly discredited in the eyes of the public and the sections of the ruling elite, the stage was set for another turn of the wheel. The 2008 economic crisis raised more sharply the question of the priorities of the system and the government. If the government could rush to approve an eight-hundred-billion-dollar bailout of Wall Street within three weeks, why should it drag its feet when faced with requests for government aid to "Main Street" like unemployment benefits or jobs programs? If the government can nationalize AIG, why can't it deliver health care for all Americans? If so many Americans were losing their jobs and health care, why was the United States spending billions every month to prop up unpopular wars in Iraq and Afghanistan? The crisis provided a political opening that laid bare the priorities of the system and opened a debate in society about what those priorities ought to be. In other words, when Obama arrived in the Oval Office, the country stood ready for a break from the politics of the past.

Nevertheless, it was hard to say that the 2008 Democratic sweep—reversed with the GOP sweep in 2010—represented a rebirth of liberalism. In the sense that Democrats stand (slightly) to the left of Republicans on most issues, and that a Democratic victory broke years of right-wing Republican dominance, liberalism received a boost. Millions of Americans voted for Democratic candidates hoping that they would act on the issues that concerned the majority: ending the war in Iraq, fixing the mortgage crisis, providing universal health care. If the mainstream political system had made room for these "liberal" issues, people's expectations that something could be done about them would have been raised.

However, the kind of liberalism the Democratic Party represents today is no longer the counterfeit social democracy of the New Deal or Great Society. As the pillars of the New Deal coalition dissolved, the Democrats remade their party. Particularly in the 1990s, Democratic Party leaders under Bill Clinton reoriented the institution to the emerging sectors of the "New Economy," as noted in chapter 3. So when Democratic leaders got down to discussing what to do to fix the health care crisis, they produced a "universal health care" plan that preserved—and even enhanced—the dominant role of the private, profit-making insurance companies that are one of the chief culprits in the existing disaster that is U.S. health care. And as the Democratic Congress's capitulation to President George W. Bush on almost all aspects of the Iraq War foreshadowed, a Democratic administration has proved itself to be a responsible trustee of the U.S. empire. Reviewing President Obama's penchant to seek compromises with industry and conservatives during the health care reform debate, psychologist and Democratic Party consultant Drew Westen complained,

> I don't honestly know what this president believes. But I believe if he doesn't figure it out soon, start enunciating it, and start fighting for it, he's not only going to give American families hungry for security a series of half-loaves where they could have had full ones, but he's going to set back the Democratic Party and the progressive movement by decades, because the average American is coming to believe that what they're seeing right now is "liberalism," and they don't like what they see.[1]

Who's "Sitting In"?

This book has conducted a sustained argument to establish the Democratic Party as one of the main capitalist institutions in this country. So why should a study like this interest someone on the left, a trade unionist or social movement activist, any more than a book-length study of another capitalist institution, like the stock market or a major corporation? It is because the Democratic Party is a different kind of institution—one that inspires the widespread belief that it, unlike the stock market, can be a vehicle for positive social change.

Yet its history, from the Democratic fusion with the Populists through the present day, should challenge this widespread belief. Many times activists have attempted to work with or to "take over" the Democratic Party to make it a vehicle to fight on behalf of the exploited and oppressed. They have failed every time.

In the 2008 presidential campaign, politicians from both major parties recognized the public's desire for something different and embraced the idea of "change." In his speeches and advertising, Democratic nominee Barack Obama invoked images of past movements for social justice, like the movements for civil rights, abolition, and women's suffrage, and asked supporters to join his "movement."[3] As chapter 5 showed, this rhetoric actually inverted reality because the Democratic Party has played a critical role in derailing and disorienting genuine movements for social change.

Despite the rhetoric, Obama was not building a real grassroots movement for social change but an electoral campaign within the capitalist mainstream. That distinction is crucial, as author and radio host Laura Flanders, an Obama supporter, noted:

> Let's keep in mind that those hopeful base voters aren't doing all this work simply in order to get a change of personnel in the White House. It's change in their lives and their communities, as well as in the country at large that they need and want. Even a shift of power in both chambers of Congress in November 2006 has brought them precious little of that. . . . The swirl of the primary season is intoxicating—and the media love it. But real change happens on a different timetable. If you're looking for estimated times of arrival, the problem is: We don't know that timetable yet.[2]

The idea that lasting social change comes only from the ballot box—an idea that Democratic candidates promote every election cycle—helps misdirect political energy *away* from the place where, historically, social change has come in the United States. Historian Howard Zinn explained it this way:

> There's hardly anything more important that people can learn than the fact that the really critical thing isn't who is sitting in the White House, but who is sitting in—in the streets, in the cafeterias, in the halls of government, in the factories. Who is protesting, who is occupying offices and demonstrating—those are the things that determine what happens.[3]

The trends of struggle between workers and bosses, and in society as a whole, determine the level and pace of reforms much more than the outcome of any election. It is no accident that the two periods of the highest level of class and social struggle in the twentieth century—the 1930s and the 1960s—account for the main periods of expansion of the United States' meager social welfare provisions. Of course these were also the heydays of the Democratic Party's New Deal and Great Society platforms. Democratic partisans might claim this as evidence that only an electoral strategy aimed at electing Democrats would create these conditions. But it is more accurate to say that the struggle itself created these conditions—and often forced the "people's party" to act in ways that it did not intend. In 1932 Roosevelt did not campaign as a champion of working people or for social insurance. In 1965 Lyndon Johnson acknowledged that the civil rights movement forced him to work for passage of the Voting Rights Act—an action he had wanted to postpone for years.[4] Ramsey Clark, who served as attorney general in the Johnson administration, conceded that the civil rights movement was the key factor in setting LBJ's civil rights agenda:

By their actions that this is where the pressure was, and this is where the pressure had to be relieved, and this is what really motivated government action, I'm sure. I think—it's too bad, it would be nice if somehow or other government could look out there and see a situation and say that this isn't right, and let's do something about it. But that's not the way it happened. It happened because there is immense pressure and insistence and potential for friction and violence that caused us to face up to these problems and do something about it.[5]

The Lesser Evil Is Still an Evil

Many people who agree with every argument in this book may still decide to vote for a Democrat—if only to prevent a conservative Republican from wreaking further damage on the tattered social welfare state and on civil liberties. Like the proverbial atheist who, wanting to hedge his or her bets against the possibility of an afterlife, asks to receive last rites from a priest before dying, many voters will cast a vote for the lesser evil—just in case. But is voting for the lesser of two evils really a strategy to win social change or "breathing space" to organize movements from below? Consider Democrat Lyndon Johnson's election as a "peace candidate" in 1964. Once elected, Johnson escalated the war in Vietnam beyond anyone's worst nightmares.

In reviewing the left's support for the lesser-evil election of Johnson, socialist Hal Draper recalled, in the essay reprinted in the appendix to this book, when the German Social Democrats encouraged a vote for extreme conservative Field Marshal von Hindenburg against Hitler and the Nazis in 1932:

> So the Lesser Evil, Hindenburg, won; and Hitler was defeated. Whereupon President Hindenburg appointed Hitler to the chancellorship, and the Nazis started taking over . . . the people voted for the Lesser Evil and got both [the greater and lesser evil]. . . . This is exactly why 1932 is the classic case of the Lesser Evil, because even when the stakes were this high, even then voting for the Lesser Evil meant historic disaster.

Draper's historical example is dramatic, but it illustrates the importance of analyzing the Democrats and Republicans in the way that twentieth-century muckraker Ferdinand Lundberg described them: as two wings of the same "property" party. What about issues like abortion rights on which there are real differences between the two parties? At least Democrats are committed to maintaining abortion as a legally available option for women, whereas the Republicans are committed to outlawing it. This is true. But supporting Democrats just because they aren't as bad as the Republicans demonstrates the poverty of expectations among liberals and progressives—and negates the role of struggle in winning reforms. After all, the U.S Supreme Court was packed with conservative appointees when it first legalized abortion in its 1973 *Roe v. Wade* decision, while Richard Nixon, an ardent opponent of choice, occupied the White House.[6] Yet the Supreme Court felt the pressure of thousands of women and men who demonstrated for abortion rights in the preceding years in deciding to make abortion legal.

When he was running for president in 1992, Bill Clinton promised to pass a "Freedom of Choice Act" that would guarantee a woman's right to choose. After he took office, he dropped the bill because he no longer felt beholden to pro-choice activists who had mobilized the vote for him. While he vetoed efforts to ban the late-term abortion procedure misnamed "partial-birth" abortion, he nevertheless signed into law abortion bans affecting federal employees and residents of Washington, D.C., and he maintained the ban on Medicaid funding for abortion.[7]

But women's rights groups never made Clinton pay a political price for these betrayals. Meanwhile, a concerted attack on abortion rights gathered steam at the state level, while feminist leaders refused to mobilize a counteroffensive—based in part on their assumption that abortion rights were safe with a Democrat in the White House. When movements align themselves with Democrats, they can end up accepting the Democrats' definitions of what they can achieve. They learn to be "team players" and "not to rock the boat." They may express dismay that Democrats aren't standing up for the movement's demands, but that rarely stops them from getting out the Democratic vote on Election Day. And as Draper notes elsewhere in his seminal essay, when Democratic politicians are assured that progressives will vote for them anyway, they spend most of their time courting the right.

Build a Genuine Alternative

One of the great Achilles' heels of the American left has been its failure to build a sustained political alternative to the Democratic Party. There are many reasons for this; chapter 8 touched on them. Today it is common for most people and organizations that consider themselves on the "left" to be at least passive supporters of the Democratic Party. The last great period of the flowering of left, revolutionary, and socialist organizations—in the years following 1968—ended with many former revolutionaries finding their way back to "progressive" politics through the Democratic Party. Unfortunately, this means that by default the Democrats largely maintain the ability to define the left-most edge of the political spectrum. Millions of Americans then never hear any alternative political vision to what is on offer from the two capitalist parties.

Eugene V. Debs, the greatest socialist leader the American working-class movement has produced, offered a cogent argument for building a political alternative to the Democrats in 1900:

> We hear it frequently urged that the Democratic Party is the "poor man's party," "the friend of labor." There is but one way to relieve poverty and to free labor, and that is by making common property of the tools of labor.
>
> Is the Democratic Party, which we are assured has "strong socialistic tendencies," in favor of collective ownership of the means of production? Is it opposed to the wage system, from which flows in a ceaseless stream the poverty, misery and wretchedness of the children of toil?
>
> If the Democratic Party is the "friend of labor" any more than the Republican Party, why is its platform dumb in the presence of Coeur d'Alene [where the Idaho state government declared martial law against an 1899 miners' strike]? It knows the truth about these shocking outrages—crimes upon workingmen, their wives and children, which would blacken the pages of Siberia. Why does it not speak out?
>
> What has the Democratic Party to say about the "property and educational qualifications" in North Carolina and Louisiana, and the proposed general disfranchisement of the Negro race in the Southern states?
>
> The differences between the Republican and Democratic parties involve no issue, no principle in which the working class has any interest, and whether the spoils be distributed by [Republicans] Hanna and Platt, or by [Democrats] Croker and Tammany Hall is all the same to it.
>
> Between these parties socialists have no choice, no preference.[8]

Debs ran for president on the Social Democratic Party and Socialist Party tickets five times between 1900 and 1920. Debs won 6 percent of the vote in the 1912 election. The Democratic administration of President Woodrow Wilson imprisoned him for giving a speech in 1918 opposing the First World War. He spent three years in federal prison. While imprisoned, Debs won almost one million votes in the 1920 presidential election. The support Debs received in his active attempt to build an independent socialist alternative proved that socialism could take root in American soil.

Today, when the left is much weaker than it was in Debs's era, his challenge remains. If we ever hope to win support for left-wing ideas in the electoral arena, we must build a political alternative that is independent of the Democrats. Postponing that task with attempts to "take over and transform" the Democratic Party will only delay the day when working people can vote for something they can actually support, rather than always being forced to choose between "terrible" and "not as bad." The choice between Democrats and Republicans is ultimately no choice at all.

Indeed, while corporate interests largely control the political parties, real power in capitalist society lies elsewhere—control over the means of production, the means of destruction, and the means of disseminating ideas. The wealthiest one percent of the population—industrialists, bankers, and media barons—controls all these "means." They own the major corporations and the media. Through their control over the state, they defend their privileges and power. No less an authority than Democratic president Woodrow Wilson explained it this way:

> Suppose you go to Washington and try to get at your government. You will always find that while you are politely listened to, the men really consulted are the men who have the big stake—the big bankers, the big manufacturers, and the big masters of commerce. . . . The masters of the government of the United States are the combined capitalists and manufacturers of the United States.[9]

Ordinary working-class Americans, by contrast, have no say over their working conditions, whether they will be "downsized" out of jobs, or whether their wages and benefits will be cut.

Working people do not elect the top judges, the generals, the police, or the bureaucrats who run Washington—all of whom are appointed, not elected. And working people have no means to control the candidates they elect once they have taken office.

As argued above, this doesn't mean that workers are powerless to change the conditions of their lives. Ordinary people have always fought for their right to a decent life. In the United States, the abolition of slavery, the right to form trade unions, the eight-hour work day, the end of the Vietnam War, the end of Jim Crow segregation in the South, and the right to vote for Blacks and women were not won at the ballot box. They were won in struggles of ordinary people from below.

If we want to end oppression and exploitation for good, we need to fight for the kind of society to which Debs committed himself: a socialist society in which human needs are not sacrificed for the profits of the rich. In a socialist society, workers would take control of the factories and offices. The repressive apparatuses of the state—from prisons to the military—would be brought under democratic control and then abolished. George Orwell, describing revolutionary Barcelona in 1936, gave us a glimpse of that kind of alternative vision:

> When one came straight from England the aspect of Barcelona was something startling and overwhelming. It was the first time that I had ever been in a town where the working class was in the saddle. . . . Every shop and cafe had an inscription saying that it had been collectivized; even the bootblacks had been collectivized and their boxes painted red and black. Waiters and shop-walkers looked you in the face and treated you as an equal. Servile and even ceremonial forms of speech had temporarily disappeared. Nobody said "Señor" or "Don" or even "Usted"; everyone called everyone else "Comrade" and "Thou", and said "Salud!" instead of "Buenos días." Tipping was forbidden by law; almost my first experience was receiving a lecture from a hotel manager for trying to tip a lift-boy. There were no private motor-cars, they had all been commandeered, and all the trams and taxis and much of the other transport were painted red and black. The revolutionary posters were everywhere, flaming from the walls in clean reds and blues that made the few remaining advertisements look like daubs of mud. Down the Ramblas, the wide central artery of the town where crowds of people streamed constantly to and fro, the loudspeakers were bellowing revolutionary songs all day and far into the night. And it was the aspect of the crowds that was the queerest thing of all. In outward appearance it was a town in which the wealthy classes had practically ceased to exist. Except for a small number of women and foreigners there were no "well-dressed" people at all. Practically everyone wore rough working-class clothes, or blue overalls, or some variant of the militia uniform. All this was queer and moving. There was much in it that I did not understand, in some ways I did not even like it, but I recognized it immediately as a state of affairs worth fighting for.[10]

In the first two years of the Obama administration, two national polls, including one by the conservative Rasmussen Reports, found that more than one-third of Americans held a positive view of "socialism." Gallup found 36 percent of Americans voicing positive views of socialism, compared to the 18 percent of Americans who identified themselves as Tea Party supporters in a *New York Times*/CBS survey. Who would have thought that in "center-right" America, potential supporters of socialism outnumber Tea Party supporters by two to one?[11]

These statistics tell us that there are millions of people who could potentially be mobilized against the right's and corporate America's plans to further immiserate working people. The "Occupy" movement that burst out in 2011 offered a glimpse of what was possible. We face the challenge of building organizations to fight effectively for working people's demands. But we also face the challenge of building a mass-based political alternative to the Democrats. Without that, we will continue to find ourselves facing the same Hobson's choice between "terrible" (the GOP) and "not as bad" (the Democrats).

A socialist organization to connect today's fights—for higher wages, for health care, and against racism, sexism, and homophobia—is key to the fight for a future socialist society. One of the first steps to build a socialist organization is the one Debs advocated more than a century ago. That is to recognize the Democratic Party as one of the chief pillars of the system that perpetuates exploitation and oppression, and to build a socialist alternative to it. I hope that this book has helped to make that case.

Who's Going to Be the Lesser Evil in '68?

Hal Draper

In 1968, when the presidential sweepstakes come up again, liberals all over the country are likely to face the California Syndrome. At the risk of sounding like a Californian, I'm referring to the political pattern that was acted out in the recent Brown[1]-Reagan contest in that state—whose denizens have this in common with New Yorkers, that they tend to think that whatever is happening in their state is What's Happening. Sometimes it is.

In '68 the problem is going to be: vote for Lyndon Johnson[2] again or not. Among all those schizophrenic people you know whose heart is in the famous Right Place—viz. a little left of center—ulcers are going to ulcerate, psychiatrists' couches will get political, and navels will be contemplated with a glassy stare. Johnson or Nixon? Johnson or Romney[3]? Johnson or Reagan[4]? Johnson or anybody? As a matter of fact, even before this point is reached, there bids fair to be a similar pattern inside the Democratic Party machine itself: Johnson or Kennedy-Fulbright,[5] or its equivalent.

Now radicals have been wont to approach this classic problem with two handy labels, which in fact are fine as far as they go. One is called the Tweedledum-Tweedledee pattern, and the other is called the Lesser Evil pattern. Neither of these necessarily quite describes What's Happening. To see why, let's take a quick look at both of them in terms of 1968.

(1) The '68 race could be a Tweedledum-Tweedledee affair, and it may be. For example, Johnson versus Governor Romney. One can defy even Max Lerner[6] to insert even a razor-thin sentence between the politics respectively represented by these two millionaires. In fact, there is bound to be a sector of liberal sentiment which would indeed see the Lesser Evil in Romney, since there is as yet no evidence that Romney is quite as rascally a liar as the present Leader of the Free World. But roughly speaking, these two are politically indistinguishable: this is the defining characteristic of the Tweedledum-Tweedledee pattern. (The sociological label for this invented by the professorial witch-doctors is Consensus Politics.)

(2) In contrast, the Lesser Evil pattern means that there is a significant political difference between the two candidates, but—.

To explain the "but," let's take—for reasons that will appear—not a current example, but the classic example.

The day after Reagan's election as governor of California, a liberal pro-Brown acquaintance met me with haggard face and fevered brow, muttering "Didn't they ever hear of Hitler? Didn't they ever hear of Hitler?" Did he mean Reagan was Hitler? "Well," he said darkly, "look how Hitler got started..." A light struck me about what was going on in his head. "Look," I said, "you've heard of Hitler, so tell me this: how did Hitler become chancellor of Germany?"

My pro-Brown enthusiast was taken aback: "Why, he won some election or other—wasn't it—with terror and a Reichstag fire and something like that." "That was after he had already become chancellor. How did he become chancellor of Germany?"

Don't go away to look it up. In the 1932 presidential election the Nazis ran Hitler, and the main bourgeois parties ran Von Hindenburg, the Junker general who represented the right wing of the Weimar republic but not fascism. The Social-Democrats, leading a mass workers' movement, had no doubt about what was practical, realist, hard-headed politics and what was "utopian fantasy": so they supported Hindenburg as the obvious Lesser Evil. They rejected with scorn the revolutionary proposal to run their own independent candidate against both reactionary alternatives—a line, incidentally that could also break off the rank-and-file followers of the Communist Party, which was then pursuing the criminal policy of "After Hitler we come" and "Social-fascists are the main enemy."

So the Lesser Evil, Hindenburg, won; and Hitler was defeated. Whereupon President Hindenburg appointed Hitler to the chancellorship, and the Nazis started taking over.

The classic case was that the people voted for the Lesser Evil and got both.

Now 1966 America is not 1932 Germany, to be sure, but the difference speaks the other way. Germany's back was up against the wall; there was an insoluble social crisis; it had to go to revolution or fascism; the stakes were extreme. This is exactly why 1932 is the classic case of the Lesser Evil, because even when the stakes were this high, even then voting for the Lesser Evil meant historic disaster. Today, when the stakes are not so high, the Lesser Evil policy makes even less sense.

In 1964, you know all the people who convinced themselves that Lyndon Johnson was the lesser evil as against Goldwater,[7] who was going to do Horrible Things in Vietnam, like defoliating the jungles. Many of them have since realized that the spiked boot was on the other foot; and they lacerate themselves with the thought that the man they voted for "actually carried out Goldwater's policy."[8] (In point of fact, this is unfair to Goldwater: he never advocated the steep escalation of the war that Johnson put through; and more to the point, he would probably have been incapable of putting it through with as little opposition as the man who could simultaneously hypnotize the liberals with "Great Society" rhetoric.)

So who was really the Lesser Evil in 1964? The point is that it is the question which is a disaster, not the answer. In setups where the choice is between one capitalist politician and another, the defeat comes in accepting the limitation to this choice.

New Development

For the moment, so much for the Lesser Evil pattern. But there is an interesting difference between the classic case (Hitler and Hindenburg in 1932) and the Johnson-Goldwater case. There really was a significant political difference between Hitler and Hindenburg; the general himself would never have fascized Germany. If he called the Nazi to the chancellorship, it was because he believed that the imposition of government responsibility was the way to domesticate the wild-talking Nazis, that the burden of actually having to run the country would turn the "irresponsible" extremists into tame politicians like all the others, in the pattern usually seen (as with the Hubert Humphreys[9]). But Hindenburg himself was not a Hitler and he really was a Lesser Evil. What the classic case teaches is not that the Lesser Evil is the same as the Greater Evil—this is just as nonsensical as the liberals argue it to be but rather this: that you can't fight the victory of the rightmost forces by sacrificing your own independent strength to support elements just the next step away from them.

This latter pattern is what has been going on in this country for the last two decades. Every time the liberal labor left has made noises about its dissatisfaction with what Washington was trickling through, all the Democrats had to do was bring out the bogy of the Republican right.

The lib-labs would then swoon, crying "The fascists are coming!" and vote for the Lesser Evil. In these last two decades, the Democrats have learned well that they have the lib-lab vote in their back pocket, and that therefore the forces to be appeased are those forces to the right. The lib-labs were kept happy enough if Hubert Humphrey showed up at a banquet to make his liberal speeches; or, before that, by the Kennedy myth which bemused them even while the first leader on this planet poised his finger over the nuclear-war button and said "Or else!" With the lib-lab votes in a pocket, politics in this country had to move steadily right-right-right—until even a Lyndon Johnson could look like a Lesser Evil. This is essentially why—even when there really is a Lesser Evil—making the Lesser Evil choice undercuts any possibility of really fighting the Right.

But now notice this: when the Lesser Evil named Johnson was elected in 1964, he did not call in the Greater Evil to power, as did Hindenburg. He did not merely act in so flabby a manner that the right-wing alternative was thereby strengthened—another classic pattern. These patterns would have been old stuff, the historic Lesser Evil pattern in full form.

What was bewildering about Johnson was that the Lesser Evil turned out to be the Greater Evil, if not worse. Was it then the Tweedledum-Tweedledee pattern, after all? Am I merely then saying that the apparent difference between Johnson and Goldwater (even within the framework of capitalist politics) was just an illusion? Is the conclusion merely that all capitalist politicians have to be the same, that therefore the case against voting for the Lesser Evil is that there is no Lesser Evil?

I don't think that's the answer; I think there is a third pattern around, which is neither Tweedledee-Tweedledum nor the classic Lesser Evil choice. If the Johnson-Goldwater contest was one example, then an even better one was provided by the recent Brown-Reagan race. For Pat Brown really is a liberal, whatever you may think of Johnson; and thereby hangs the tale.

Because this genuine liberal, Pat Brown, acted for eight years as governor of California in no important respect differently from what a conservative Republican would have done. The operative word is acted. He sold out the water program to the big landholding companies as his two Republican predecessors never dared to do. He fought tooth and nail for the bracero system[10] as no Republican governor of an agricultural state dared to do.

It was he (not Clark Kerr[11]) who in 1964 unleashed an army of police against the Berkeley students. After the Watts uprising, it was he who named John J. McCone's commission to whitewash the whole business, and who then supported the right wing's anti-riot law to intimidate the ghetto. It was Brown who gave the liberal Democratic CDC the final decapitation when he personally mobilized all his strength to oust Si Casady as CDC head.[12] If half of this had been done by a Reagan, the lib-labs would be yelling "Fascism" all over the place. (As they will during the next four years, no doubt.)

And I repeat that I don't think this took place simply because Pat Brown was a Tweedledee reflecting image of Reagan. Here is a somewhat different interpretation:

A profound change has taken place in this country since the days of the New Deal—has taken place in the nature of capitalist politics, and therefore in the two historic wings of capitalist politics, liberalism and conservatism. In the 1930s there was a genuine difference in the programs put before capitalism by its liberal and conservative wings. The New Deal liberals proposed to save capitalism, at a time of deepgoing crisis and despair, by statification—that is, by increasing state intervention into the control of the economy from above. It is notorious that some of the most powerful sectors of the very class that was being saved hated Roosevelt like poison. (This added to the illusions of the "Roosevelt revolution" at the time, of course.) Roosevelt himself always insisted that a turn toward state-capitalist intervention was necessary to save capitalism itself; and he was right. In fact, the New Deal conquered not only the Democratic but the Republican Party. When Roosevelt's New Deal and Truman's Fair Deal were succeeded by Eisenhower's regime, the free-enterprise-spouting Republican continued and even intensified exactly the same social course that Roosevelt had begun. (This is the reality behind the Birchite charge that Eisenhower is a "card-carrying Communist"!)[13]

In the three and a half decades since 1932, and before, during, and after a Second World War, which intensified the process, the capitalist system itself has been going through a deepgoing process of bureaucratic statification.[14] The underlying drives are beyond the scope of this article; the fact itself is plain to see. The liberals who sparked this transformation were often imbued with the illusion that they were undermining the going system; any child can now see that they knew not what they did. The conservatives who denounced all the steps in this transformation, and who had to be dragged kicking and screaming into the new stage, were also imbued with the very same illusion. But even Eisenhower—who has never been accused of being an egghead, and who, before he was nominated for the presidency, made exactly the same sort of free-enterprise-hurrah speeches as Reagan was paid to make for General Electric—even he was forced to act, in the highest office, no differently from a New Deal Democrat. Because that is the only way the system can now operate.

Fruits of Lesser-Evilism

Under the pressure of bureaucratic-statified capitalism, liberalism and conservatism converge. That does not mean they are identical, or are becoming identical. They merely increasingly tend to act in the same way in essential respects, where fundamental needs of the system are concerned. And just as the conservatives are forced to conserve and expand the statified elements of the system, so the liberals are forced to make use of the repressive measures which the conservatives advocate: because the maintenance of the system demands it.[15] Just as when Truman vetoed Taft-Hartley and then invoked it against striking workers. What is more, because the liberal politicians can point a warning finger toward the right and because the lib-labs will respond to it, they are even more successful than the conservatives in carrying out those measures which the conservatives advocate. It is not necessary to claim that even that pitiful man, Hubert Humphrey, is merely a hypocrite. No, I fully believe, myself, that he is as sincere a liberal as the next lib-lab specimen. It is liberalism which requires the examination, not Humphrey's morals. Nor was that even more pathetic man, Adlai Stevenson, simply a rascal when he found himself lying like a trooper at the UN in the sight and knowledge of the whole world.

So besides Tweedledee-Tweedledums and besides the Lesser Evils who really are different in policy from the Greater Evils, we increasingly are getting this third type of case: the Lesser Evils who, as executors of the system, find themselves acting at every important juncture exactly like the Greater Evils, and sometimes worse. They are the product of the increasing convergence of liberalism and conservatism under conditions of bureaucratic capitalism. There never was an era when the policy of the Lesser Evil made less sense than now.

That's the thing to remember for 1968, as a starter.

This article was first published in the *Independent Socialist*, January-February 1967.

Notes

Introduction: What Happened to the New Era?

1. Robert Kuttner, *Obama's Challenge* (White River Junction, VT: Chelsea Green Publishing, 2008), 1.
2. David Frum, "Beware the Democratic Sea-Change," *Financial Times*, February 6, 2008.
3. Polling data on presidential approval and direction of country are taken from www.pollingreport.com, accessed on October 27, 2011.
4. Keith Johnson, "State-Level Wins Augur More GOP Safe Seats," *Wall Street Journal*, November 4, 2010.
5. Income and poverty figures reported in Catherine Dodge, "Decline in U.S. Income Raises Stakes in 2012 Presidential Race," Bloomberg Business Week, September 14, 2011, at www.businessweek.com/news/2011-09-14/decline-in-u-s-income-raises -stakes-in-2012-presidential-race.html, accessed on October 27, 2011.
6. Figures on foreclosure cited in Eric Dash, "As Lenders Hold Homes in Foreclosure, Sales Are Hurt," New York Times, May 22, 2011.
7. Elizondo quoted in Steven Greenhouse, "Unions Find Members Slow to Rally Behind Democrats," *New York Times*, September 17, 2010.
8. Gary Langer, "Obama's No Shows: 29 Million," ABC News, at http://blogs.abcnews .com/thenumbers/2010/11/obamas-no-shows-29-million.html.
9. In ancient Roman mythology, Janus, the god of beginnings and transitions (and the namesake for the month of January), had two faces on the same head that looked in opposite directions.
10. Jerome Armstrong and Marcos Moulitzas Zúniga, *Crashing the Gate* (White River Junction, VT: Chelsea Green Publishing, 2006), 24.
11. See Mike Davis, *Prisoners of the American Dream* (New York: Verso, 1985).

Chapter One: "History's Second-Most Enthusiastic Capitalist Party"

1. Excerpts from Obama's speech in Cincinnati on September 22, 2012, reported in Lucy Madison, "Obama: 'I'm a Warrior for the Middle Class,'" *Political Hot Sheet*, CBS News, September 22, 2012 at www.cbsnews.com/8301-503544_162 -20110333-503544.html.

2. The comparison of Obama's and McCain's receipts appears in the summary of the 2008 presidential election on the website for the Center for Responsive Politics, the most authoritative source on the role of money in U.S. politics. See www.opensecrets.org/pres08/summary.php?cycle=2008&cid=N00009638. The paltry labor contribution may be somewhat distorted as organized labor provides millions of hours of "in-kind" donations (its members' phone-banking, door-knocking, etc.) and funnels millions through ideological and other "get-out-the-vote" organizations working for Democrats.

3. Kevin P. Phillips, "A Capital Offense; Reagan's America," *New York Times Magazine*, June 17, 1990.

4. Ferdinand Lundberg quoted in G. William Domhoff, *Fat Cats and Democrats* (Englewood Cliffs, NJ: Prentice Hall, 1972), 26–27.

5. Kenneth Janda, *Political Parties: A Cross-National Survey* (New York: The Free Press, 1980), 185–89. Just how far removed the party is from even the Democratic electorate can be measured in the role of "superdelegates." These Democratic leaders—mainly elected politicians and DNC members—account for more than one-fourth of delegates to the Democratic convention, while primary elections assign the other three-quarters. The superdelegates are fully within their rights to defy Democratic voters to choose an "establishment" candidate to back for president.

6. For a description of this type of party, see Carl Schorske's description of the German Social Democratic Party in his *German Social Democracy, 1905–1917* (Cambridge, MA: Harvard University Press, 1983).

7. For a discussion of the Democratic Party within this framework, see Alan Ware, *The Breakdown of Democratic Party Organization, 1940–1960* (Oxford: Clarendon Press, 1985), 12–15.

8. Mike Royko, *Boss: Richard J. Daley of Chicago* (New York: Signet Classics, 1971), 77–78.

9. Tom Vanden Brook, "Indictments and Allegations Cloud Windy City," *USA Today*, October 4, 2005.

10. "Excerpts from the Democratic Platform: A Revival of Hope," *New York Times*, July 20, 1988, 14.

11. "What We Stand For" on the Democratic Party website, www.dnc.org/a/party/ stand.html.

12. Program on International Policy Attitudes, "Most Iraqis Want U.S. Troops Out in a Year," September 27, 2006, www.worldpublicopinion.org/pipa/articles/ brmiddleeastnafricara/250.php. Data on U.S. support for troop withdrawal is from "U.S. Public Opinion in Line with Iraq Study Group's Proposal," December 5, 2006, www.worldpublicopinion.org/pipa/articles/brunitedstatescanadara/283.php.

13. See Stephen Zunes, "The Foreign Policy Agenda of the Democratic Front-Runners: Comparisons on Some Key Issues," www.commondreams.org, January 25, 2008.

14. Political scientists and reformers have for years clamored for the United States to adopt a "responsible" political party system—the concept that political parties with firm positions compete for election on a political program that, once elected,

they carry out. In Congress, they would vote as a bloc and party leaders would be able to punish members who voted against the majority opinion. This is closer to the model of a parliamentary system than to the American party system.

15. Jesse Jackson's contribution to sidebar feature, "What Blacks Can Expect from Clinton," *Jet*, December 28, 1992, 6.
16. Thomas L. Friedman, "The Transition: Plans and Policies; Aides Say Clinton Will Swiftly Void G.O.P. Initiatives," *New York Times*, November 6, 1992.
17. "Press Briefing with Bentsen, Rubin and Tyson," *U.S. Newswire*, December 20, 1993.
18. James Petras and Morris Morley, *Latin America in the Time of Cholera* (New York: Routledge, 1992), 165.
19. Ibid., 166.
20. James O'Connor, *The Fiscal Crisis of the State* (New York: St. Martin's Press, 1973), 68.
21. Ibid., 69.
22. Phillips, *Wealth and Democracy*, 41, 55.
23. Frederick Engels, "1891 Introduction," in Karl Marx, *The Civil War in France*. It can be found at www.marxists.org/archive/marx/works/1871/civil-war-france/postscript.htm.
24. Thomas Ferguson, *Golden Rule: The Investment Theory of Party Competition and the Logic of Money-Driven Political Systems* (Chicago: University of Chicago Press, 1995), 132.
25. Ibid., 145.
26. See Ferguson, *Golden Rule*, 150–59; and Thomas Ferguson, "Industrial Conflict and the Coming of the New Deal: The Triumph of Multinational Liberalism in America," in Steven Fraser and Gary Gerstle, eds., *The Rise and Fall of the New Deal Order* (Princeton, NJ: Princeton University Press, 1989), 19–24.
27. Edward Berkowitz and Kim McQuaid, *Creating the Welfare State: The Politial Economy of Twentieth-Century Rerform* (New York: Praeger Publishers, 1980), 92.
28. Sharon Smith, *Subterranean Fire: A History of Working-Class Radicalism in the United States* (Chicago: Haymarket Books, 2006), 118–19.
29. *New York Times* report quoted in Ferguson, *Golden Rule*, 156.
30. Hal Draper, "Who Will Be the Lesser Evil in '68?" in this volume.
31. Thomas Ferguson and Joel Rogers, *Right Turn: The Decline of the Democrats and the Future of American Politics* (New York: Hill & Wang, 1986), 79.
32. Kevin Phillips, *Wealth and Democracy: A Political History of the American Rich* (New York: Broadway Books, 2002), 541.
33. Mike Davis, *In Praise of Barbarians: Essays Against Empire* (Chicago: Haymarket Books, 2006), 21.
34. These data come from the profile of political parties' fundraising and expenditures for the 2010 election cycle appearing on the Center for Responsive Politics' website on October 16, 2011. These are based on party filings with the Federal Election Commission made public in April and May 2011. The industry sectors are as defined by the Center for Responsive Politics: agribusiness, communications/electronics, construction, defense, energy and natural resources, finance/insurance/real estate, health, ideological/single issue, labor, lawyers and lobbyists, miscellaneous business, other, and transportation. For further explanation, see www.opensecrets.org/industries/index.php.
35. Michael Brush, "Why Politicians Are Worth Buying," *MSN Money*, February 2, 2007, http://articles.moneycentral.msn.com/Investing/CompanyFocus/Why PoliticiansAreWorthBuying.aspx, accessed on July 20, 2008.

36. Thomas Ferguson, "Bill's Big Backers," *Mother Jones*, November/December 1996. Figures on cable TV and phone rates are from Common Cause, "The Fallout from the Telecommunications Act of 1996: Unintended Consequences and Lessons Learned," www.commoncause.org/atf/cf/%7BFB3C17E2-CDD1-4DF6 -92BE-BD4429893665%7D/FALLOUT_FROM_THE_TELECOMM_ACT_5-9 -05.PDF. The figure of telecommunications contributions to the Democratic Party in 1996 comes from www.opensecrets.org/bigpicture/stats.asp?cycle=2006& display=A&type=W. All were accessed on January 13, 2008.

37. All these facts come from Neel's official biography, published on the website of Vanderbilt University, where he now serves as a faculty member. See http:// sitemason.vanderbilt.edu/files/c/c4uDeM/Neel%20Roy%20BIOROYNEEL.pdf, accessed on January 13, 2008.

38. 2006 figures from "The Price of Admission" at www.opensecrets.org/bigpicture/ stats.asp?cycle=2006&display=A&type=W. 1986 figures from U.S. Federal Election Commission, *FEC Reports on Financial Activity Final Report, 1985–86. U.S. Senate and House Campaigns* (Washington, D.C.: U.S. Government Printing Office, 1988), xi.

39. Mike Allen, "MCI Center's Menu: Ribs and a Record Democratic Fundraiser," *Washington Post*, May 24, 2000; Ken Foskett, "Democrats Raise Record Amount," *Atlanta Journal Constitution*, May 25, 2000.

40. "Soft Money Lives: Democrats Take in $12 Million in Gifts," *New York Times*, March 22, 2002.

41. "Soros Says Kerry's Failings Undermined Campaign against Bush," January 30, 2005, reprint from Bloomberg.net at www.truthout.org/cgi-bin/artman/exec/ view.cgi/40/8662, accessed on December 12, 2007.

42. See George Soros, "Why We Must Not Reelect President Bush," speech delivered to National Press Club, September 28, 2004, reprinted on www.commondreams .org/views04/0928-16.htm.

43. Domhoff, *Fat Cats and Democrats*, 114.

44. Figures derived from www.opensecrets.org/parties/indus.php?cycle=2008&cmte =DPC, under "Receipts by sector." Accessed on October 15, 2011.

45. Long quoted in Ira Katznelson and Mark Kesselman, *The Politics of Power: A Critical Introduction to American Government* (New York: Harcourt, Brace and Jovanovich, 1975), 259.

46. Quoted in *Congressional Quarterly, Elections '86* (Washington, D.C.: Congressional Quarterly, 1986), 60.

47. Jake Lewis of the House Banking Committee, quoted in Alexander Cockburn and Ken Silverstein, *Washington Babylon* (New York: Verso, 1996), 67.

48. See McQuaid, passim.

49. Harry Frankel (aka Harry Braverman), "Capitalism and Democracy," *New International* 13 no. 5 (September 1952), 144–49.

50. Jacob S. Hacker and Paul Pierson, *Winner-Take-It Politics* (New York: Simon & Schuster, 2010), 218 (location 3655 in Kindle Books).

51. Cockburn and Silverstein, *Washington Babylon*, 97.

52. "Managed competition" was aimed at co-opting the largest insurance companies into the Clinton plan. Ironically, this provoked a backlash from smaller insurance companies, who felt they would lose the most in a managed-care system. As a result, the smaller insurance companies were the "shock troops" that defeated the Clinton plan.

53. See Vicente Navarro, "Getting the Facts Right: Why Hillary's Health Care Plan

Really Failed," published in *CounterPunch*, November 12, 2007. The characterization of Enthoven as "the father of managed competition" comes from his website: http:/healthpolicy.stanford.edu/people/alaincenthoven.

54. Gregg Easterbrook, "The Business of Politics," *Atlantic*, October 1986, www.theatlantic.com/politics/polibig/eastbusi.htm.

55. K Street is the location in Washington, D.C., of many leading lobbying groups. Politicians refer to the lobbying industry by the shorthand "K Street" in the same way that the media refers to the finance industry as "Wall Street."

56. Jonathan Weisman and Shailagh Murray, "After Abramoff, a GOP Scramble," *Washington Post*, January 6, 2006.

57. Brody Mullins, "Corporate Contributions Shift to the Left," *Wall Street Journal*, June 19, 2006.

58. *The Hill* quoted in David Sirota, "Big Money versus the Grassroots: The Fight for the Heart of the Democratic Party, *Washington Spectator*, September 5, 2006.

59. Robert Pear, "Business Lobby Presses Its Agenda Before '08 Vote," *New York Times*, December 2, 2007.

60. Katznelson and Kesselman, *Politics of Power*, 278.

61. Domhoff, *Fat Cats and Democrats*, 111.

62. Cockburn and Silverstein, *Washington Babylon*, 214–15. Figures on donations from 210.

63. Ibid., 223.

64. Howie Hawkins, "Introduction: The Green Party's Missed Opportunity in 2004—and the Opportunity Still at Hand" in Howie Hawkins, ed., *Independent Politics: The Green Party Strategy Debate* (Chicago: Haymarket Books, 2006), 40.

65. Thomas Harrison, "Election 2000: Infamy and Hope" *New Politics* 8 no. 2 (Winter, 2001).

66. Burnham quoted in Martin P. Wattenberg, "The Crisis of Electoral Politics," *Atlantic*, May 1997.

67. Katha Pollitt, "The Strange Death of Liberal America," *Nation*, August 26, 1996. Pollitt's criticisms of "lesser evil" politics were short-lived, as she later backed Democratic candidates in 2000 and 2004 while criticizing Ralph Nader's third-party efforts.

68. Sheldon S. Wolin, *Democracy Incorporated: Managed Democracy and the Specter of Inverted Totalitarianism* (Princeton, NJ: Princeton University Press, 2008), 203, locations 4122-4124 in Kindle Books.

Chapter Two: The Party of Slavery Becomes the "Party of the People"

1. On Jay's treaty, see William Nisbet Chambers, *Political Parties in a New Nation: The American Experience, 1776–1809* (London: Oxford University Press, 1963), 80.

2. Harry Frankel, "The Jackson Period of American History," *Fourth International* 7 no. 12 (December 1946): 365–68.

3. Ibid.

4. James McPherson, *Battle Cry of Freedom: The Civil War Era* (New York: Oxford University Press, 1988), 26–30.

5. Ibid., 30–31.

6. Peter Camejo, *Racism, Revolution, Reaction, 1861–1877* (New York: Monad Press, 1976), 21.

7. McPherson, *Battle Cry of Freedom*, 690.

8. On the role of the Copperheads or "Peace Democrats" in the riots, see Iver

Bernstein, *The New York City Draft Riots: Their Significance for American Society and Politics in the Age of the Civil War* (New York: Oxford University Press, 1990), 11–14. In the end, the pro-war conservative Democrats of Tammany Hall engineered a compromise that allowed the draft to go forward, but awarded city grants to those who wanted to buy their way out of service. This deal became the cornerstone of the Boss Tweed machine after the war.

9. Mike Davis, *Prisoners of the American Dream: Politics and Economy in the History of the U.S. Working Class* (London: Verso, 1986), 26. By "class consciousness," Davis means "political class consciousness" that would be manifested in the creation of a stable, mass-based labor party. It should be remembered that in this period, American workers fought some of the largest and most militant mass strikes ever seen.

10. Irving Bernstein, *The Lean Years: A History of the American Worker 1920–1983* (Boston: Da Capo Press/Houghton Mifflin), 84.

11. Quoted in Kenneth S. Davis, *FDR: The New Deal Years, 1933–37* (New York: Random House, 1986), 372, 675.

12. Thomas Ferguson and Joel Rogers, *Right Turn: The Decline of the Democrats and the Future of American Politics* (New York: Hill & Wang, 1986), 130.

13. Figures from Michael Goldfield, *The Decline of Organized Labor in the United States* (Chicago: University of Chicago Press, 1982), 10.

14. Chris Harman, *Explaining the Crisis: A Marxist Re-Appraisal* (London: Bookmarks, 1984), 64.

15. Garner and Davis quoted in Frances Fox Piven and Richard Cloward, *Regulating the Poor: The Functions of Public Welfare* (New York: Vintage Books, 1971), 70.

16. Rhonda F. Levine, *Class Struggle and the New Deal* (Lawrence: University Press of Kansas, 1988), 24.

17. Quoted in ibid., 66.

18. Ibid., 67.

19. Rosenman's account is found in Paul Dickson and Thomas B. Allen, *The Bonus Army: An American Epic* (New York: Walker and Company, 2004), 138–39.

20. Ibid., 139.

21. Barton Bernstein, "The New Deal: The Conservative Achievements of Liberal Reform," in *Towards a New Past: Dissenting Essays in American History*, Barton Bernstein, ed. (New York: Vintage, 1969), 268.

22. Attributed to UMWA president John L. Lewis in David M. Kennedy, *Freedom from Fear: The American People in Depression and War, 1929–1945* (New York: Oxford University Press, 1999), 296.

23. Jeremy Brecher, *Strike!* (Boston: South End Press, 1972), 177.

24. Sharon Smith, *Subterranean Fire: A History of Working-Class Radicalism in the United States* (Chicago: Haymarket Books, 2006), 120.

25. Quoted in Michael Goldfield, "Worker Insurgency, Radical Organization and New Deal Labor Legislation," *American Political Science Review* 83 (1989): 1253.

26. Ferguson and Rogers, *Right Turn*, 46.

27. Thomas Ferguson, *Golden Rule: The Investment Theory of Party Competition and the Logic of Money-Driven Political Systems* (Chicago: University of Chicago Press, 1995), 156.

28. This account of Labor's Non-Partisan League, including Berle's note that labor had to "carry the ball" for Roosevelt, the description of the "embarrassingly roseate" LNPL view of FDR's labor policies, and the worries about a 1936 Roosevelt loss empowering a "real Fascist" administration, relies on Steven Fraser,

Labor Will Rule (Ithaca, NY: Cornell University Press, 1991), 352–72.

29. Art Preis, *Labor's Giant Step: The First Twenty Years of the CIO: 1936–55* (New York: Pathfinder Press, 1972), 70.

30. The reference to the "conservative coalition" is the Republican and Southern Democratic working coalition that operated in Congress from 1939 to 1963. See James T. Patterson, "A Conservative Coalition Forms in Congress, 1933–1939," *Journal of American History* 52 no. 4 (March 1966): 757–72.

31. Philip Yale Nicholson, *Labor's Story in the United States* (Philadelphia: Temple University Press, 2004), 220.

32. For a discusssion of the distinction in the Social Security Act between "security" and "welfare," see Theda Skocpol, "The Limits of the New Deal System and the Roots of Contemporary Welfare Dilemmas" in *Social Policy in the United States*, Theda Skocpol, ed. (Princeton, NJ: Princeton University Press, 1995), 211–14.

33. Lipsitz quoted in John Newsinger, "From Class War to Cold War," *International Socialism Journal* 73 (Spring 1996): 108.

34. Harman, *Explaining the Crisis*, 79.

35. Diane B. Kunz, *Butter and Guns: America's Cold War Economic Policy* (New York: The Free Press, 1997), 56.

36. Ibid., 58.

37. The theory of the "permanent arms economy" was developed by the International Socialists in the 1950s and 1960s to explain not only the high level of peacetime arms spending that Cold War adversaries maintained, but also the basis for the postwar economic boom that arms spending provided. See Michael Kidron, *Western Capitalism Since the War* (London: Weidenfeld and Nicolson, 1968).

38. Kunz, *Butter and Guns*, 63.

39. See Daniel Guerin, *100 Years of Labor in the USA* (London: Ink Links, 1979), 161–63; Nicholson, *Labor's Story in the United States*, 251.

40. Quoted in William Serrin, *Homestead: The Glory and Tragedy of an American Steel Town* (New York: Times Books, 1992), 275.

41. Ibid.

42. Quoted in David Brody, *Workers in Industrial America* (New York: Oxford University Press, 1980), 237.

43. Davis, "The New Right's Road to Power," in *Prisoners of the American Dream*, 165. Emphasis is in the original.

44. For these data and more, see Edward N. Wolff, "The Stagnating Fortunes of the Middle Class" in *Should Differences in Income and Wealth Matter?*, Ellen Frankel Paul, Fred D. Miller, and Jeffrey Paul, eds. (New York: Cambridge University Press, 2002), 59–60.

45. Smith, *Subterranean Fire*, 209.

46. Melvyn Dubofsky, *The State and Labor in Modern America* (Chapel Hill: University of North Carolina Press, 1994), 209.

47. Nelson Lichtenstein, "From Corporatism to Collective Bargaining: Organized Labor and the Eclipse of Social Democracy in the Postwar Era," in *Rise and Fall of the New Deal Order*, Gerstle and Fraser, eds. (Princeton, NJ: Princeton University Press, 1989), 140.

48. Kevin Boyle, *The UAW and the Heyday of American Liberalism, 1945–1968* (Ithaca, NY: Cornell University Press, 1995), 92–93. Montgomery quoted on p. 92.

49. Ibid.

50. Documentation of Democratic liberals' anticommunism can be found in David Caute, *The Great Fear: The Anti-Communist Purge Under Truman and Eisenhower*

(New York: Simon & Schuster, 1978), 25–33.

51. Thomas Ferguson, "Industrial Conflict and the Coming of the New Deal: The Triumph of Multinational Liberalism in America," in *Rise and Fall of the New Deal Order*, Gerstle and Fraser, eds., 27.

52. On the dynamic of "reforms from above," see Doug McAdam, *Political Process and Black Insurgency* (Chicago: University of Chicago Press, 1982). On Stevenson, see Boyle, *UAW and Heyday*, or Frances Fox Piven and Richard Cloward, *Why Americans Don't Vote* (New York: Pantheon, 1989).

53. Ahmed Shawki, *Black Liberation and Socialism* (Chicago: Haymarket Books, 2006), 166.

54. Robert Fitch, "H. Ross Perot: America's First Welfare Billionaire," *Ramparts*, November 1971, 43–45, 53.

55. Piven and Cloward, *Regulating the Poor*, 244.

56. John Dittmer, *Local People: The Struggle for Civil Rights in Mississippi* (Urbana, IL: University of Illinois Press, 1994), 374.

57. Quoted in Ibid., 372.

58. On LBJ's troubles, see Joe Allen, "Tet: Turning Point in the Vietnam War," *International Socialist Review* 56 (November–December 2007).

59. C. Eugene Steuerle and Gordon Mermin, "The Big Spending Presidents" (Washington, D.C.: Urban Institute, 1997).

60. "Bretton Woods" refers to the post–Second World War financial system, set up in 1944 at an Allied meeting in Bretton Woods, New Hampshire. The Bretton Woods agreements established the World Bank and the International Monetary Fund and fixed the exchange rate for gold in dollars. The effect was to make the U.S. dollar the world's de facto reserve currency.

61. Charles S. Maier, "The Politics of Productivity: Foundations of American International Economic Policy after World War II," *International Organization* 31 no. 4 (Autumn 1977), 607–33.

62. Quoted in Barry Eichengreen, "The Dollar and the New Bretton Woods System," text of the Henry Thornton Lecture delivered at the Cass School of Business, London, England, December 15, 2004, 11. Available at: www.econ.berkeley.edu/ ~eichengr/policy/cityuniversitylecture2jan3-05.pdf.

Chapter Three: The Rise of the New Democrats

1. The quotes on the Conference Board and the management offensive come from David Gordon, *Fat and Mean: The Corporate Squeeze of Working Americans and the Myth of Managerial "Downsizing"* (New York: Free Press, 1996), 203–205.

2. Quoted in Kim Moody, *An Injury to All: The Decline of American Unionism* (New York: Verso, 1988), 148–49.

3. Kevin Phillips, *The Politics of Rich and Poor: Wealth and the American Electorate in the Reagan Aftermath* (New York: Random House, 1990), 10.

4. Donald L. Bartlett and James B. Steele, "The Broken Promise," *Time*, October 31, 2005.

5. Francis Fox Piven and Richard Cloward, "The Historical Sources of the Contemporary Relief Debate," in *The Mean Season*, Fred Block, et. al (New York: Pantheon Books, 1987), 19.

6. On the importance of opposition to abortion to the creation of the New Right, see Sharon Smith, "Abortion Rights: The Socialist Case," in *Women and Socialism: Essays on Women's Liberation* (Chicago: Haymarket Books, 2005), 69–76. Dan T.

Carter argues for the importance of veiled appeals to racism in the "Southern strategy" that built the GOP from 1968 and beyond in *The Politics of Rage: George Wallace, the Origins of the New Conservatism and the Transformation of American Politics* (Baton Rouge: Lousiana State University, 1996).

7. Ferguson and Rogers, *Right Turn: The Decline of the Democrats and the Future of American Politics* (New York: Hill & Wang, 1986), 106.

8. David Brody, *Workers in Industrial America* (New York: Oxford University Press, 1980), 244.

9. Manning Marable, *Race, Reform and Rebellion* (Jackson: University Press of Mississippi, 1984), 184.

10. Quoted in Andrew R. Flint and Joy Porter, "Jimmy Carter: The Re-emergence of Faith-Based Politics and the Abortion Rights Issue," *Presidential Studies Quarterly* 35 (2005): 28ff.

11. "To Work—Or Not to Work," *Time*, vol. 111 no. 13 (March 20, 1978): 8–16.

12. Quoted in W. Carl Bliven, *Jimmy Carter's Economy: Policy in an Age of Limits* (Chapel Hill: University of North Carolina Press, 2002), 131.

13. AFL-CIO quote from Brody, *Workers in Industrial America*, 244. Information on the defeat of labor law reform comes from Ferguson and Rogers, *Right Turn*, 222–27.

14. On PD-59 and other of Carter's right-wing foreign policy moves, see Stephen Zunes, "Carter's Less-Known Legacy," October 18, 2002, at www.commondreams.org/views02/1018-06.htm, accessed on April 9, 2008.

15. Moody, *Injury to All*, 182. Moody also points out another reason for the Progressive Alliance's collapse: the acceptance of UAW president Fraser of Carter's bailout of Chrysler and the broader goal of labor-management cooperation. "[The unions behind the Progressive Alliance] thus slipped from rebellion against the Democrats, back into dependence," 151.

16. Mike Urquhart, "Gramm-Rudman Bill Will Hurt Us All; Could Cost 300,000 Federal Jobs," *Labor Notes*, March 1986, 3.

17. On Democrats' support for the invasion of Grenada, see *Projections of Power*, Robert M. Entman, (Chicago: University of Chicago Press, 2004), 65–68. The sordid history of Democratic complicity with the Reagan and Bush administrations' support for the UNITA thugs is recounted in George Wright, *The Destruction of a Nation* (London: Pluto Press, 1997), esp. chapters 7 and 8. For Aspin's championing of the contras, the Midgetman missile and other right-wing positions, see Andrew Rosenthal, "House, 176–90, Votes to Scrap The Midgetman," *New York Times*, July 28, 1989, and David Brooks and Peter Osterlund, "The Real Les Aspin Story," *National Review*, December 19, 1986.

18. Thomas Ferguson and Joel Rogers, "Big Business Backs the Freeze," *Nation*, July 19, 1986.

19. Information on the DBC and the DLC from Ferguson and Rogers, *Right Turn*, 8–9, Kirk quoted on p. 9, and from William Greider, *Who Will Tell the People?* (New York: Touchstone, 1992), 263. It's interesting to note that Gephardt in the 1990s and 2000s promoted himself as a pro-labor populist.

20. Trade union density figures are from "Trade Union Density (%) in OECD Countries, 1960–2002," Organization of Economic Cooperation and Development, at www.oecd.org/dataoecd/25/42/39891561.xls, accessed April 9, 2008. Figures on the ratio of profits to stockholder equity are found in the *Economic Report of the President, 2003* (Washington, D.C.: U.S. Government Printing Office, 2003), Table B-94, 385.

21. Robert Dreyfuss, "How the DLC Does It," *American Prospect*, April 22, 2001. The

book that Dreyfuss cites is Kenneth S. Baer, *Reinventing Democrats* (Lawrence: University of Kansas Press, 2000).

22. Norman Solomon, *False Hope: The Politics of Illusion in the Clinton Era* (Monroe, ME: Common Courage Press, 1994), 27.

23. H. Ross Perot was a Republican billionaire who ran a "centrist" campaign emphasizing protectionism and a balanced budget. He won nearly 19 percent of the total popular vote, the highest showing for a third party in eighty years. Although subsequent surveys showed he drew votes equally from the Democrats and the Republicans, his campaign mostly hurt the incumbent president, George H. W. Bush, and helped Clinton. See Steven J. Rosenstone, Roy L. Behr, and Edward H. Lazarus, *Third Parties in America*, 2nd ed. (Princeton, NJ: Princeton University Press, 1996), especially chapter 9.

24. Peter Baker and John F. Harris, "Clinton Admits to Lewinsky Relationship, Challenges Starr to End Personal 'Prying,'" *Washington Post*, August 18, 1998.

25. Ronald Brownstein, "Clintonism," *U.S. News and World Report*, January 26, 1998.

26. Quoted in Philip A. Klinkner, "Bill Clinton and the New Liberalism," in *Without Justice for All*, Adolph Reed Jr., ed. (Boulder, CO: Westview Press, 1999), 15.

27. See James Hormey and Robert Greenstein, "Is the Clinton Budget a 'Big Government' Proposal?" Center for Budget and Policy Priorities, March 14, 2000, www.cbpp.org.

28. David Frum, "When the Economy Turns," *Weekly Standard* 4 no. 19 (February 1, 1999).

29. These plans, along with many other later-broken promises, were outlined in the campaign's mass-produced manifesto, Bill Clinton and Al Gore, *Putting People First: How We Can All Change America* (New York: Three Rivers Press, 1992).

30. E. J. Dionne, *They Only Look Dead: Why Progressives Will Dominate the Next Political Era* (New York: Simon & Schuster, 1996), 113.

31. On the Democratic mania for deregulation, see James Ridgeway, "It's the Deregulation, Stupid," *Mother Jones*, March 28, 2008.

32. For an exposé of the Clinton-Gore first-term environmental record, see Alexander Cockburn and Ken Silverstein, *Washington Babylon*, 187–247. Browner's quote is from page 235.

33. See "Remarks by the President on the House Vote on the Budget Package," the White House, August 5, 1993, available at www.clintonfoundation.org/legacy/080593-speech-by-president-in-the-rose-garden.htm, accessed April 9, 2008.

34. Quoted in Robert D. Reich, "Coolidge's Democratic Disciples," *New York Times*, February 8, 2000.

35. Joel Geier, "Can the U.S. Escape the Global Crisis?," *International Socialist Review* 6 (Spring 1999), 40.

36. The U.S. economy was considered so strong by 2000 that the International Monetary Fund devoted a section to "How Much Longer Will the Expansion in North America Continue?" in its *World Economic Outlook*, issued in 2000. See International Monetary Fund, *World Economic Outlook* (Washington, D.C.: International Monetary Fund, 2000).

37. John E. Schwartz, "The Hidden Side of the Clinton Economy," *Atlantic Monthly*, October 1998.

38. Isaac Shapiro and Robert Greenstein, "The Widening Income Gulf," Center for Budget and Policy Priorities, September 5, 1999.

39. See U.S. Census Bureau, *Poverty in the United States: 2000* (Washington, D.C.: U.S. Government Printing Office, 2000).

40. See David E. Rosenbaum and Steve Lohr, "With a Stable Economy, Clinton Hopes for Credit," *New York Times*, August 6, 1996.

41. Peter Edelman, "The Worst Thing Bill Clinton Has Done," *Atlantic Monthly*, March 1997.

42. Ibid.

43. Liz Schott, Robert Greenstein, and Wendell Primus, "The Determinants of Welfare Caseload Decline: A Brief Rejoinder," Center for Budget and Policy Priorities, June 22, 1999.

44. Ed Lazere, "Welfare Balances After Three Years of TANF Block Grants," Center for Budget and Policy Priorities, January 12, 2000.

45. See Sam Elkin and Robert Greenstein, "Much of the Projected Non Social Security Surplus Is a Mirage," July 12, 1999, Center for Budget and Policy Priorities, July 12, 1999.

46. On the cuts in Medicare, see Robert Pear, "Health Providers and Elderly Clash on Medicare Funds," *New York Times*, May 15, 2000. On the decline of home health care, see the *New York Times* editorial "The Plunge in Home Health Care," April 25, 2000.

47. For a critique of the drift in Medicare policy, see Judith Feder and Marilyn Moon, "Can Medicare Survive Its Saviors?," *American Prospect* 44 (May/June, 1999). For a clear critique of plans to privatize Social Security, see Mark Weisbrot and Dean Baker, *Social Security: The Phony Crisis* (Chicago: University of Chicago Press, 1999).

48. Gwen Ifill, "The Free-Trade Accord: Estranged, Not Divorced," *New York Times*, November 9, 1993.

49. Quoted in Lee Sustar, "A New Labor Movement?" *International Socialist Review* 1 (Summer 1997), 21.

50. For a critique of this program see Peter Lurie, Marti Long, and Sidney M. Wolfe, "Reinventing OSHA: Dangerous Reductions in Enforcement During the Clinton Administration," *Public Citizen*, 1999, at www.citizen.org/publications/release .cfm?ID=6693, accessed April 16, 2008.

51. For an eyewitness report of the 1999 "Battle of Seattle" and an evaluation of labor's role in it, see editorial "WTO: Crashing the Bosses' Party" and Lee Sustar, "Take the Spirit of Seattle Across the U.S.," *International Socialist Review* 10 (Winter 2000), 1–5.

52. The administration bragged about this on the "Reinventing Government" website. See National Partnership for Reinventing Government, "Reinvention@ workforyou: Creating a Culture of Change and Reconnecting Americans to Their Government," http://govinfo.library.unt.edu/npr/whoweare/history2.html.

53. Figures are from U.S. Bureau of Justice Statistics, *Sourcebook of Criminal Justice Statistics Online*, available at www.albany.edu/sourcebook/, accessed on April 6, 2008.

54. For details on the impact of these repressive Clinton-era laws that presaged the 2001 PATRIOT Act, see "Testimony of Legislative Counsel Gregory T. Nojeim on the Use of Secret Evidence in Immigration Proceedings Before the House Judiciary Committee," May 23, 2000, at www.aclu.org/immigrants/evidence/ 11767leg20000523.html.

55. The Supreme Court declared the Communications Decency Act of 1996 unconstitutional in *Reno v. American Civil Liberties Union*, 521 U.S. 844 (1997), and in *Shea v. Reno*, 930 F. Supp. 916; 1996 U.S. Dist.

56. Philip A. Klinkner, "Bill Clinton and the New Liberalism," in *Without Justice for*

All, Adolph Reed, ed., 25.

57. See Marc Cooper, "Letter from California: What Cost Victory?" *Nation*, November 4, 1996, 11–15.

58. Quoted in Klinkner, "Bill Clinton and New Liberalism," 26–27.

59. Quoted in Katherine S. Manegold, "Clinton Ire on Appointments Startles Women," *New York Times*, December 23, 1992.

60. Elizabeth Schulte, "The New Assault on a Woman's Right to Choose," *International Socialist Review* 12 (June–July 2000), 46. Clinton said he would sign the "partial-birth" abortion ban if its wording were changed.

61. "Don't ask, don't tell" was the "compromise" policy on gay service members that the Clinton administration worked out with the Pentagon. The new regulation called for military officials not to ask service members to disclose their sexual orientation. But it left intact the right of the military to discharge any gay service members who disclosed their sexual orientation or who were later discovered to be gay.

62. See Lance Selfa, "Gay Politics in the U.S.: Which Way Forward?" *International Socialist Review* 6 (Spring 1999), 15–20.

63. Kevin Phillips, *Wealth and Democracy: A Political History of the American Rich* (New York: Broadway Books, 2002), 343.

64. John R. MacArthur, "Democrats Have No One to Blame but Themselves," *Toronto Globe & Mail*, November 8, 2002.

65. Anis Shivani, "Conservative Politics in an Era of Dealignment," Counterpunch, January 4, 2003, www.counterpunch.org/shivani01042003.html.

66. William Greider, "Clinton's Lost Presidency," *Nation*, February 14, 2000, 11–18.

67. Quoted in Henry J. Pulizzi, "Bush Rebuts Greenspan's Critique of Fiscal Policy," *Wall Street Journal*, September 19, 2007.

68. "Statement from DLC Founder Al From," July 5, 2011, on www.dlc.org.

Chapter Four: From "Hope" to Hopeless: The Democrats in the Obama Era

1. Susan Page and Mimi Hall, "Poll: Americans Believe Obama Will Deliver Despite Down Times," *USA Today*, January 15, 2009, at www.usatoday.com/news/washington/2009-01-15-obamapoll_N.htm, accessed on December 13, 2011.

2. Keith Johnson, "State-Level Wins Augur More GOP Safe Seats," *Wall Street Journal*, November 4, 2010.

3. Andrew Kohut, "Post-Election Perspectives," Remarks at the Pew Research Center Second Annual Warren J. Mitofsky Award Dinner, on Behalf of the Roper Center Newseum, Washington DC, November 13, 2008, at http://pewresearch.org/pubs/1039/post-election-perspectives.

4. Gerald F. Seib, "Business Warms to Obama, but Frictions Loom on Climate," January 8, 2009 at http://online.wsj.com/article/SB123146552810966837.html.

5   See Alistair Barr, "Industry giants support more regulation," *MarketWatch*.com, November 13, 2008, at www.marketwatch.com/news/story/industry-giants-support-more-regulation/story.aspx?guid=%7B06D486AB-87B7-442B-A177-E4CF7C28EE5A%7D.

6. Public Policy Polling, "Takeaways from Massachusetts," January 19, 2010, at http://publicpolicypolling.blogspot.com/2010/01/takeaways-from-massachusetts.html, accessed on December 13, 2011.

7.   E.J. Dionne, "Dems Are Losing the Message War," Real Clear Politics, February 18, 2010, at www.realclearpolitics.com/articles/2010/02/18/why_the_democrats_are_losing_104458.html, accessed on December 13, 2011.

8.   See Sheldon S. Wolin, "Preface to the Paperback Edition," *Democracy Incorporated* (Princeton: Princeton University Press, 2009).

9.   Even Republican leaders acknowledged this. Rep. Tom Davis, head of the Republican Congressional Campaign Committee before he decided to retire in 2008, wrote in a memo to his colleagues that "if we were a dog food, they would take us off the shelf." Quoted in Tom Hamburger and Peter Wallsten, "GOP Torn by Change It Can Believe In," *Los Angeles Times*, May 18, 2008.

10.   For a great dissection of the creation and marketing of the "Obama phenomenon," see Paul Street's *Barack Obama and the Future of American Politics* (Herndon, VA: Paradigm Publishers, 2008).

11.   Federal Election Commission figures available at www.opensecrets.org/pres08/index.php. Industrial sector data can be found in "Contributions by Sector" at www.opensecrets.org/pres08/sectorall.php?cycle=2008.

12.   Ann Zimmerman and Kris Maher, "Wal-Mart Warns of Democratic Win," *Wall Street Journal*, August 1, 2008.

13.   Ken Silverstein, "Barack Obama, Inc.: The Birth of a Washington Machine," *Harpers*, November 2006, at www.harpers.org/archive/2006/11/0081275, accessed on December 13, 2011.

14.   Michael Luo and Christopher Drew, "Obama and McCain Lag in Naming 'Bundlers' Who Rake in Campaign Cash," *New York Times*, July 11, 2008. According to my calculations, if these 507 bundlers hit their targets, they would be responsible for raising at least fifty-two million dollars for Obama.

15.   Campaign Finance Institute, "Reality Check: Obama Received About the Same Percentage from Small Donors in 2008 as Bush in 2004," November 24, 2008, at www.cfinst.org/press/PReleases/08-11-24/Realty_Check_-_Obama_Small_Donors.aspx, accessed on December 13, 2011.

16.   Quoted in "Obama's Mixed Message," *International Socialist Review* 64, March-April 2009, www.isreview.org/issues/64/ed-obama.shtml, accessed January 20, 2012.

17.   Ezra Klein, "Waiting for Barack," *American Prospect*, October 10, 2006.

18.   Thomas Friedman, "Dumb as We Wanna Be," *New York Times*, April 30, 2008.

19.   Edward Luce, "Obama Holds Bipartisan Economy Talks," *Financial Times*, July 29, 2008.

20.   Jonathan Greenberger, "Obama Slams Clinton for Iraq Vote," May 17, 2007, ABC News Political Radar Blog, http://blogs.abcnews.com/politicalradar/2007/05/obama_slams_cli.html. Greenberger notes that Obama had earlier told the *New Yorker*, "it's not clear to me what differences [Clinton and I have] had since I've been in the Senate" and "I think what people might point to is our different assessments of the war in Iraq, although I'm always careful to say that I was not in the Senate, so perhaps the reason I thought it was such a bad idea was that I didn't have the benefit of U.S. intelligence." On all Iraq-related votes through 2007, Clinton and Obama took opposite sides only once, when he voted to confirm Gen. George Casey as army chief of staff and she voted against. In his *Barack Obama and the Future of American Politics*, Paul Street notes how the Democratic candidates' convergence on a position of grudging acceptance of the Iraq War effectively took the war out of contention for the general election.

21. David Brooks, "Obama Admires Bush," *New York Times*, May 16, 2008.
22. Barack Obama, "Renewing American Leadership," *Foreign Affairs*, July/August 2007, www.foreignaffairs.org/20070701faessay86401/barack-obama/renewing-american -leadership.html.
23. See "An Open Letter to Barack Obama," *The Nation*, July 30, 2008, at www .thenation.com/doc/20080818/open_letter. Signatories include most of the regular columnists and contributors to the *Nation*, Tim Carpenter of Progressive Democrats of America, historian Howard Zinn, sociologist Frances Fox Piven, *Black Commentator* editor Bill Fletcher Jr., the novelist Walter Mosley, and former Howard Dean 2004 Internet guru Zephyr Teachout.
24. Obama's comments recorded in Michael Powell, "Obama Moves to Reassure his 'Friends on the Left'," *International Herald Tribune*, July 9, 2008.
25. Read the entire statement at http://progressivesforobama.blogspot.com.
26. Glen Ford, "'Progressives for Obama' Fool Themselves," *Black Agenda Report*, July 9, 2008.
27. Ron Suskind, *Confidence Men: Wall Street, Washington and the Education of a President* (New York: HarperCollins, 2011), 353.
28. Ezra Klein, "Could this time have been different?" *Washington Post*, October 8, 2011.
29. See the criticism of the Treasury's housing policies at Yves Smith's nakedcapitalism .com blog, e.g., "Quelle Surprise! Treasury Mortgage Mod Program Produces Zero Permanent Mods," November 29, 2009, at www.nakedcapitalism.com/2009/11/ quelle-surprise-treasury-mortgage-mod-program-produces-zero-permanent -mods.html.
30. Quoted in Ron Suskind, *Confidence Men: Wall Street, Washington and the Education of a President* (New York: HarperCollins, 2011), 234.
31. Suskind, *Confidence Men*, 242.
32. Andrea Orr, "Tracking the Recovery: Big Banks Seen as Big Beneficiaries of Government Economic Policies," Economic Policy Institute, October 6, 2009, at www.epi.org/publication/big_banks_seen_as_big_beneficiaries_of_government _economic_policies/, accessed on December 24, 2011.
33. Viral Acharya, Matthew Richardson and Richard Sylla, "A Critical Assessment of the Wall Street Reform and Consumer Protection Act," www.nakedcapitalism.com, October 21, 2010, accessed on December 24, 2011.
34. Suskind, *Confidence Men*, 390.
35. Jeff Karoub, "Workers say Obama Treated Autos Worse than Wall St," Associated Press, March 31, 2009.
36. Obama appointed the Council in 2011 under the chairmanship of General Electric CEO Jeffrey Imhelt. See www.whitehouse.gov/administration/advisory-boards/jobs -council/meetings.
37. Arun Gupta, "Hope Has Left the Building," *Indypendent*, January 8, 2010, at www.indypendent.org/2010/01/07/hope-left/.
38. I am not using the term "center-right" for effect. It's an accurate assessment of the Obama administration's economic policies. No less an authority than Lawrence Fink, the billionaire CEO of BlackRock, the multinational investment firm, said after meeting Obama: "The president is much more of a centrist . . . in some ways he might even be called right of what used to be called center." See Suskind, *Confidence Men*, 455.
39. Obama quoted in Gerald F. Seib, "Obama, Business Leaders Inch Toward Rapprochement," *Wall Street Journal*, February 5, 2010, A2.

40. To see how pervasive the influence of corporate money is, see the account of the "conscience of Congress," the Congressional Black Caucus, in Eric Lipton and Eric Lichtblau, "In Black Caucus, a Fundraising Powerhouse," *New York Times*, February 10, 2010, at www.nytimes.com/2010/02/14/us/politics/14cbc.html.

41. For example, see the statement by leading members of Physicians for a National Health Program, "A False Promise of Reform," March 22, 2010, at www.pnhp .org, accessed on December 24, 2011.

42. Physicians for a National Health Program, "Barack Obama on Single Payer in 2003," at www.pnhp.org/news/2008/june/barack_obama_on_sing.php, accessed on January 16, 2012.

43. See Physicians for a National Health Program, "Obama to Single-Payer Advocates: Drop Dead," March 3, 2009, and "Dr. Oliver Fein Reports on the White House Health Summit," March 9, 2009, both available at the Physicians for a National Health Program website, www.pnhp.org, accessed on January 16, 2012.

44. ProCon.org, "History of the Individual Health Insurance Mandate, 1989-2010: Republican Origins of Democratic Health Care Provision," February 25, 2011, at http://healthcarereform.procon.org/view.resource.php?resourceID=004182.

45. From Chad Terhune and Keith Epstein, "The Health Insurers Have Already Won," *Bloomberg Businessweek*, August 6, 2009.

46. See Sunlight Foundation, "Visualizing the Health Care Lobbyist Complex, July 22, 2009, at http://sunlightfoundation.com/projects/2009/healthcare_lobbyist _complex/, accessed on December 24, 2011.

47. David K. Kilpatrick, "Obama Is Taking an Active Role in Talks on Health Care Plan," *New York Times*, August 12, 2009, at www.nytimes.com/2009/08/13/health /policy/13health.html and Ryan Grim, "Internal Memo Confirms Big Giveaways In White House Deal With Big Pharma." Huffington Post, September 13, 2009, at www.huffingtonpost.com/2009/08/13/internal-memo-confirms-bi_n_258285 .html, both accessed on December 11, 2011.

48. Glenn Greenwald, "White House as Helpless Victim on Health Care," *Salon*, December 16, 2009, at www.salon.com/2009/12/16/white_house_5/, accessed on December 11, 2011.

49. Suzy Khimm, "Howard Dean Walks It Back," *Newsweek*, December 20, 2009, at www.thedailybeast.com/newsweek/blogs/the-gaggle/2009/12/20/howard-dean -walks-it-back.html, accessed on December 11, 2011.

50. For an insightful review of the origin and base of the Tea Party, see Paul Street and Anthony Dimaggio, *Crashing the Tea Party* (Herndon, VA: Paradigm Publishers, 2011).

51. See Stanford University with the Robert Wood Johnson Foundation, The Associated Press 2010 Health Care Reform Survey conducted by Knowledge Networks, August 31–September 7, 2010, at http://surveys.ap.org/data/ KnowledgeNetworks/Health%20Reform%20Topline%20for%20Posting.pdf.

52. David McNally, *Global Slump* (Oakland, CA: PM Press, 2011), 4.

53. A preview of the commission's report—which takes aim at Social Security, Medicaid, and the federal workforce—came with the November 10, 2010 release of the wish list of commission co-chairs Erskine Bowles and Alan Simpson. See Megan Carpentier, "Fiscal Commission Co-Chairs Simpson and Bowles Release Eye-Popping Recommendations," Talking Points Memo, November 10, 2010, at http://tpmdc.talkingpointsmemo.com/2010/11/deficit-commission-co-chairs -simpson-and-bowles-release-eye-popping-recommendations.php.

54. Gerald Seib, "Obama Targets a 'Grand Bargain' to Fix Budget Mess," *Wall Street Journal*, January 16, 2009, at http://blogs.wsj.com/capitaljournal/2009/01/16/obama -targets-a-grand-bargain-to-fix-budget-mess/, accessed on December 11, 2011.

55. Frank Newport, "Americans Favor Jobs Plan Proposals, Including Taxing Rich," Gallup Poll, September 20, 2011, at www.gallup.com/poll/149567/Americans -Favor-Jobs-Plan-Proposals-Including-Taxing-Rich.aspx, accessed on December 11, 2011.

56. Elizondo quoted in Steven Greenhouse, "Unions Find Members Slow to Rally Behind Democrats," *New York Times*, September 17, 2010.

57. Gary Langer, "Obama's No Shows: 29 million," ABC News, at http://blogs .abcnews.com/thenumbers/2010/11/obamas-no-shows-29-million.html.

58. "CNN Poll: Drop in Liberal Support Pushes Obama Approval Rating Down," PoliticalTicker, July 22, 2011, at http://politicalticker.blogs.cnn.com/2011/07/22/ cnn-poll-drop-in-liberal-support-pushes-obama-approval-rating-down/, accessed December 11, 2011.

59. See Street and Dimaggio, *Crashing the Tea Party*, on the racism of Tea Party supporters.

60. On the Gates and Sherrod incidents, see Patricia Zengerle, "Analysis: Race Issues Beset Obama's "Post-Racial" Presidency," Reuters, July 21, 2010 at www.reuters .com/article/2010/07/21/us-usa-politics-obama-race-idUSTRE66K6JN20100721, accessed on January 16, 2012. For Michele Obama's remarks on obesity, see Lynn Sweet, "Michelle Obama in NAACP Speech, Compares Crusade Against Obesity to Civil Rights Battles," *Chicago Sun-Times*, July 13, 2010.

61. John McWhorter, "Why Won't Obama End the War on Drugs?" National Public Radio, June 17, 2011, at www.npr.org/2011/06/17/137243512/the-root-why-wont -obama-end-the-war-on-drugs, accessed on January 16, 2012.

62. Lyndra Vassar, "Tavis Smiley and Cornel West Criticize President Obama, Steve Harvey Responds," *Essence*, August 13, 2011, at www.essence.com/2011/08/13/ tavis-smiley-and-cornel-west-criticize-president-obama-steve-harvey-responds /#ixzz1jdSivgiq, accessed on January 16, 2012.

63. Quoted in Keeanga-Yamahtta Taylor, "No He Won't for Black America," *Socialist Worker*, September 29, 2011, at http://socialistworker.org/2011/09/29/no-he-wont -for-black-america, accessed December 11, 2011.

64. For a socialist critique of the Obama administration's environmental policies, see Chris Williams, "Sacrificing the Earth," *International Socialist Review* 79 (September-October, 2011) and his *Ecology and Socialism* (Chicago: Haymarket Books, 2010).

65. Peter Wallsten and Jia Lynn Yang, "Obama's Support for Nuclear Power Faces a Test," *Washington Post*, March 18, 2011, at www.washingtonpost.com/politics/ obamas-support-for-nuclear-power-faces-a-test/2011/03/18/ABQLu8r_story.html, accessed on January 16, 2012.

66. For a balance sheet on the Copenhagen climate change summit, see John Vidal, Allegra Stratton and Suzanne Goldenberg, "Low Targets, Goals Dropped: Copenhagen Ends in Failure," *Guardian* (UK), December 18, 2009. For details on the administration's cave-in on the EPA ozone standards, see John M. Broder, "Obama Administration Abandons Stricter Air-Quality Rules," *New York Times*, September 2, 2011. Daniel J. Weiss of the normally administration-friendly Center for American Progress criticized the White House for "[granting] an item on Big Oil's wish list at the expense of the health of children, seniors and the infirm."

67. "Vulnerable to Disaster around the World," interview with Harvey Wasserman,

Socialist Worker, March 21, 2011, at http://socialistworker.org/2011/03/21/ vulnerable-to-disaster, accessed January 20, 2012.

68. Jeffrey St. Clair, "Obama and the Man in the Hat," *Counterpunch,* May 13-15, 2011, at www.counterpunch.org/2011/05/13/obama-and-the-man-in-the-hat, accessed on January 16, 2012.

69. See the videos of Obama's 2008 promises at http://fairimmigration.org/change -takes-courage/obamas-unfulfilled-immigration-promises/, accessed on January 18, 2012.

70. Shaun Harkin and Nicole Colson, "Resisting Juan Crow in Alabama, "*Socialist Worker,* November 29, 2011, at http://socialistworker.org/2011/11/29/resisting -juan-crow-in-alabama, accessed January 20, 2012.

71. Mary O'Toole, "Analysis: Obama Deportations Raise Immigration Policy Questions," Reuters, September 20, 2011, at www.reuters.com/article/2011/09/ 20/us-obama-immigration-idUSTRE78J05720110920, accessed January 18, 2012.

72. Kung Li, "Voices: Obama Skewers the Immigrant Justice Movement," *Facing South,* August 25, 2011, at www.southernstudies.org/2011/08/voices-obama -skewers-the-immigrant-justice-movement.html, accessed January 18, 2012.

73. See David Moberg, "The Meaning of 'Massachusetts Working-Class Revolt,'" *In These Times,* January 22, 2011, at www.inthesetimes.com/working/entry/5460 /the_meaning_of_massachusetts_working-class_revolt/, accessed December 11, 2011; Michael O'Brien, "AFL-CIO Blames 'Working-Class Revolt' for Brown Election," *The Hill,* January 21, 2011, at http://thehill.com/blogs/blog-briefing-room /news/77365-afl-cio-cites-working-class-revolt-in-special-election-aftermath?page =2#comments, accessed December 11, 2011.

74. Bureau of Labor Statistics, US Department of Labor, "Major Work Stoppages in 2009," Economic News Release at www.bls.gov/news.release/wkstp.nr0.htm.

75. After Arizona passed its draconian anti-immigrant law in 2010, a grassroots protest movement erupted. In the absence of that movement, it's not clear that the Justice Department would have filed its 2010 court challenge to the law. Similarly, hundreds of environmental activists were arrested in protests at the White House over the U.S. State Department's support for the planned Keystone XL gas pipeline from Canada. Following the protests, the White House announced that it would put off a final decision on the pipeline until after the 2012 election. These cases illustrate a couple of points: first, that protest does work; second, that grassroots activism, rather than Beltway lobbying, forced the White House to act.

76. Jane Hamsher, "Rahm Goes Apeshit on Liberals in the Veal Pen," *Firedoglake,* August 9, 2009, at http://fdlaction.firedoglake.com/2009/08/07/rahm-goes -apeshit-on-liberals-in-the-veal-pen/. Among the regular attendees at this meeting are, according to Hamsher, Rock the Vote, the unions, the Leadership Conference on Civil and Human Rights, the Sierra Club, Health Care For America Now!, Bob Creamer (liberal Rep. Jan Schakowsky's husband) of Americans United for Change, Center for American Progress, Media Matters, MoveOn, Campaign for America's Future. The most plugged-in union is SEIU and its coalition Change To Win.

77. Katrina vanden Heuvel, "Progressives Don't Hate Ourselves," *Washington Post,* November 29, 2011, at www.washingtonpost.com/opinions/progressives-dont-hate -ourselves/2011/11/28/gIQAQI6T6N_story.html, accessed on December 11, 2011.

78. The October 2 "One Nation" rally organized by a coalition of groups, including the AFL-CIO and the NAACP, brought out hundreds of thousands of working people. But instead of making the rally a focal point in a fight for jobs, the

organizers kept its focus on getting out the vote for the Democrats.

79. Tom Hamburger, "Labor Unions Find Themselves Card Checkmated," *Los Angeles Times*, May 19, 2009.

80. Brody Mullins and John D. McKinney, "Campaign's Big Spender," *Wall Street Journal*, October 22, 2010.

81. Theda Skocpol, "The Democrats' Learned Timidity," *New York Times*, January 20, 2010, at http://roomfordebate.blogs.nytimes.com/2010/01/20/the-democrats-day -after/#theda, accessed on December 12, 2011.

82. All quotes from Kevin Baker, "Barack Hoover Obama: The Best and the Brightest Blow It Again," *Harper's*, July, 2009, at www.harpers.org/archive/2009/ 07/0082562, accessed on December 12, 2011.

83. Stanley Aronowitz, "Let's Break from the Party of War and Wall Street," *Indypendent*, January 8, 2010, at www.indypendent.org/2010/01/07/break-from -the-party/. While campaign finance data show that Democrats have been increasingly successful in winning Wall Street and hedge fund money since the Clinton years, it's too easy to label it a "party of finance capital." Wall Street still plays both sides of the aisle, and has recently shifted contributions to the GOP to pressure congressional Democrats to water down financial reform legislation. See Brody Mullins and Neil King Jr., "GOP Chases Wall Street Donors," *Wall Street Journal*, February 4, 2010.

84. Rick Ellis, "Updated: 'Occupy' Crackdowns Coordinated with Federal Law Enforcement Officials," *Minneapolis Top News Examiner*, November 15, 2011, at www.examiner.com/top-news-in-minneapolis/were-occupy-crackdowns-aided -by-federal-law-enforcement-agencies, accessed December 24, 2011.

85. Matt Taibbi, "Obama and Jobs: Why I Don't Believe Him Anymore," reprinted at CommonDreams.org, September 6, 2011, at www.commondreams.org/view/2011/ 09/06-6, accessed on December 13, 2011.

Chapter Five: Social Movements and the "Party of the People"

1. The Constitution can be viewed online at www.usconstitution.net/const.html.

2. Frederick Douglass, "The Significance of Emancipation in the West Indies," speech delivered at Canandaigua, New York, August 3, 1857, in *The Frederick Douglass Papers. Series One: Speeches, Debates, and Interviews*, vol 3: 1855-63, ed. John W. Blassingame (New Haven, CT: Yale University Press), 204.

3. See Sharon Smith's discussion of these pecularities of American capitalism in *Subterranean Fire: A History of Working-Class Radicalism in the United States* (Chicago: Haymarket Books, 2005), chapter 2.

4. G. William Domhoff, *Fat Cats and Democrats* (Englewood Cliffs, NJ: Prentice-Hall, 1972), 30–31.

5. Michael Schwartz, *Radical Protest and Social Structure* (Chicago: University of Chicago Press, 1976), 13.

6. See ibid., 3–16, for more discussion about the origins of the Farmers' Alliance and the class nature of the Democratic Party.

7. Robert C. McMath Jr., *American Populism: A Social History, 1877–1898* (New York: Hill & Wang, 1993), 148.

8. See the details at Dave Leip's "Atlas of U.S. Presidential Elections" at www .uselectionatlas.org/RESULTS/party.php?year=1892&type=national&no=3&f=1 &off=0&elect=0, accessed on April 26, 2008. Weaver won Nevada, Idaho, North Dakota, Kansas, and Colorado.

9. Quoted in McMath, *American Populism*, 156.
10. Lawrence Goodwyn, *The Populist Moment* (New York: Oxford University Press, 1978), 232–33. The Populist demand for "free silver" was a demand for the government to stimulate the economy through inflation. Indebted farmers would receive relief by being able to pay back their debts in inflated dollars. The government-maintained gold standard for money had, on the other hand, a deflationary impact, which aided banks and other of the farmers' creditors. This was why William Jennings Bryan, in his speech at the 1896 Democratic convention, famously charged that farmers were being "crucified on a cross of gold."
11. Ibid., 231.
12. Robert E. Cherny, "The Democratic Party in the Era of William Jennings Bryan," in *Democrats and the American Idea*, Peter B. Kovler, ed. (Washington, D.C.: Center for National Policy Press, 1992), 179.
13. Lloyd, quoted in McMath, *American Populism*, 203.
14. Howard Zinn, *A People's History of the United States, 1492–Present* (New York: HarperCollins, 1995), 295.
15. Ahmed Shawki, *Black Liberation and Socialism* (Chicago: Haymarket Books, 2006), 79.
16. AFL official Ed McGrady quoted in Arthur M. Schlesinger, *The Crisis of the Old Order, 1919–1933* (New York: Houghton-Mifflin, 1957), 176.
17. Julian E. Zelizer, "The Forgotten Legacy of the New Deal: Fiscal Conservatism and the Roosevelt Administration, 1933–1938," *Presidential Studies Quarterly* 30 no. 2 (2000), 331ff.
18. See the 1932 Democratic Party platform at the website of the American Presidency Project, www.presidency.ucsb.edu/showplatforms.php?platindex=D1932.
19. John Braeman, Robert H. Bremner, and David Brody, *The New Deal: The National Level* (Columbus: Ohio State University Press, 1975), 57.
20. This characterization of the "uprising" for union recognition, including the quote from the AFL convention report, is from Frances Fox Piven and Richard A. Cloward, *Poor Peoples' Movements: Why They Succeed, How They Fail* (New York: Vintage, 1977), 114.
21. The 1934 figures are from Smith, *Subterranean Fire*, 104. The 1937 figures are from Art Preis, *Labor's Giant Step* (New York: Pathfinder Press, 1974), 121.
22. Read about these three "turning point" strikes in Smith, *Subterranean Fire*, 104–13.
23. Richard O. Boyer and Herbert M. Morais, *Labor's Untold Story* (Pittsburgh, PA: United Electrical, Radio and Machine Workers of America, 1955), 276.
24. Irving Bernstein, "Americans in Depression and War," U.S. Department of Labor website, at www.dol.gov/oasam/programs/history/chapter5.htm, accessed on April 26, 2008.
25. David M. Kennedy, *Freedom from Fear: The American People in Depression and War, 1929–1945* (New York: Oxford University Press, 1999), 297–98.
26. This description of the Liberty League comes from Edward Berkowitz and Kim McQuaid, *Creating the Welfare State: The Political Economy of Twentieth Century Reform* (New York: Praeger Publishers, 1980), 90.
27. Quoted in Douglas B. Craig, *After Wilson: The Struggle for the Democratic Party, 1920–1934* (Chapel Hill: University of North Carolina Press, 1992), 288.
28. Dan La Botz, "The New Deal at 75—Lessons for Today: Confronting the Economic Crisis," April 9, 2008, *Counterpunch*, www.counterpunch.org/labotz04092008.html, accessed on April 26, 2008.
29. Stephen Fraser, *Labor Will Rule: Sidney Hillman and the Rise of American Labor*

(Ithaca, NY: Cornell University Books, 1991), 323.

30. Ibid., 335–36.
31. Lewis quoted in Seymour Martin Lipset and Gary Marks, *It Didn't Happen Here: Why Socialism Failed in the United States* (New York: W.W. Norton, 2000), 212.
32. Preis, *Labor's Giant Step*, 96.
33. Lipset and Marks, *It Didn't Happen Here*, 72.
34. Mike Davis, *Prisoners of the American Dream: Politics and Economy in the History of the US Working Class* (New York: Verso, 1986), 67.
35. Smith, *Subterranean Fire*, 121.
36. Nelson Lichtensten quoted in Kim Moody, "Stumbling in the Dark: American Labor's Failed Response," in *The Year Left*, vol. 1, Mike Davis, Fred Pfeil, and Michael Sprinker, eds. (London: Verso, 1985), 88. CIO-PAC was the forerunner of the modern-day AFL-CIO's Committee on Political Education (COPE).
37. Preis, *Labor's Giant Step*, 29.
38. Ibid., 113–20.
39. Smith, *Subterranean Fire*, 158.
40. Piven and Cloward, *Poor People's Movements*, 167.
41. This point will be developed further in chapter 5.
42. Preis, *Labor's Giant Step*, 276. See also Davis, *Prisoners of American Dream*, 86.
43. "Special Message to the Congress Urging Legislation for Industrial Peace," May 25, 1946, available at Harry S. Truman Library and Museum at www.trumanlibrary.org/publicpapers/index.php?pid=1567&st=railroad+strike&st1=Congress, accessed July 15, 2008.
44. Ronald L. Filippelli and Mark D. McCulloch, *Cold War in the Working Class: The Rise and Decline of the United Electrical Workers* (Albany: State University of New York Press, 1995), 108.
45. Quoted in Preis, *Labor's Giant Step*, 294.
46. For a discussion of the provisions of the Taft-Hartley Act, see Melvyn Dubofsky, *The State and Labor in Modern America* (Chapel Hill: University of North Carolina Press, 1994), 201–207.
47. Preis, *Labor's Giant Step*, 316. In the congressional votes overriding Truman's veto of Taft-Hartley, House Democrats voted for the Act 106–71 and Senate Democrats voted to uphold Truman's veto by a vote of 20–22.
48. Kevin Boyle, *The UAW and the Heyday of American Liberalism* (Ithaca, NY: Cornell University Press, 1995), 51.
49. James R. Fuchs, interview with Andrew J. Biemiller, Washington, D.C., July 29, 1977, archived at the Harry S. Truman Library, Independence, MO, at www.trumanlibrary.org/oralhist/biemiller.htm#transcript, accessed on May 3, 2008.
50. Jerry N. Ness, interview with Clark Clifford, May 10, 1971, www.trumanlibrary.org/oralhist/cliford4.htm#213, accessed on May 3, 2008. Clifford went on to become a Democratic elder and fixture in the Washington establishment. He served as defense secretary during the Vietnam War under LBJ.
51. John Anderson, *The Taft-Hartley Act* (Seattle, WA: Hera Press, 1977).
52. Zinn, *People's History of the United States*, 420–21.
53. Davis, *Prisoners of American Dream*, 1–92. See Filippelli and McCulloch for the history of the CIO-sponsored dismemberment of the left-led United Electrical Workers union.
54. Ellen Schrecker, "McCarthyism's Ghosts: Anticommunism and American Labor," *New Labor Forum*, vol. 5 (Spring/Summer 1999), 7–17.
55. Dubofsky, *State and Labor*, 215.

56. Jack M. Bloom, *Class, Race and the Civil Rights Movement* (Bloomington: Indiana University Press, 1987), 69.

57. Nelson Lichtenstein, *State of the Union: A Century of American Labor* (Princeton, NJ: Princeton University Press, 2003), 113.

58. Michael K. Honey, "Operation Dixie, the Red Scare, and the Defeat of Southern Labor Organizing," in *American Labor and the Cold War: Grassroots Politics and Postwar Political Culture*, Robert W. Cherny, William Issel, and Kieran Walsh Taylor, eds. (Rutgers, NJ: Rutgers University Press, 2004), 226.

59. Preis, *Labor's Giant Step*, 377.

60. Davis, *Prisoners of American Dream*, 93.

61. Human Rights Watch, "Unfair Advantage: Workers' Freedom of Association in the United States Under International Human Rights Standards" (New York: Human Rights Watch, 2000), www.hrw.org/reports/2000/uslabor/.

62. J. David Greenstone, *Labor in American Politics* (New York: Vintage Books, 1969), 80.

63. Davis, *Prisoners of American Dream*, 99–100.

64. Details of this meeting are described in Taylor Branch, *Parting the Waters: America in the King Years, 1954–63* (New York: Simon & Schuster, 1988), 405–407.

65. Ibid., 476.

66. This account of Kennedy's meeting with the civil rights activists is reported in Ronald Steel, *In Love with the Night: The American Romance with Robert Kennedy* (New York: Simon & Schuster, 2000), 159.

67. This conversation is recorded in Branch, *Parting the Waters*, 797.

68. Quoted in David J. Garrow, *Bearing the Cross: Martin Luther King, Jr. and the Southern Christian Leadership Conference* (New York: HarperCollins, 2004), 282.

69. Manning Marable, *Black American Politics: From the Washington Marches to Jesse Jackson* (New York: Verso, 1985), 95.

70. Quoted in John Dittmer, *Local People: The Struggle for Civil Rights in Mississippi* (Champaign: University of Illinois Press, 1995), 290. Connally later switched parties to become a Republican and served in President Nixon's cabinet.

71. Peter B. Levy, *The New Left and Labor in the 1960s* (Chicago: University of Illinois Press, 1994), 39–40.

72. Most of this account of the MFDP comes from Harvard Sitkoff, *The Struggle for Black Equality, 1954–1980* (New York: Hill & Wang, 1981), 167–186. For an excellent summary of the MFDP's conflict with the Democrats, see Aaron Hess and Elizabeth Wrigley-Field, "How the Democratic Party Shut Out the Mississippi Freedom Democratic Party," *International Socialist Review* 38 (November–December, 2004).

73. Dittmer, *Local People*, 317–18.

74. August Meier and Elliott Rudwick, *CORE: A Story in the Civil Rights Movement* (Urbana: University of Illinois Press, 1975), 363–64.

75. Sitkoff, *Struggle for Black Equality*, 185.

76. Malcolm X, "The Ballot or the Bullet," in *Malcolm X Speaks*, George Breitman, ed. (New York: Grove Press, 1965), 139.

77. Malcolm's expression refers to the "Mau Mau" uprising, an anticolonial insurgency of Kenyans against British colonial rule from 1952 to 1960.

78. These figures are from an FBI report quoted in *Agents of Repression: The FBI's Secret Wars Against the Black Panther Party and the American Indian Movement*, Ward Churchill and Jim Vander Wall (Boston: South End Press, 1988), 63.

79. For a brief outline of the BPP's ideology, see Alphonso Pinckney, *Red, Black and*

Green: Black Nationalism in the United States (Cambridge: Cambridge University Press, 1976), 99–107.

80. Martin Glaberman, "Dodge Revolutionary Union Movement," *International Socialism*, no. 36 (April/May 1969), 9.

81. Allen, *Vietnam: The (Last) War the U.S. Lost*, (Chicago: Haymarket Books, 2008), 154–55.

82. Marable, *Race, Reform and Rebellion*, 102–103.

83. Hoover quoted in Pinckney, *Red, Black and Green*, 104. Glaberman, "Dodge Revolutionary Union Movement," makes the point about the connection of the 1967 Detroit riot to the founding of DRUM.

84. Adam Cohen and Elizabeth Taylor, *American Pharoah: Mayor Richard J. Daley—His Battle for Chicago and the Nation* (Boston, MA: Little, Brown, 2000), 501.

85. Boyle, *UAW and Heyday*, 253–54.

86. Dan Georgakas and Marvin Surkin, *Detroit: I Do Mind Dying* (New York: St. Martin's Press, 1975), 231.

87. Boyle, *UAW and Heyday*, 254.

88. Robert L. Allen, *Black Awakening in Capitalist America* (New York: Anchor Books, 1969), 139.

89. Figures from Manning Marable, "Forward," in *The New Black Vote: Power Politics in Four American Cities*, Rod Bush, ed. (San Francisco: Synthesis Publications, 1984), 3–5; *1987 Information Please Almanac* (Boston: Houghton-Mifflin, 1987), 48.

90. Manning Marable, *How Capitalism Underdeveloped Black America* (Boston: South End Press, 1983), 38.

91. William K. Stevens, "Persevering Political Survivor: Willie Wilson Goode," *New York Times*, November 5, 1987.

92. Women's Research and Education Institute, *The American Woman 1988–89* (New York: W.W. Norton, 1988), 341.

93. Sarah Evans, *Personal Politics: The Roots of Women's Liberation in the Civil Rights Movement and the New Left* (New York: Random House, 1979), 221.

94. Jane J. Mansbridge, *Why We Lost the ERA* (Chicago: University of Chicago Press, 1986), 127, 130–31.

95. In the 1980s, pollsters noted a marked tendency for the majority of women to vote for Democrats while the majority of men voted Republican. An attempt to exploit this "gender gap" in the 1984 presidential election led the Democrats to nominate Representative Geraldine Ferraro (D-NY) for vice president. But in 1984, Mondale and Ferraro lost in a landslide to the GOP's Ronald Reagan and George H. W. Bush, and the majority of women actually voted for Reagan. On the decision to nominate Ferraro, see Mary Frances Berry, *Why the ERA Failed: Politics, Women's Rights, and the Amending Process of the Constitution* (Bloomington: Indiana University Press, 1988), 115–16.

96. Martha Burk, "Is Bill Clinton a Feminist?" *Nation*, February 8, 1993. The Freedom of Choice Act would have written the *Roe v. Wade* decision into law.

97. Nicole Colson, "Have the Democrats Surrendered on Abortion Rights?" *Socialist Worker*, February 4, 2005.

98. Gay Left Collective, ed., *Homosexuality: Power and Politics* (London: Allison and Busby, 1980), 67.

99. Carter told the gay *Advocate* magazine: "I do not feel that people should be abused because of their sexual preference, but I don't know how we could deal with the issue of blackmail in federal security jobs. But with that possible exception, I would probably support this legislation." The risk of blackmail had been

the standard justification for anti-gay provisions in the federal employment code! Carter quoted in Randy Shilts, *Conduct Unbecoming: Gays and Lesbians in the U.S. Military* (New York: St. Martin's Press, 1993), 275.

100. David Rayside, *On the Fringe: Gays and Lesbians in Politics* (Ithaca, NY: Cornell University Press, 1998), 287.

101. Quoted in Chris Bull, "Feeling His Pain," *Advocate*, October 13, 1998, 28.

102. Sarah Wildman, "Wedding Bell Blues," *American Prospect*, December 6, 2004.

103. See Nate Silver, "Gay Marriage Opponents Now in a Minority," *Five Thirty Eight* blog in the *New York Times*, April 20, 2011, at http://fivethirtyeight.blogs.nytimes.com/2011/04/20/gay-marriage-opponents-now-in-minority/; Ed O'Keefe and Jon Cohen, "Most Back Repealing 'Don't Ask, Don't Tell,' Poll Says", Washington Post, December 15, 2010, at http://voices.washingtonpost.com/federal-eye/2010/12/most_back_repealing_dont_ask_d.html, both accessed on November 9, 2011.

104. Ben Smith and Maggie Haberman, "Gay Donors Fuel President Obama's 2012 Campaign," *Politico*, May 9, 2011, at www.politico.com/news/stories/0511/54539.html, accessed on November 9, 2011.

105. Sharon Smith, "The Pro-War Democrats' Antiwar Enablers," *Socialist Worker*, December 7, 2007, 3. Smith quotes UFPJ adviser Phyllis Bennis's commentary: "It is very hard, at an emotional level, for people to understand that none of the presidential candidates likely to win in 2008 is committed to ending the war. . . . Still, it matters very much who gets elected in 2008." Read Bennis's commentary at www.peaceworkmagazine.org/deepening-majority-anti-war-organizing-election-year.

106. Michael T. Heaney and Fabio Rojas, "Partisan Dynamics of Contention: Demobilization of the Antiwar Movement in the United States, 2007–2009," *Mobilization: An International Journal* 16 (1), 49.

107. Robert Brenner, "The Paradox of Social Democracy: The American Case," in *The Year Left*, vol. 1, Mike Davis, Fred Pfeil, and Michael Sprinker, eds., 36–37.

108. Andrew Cole, "Why the Wisconsin Recall Failed," *Socialist Worker*.org, August 23, 2011, at http://socialistworker.org/2011/08/23/why-the-wisconsin-recall-failed, accessed on November 9. 2011. Please also consult the embedded links in the cited article.

109. Peter Miguel Camejo, "The Avocado Declaration," in *Independent Politics: The Green Party Strategy Debate*, Howie Hawkins, ed. (Chicago: Haymarket Books, 2006), 64.

Chapter Six: Defenders of the Empire

1. G. William Domhoff, *Who Rules America Now?* (Englewood Cliffs, NJ: Prentice Hall, 1983), chapter 5.

2. See "The Missile Gap Flap," *Time*, February 17, 1961.

3. On Mondale's call for a "quarantine" of Nicaragua, see the transcript of the second presidential debate with Reagan in 1984 at www.pbs.org/newshour/debatingourdestiny/84debates/2prez1.html, accessed June 8, 2008.

4. Andrew Bacevich, *American Empire* (Cambridge, MA: Harvard University Press, 2002), 200.

5. Holbrooke was the Carter administration's ambassador in Indonesia, a post that went to Wolfowitz when the Reagan administration took over in 1981. Holbrooke and Wolfowitz essentially acted as a tag team in running U.S. policy toward East Timor and the Suharto dictatorship in Indonesia throughout the 1970s and 1980s. See Tim Shorrock, "Paul Wolfowitz, Reagan's Man in

Indonesia, Is Back at the Pentagon," *Foreign Policy in Focus*, February 2001, at www.fpif.org.

6. Editorial, "Coddling China, Constructively," *New York Times*, November 18, 1993.

7. Quoted in Anthony Lewis, "Abroad at Home; The Two Clintons," *New York Times*, February 22, 1993.

8. Gwen Ifill, "Campaign 1992: Interview; Clinton Seeking Forceful Image as a Leader in Foreign Affairs," *New York Times*, June 28, 1992.

9. Quoted in James Traub, "The Bush Years; W.'s World," *New York Times*, January 14, 2001.

10. See Robert Kagan and William Kristol, "National Humiliation," *Weekly Standard*, April 9, 2001.

11. Sherry Wolf reviews the Democrats' history as a party of imperialism and war in "The Democrats and War: Not a Lesser Evil," *International Socialist Review* 26 (November–December 2002), 39–46.

12. See the chronology of the Spanish-American War in Donald H. Dyal, Brian B. Carpenter, and Mark A. Thomas, eds., *Historical Dictionary of the Spanish-American War* (Boulder, CO: Greenwood Press, 1996), xi–xii.

13. Twain quoted in Howard Zinn, *A People's History of the United States*, 321.

14. Neil Gabler, "The Splendid Little War," *Salon*, February 21, 2003. President Roosevelt's support for an "international police power" became known as the "Roosevelt Corollary" of the Monroe Doctrine.

15. Quoted in Arthur Schlesinger, *The Crisis of the Old Order: The Age of Roosevelt, 1919–1933* (New York: HarperCollins, 2002), 364. An interesting side note to this story is that Franklin Roosevelt, who served as Wilson's assistant naval secretary, claimed in his 1920 campaign for vice president that he wrote the Haitian constitution!

16. Quoted in Sidney Lens, *The Forging of the American Empire: From the Revolution to Vietnam: A History of U.S. Imperialism* (Chicago: Haymarket Books, 2003), 195.

17. For a discussion of "Wilsonianism" and its influence on modern U.S. foreign policy, see Kevin J. Cole, "The Wilsonian Model of Foreign Policy & the Post-Cold War World," *Air and Space Power Journal*, July 26, 1999, www.airpower .maxwell.af.mil/airchronicles/cc/Cole.html.

18. For an interpretation of U.S. entry into the war along these lines, see Paul Birsdall, "Neutrality and Economic Pressures, 1914–1917" in *The Shaping of American Diplomacy*, William Appleman Williams, ed. (Chicago: Rand-McNally, 1956), 560–67.

19. Quoted in Williams, *Shaping of American Diplomacy*, 550–51.

20. E. H. Carr, *The Bolshevik Revolution* (New York: W.W. Norton, 1953), 10–11.

21. Lens, *Forging of American Empire*, 267.

22. Quoted in ibid.

23. Williams, *Shaping of American Diplomacy*, 614.

24. Leon Trotsky, "War and the Fourth International," in *Writings of Leon Trotsky 1933–34* (New York: Pathfinder Press, 1972), 301–302.

25. Quoted in Lens, *Forging of American Empire*, 307.

26. Lens, *Forging of American Empire*, 321.

27. See Warren F. Kimball, "Franklin D. Roosevelt and World War II," *Presidential Studies Quarterly* 34, no. 1 (2004), 83ff.

28. Quoted in Gabriel Kolko, *The Politics of War* (New York: Pantheon Books, 1990), 321.

29. Franklin Delano Roosevelt, "Address to Congress," January 6, 1941, *Congressional Record*, 1941, vol. 87, pt. I.

30. For more on the march on Washington, see Marable, *Black American Politics*, 79–87.
31. See Lance Selfa, *The Struggle for Palestine* (Chicago: Haymarket Books, 2002), 15.
32. Richard Hofstadter, *The American Political Tradition* (New York: Vintage Books, 1974), 454–55.
33. "Kill Japs..." and Elliott Roosevelt statements are quoted in John W. Dower, *War Without Mercy: Race and Power in the Pacific War* (New York: Pantheon Books, 1986), 55.
34. These issues, including Eisenhower's reservations, are neatly summarized in Gar Alperovitz, "Hiroshima: Historians Reassess," *Foreign Policy 99* (Summer 1995), 15ff.
35. Information on Justice Radhabinod Pal's dissent comes from Dower, *War Without Mercy*, 38.
36. The figure is cited in editorial, "U.S. Military Bases and Empire," *Monthly Review*, March 2002.
37. Quoted in Gabriel Kolko, *The Politics of War: The World and United States Foreigh Policy, 1943–1945* (New York: Pantheon Books, 1990), 258.
38. Diane B. Kunz, "The Marshall Plan Reconsidered: A Complex of Motives," *Foreign Affairs*, May/June 1997.
39. Quoted in Tariq Ali, "NATO's Balkan Crusade," in *Masters of the Universe? NATO's Balkan Crusade*, Tariq Ali, ed. (New York: Verso, 2000), 359.
40. Quoted in Lawrence S. Wittner, *Cold War America* (New York: Praeger Publishers, 1974), 67.
41. NSC-68: United States Objectives and Programs for National Security (April 12, 1950), Section VI. To read the entire National Security Coucil document, see www.fas.org/irp/offdocs/nsc-hst/nsc-68.htm.
42. For more details on this history, see *Class Struggles in Eastern Europe 1495–83*, Chris Harman (London: Pluto Press, 1983), and *Neither Washington Nor Moscow: Essays on Revolutionary Socialism*, Tony Cliff (London: Bookmarks, 1982).
43. President Harry S. Truman, address before a joint session of Congress, March 12, 1947, retrieved August 12, 2008 from Academic Search Complete database.
44. Quoted in Noam Chomsky, *Towards a New Cold War: Essays on the Current Crisis and How We Got There* (New York: The New Press), 21.
45. Christopher Layne, "From Preponderance to Offshore Balancing: America's Future Grand Strategy," in *America's Strategic Choices*, Michael E. Brown, Owen R. Coté Jr., et al., eds. (Cambridge, MA: MIT Press, 1997), 257.
46. Quoted in Marilyn B. Young, *The Vietnam Wars, 1945–1990* (New York: Harper Perennial, 1991), 79.
47. Ibid. For information on Johnson touting Diem as the "Winston Churchill of Southeast Asia," see p. 79; for Johnson's advising of Humphrey that "now it's happening here," see p. 102; and for figures on numbers of advisers, see p. 103.
48. Lens, *Forging of American Empire*, 421.
49. "The Blueprint for an Americanized War," from *Pentagon Papers*, reprinted in *Vietnam and America: A Documentary History*, Marvin E. Gettleman, et al., eds. (New York: Grove Press, 1995), 239–45.
50. "The Gulf of Tonkin 'Incidents' and Resolution," from "Pentagon Papers," in *Vietnam and America: The Most Comprehensive Documented History of the Vietnam War*, Gettleman, Franklin, et. al., eds., 246–52.
51. For an excellent overview and analysis of the Vietnam War, see Joe Allen's *Vietnam: The (Last) War the U.S. Lost* (Chicago: Haymarket Books, 2008).
52. Figure from Edwin Warner, "Dueling over Defense," *Time*, September 1, 1980.

53. One can read the declassified version of Presidential Directive 59 at www.jimmy-carterlibrary.org/documents/pddirectives/pd59.pdf, accessed March 8, 2008.
54. Zinn, *People's History of United States*, 554.
55. Quoted in Maryam Poya, "Long Live the Revolution . . . Long Live Islam?" in *Revolutionary Rehearsals*, Colin Barker, ed. (London: Bookmarks, 1987), 136.
56. See Israel Shahak, *Open Secrets: Israeli Foreign and Nuclear Policies* (London: Pluto Press, 1997), 78.
57. On Carter's firing of Young, see Naseer H. Aruri, *The Obstruction of Peace: The U.S., Israel and the Palestinians* (Monroe, ME: Common Courage Press, 1995), 265–66.
58. Cited by Agence France Presse, January 14, 1998. See also: Greg Guma, "Cracks in the Covert Iceberg," *Toward Freedom*, May 1998, 2; Leslie Feinberg, "Brzezinski Brags, Blows Cover: U.S. Intervened in Afghanistan First," *Workers World*, March 12, 1998.
59. Nafeez Mosaddeq Ahmed, "Afghanistan, the Taliban and the United States," available on the Media Monitors Network website at www.mediamonitor.net or at www.isreview.org/issues/20/ahmed_afghanistan.shtml.
60. Jimmy Carter, 1980 State of the Union Address, Jimmy Carter Library website, www.jimmycarterlibrary.org/documents/speeches/su80jec.phtml.
61. A good short description of this plan for direct U.S. intervention in the Gulf is Sheila Ryan, "Countdown for a Decade: The U.S. Build-up for War in the Gulf," in *Beyond the Storm: A Gulf Crisis Reader*, Phyllis Bennis and Michel Moushabeck, eds. (New York: Olive Branch Press, 1991), 91–102.
62. Lawrence Korb, "Sized Up," *Foreign Affairs* 79 no. 2 (March–April 2000), 150.
63. The GAO estimate of $112 billion to repair schools is cited in Brookings Institution, *The Future of Children* 7, No. 3, "Financing Schools" (Winter 1997), 127–32.
64. Korb, "Sized Up," 149.
65. Robert L. Borosage, "Money Talks: The Implications of U.S. Budget Priorities," in *Global Focus: U.S. Foreign Policy at the Turn of the Millennium*, Martha Honey and Tom Barry, eds. (New York: St. Martin's Press, 2000), 12. These figures count the number of times presidents are required, under the 1973 War Powers Act, to notify Congress when they send troops abroad to face "imminent hostilities."
66. Madeleine Albright, interview by Leslie Stahl, *60 Minutes*, CBS, May 12, 1996.
67. Clinton waived human rights conditions in approving the $1.3 billion aid package. See Human Rights Watch, "Clinton's Colombia Waiver 'a Grave Mistake,'" *Human Rights News*, August 23, 2000, at www.hrw.org/english/docs/2000/08/23/colomb730.htm, accessed June 9, 2008.
68. Michael Mandelbaum, "A Perfect Failure: NATO's War Against Yugoslavia," *Foreign Affairs* 78 no. 5 (September/October 1999), 6–7.
69. Quoted in Michael T. Klare, "US Aims to Win on All Fronts," *Le Monde Diplomatique*, May 1999.
70. Ibid.
71. Wolfowitz was the chief author of the 1992 Defense Policy Guidance document that anticipated the Bush Doctrine's central themes: ". . . we endeavor to prevent any hostile power from dominating a region whose resources would, under consolidated control, be sufficient to generate global power." When word of this document leaked to the *New York Times*, it caused a scandal that led the Pentagon and the George H. W. Bush administration to repudiate it. See Michael T. Klare, *Rogue States and Nuclear Outlaws: America's Search for a New Foreign Policy* (New York: Hill & Wang, 1995), 100–104.
72. William Hartung, "Elections and the War," *Baltimore Chronicle*, December 4, 2002.

73. Perry Anderson, "Force and Consent," *New Left Review* 17 (September–October 2002).
74. Andrew J. Bacevich, "Not-So-Special Operation: Bush Adopts the Clinton Way of War," *National Review*, November 19, 2001.
75. See Rahul Majahan, *Full Spectrum Dominance: U.S. Power in Iraq and Beyond* (New York: Seven Stories Press, 2003), 9, 51–54.
76. Andrew J. Bacevich, "Bush's Grand Strategy," *American Conservative*, November 4, 2002.
77. Typical of this analysis is Sydney Blumenthal, "America's Military Coup," *Guardian*, May 13, 2004.
78. See Thomas Ferguson and Joel Rodgers, *Right Turn: The Decline of the Democrats and the Future of American Politics* (New York: Hill & Wang, 1986), 31, 37, on the McGovern campaign.
79. Kim Moody, *An Injury to All: The Decline of American Unionism* (New York: Verso, 1988), 288–93.
80. See Political Research Associates' dossier on Social Democrats USA at www .publiceye.org/research/Group_Watch/Entries-118.htm. This is a fascinating look at the connections between the right wing of the AFL-CIO and the neoconservative establishment.
81. For background on the neoconservatives, see Alain Frachon and Daniel Vernet, "The Strategist and the Philosopher," June 2, 2003, at www.counterpunch.org/ frachon06022003.html. Article originally published in *Le Monde Diplomatique*, April 16, 2003. Translated by Norman Madarasz. On the connections between the neoconservatives and radicals, see John B. Judis, "Trotskyism to Anachronism: The Neoconservative Revolution," *Foreign Affairs* vol. 74, no. 4 (July/August 1995).
82. For more on the CDM, see www.publiceye.org/research/Group_Watch/Entries -26.htm. In an even more bizarre connection between these right-wing Democrats and the current crop running Bush foreign policy, CDM housed the offices of "Team B," a right-wing cabal George H. W. Bush set up inside the CIA to provide intelligence intended to undermine President Ford's détente plans with the Soviet Union. Team B fed back-channel information to then–defense secretary Donald Rumsfeld that helped Rumsfeld sink SALT I negotiations. Many observers today say that Rumsfeld's current "Office of Special Plans" is modeled on Team B—a connection that isn't so far-fetched when you consider that Wolfowitz was a member of Team B.
83. A good example of this, appearing in the issue of *Foreign Affairs* on the newsstands during the 2004 election, was Robert W. Tucker and David C. Hendrickson, "The Sources of American Legitimacy," which argued, "The United States has assumed many of the very features of the 'rogue nations' against which it has rhetorically—and sometimes literally—done battle over the years. The legitimacy of U.S. power has, at a minimum, been eroded significantly, and at certain moments—for instance, in the general revulsion to reports of widespread torture in Iraq—it seems to have vanished entirely." See the article at www.foreignaffairs.org/20041101faessay83603/robert-w-tucker-david-c -hendrickson/the-sources-of-american-legitimacy.html, accessed June 8, 2008.
84. Quoted in Charles Babington, "Hawkish Democrat Joins Call for Pullout," *Washington Post*, November 18, 2005, A01.
85. On the eve of the November election, Democrats had outraised Republicans by $559 million to $555 million. See Federal Election Commission, "Congressional Campaigns Spent $966 Million Through Mid-October," Federal Election

Commission press release, November 2, 2006, at www.fec.gov/press/press2006/20061102can/20061102can.html, accessed March 16, 2008.

86. "The Nobel Peace Prize 2009," Nobelprize.org October 30, 2011, at www.nobelprize.org/nobel_prizes/peace/laureates/2009/.

87. See "Balance-sheet of US Imperialism," in *International Socialist Review* 61 (September–October, 2008) at www.isreview.org/issues/61/feat-achcarint.shtml, accessed on January 15, 2012.

88. For analysis for the international agreement that codified Zelaya's return, see Todd Gordon and Jeffery R. Webber, "From Cartagena to Tegucigalpa: Imperialism and the Future of the Honduran Resistance," *The Bullet* (Socialist Project), July 6, 2011, at www.socialistproject.ca/bullet/524.php, accessed November 5, 2011.

89. Manuel Perez-Rocha, "Obama in Latin America: Another Missed Opportunity," *Foreign Policy in Focus*, March 24, 2011, at www.fpif.org/articles/obama_in_latin_america_another_missed_opportunity, accessed on January 15, 2012.

90. Dafna Lizner, "Obama Makes Indefinite Detention and Military Commissions His Own," *Pro Publica*, March 8, 2011, at www.propublica.org/article/obama-makes-indefinite-detention-and-military-commissions-his-own, accessed on October 30, 2011.

91. Glenn Greenwald, "Confirmed: Obama Authorizes Assassination of U.S. Citizen," *Salon*, April 7, 2011, www.salon.com/2010/04/07/assassinations_2/, accessed on October 30, 2011.

92. Klaus Brinkbäumer and John Goetz, "Taking Out Terrorists by Remote Control," *Der Spiegel* Online, October 12, 2011, at www.spiegel.de/international/world/0,1518,722583,00.html, accessed on October 30, 2011.

93. See Deepa Kumar's analysis of the Obama speech in "Looking Beyond the Symbolism," *Socialist Worker*, June 12, 2009, at http://socialistworker.org/2009/06/12/looking-beyond-symbolism.

94. Jim Lobe, "Obama Seeks to Quiet Outrage Over Gaza Raids," InterPress News Agency, June 1, 2010, at http://ipsnews.net/news.asp?idnews=51679, accessed November 5, 2011.

95. See Juan Cole, "Palestine, Bahrain and US Hypocrisy," *Informed Comment*, September 24, 2011, at www.juancole.com/2011/09/palestine-bahrain-and-us-hyprocrisy.html, accessed November 5, 2011.

96. Stephen M. Walt, "What Intervention in Libya Tells Us about the Neocon-Liberal Alliance", *Foreign Policy*, March 21, 2011, at http://walt.foreignpolicy.com/posts/2011/03/21/what_intervention_in_libya_tells_us_about_the_neocon_liberal_alliance, accessed on November 5, 2011.

97. For an assessment of post-Qaddafi Libya, see Phyllis Bennis, "Libya: Too Soon to Declare Victory", Institute for Policy Studies, August 22, 2011, at www.ips-dc.org/articles/libya_too_soon_to_declare_victory, accessed November 5, 2011.

98. John Pilger, "US Combat Troops Descend on Africa", *Truthout*, October 20, 2011, at www.truth-out.org/us-combat-troops-descend-africa/1319125424, accessed on January 15, 2012.

98. Thom Shanker and Steven Lee Myers, "U.S. Planning Troop Buildup in Gulf After Exit From Iraq," *New York Times*, October 29, 2011.

Chapter Seven: Can the Left Take Over the Democratic Party?

1. See Progressive Democrats of America, "What Is PDA?," at www.pdamerica.org/

about/what-is-pda.php, accessed June 14, 2008.

2. Laura Flanders's *Blue Grit: True Democrats Take Back Politics from the Politicians* (New York: Penguin Group, 2007) recounts several stories of activists and unions taking over moribund local and state Democratic Party organizations.

3. See Eric Chester, *Socialists and the Ballot Box* (New York: Praeger, 1985), 131–47, for an account of the realignment perspective.

4. Quoted in Maurice Isserman, *The Other American: The Life of Michael Harrington* (New York: Public Affairs, 2000), 187.

5. Progressive Democrats of America, "PDA Inside/Outside Strategy," at www.pdamerica.org/about/strategy.php.

6. The DSA's "Where We Stand" document explained this shift: "Democratic socialists reject an either-or approach to electoral coalition building, focused solely on a new party or on realignment within the Democratic Party. The growth of PAC-driven, candidate-based, entrepreneurial politics in the last 25 years leaves little hope for an immediate, principled electoral response to the rightward, pro-corporate drift in American politics. The fundamental task of democratic socialists is to build anti-corporate social movements capable of winning reforms that empower people. Since such social movements seek to influence state policy, they will intervene in electoral politics, whether through Democratic primaries, non-partisan local elections, or third party efforts. Our electoral work aims at building majoritarian coalitions capable of not only electing public officials on the anti-corporate program of these movements, but also of holding officials accountable after they are elected." See it at www.dsausa.org/about/where.html, accessed July 18, 2008.

7. Spidel interviewed in William Rivers Pitt, "Ordinary Heroes and the Rising Power of the Roots," *Truthout*, January 27, 2005, www.truthout.org/docs_05/012805U.shtml.

8. See Joe Libertelli, "New Organization, 'Progressive Democrats of America,' Emerges After Democratic Convention," at www.opednews.com/libertelli_080104_new_org.htm. Spidel describes his job at PDA in very un-grassroots sounding ways: "I serve as Deputy Director, and to an extent as political director. My niche is the strategy component. I take the relationships Tim Carpenter builds on the Hill, along with the desires of our grassroots organizers and the caucuses that tell us what their priorities are, I take those and balance them out into an executable strategy. I dictate the direction of the activism—targeting congressional districts, ballot initiatives, aiming the fire of the grassroots at the targeted spot. I take the initiatives of the policy board and organize them into effective action."

9. See PDA board member David Swanson's response to my criticism of PDA in *Socialist Worker*, April 8, 2005, available online at www.socialistworker.org/20051/538/538_08_DebatingthePDA.shtml.

10. "New Political Organization to Be Launched in Boston: Progressive Democrats of America," July 20, 2004, available online at www.commondreams.org/news2004/0720-06.htm.

11. Medea Benjamin, contribution to "Looking Back, Looking Forward: A Forum," *Nation*, December 20, 2004.

12. Peter Camejo, "The Crisis in the Green Party: The Magic Number 39 & My Meetings with Cobb, Kucinich and the GPUS SC," www.greens4democracy.net/.

13. Spidel, "Ordinary Heroes," *Truthout*, January 27, 2005.

14. Quoted in Charley Underwood, "A Kucinich Delegate in Boston and the Totalitarian Democratic Party," *Bella Ciao*, August 1, 2004, available online at

www.bellaciao.org/en/article.php3?id_article=2305.

15. Quoted in Mark Naymik, "Many Kucinich Backers Are Out There, Way Out," *Cleveland Plain Dealer*, March 9, 2003.

16. On the Bush-Kerry exchange, see William Saletan, "Would Kerry Vote Today for the Iraq War?" *Slate*, August 12, 2004, at www.slate.com/id/2105096.

17. Libertelli, "John Kerry's Statement on the Iraq War; Political Ecology 101," at www.pdamerica.org.

18. Ibid.

19. See Cindy Sheehan, "Why I Am Leaving the Democratic Party," *Counterpunch*, May 28, 2007, at www.counterpunch.org.

20. See "Strategizing with Leaders of the Anti-War Movement," a transcript of a conference call between leading antiwar activists and Democratic Congress members organized by the Network of Spiritual Progressives, www.spiritualprogressives .org/article.php?story=20070907191110516.

21. Glenn Greenwald, "Barack Obama Is Gutting the Core Principles of the Democratic Party," *Guardian*, July 21, 2011.

22. Jane Hamsher, "Bernie Sanders to Primary Obama? Don't Make Me Laugh," *Firedoglake*.com, July 31, 2011, at http://fdlaction.firedoglake.com/2011/07/31/ bernie-sanders-to-primary-obama-dont-make-me-laugh/, accessed December 20, 2011.

23. Read Joshua Frank's account of the DLC's "assassination" of Dean in *Left Out!: How Liberals Helped Reelect George W. Bush* (Monroe, ME: Common Courage Press, 2005), 103–11.

24. On the beginnings of the campaign of Democratic sabotage of Sinclair's campaign, see Greg Mitchell, *The Campaign of the Century: Upton Sinclair's Race for Governor of California and the Birth of Media Politics* (New York: Random House, 1992), 214.

25. Dawson operated a patronage machine on Chicago's Black South Side that worked to "get out the vote" for Democrats in the city. In some ways, the Dawson machine was a replica in Chicago's Black neighborhoods of the citywide Democratic machine. While the city machine under Daley gave Dawson wide latitude in running the Black South Side Democratic machine, the Dawson machine was always subservient to the city machine and to Daley. For that reason, his political operation was referred to as a "submachine."

26. The Emmett Till case revolved around the lynching of fourteen-year-old Chicagoan Emmett Till who was accused of "whistling at a white woman" during a stay with relatives in Money, Mississippi. Till's mother, Mamie Till Bradley, insisted that Emmett's maimed body be returned to Chicago and displayed in an open casket during his funeral. As many as fifty thousand people turned out at Till's funeral, which became a major touchstone in the growing movement for civil rights.

27. Adam Cohen and Elizabeth Taylor, *American Pharaoh: Richard J. Daley—His Battle for Chicago and the Nation* (Boston: Little, Brown, 2000), 206–207.

28. Alexander Cockburn, "The Democrats and Their Conventions," *CounterPunch*, July 26, 2004, at www.counterpunch.org/cockburn07262004.html.

29. Sheila Collins, *The Rainbow Challenge: The Jackson Campaign and the Future of U.S. Politics* (New York: Monthly Review Press, 1986), 105.

30. Adolph L. Reed Jr., *The Jesse Jackson Phenomenon: The Crisis of Purpose in Afro-American Politics* (New Haven, CT: Yale University Press, 1986), 14–15.

31. *Guardian* [US], April 30, 1986, 15.

32. For information on Jackson's relationship with King, see David Garrow, *Bearing*

the Cross (New York: William Morrow and Co., 1987), 584–86, 562. For the quote by Jackson, see George Packer, "Trickle-Down Civil Rights," *New York Times*, December 12, 1999.

33. See Lee Sustar, "The Black Political Convention of 1972," *Socialist Worker*, April 1988. Also see Marable, *Black American Politics*, 266.

34. Paul Hockenos, *Guardian* [US], February 17, 1988, 1.

35. "Jackson Names 2 to Head Campaign," *New York Times*, November 14, 1987, 1, 35.

36. Sustar, "A Rainbow Solution?" *Socialist Worker*, November 1987.

37. See "Jesse Jackson on Arafat & the PLO," *Against the Current* 15 (July/August 1988), 18.

38. "Briefing," *New York Times*, March 22, 1988.

39. Information on Bentsen from James Ledbetter and Ariel Kaminer, "'Special Interests' Get Their Veep," *Guardian* [US], August 3, 1988.

40. David E. Rosenbaum, "The Democrats in Atlanta; With Palestinian Issue Put Aside, Platform Is Adopted," *New York Times*, July 20, 1988.

41. Jackson adviser Robert Borosage quoted in editorial, "Deal, Jesse, Deal," *Socialist Worker*, July 1988.

42. Jo Seidita, "The Hollow Men," *Progressive*, September 1988, 6.

43. Quoted in Maureen Dowd, "Dukakis and Bush Spar on Conservatism," *New York Times*, June 8, 1988.

44. "Open Letter from Tom Hayden," October 4, 2004, at www.pdamerica.org/articles/news/hayden_letter.php.

45. Mark S. Kamleiter, "Conflict in the Green Party: A Response," July 30, 2005, www.greens4democracy.net/.

Chapter Eight: Why Is There No Alternative?

1. Russell Baker, "In the Attic? Hillary?" *New York Times*, August 3, 1996.

2. Office of the Attorney General of New York, "Voting Matters in New York," February 12, 2001, 18–31. The quote is from *Illinois State Bd. of Elections v. Socialist Workers Party*, 440 U.S. 173, 184 n15 (1979). See www.oag.state.ny.us/press/reports/voting.pdf, accessed June 15, 2008.

3. Eric Thomas Chester, *True Mission: Socialists and the Labor Party Question in the U.S.* (London: Pluto Press, 2004), 22.

4. James Weinstein, *The Decline of Socialism in America: 1912–1925* (New York: Vintage, 1967), 93, 103.

5. Smith, *Subterranean Fire*, 24. Daniel Guerín, *100 Years of Labor in the U.S.A.*, translated by Alan Adler (London: Ink Links, 1979), 105.

6. Bert Cochran, *Labor and Communism* (Princeton, NJ: Princeton University Press, 1977), 133–38.

7. For membership figures and SDS history, see Kirkpatrick Sale, *SDS* (New York: Random House, 1973). Membership figure quoted on 479.

8. Benjamin I. Page and Mark P. Petracca, *The American Presidency* (New York: McGraw Hill and Co., 1983), 135–136.

9. Quoted in Stanley Karnow, *Vietnam: A History* (New York: Viking Press, 1983), 326.

10. Kim McQuaid, *Big Business and Presidential Power* (New York: William Morrow, 1982), 231–33.

11. Hal Draper, "Who's Going to Be the Lesser Evil' in '68?" in this volume.

12. See Dave Friedman, "The Roots of Repression," in *The New Left of the Sixties*, Michael Friedman, ed. (Berkeley, CA: Independent Socialist Press, 1972), 242ff

for a socialist critique of this "guerrilla war" perspective.

13. Max Elbaum, *Revolution in the Air: Sixties Radicals Turn to Lenin, Mao and Che* (New York: Verso Books, 2002), 127–28.
14. Ibid., 249.
15. Ibid.
16. Eric Chester, *Socialists and the Ballot Box* (New York: Praeger, 1985), 143.
17. See ibid., 131–47, for an account of the realignment perspective.
18. Elbaum, *Revolution in the Air*, 250.
19. Chester, *Socialists and Ballot Box*, 146.
20. *New York Times*, "Jackson Seeking Socialist Backing," *New York Times*, December 5, 1987.
21. Robert Brenner, "The Paradox of Social Democracy: The American Case," in *The Year Left*, vol. 1, Mike Davis, Fred Pfeil, and Michael Sprinker, eds. (London: Verso, 1985), 65.
22. See Democratic Socialists of America, "Where We Stand," www.dsausa.org/about/where.html.
23. Ibid.
24. Ibid.
25. See editorial, "Reasonable Differences," in *Democratic Left* (Fall 2000), 1, and the exchange in the letters to the editor on pages 3 and 15. Judging from the letters to the editor, it appears that the DSA rank and file was much more favorable to an endorsement of Nader than its political committee was.
26. Democratic Socialists of America Political Action Committee, "Socialists Urge Support for Kerry," press release issued July 23, 2004. See a copy at www.dsaboston .org/yradical/yr2004-09.pdf, accessed June 15, 2008.
27. "Resolution on the 2008 Presidential Election," *Democratic Left*, XXXVI, Summer 2008, 1.
28. Bodgan Denitch, "This Election is Different—A Potential Catastrophe," *Democratic Left*, XXXVI, Fall 2008, 1.
29. See José Corrêa Leite, *The World Social Forum: Strategies of Resistance* (Chicago: Haymarket Books, 2005), 21–53, for a description of the political context of the early twenty-first century.
30. See Michael Goldfield, *The Decline of Organized Labor in the United States* (Chicago: University of Chicago Press, 1987).
31. Quotes are from "Ralph Nader: Taking on the Parties of Big Business" and "You Can't Spoil a System That's Spoiled to the Core," in *International Socialist Review* (October–November 2000), 9–12.
32. See the analysis of the Nader vote in my "What the Voters Really Said in 2000," *International Socialist Review* (February–March 2001), 21–23.
33. The first quote is from Medea Benjamin, "Want to Get Rid of Bush and Grow the Greens? Support David Cobb," reprinted at www.harriscounty-greenparty .org/campaigns/2004/BenjaminForCobb2004.htm, accessed June 15, 2008. The second quote is from Medea Benjamin, Peter Coyote, John Eder, Daniel Ellsberg, et al., "Vote Kerry and Cobb: An Open Letter to Progressives," reprinted in *Independent Politics: The Green Party Strategy Debate*, Howie Hawkins, ed. (Chicago: Haymarket Books, 2006), 213.
34. Quoted in Joshua L. Weinstein, "LaMarche Says She'll Vote for Whoever Can Beat Bush," *Portland Press Herald*, June 30, 2004.
35. See Rachel Odes, "Missing Documents and Summary of Documents Not Included" in *Independent Politics*, Hawkins, ed., 51–56, for examples of these liberal

attacks on Nader.

36. Joshua Frank, "Narcissism Runs Rampant: Diagnosing the Green Party" in ibid., 253–256.

37. Howie Hawkins, "The Green Party's Missed Opportunity in 2004—and the Opportunity Still at Hand," in ibid., 47.

Conclusion: Is the Lesser Evil Good Enough?

1. Drew Westen, "Leadership, Obama Style, and the Looming Losses in 2010: Pretty Speeches, Compromised Values, and the Quest for the Lowest Common Denominator," *Huffington Post,* December 20, 2009, at www.huffingtonpost.com/drew-westen/leadership-obama-style-an_b_398813.html, accessed December 20, 2011.

2. Laura Flanders, "Grassroots: The Democratic Party's Real Hope for Change," *Alternet,* February 8, 2008, at www.alternet.org/story/76365/?page=entire.

3. Howard Zinn, "The Signs of Resistance," interview by Anthony Arnove, *Socialist Worker,* February 16, 2001.

4. Historian Taylor Branch made this point in his presentation on "Progressive Movement in a Democratic Era: The Lessons of King and the Civil Rights Movement" at the Campaign for America's Future Take Back America conference, March 18, 2008, Washington, D.C. At the same event, former Johnson administration official Roger Wilkins said the Civil Rights Act of 1964 would never have been passed had it not been for the movement's activism. See their speeches at www.ourfuture.org/video/tba-2008-progressive-movement-democratic-era-lessons-king-and-civil-rights-movement.

5. Ramsey Clark interview with Harri Blake, Oral History Interview II, February 11, 1969, in the oral history archive of the Lyndon Baines Johnson Presidential Library, Austin, Texas, at www.lbjlib.utexas.edu, accessed on June 15, 2008.

6. Sharon Smith, *Women and Socialism: Essays on Women's Liberation* (Chicago: Haymarket Books, 2005), 90–92.

7. Ibid., 79–80.

8. Eugene V. Debs, "The Outlook for Socialism in the United States," *International Socialist Review,* September 1900.

9. Woodrow Wilson, *The New Freedom: A Call for the Emancipation of the Generous Energies of a People* (New York: Doubleday, 1913), 57–58.

10. George Orwell, *Homage to Catalonia* (San Diego, CA: Harcourt, 1980).

11. See Gallup, "Socialism Viewed Positively by 36 Percent of Americans," February 4, 2010, at Gallup.com; Kate Zernike and Megan Thee-Brenan, "Poll Finds Tea Party Backers Wealthier and More Educated," *New York Times,* April 14, 2010.

Appendix: Who's Going to Be the Lesser Evil in '68?

Notes to this essay were added for its republication in the *International Socialist Review* 34, April–May 2004.

1. Edmund G. "Pat" Brown (Democrat): California state attorney general, 1951–59; governor of California, 1959–67.

2. Lyndon B. Johnson: The Texas Democratic vice president was sworn in as president in 1963 after the assassination of John F. Kennedy. He went on to win election to a full term in a landslide against GOP candidate Barry Goldwater in the

presidential race in 1964. At the time of the writing of this article, Johnson was planning to run as president, but he later announced he would not seek another term as president after the January 1968 Tet Offensive exposed the U.S.'s inability to win the war in Vietnam and his poll figures dropped precipitously.

3. George W. Romney served three consecutive terms as governor of Michigan, from 1962 to 1968. He was chairman of American Motors Corporation from 1954–62 and a contender for the 1968 Republican presidential nomination. His son Willard (a.k.a. Mitt) is the 2012 GOP presidential contender and former Massachusetts governor.

4. At this time, Ronald Reagan was the Republican governor of California. He later (1980) was elected president and served two terms. His presidency personified the new drift to the right in U.S. politics—a ruling-class backlash against the political and social movements of the 1960s and early 1970s. He was famous, like the current president, for making inane statements such as "Trees cause more pollution than automobiles do."

5. This refers to a hypothetical 1968 presidential ticket of Senator Robert F. Kennedy and Senator J. William Fulbright. Kennedy served as attorney general in brother John F. Kennedy's brief presidential administration, and then became a senator in 1964. He was assassinated on June 5, 1968. Fulbright of Arkansas (who once employed Bill Clinton as an intern) was chair of the Senate Foreign Relations Committee. Fulbright was an early Vietnam hawk who became a leading establishment opponent of the war.

6. A well-known liberal newspaper columnist of the day.

7. Barry Goldwater was the Republican presidential nominee who ran against Johnson in 1964. He advocated using nuclear weapons to defoliate Vietnam.

8. Johnson ran for president in 1964 promising to de-escalate the war in Vietnam. When he won the election, he did the opposite, sending hundreds of thousands more troops.

9. Hubert Humphrey was elected as vice president with President Johnson on the Democratic ticket in 1964, and he was his party's unsuccessful presidential candidate in 1968.

10. The Bracero Program was a post–Second World War government-sponsored plan aimed at importing low-paid Mexican labor to the United States. Mexicans under this program were allowed to come and work in the United States, but were required to return to Mexico when their work term expired.

11. President of the University of California system during the Berkeley students' famous free-speech fights in 1964.

12. Original note by author: The reader is referred to the October 1966 issue of *Ramparts* magazine for a brilliant (and detailed) exposition of all this, including an analysis of how it all could be done by a man who really is a liberal. *Ramparts* does this in terms of concrete facts; in this article I am generalizing.

13. It is worth noting that although the trend toward statification that Draper describes began to shift by the late 1970s toward "globalization," i.e., more neoliberal capitalist policies, the same political pattern was apparent. Not only Republicans Reagan and Bush, but also Democrat Clinton, carried out the neoliberal policies. Therefore, Draper's point that liberalism and conservatism tend to converge around the particular historic interests of the ruling class still applies.

14. "Birchite" refers to the John Birch Society, a hardline anticommunist organization.

15. Adlai Stevenson was the U.S. diplomat and Democratic politician; governor of Illinois 1949–1953; Democratic presidential candidate 1952, 1956; U.S.

ambassador to the UN 1961–1965. Famous for making a presentation to the UN in 1962 revealing the presence of Russian nuclear missiles in Cuba. Stevenson's presentation denied important facts. For example, the United States had recently launched an armed CIA invasion of Cuba—landing at the Bay of Pigs in April 1961. Stevenson denied U.S. involvement. Stevenson also left out of his presentation the fact that the United States had placed nuclear missiles in Turkey that were pointed at the Soviet Union.

Index

About Haymarket Books

Haymarket Books is a nonprofit, progressive book distributor and publisher, a project of the Center for Economic Research and Social Change. We believe that activists need to take ideas, history, and politics into the many struggles for social justice today. Learning the lessons of past victories, as well as defeats, can arm a new generation of fighters for a better world. As Karl Marx said, "The philosophers have merely interpreted the world; the point, however, is to change it."

We take inspiration and courage from our namesakes, the Haymarket Martyrs, who gave their lives fighting for a better world. Their 1886 struggle for the eight-hour day reminds workers around the world that ordinary people can organize and struggle for their own liberation.

For more information and to shop our complete catalog of titles, visit us online at www.haymarketbooks.org.

Also from Haymarket Books

American Insurgents
A Brief History of American Anti-Imperialism | Richard Seymour
978-1-60846-162-2 | $17.00

Education and Capitalism
Struggles for Learning and Liberation | Edited by Jeff Bale and Sarah Knopp
978-1-60846-147-9 | $17.00

Islamophobia and the Politics of Empire
Empire Abroad and at Home | Deepa Kumar | 978-1-60846-211-7 | $17.00

No One Is Illegal
Fighting Racism and State Violence on the U.S.-Mexico Border
Justin Akers Chacón and Mike Davis | 978-1-931859-35-6 | $18.00

Rich People Things
Real-Life Secrets of the Predator Class | Chris Lehmann | 978-1-60846-152-3 | $16.95

Sexuality and Socialism
History, Politics, and Theory of LGBT Liberation | Sherry Wolf
978-1-931859-79-0 | $12.00

Subterranean Fire
History of Working-Class Radicalism in the United States | Sharon Smith
978-1-931859-23-3 | $16.00

The United States of Fear
Tom Engelhardt | 978-1-60846-154-7 | $16.95

Vietnam
The (Last) War the U.S. Lost | Joe Allen | 978-1-931859-49-3 | $14.00